Informal Logic
Issues and Techniques

In this insightful critique of informal logic and critical thinking strategies and techniques, Wayne Grennan examines argument evaluation techniques currently used in both formal and informal logic texts and, finding them lacking, proposes a new system of evaluation.

Grennan bases his evaluation of arguments on two criteria: logical adequacy and pragmatic adequacy. He asserts that the common formal logic systems, while logically sound, are not very useful for evaluating everyday inferences, which are almost all deductively invalid as stated. Turning to informal logic, he points out that while more recent informal logic and critical thinking texts are superior in that their authors recognize the need to evaluate everyday arguments inductively, they typically cover only inductive fallacies, ignoring the inductively sound patterns frequently used in successful persuasion. To redress these problems, Grennan introduces a variety of additional inductive patterns.

Concluding that informal logic texts do not encourage precision in evaluating arguments, Grennan proposes a new argument evaluation procedure that expresses judgments of inferential strength in terms of probabilities. Based on theories of Stephen Toulmin, Roderick Chisholm, and John Pollock, his proposed system allows for a more precise judgment of the persuasive force of arguments.

WAYNE GRENNAN is associate professor of philosophy, St Mary's University.

Informal Logic

Issues and Techniques

WAYNE GRENNAN

McGill-Queen's University Press
Montreal & Kingston · London · Buffalo

© McGill-Queen's University Press 1997
ISBN 0-7735-1542-9

Legal deposit second quarter 1997
Bibliothèque nationale du Québec

Printed in the United States on acid-free paper

This book has been published with the help of a grant from the
Humanities and Social Sciences Federation of Canada, using funds
provided by the Social Sciences and Humanities Research Council
of Canada. Funds have also been provided by Saint Mary's University.

Canadian Cataloguing in Publication Data

Grennan, Wayne, 1938–
    Informal logic: issues and techniques
    Includes bibliographical references and index.
    ISBN 0-7735-1542-9
    1. Logic. I. Title.
    BC177.G74 1997   160   C97-900139-0

This book was typeset by Typo Litho Composition Inc.
in 10/12 Baskerville.

Contents

Tables

Figures

Preface

This book is intended to provide food for thought for those teaching informal logic or critical thinking, and especially for those who are writing, or thinking of writing, a text in these areas. As such, it contains (1) assessments of the argument-evaluation techniques commonly found in available texts, (2) some new evaluation techniques, and (3) a system for evaluation relying on expressing inference and premiss judgments in probabilities.

This is not an informal logic or critical thinking textbook, although it might be seen as an essay about texts. Extended critiques of currently used evaluation techniques have no place in a text, nor have the detailed justifications that are given for the new techniques I advocate. This is not to say that these new techniques are unsuitable for text inclusion. On the contrary, they have been developed with this purpose in mind. All of them have been tested in introductory courses.

To characterize this work in another way, the argument-evaluation system presented here represents an answer to an important question posed by Ralph Johnson and Anthony Blair at the First International Symposium on Informal Logic when they asked, "Are the validity/ soundness criteria of evaluation inappropriate or outmoded? If so, what should replace them?"

The evaluation system presented here is applicable to both deductive and inductive argument, but since most everyday argument is inductive, I am primarily concerned with inductive argument patterns. Moreover, I concentrate on the identification and analysis of patterns whose instances normally provide good (but not, of course, logically sufficient) grounds for accepting their conclusions. The theory I rely on has been provided by Toulmin, Chisholm, and, most recently, Pollock, who calls reasoning with these patterns "defeasible reasoning."

In the course of supplying an answer for the question posed by Johnson and Blair, I take seriously the advice of Thomas Tomko: "Informal Logic is not a field that can be developed by philosophers alone. Input from other disciplines, such as cognitive psychology, will not only be useful, but necessary" (1979, 358). Of the "other disciplines" he refers to, I have found the rhetoric/speech communication field to be most useful. Perhaps in reading this, other logicians who have not as yet made meaningful contact with these fields will gain some appreciation of how these disciplines have a bearing on some issues in informal logic.

My intellectual debts will be obvious from my literature references. Other influences of a more collegial kind are Shelagh Crooks, Sheila Kindred, and Sheldon Wein, colleagues at Saint Mary's University who read most or all of the manuscript. I appreciate their camaraderie and all their comments and suggestions, some of which influenced the essay, some of which did not.

Finally, I want to thank Eleanor for her support and tolerance. Projects of this magnitude inevitably limit the amount of companionship a spouse can provide.

Informal Logic

1 Arguments

This book will present a procedure for evaluating arguments conceived as the products of utterances that are themselves best regarded as speech act complexes. As products of utterances they are sets of propositions produced by S, the utterer, with the intention of persuading someone, H, that s/he ought to believe one part of the set (the conclusion) because of the remainder of the set, the premisses.[1] (I am discussing arguments with only one inference step in this chapter.)

The recipient of an argument, H, who wishes to evaluate it, must answer, at the most general level, one question:

(1a) To what degree ought I to accept this conclusion as true on the basis of this argument?

In the terminology I shall use, the question can be rephrased as

(1b) How much "conclusion support" does this argument provide?

Since conclusion-support decisions are a joint function of inference and (uninferred) premiss evaluations, the question resolves itself into two subquestions that can be stated in traditional form as

(2a) Are the (uninferred) premisses true?
(3a) Are the inferences valid?

For reasons that will become apparent later, I shall also express these questions differently:

(2b) How much "epistemic support" do the (uninferred) premisses provide for the conclusion?
(3b) How much "logical support" do they provide?

In what follows I shall argue that questions 2a and 3a embody an approach to argument evaluation that is far too crude, given the relevant properties of natural argumentation. By "natural argumentation" I refer to utterances that we encounter outside the "traditional" logic texts, in everyday life. Furthermore, I shall argue, the appropriate level of sophistication requires conceiving the answers to questions 2b and 3b in probabilistic terms, since conclusion support is the mathematical product of epistemic and logical support. Thus, in a two-assertion argument with premiss P and conclusion C, the answer to 2b is a value of "$p(P)$," and the answer to 3b is a value of "$p(C/P)$" (to be read as "the probability of C, given P").

The answer to question 1b can be expressed mathematically as

$$\text{Conclusion support} = p(C) = p(P) \times p(C/P).\text{[2]}$$

The value of $p(C)$ found using this formula ought to be regarded as representing the probability of C given the argument. That is, it is a measure of what the evaluator regards as the value of P in proving C.

Not all of the above theses need to be defended for any particular reader, but each may require a defence for some reader. This depends on the reader's previous exposure to logic and argumentation theory. I shall begin with the most fundamental matter: setting out an account of what an argument is, as it is to be found in a written or printed passage or in an oral utterance.

1.1 ARGUMENTS AS SPEECH ACTS

In this book I shall be concerned with one of two related but distinct concepts of argument. These concepts are distinguished by O'Keefe as "the speech act 'making an argument' and the argument conveyed by that speech act" (Cox and Willard 1982, 12). Here we have the crucial distinction between arguments as a particular kind of utterance act or performance and as the product of such an act. The utterance act represents a complex of uttered propositions. The product can be conceived as a corresponding complex of propositions that might be said to be "embodied" in the utterance and that is created by the utterance.

It is this concept of argument that will be important here, because it is this sort of entity that has logical properties.

Utterances representing arguments may be contributions to a dialogue between two persons who disagree over the truth of a claim, or a one-way activity of presenting reasons in support of a claim aimed at persuading someone to accept the claim. In this book I will be concerned only with the latter kind of performance and, more specifically, primarily with written arguments. Others have been examining the dialogue with considerable success (see especially van Eemeren and Grootendorst 1983; Jacobs and Jackson 1982). However, much of what I will say is relevant to dialogical argumentation because within a dialogue at any point, one individual acts as S and the other as H, and S's utterance is intended to help persuade H to accept some previously stated position.

1.1.1 *The Speech Act Concept of Argument*

Since unidirectional argumentation is the subject matter for investigation, the concept used here can be analyzed in terms of speech act theory. The conceptual resources of this theory, as pioneered by J.L. Austin and refined by John Searle, have led to its exploitation by a number of argumentation scholars, including van Eemeren and Grootendorst (1983). In what follows I shall rely on Searle's (1969) work.[3]

In speech act theory the most fundamental distinction is that between an utterance act, an illocutionary act, and a propositional act (Searle 1969, 24). When S (the persuader) writes, "Massive student protests are occurring daily in China," S is uttering a string of English words that, by virtue of syntactical rules of the language, qualifies as the utterance of a sentence. In making this utterance, S has performed an illocutionary act by virtue of compliance with another set of rules that qualifies the utterance as an assertion (66–7). Furthermore, S has uttered a particular assertion by virtue of the propositional act that has also been performed. Such propositional acts consist of two "sub-acts": referring and predicating.

Searle conceives that making an assertion involves the utilization of, and compliance with, two sorts of rules: rules governing the use of a (frequently suppressed) illocutionary force indicator[4] and rules that determine the content of the propositional act – that is, rules that determine what is asserted.

Searle identifies four types of rules or conditions with which we must comply in performing illocutionary acts: (1) propositional content conditions, (2) preparatory conditions, (3) sincerity conditions, and (4) essential conditions. For asserting, these are (1) the propositional content condition: any proposition p; (2) preparatory conditions: (i) S has evidence for the truth of p, and (ii) it is not obvious to both S and H that H knows p; (3) the sincerity condition: S believes p; and (4) the essential condition: the assertion counts as an undertaking to the effect that p represents an actual state of affairs (1969, 66).

For the reader inclined to question the sincerity condition on the ground that lies are assertions too, it is important to note that Searle makes a distinction between the "non-defective performance of the act" of asserting and successful, yet defective, performances (1969, 54). Some clarification of this distinction is desirable.

Searle provides the most detailed analysis for the illocutionary act of promising. Before presenting his analysis, he declares that "In order to give an analysis of the illocutionary act of promising I shall ask what conditions are necessary and sufficient for the act of promising to have been successfully and non-defectively performed in the utterance of a given sentence." The above analysis of the illocutionary act of asserting is intended to meet Searle's requirement for a "successful and non-defective" performance. Searle uses this conjunction of terms because he recognizes that "In some cases, a condition may indeed be intrinsic to the notion of the act in question and not satisfied in a given case, and yet the act will have been performed nonetheless" (1969, 54). The distinction he seems to be making here is one between necessary conditions for paradigmatic performances ("successful" ones) and non-paradigmatic but clear cases ("defective" ones). In the analysis of promising, for example, he declares that "insincere promises are promises nonetheless" (62), and apparently he would describe them as defective. In what follows I shall use the terms "paradigmatic cases" and "(non-paradigmatic) clear cases" instead of "successful" and "defective."[5]

Besides paradigmatic and other clear cases of asserting there are, presumably, borderline cases. For example, S and H are gathering apples from around a tree in a pasture, and S notices a third party approaching; S says, "Here comes a bull," but it is not clear immediately to H whether this statement is a warning or simply an assertion based on observation.

The Searlean analysis for the illocutionary act of asserting, then, is supposed to contain all the necessary conditions for a paradigmatic case, and the set of such conditions is supposed to be sufficient for an utterance to count as a paradigmatic assertion.

I will now extend the speech act analysis for asserting to utterances that count, by virtue of particular linguistic rules, as arguments. As illocutionary acts, arguments are to be conceived as logically concatenated assertions.[6] Thus, we will find that a speech act analysis for a paradigmatic case of an uttered argument will embody conditions for asserting, along with some additional ones. Van Eemeren and Grootendorst have made a significant contribution to the completion of this analysis. Relying mostly on Searle (1969), they conceive of arguments as concrete speech act complexes (1983, sec. 2.5), since they recognize that arguments consist of more than one speech act.

Van Eemeren and Grootendorst are interested in dialogue contexts in which argumentation occurs, rather than in the discrete, self-contained arguments that occur most commonly in print form. Thus, in what follows I have adapted their analysis for the latter sort of case. The main difference has to do with the fact that in paradigm cases of argumentation in print, the conclusion is explicitly uttered, whereas in dialogue they conceive the "opinion" being debated as being known to both parties before the occurrence of the kind of utterances they wish to analyze – which are assertives advanced in favour of or against that opinion.

The type of case to be studied in this work is one in which, in the paradigmatic case, a claim has been advanced by S and S has presented other assertions that S considers to be epistemic support for that claim. These latter assertions stand as premises for the claim, which represents a conclusion.[7]

Given this concept of argument, the simplest paradigmatic argument must contain two assertions – a premiss and a conclusion – and an argument indicator-word or phrase. To use a chemistry metaphor, we can say that an argument is a special type of complex: it is a logical compound, not an aggregate, because its constituents become more than a collection of assertions when uttered as an argument. (Compare it with two gases, oxygen and hydrogen, which, when brought together in certain circumstances, combine chemically to form water, something with entirely different properties.) A narrative consists of several assertions ("elements") that become an entity, an argument ("molecule"), by the addition of an argument indicator-word imputing a logical connection between the assertions.

Using "P" to stand for the premiss or set of premises and "C" to stand for the conclusion, and assuming a single inference in the argument, we can set out the conditions for a paradigmatic illocutionary act of arguing as follows:

A Propositional Content Condition
   Utterances P and C, contained within utterance U, can be correctly construed as asserted propositions.
B Preparatory Conditions
   1 S believes that H does not fully accept C (i.e., does not regard C as clearly true).
   2 S believes that H will/does accept P.

3 *S* believes that *H* will accept *P* as providing adequate logical support for *C.*

c Sincerity Conditions

1 *S* believes that *P* is epistemically acceptable.

2 *S* believes that *P* is adequate logical support for *C.*

D Essential Condition

Uttering *U* counts as an attempt by *S* to convince *H* that *C* is epistemically acceptable on grounds that *P.*

Condition (A) simply reflects the conceptual fact that an argument consists of a relationship between entities bearing truth values. The phrase "can be construed" is needed because we sometimes utter arguments that do not seem at first sight to clearly consist of assertions. For example: Sam is a passenger in a car being driven by Freda, and it is just past sunset; since Freda has not as yet turned the lights on, Sam says impatiently, "It's getting dark, so turn on the lights." Here it is not unnatural to construe the utterance as an argument; Sam is trying to persuade Freda to turn the lights on. But Sam seems to have uttered an assertion followed by a request or perhaps even an order (for example, they might be travelling in a military vehicle, and Sam might be in charge of it).

If Sam has given an order, it will not be correct to construe his utterance as an argument, since orders are not attempts to persuade. Indeed, they are clear attempts to evoke action without persuasion. If he has given an order, we cannot construe the first part of the utterance as the premiss of an argument. We must instead take it to be an explanation for the issuing of the order.

On the other hand, if the second part of the utterance is a request, we can rely on a distinction between utterance meaning and speaker's meaning that will enable us to fit the example to the Searlean model presented above. We can regard Sam's meaning as more adequately expressed by "It's getting dark, so you ought to turn on the lights." If Sam would accept this as expressing what he meant, then the second part of the sentence represents an assertion, since it has a truth value; that is, the utterance of the entire sentence would be the utterance of two assertions, with the former intended to persuade Freda of the truth of the latter. If this is an adequate interpretation of Sam's utterance, it meets Condition A.

Condition B is intended to exclude various kinds of infelicities and misfirings in the attempt to utter an argument, infelicities that are incompatible with the argument utterances having a purpose. Condition B1 provides the explanation for *S*'s utterance. If *S* thought that *H* did accept *C*, uttering *U* would be pointless. This condition can be regarded as compliance with Grice's cooperative principle: "make your conversational contribution such as is required, at the stage at which it occurs, by the accepted purpose or direction of the talk exchange in which you are engaged" (1975, 45).

Condition B2 is needed to exclude another kind of exercise in futility. Clearly, H will not be persuaded to accept C on grounds that P if H does not believe P. Successful persuasion requires selecting premisses that H regards as providing epistemic support for C.

Condition B3 will expresses the idea that S believes that H will recognize C as being inferrable from the premisses. Again, it would be irrational to utter U in the hope of persuading H that C unless it was thought that B3 was true.

The set of sincerity conditions, C, are necessary conditions only for paradigm cases. As Searle observed in connection with promising and as I observed in connection with asserting, there can be clear cases of these illocutionary acts that are not sincere. The same holds true, by extension, for arguing. Many illustrations of this occur when lawyers plead cases and when participants in formal debates are assigned the affirmative position when they actually believe the negative position.

Van Eemeren and Grootendorst (1983, 195) argue that these conditions ought to be called "responsibility conditions," and I am disposed to agree, for several reasons. First, S is committed to defending the epistemic acceptability of P and C, should H subsequently mount a challenge. This is an ethical requirement rather than a logical one. A presumptive obligation to say only what one takes to be true is operative in everyday life. This obligation is not operative in formal contexts such as courtroom advocacy and formal debate.

Failure to observe this sincerity obligation will have no serious effect on S's attempt to persuade H if H finds P acceptable on the evidence H already has and H is able to judge independently that P provides adequate logical support for C. On the other hand, if H accepts P because S asserts it (for example, when S is an expert in a science) or if H accepts that P provides adequate logical support because S presents the argument (for example, when S is a mathematician presenting a long proof for an easily understood conclusion from fairly obvious premisses) then S will be guilty of misleading H and possibly engaging in manipulation.

In view of all this, the sincerity conditions for clear cases of uttered arguments can be replaced by responsibility conditions:

c Responsibility Conditions
   1 S is committed to affirming P.
   2 S is committed to affirming that the truth of P guarantees the truth of C.

Condition D, the essential condition, is, in effect, a definition of the illocutionary act of presenting an argument. Searle has chosen the expression "counts as" to reflect the fact that the rules that enable the performance of the act are constitutive and not purely regulative. The central hypothesis of his speech act theory is that "the semantic structure of a language may be regarded as a conventional realization of a series of sets of underlying constitutive rules, and that speech acts are acts characteristically performed by uttering expressions in accordance with these sets of constitutive rules" (1969, 37).

1.1.2 *Argument Utterance Effects*

Argument utterances are essentially instances of attempts to communicate. An utterance that meets the conditions set out in the last section represents a successful argument utterance in the sense that it counts as a paradigm case of it. But such an utterance is only an *attempt* to convince (condition D). In the performance of an illocutionary act no reference needs to be made to how the act affects *H*. Thus, successful performance of the act is distinct from successfully convincing *H* that *C*.

To successfully convince, two additional events must occur: the illocutionary act of *S* must bring about an illocutionary effect in *H*, and the illocutionary effect must result in *H* being convinced that *C*. In speech act terminology the latter occurrence is a "perlocutionary" effect. It has been called the "inherent" perlocutionary effect to distinguish it from "consecutive" perlocutionary consequences, that is, "all other consequences of the speech act" (van Eemeren and Grootendorst 1983, 24).

1.1.2.1 *The Illocutionary Effect: Getting the Message.* Speaker *S* having uttered something of the form "*P,* so *C,*" has *H* gotten the message? The occurrence of the illocutionary effect in *H* is supposed to be brought about by *S*'s performance of the illocutionary act of presenting an argument. Clearly, the occurrence of the illocutionary effect depends on *H* and factors that promote or inhibit *H*'s recognition that *S* has uttered an argument. To identify the conditions under which the illocutionary effect occurs we must begin by noting that getting the message is, in part, identifying the propositional act. That is, *H* must recognize what *S* means.

Searle provides the following analysis of "*S* utters sentence *T* and means literally what he says": "*S* utters *T* and (a) *S* intends (i-1) the utterance *U* of *T* to produce in *H* the knowledge ... that the states of affairs specified by (certain of) the rules of *T* obtain (call this the illocutionary effect, "IE"); (b) *S* intends *U* to produce IE by means of the recognition of *i*-I; (c) *S* intends that *i*-I will be recognized in virtue of (by means of) *H*'s knowledge of (certain of) the rules governing (the elements of) *T*" (1969, 49–50).

In recognizing that *S* is uttering an argument, *H* needs to recognize not just the propositional content of the assertions made but also that *S* intends (*i*-H) *H* to come to believe *C* on the ground that *P.* Speaker *S* can arrange for *H* to recognize *i*-H by using one or more inference indicator-words. This is to be done by relying on *H*'s knowledge of the rules governing these words. Thus, an arguer might say, "Harry was born in Bermuda; therefore he is a British citizen." We can compare this with "Harry is a British citizen, and he was born in Bermuda." In both cases two assertions are made, but in the former case the presence of the inference indicator-term "therefore" entitles *H* to identify the speaker's whole utterance as an argument.

When *S* does not include such words, *S* can still be said to be uttering an argument when *S* intends to have *H* recognize *i*-H through the propositional content of *P* and *C.* For example, in some circumstances the utterance "Harry was born in Bermuda; he is a British citizen" would count as an argument. For example, if we were disagreeing over whether Harry was a British citizen or not, you might utter this as an illocutionary act of arguing, and IE would very likely occur, because I am aware that we are engaged in the enterprise of reaching agreement about Harry's citizenship. *S*'s chance of getting *H* to recognize *i*-I under such conditions is diminished, of course. There is the distinct possibility that you intended to proffer an explanation instead of an argument. You may be explaining for my benefit why you believe that Harry is a British citizen.

This possibility brings to the fore the distinction between what an utterance counts as and what it is intended to be. Ideally, to communicate successfully, one will choose the words that most effectively communicate one's message, so that there is a match between intention and what the utterance counts as. This is the sort of case that Searle is concerned with: *S* means literally what he says.

The lack of fit in this respect was of particular interest to Wittgenstein, who, in typically enigmatic fashion, says somewhere, "Say 'it's cold here' and mean 'it's warm here.'" I take his point to be that a rational individual who wishes to convey that it is warm here, cannot convey this message by this utterance. Rules governing the sentence make it a completely inappropriate device for the purpose. What the utterance of a sentence counts as in a particular context is determined by rules governing the elements in it, and a speaker's intent cannot alter this. Thus, the person to whom an utterance is directed is entitled to interpret the message in terms of the utterance content. Should *S* say

"Roses are red, so violets are blue," H is entitled to regard this as an argument and cannot be faulted by S if H advances a highly negative view of the quality of the argument.

Whether an utterance represents an argument, then, is primarily a matter of semantic and syntactic rules. But from the point of view of argument evaluation, the only matter of interest is whether or not the would-be evaluator takes it to be an argument.

In summary, then, the illocutionary effect (IE) occurs following a paradigmatic illocutionary act of argumentation when the following conditions are jointly met:

(a) H recognizes S's intention to produce in H the knowledge that U is an attempt to convince H that C on the grounds of the logical support that S regards P as providing for C;

(b) H's recognition of this intention is brought about by means of H's knowledge of the rules governing P and C and any argument indicator terms occurring in U. (This condition is required to ensure that the successful communication occurs through linguistic meaning, excluding cases in which success comes about fortuitously, for example, by guessing.)

1.1.2.2 *The Inherent Perlocutionary Effect: Convincing.* H gets the message if H recognizes the essential condition for the performance of the illocutionary act of presenting that particular argument: S's utterance counts as an attempt by S to convince me (H) that C is epistemically acceptable on the ground that P.

The ideal conditions for H becoming convinced that C by S's utterance correspond to S's beliefs set out in the preparatory conditions:

1 H did not accept C prior to S's utterance.
2 H accepts P.
3 H regards P as providing adequate logical support for C.

I shall argue later that it is not irrational to be convinced by an argument even though one does not assign a value of 1 to $p(P)$ and $p(C/P)$. It is necessary only that, using the product rule $p(P) \times p(C/P)$, one arrives at a relatively high value of $p(C)$. That is, given the alternatives "C is true," or "C is false," or "the argument does not entitle me to choose either alternative," the value of $p(C)$ must be high enough so that it is rational to say that C is true.

How high is high enough? Well, consider a thought experiment. A die is rolled, and two people bet on the outcome. One person says, "I bet $X that it's a six." As the other person, most of us would be enthusiastic to bet the same amount that it is not a six, even if *X* is a fairly large number, on the ground that the probability that it is not six is 83 percent. How much we would bet is determined, in this scenario, primarily by how much we can afford to lose. Speaking personally, I might be prepared to wager a month's pay on a single roll. I suspect many would not find this to be irresponsible.

This example suggests that if forced to choose, most of us would be willing to regard a proposition as true when the evidence makes it at least 80 percent probable.

1.2 ARGUMENTS AS SPEECH ACT PRODUCTS

Utterances that represent arguments can be conceived, I have claimed, as speech act complexes. According to Searle, such utterances involve performing three distinct kinds of acts. "Let us assign names to these under the general heading of speech acts: (a) Uttering words (morphemes, sentences) = performing *utterance acts*. (b) Referring and predicating = performing *propositional acts*, (c) Stating, questioning, commanding, promising, etc. = performing *illocutionary acts*." (1969, 23–4) Searle goes on to stress that these distinct acts are not "separate things that speakers do, as it happens, simultaneously, as one might smoke, read and scratch one's head simultaneously, but rather that in performing an illocutionary act one characteristically performs propositional and utterance acts ... utterance acts and propositional acts stand to illocutionary acts in the way in which, e.g., making an "x" on a ballot paper stands to voting" (24).

Now, since we can regard an argument as a speech act complex, we can regard it also, by virtue of the relationships described above, as an illocutionary act complex. The particular illocutionary acts involved are, of course, assertions. Furthermore, we can also regard the illocutionary act complex as a propositional act complex, with each assertion representing an asserted proposition. And since it is the proposition that has the property of bearing a truth value, in evaluating arguments from the perspective of attempts to persuade, it is arguments as propositional complexes that are of interest.

From the point of view of many argumentation scholars, treating arguments as propositional complexes requires some defence. Non-logicians complain that conceiving of arguments as propositional complexes is unsatisfactory. Perhaps the most vehement critic is Charles Willard, who supports O'Keefe's "argument$_2$" (argument as interaction) concept as the "organizing model for argumentation" (Willard 1979, 21), in preference to "argument$_1$," the propositional product concept. He maintains that "Arguments are fleeting ephemeral phenomena, akin in this respect to other kinds of interaction. The assumption that they consist uniquely of propositions is arbitrary" (28).

I do not, nor would most other logicians, take the view that there is nothing more to an argument than a set of propositions. It may appear that we hold this view because logic texts generally ignore everything except the propositional product. But this is explained by our exclusive interest in the logical quality of arguments, which can be determined by considering them as propositional complexes. This is not to say that logicians need not ever consider arguments as speech acts, though. Sometimes the words uttered may not be the best ones in which to express argument content. We may have to rely on the utterer's intentions to establish the most accurate wording.

It is correct that "A product-oriented approach to argumentation provides no insight into the conditions that have to be fulfilled for a constellation of speech utterances to count as argumentation" (van Eemeren and Grootendorst 1983, 9). But in the theoretical study of argument from the logician's point of view, one is interested in the product of utterances that count as arguments. By virtue of the fact that logic is a specialty within the field of argumentation studies, it is appropriate for the logician to regard arguments as propositional complexes. Those who complain about the narrowness of the propositional-complex conception of argument may be protesting about the unhealthy influence that this conception has enjoyed by virtue of its use by logicians, which amounts to a complaint about the unhealthy influence of logicians in the field of argumentation studies. Such complaints are well-founded, it seems to me.

Logicians (that is, formal logicians) as a group have enjoyed an academic prestige that rhetoricians and other argumentation scholars have not. This essay represents evidence that times have changed, that the role of formal logic as a specialty in the field of argumentation studies must be regarded as much smaller than previously thought. Furthermore, while the propositional-complex concept of argument is the one informal logicians will normally work with, it is essential to keep the broader concept, the speech act concept, in mind. In particular, it must be remembered that arguments as uttered propositional complexes are intended to persuade. This has a bearing on what may count as a genuine argument.

The preparatory conditions 1 and 2, cited above, entail that S believes that H regards the initial probability of P as greater than that of C. And if H does not regard P as more probable than C, the argument cannot be persuasive. Thus, if we regard arguments as persuasive devices, as I intend to in this essay, we must exclude some propositional patterns as argument patterns, on the ground that normally their conclusions are better known than their premisses. *Petitio* patterns are examples.

1.3 CONCLUSION

In this first chapter I have discussed two concepts of argument, each of which is based on the speech act theory of language use. The first concept is that of an argument as an illocutionary act complex, that is, an assertion complex. The second is the concept of an argument as the product of an utterance, a propositional complex. This is the concept of interest here.

2 Current Argument-Evaluation Techniques

The presentation of another argument-evaluation procedure is defensible only to the extent that the extant ones are deficient. In this chapter I want to describe and critique the more popular approaches to argument evaluation found in the textbooks designed for undergraduate courses offered by philosophy departments in American and Canadian universities. They will be examined in terms of how well they equip anyone who masters their techniques for the evaluation of everyday argumentation.

Two distinct approaches are now common. The first one I will discuss can be called the "traditional approach," but of course this is a tendentious label, suggesting as it does that other approaches are unorthodox or perhaps, more positively, progressive. The second is the "informal logic" approach distinguished by its orientation toward everyday argument and the abandonment of formal techniques.

For each type I will first discuss the evaluation procedure presented, if there is one. The importance of having such a procedure should be evident when argument evaluation is conceived as arriving at conclusion-support judgments, since this approach involves more than one evaluation step. Second, I will examine the particular evaluation techniques from the point of view of their usefulness in evaluating everyday argument. Third, I will review the shortcomings of each approach, that is, kinds of everyday argument for which the texts do not furnish any evaluation techniques.

2.1 THE TRADITIONAL APPROACH

The traditional approach, as I have called it, is exemplified by Irving Copi's *Introduction to Logic*, first published in 1953 and now in its ninth edition.[1] It is my understanding that it is the biggest seller among the traditional texts. From the late fifties until the mid-seventies Copi's text and its "clones" published by others had hegemony in American and Canadian universities teaching "baby" logic (introductory logic courses that covered more than symbolic logic systems).

2.1.1 *Evaluation Techniques*

The Copi-style text usually offers thorough presentations of three inference-evaluation techniques, using three highly developed logical systems: (1) syllogistic systems, (2) a deduction version of the propositional calculus,[2] and (3) a deduction version of the predicate calculus. In what follows I discuss the usefulness of these three systems as techniques for evaluating the inferences of everyday arguments.[3] To save time and space I will assume, on the reader's part, some familiarity with each system.

2.1.1.1 *Syllogistic.* Of the three systems, syllogistic is narrowest in the scope of its usefulness and, as students of symbolic logic will be aware, is considered to have been logically superseded by the more powerful predicate calculus, which can identify valid class reasoning in cases in which syllogistic cannot (Tapscott 1976, 401). Yet, syllogistic is superior in an important way – its rules allow it to function as a decision procedure, whereas the other two systems are not really decision procedures at all (see further discussion of this point in chapter 5). In this respect syllogistic is a more practical system for evaluating inferences representing class reasoning.

Regrettably, however, it is confined to dealing primarily with arguments that can be cast in standard syllogistic form.[4] That is, exactly three classes (terms) are mentioned with one term occurring in each of two premises (the "middle term") but not in the conclusion; and each assertion must be formulated as one of four standard types: A, E, I, or O (see Copi 1982, sec. 5.1, 6.1). This sort of class reasoning must be cast in a standard form because the decision criteria consist of a set of rules that are expressed in terms of a standard form. In his version, Copi (1982, 227–31) has six such rules. Such a set of rules enables the user to identify valid and invalid syllogisms once the argument has been written as a standard-form categorical syllogism.

Unfortunately, not many arguments we encounter in everyday life are expressed in standard syllogistic form or have the potential for being rewritten in standard form. And even if they do have that potential, converting them is not always straightforward. In most natural languages there is much stylistic variation, allowing people to express categorical propositions in a number of different ways. For instance, "Only X's are Y's" is expressed in standard form as "All Y's are X's." It is, I have found, difficult to get students to appreciate this, and a number of other intuitively implausible equivalencies, without resorting to graphic representations such as the Venn diagram.

Happily, the Copi-style texts usually include, as an adjunct to classical syllogistic, the Venn-diagram method for evaluating class reasoning. The Venn-diagram method for syllogism testing utilizes a diagram format that enables us to graphically represent categorical syllogistic assertions, whether they are in standard form or not. Indeed, it has the advantage of being able to test the validity of class reasoning involving only two classes, such as the patterns associated with the traditional square of opposition (see Copi 1982, 188–9). For example, the pattern "All X's are Y's so all Y's are X's," a fallacy of conversion, can be shown to be invalid using the Venn approach.

2.1.1.2 *Propositional Deduction.* The most serious limitation of the propositional deduction system is that it is a proof procedure, not a decision procedure. That is, this system can show that some arguments cast in its "language" are formally valid, but it cannot demonstrate that invalid ones are invalid. For example, there are rules and axioms that allow us to discover that an argument of the pattern "If A then B, and if B then C, therefore if A then C" is formally valid in the propositional calculus. But there are no such rules to demonstrate that "If A then B, and if C then B, therefore if A then C" is formally invalid. The best that can be done is to infer, from failures to construct a proof, that the argument is formally invalid. This, of course, is an inductive inference.

This deficiency is obscured in the textbooks by the common practice of furnishing sets of arguments that we are told in advance are valid. Speaking from experience, should an argument actually be invalid but not transparently so, we will so conclude only after a number of attempts at proving validity have failed. Defenders of these systems respond by pointing out that they are proof procedures, not decision procedures, but this disclaimer is seldom stated and never stressed in their texts.

Since inference evaluation normally begins in a state of uncertainty about the quality of the inference, axiomatic deductive systems such as the propositional calculus are limited in practical use for testing inferences in everyday arguments. Another limitation is purely practical, but significant nonetheless: acquiring competence in testing argument patterns is not easy, and once done, it is possible to retain one's skill only by continual use. Anyone who has more or less mastered such a system can attest to both these facts. More seriously, the experience of those of us who have taught these systems indicates that only a minority of people can master them.

Finally, given competence, how useful is it? The propositional calculus is useful only for examining inferences that involve at least one disjunction (or logical equivalent, such as $-(-p \,\&\, -q)$) or at least one conditional (or logical equivalent, such as $-p \lor q$), or at least one biconditional, or equivalent. (Arguments containing a conjunction as a premiss can be regarded as cases in which the conjuncted proposition represents two separate assertions.) Arguments lacking disjunctions and conditionals will have their propositions symbolized as single letters, and no such arguments can be deductively valid within the system ("p therefore q" is invalid, as is "p and q therefore r," and "p and q and r therefore s"). Thus, there is no point in testing these inferences in this way.

In everyday argumentation, or at least in such argumentation as found outside legal and philosophical circles, disjunctions and conditionals do not frequently occur, and biconditionals are rare indeed.[5] Conditionals occur more frequently than disjunctions, but perhaps the majority of them really represent arguments, arguments arising when S is not certain of the truth of a premiss. (For example, we are dining and I notice that you have not touched the beets on your plate; I am pretty sure, but not certain, that you intend to leave them, but I love beets, so I say, "If you aren't going to eat those beets, you ought to give them to me." Had I been certain of your intentions, I would have said instead, "You aren't going to eat those beets, so you ought to give them to me.")

Thus, it appears that only a relatively small proportion of everyday arguments are usefully tested with the propositional calculus, so that it is difficult to justify the effort needed to learn the system and maintain competence.

2.1.1.3 *Predicate Deduction.* The opportunity to apply the predicate deduction systems in the evaluation of everyday argument is somewhat greater than for propositional logic. As noted already, the predicate calculus is much more powerful than syllogistic for testing inferences in class reasoning. Specifically, it can be used to show validity regardless of how many classes are mentioned. On the other hand, the extra power in demonstrating inference validity is offset by the total inability to show invalidity. This is because it is only a proof procedure, not a decision procedure. It can be used to reduce arguments to a form in which a decision procedure can be applied, however.

As with propositional logic, we must ask whether predicate logic is useful enough to justify the effort needed to master the system and maintain mastery. My experience, and the testimony of others who have tried it, convinces me that learning how to write everyday arguments in the language of predicate logic is even more difficult than learning to cast them in propositional form. And being even more difficult to acquire, it is even more difficult to retain.

While there may be a greater proportion of everyday arguments that can be written in the language of predicate logic, most of them are invalid, a good many because they represent enthymemes. For example, the inference claim in "Elvis is a man, so Elvis is mortal" can be written semi-symbolically as "If *Fa* then *Ga*." This is not an instance of a deductive pattern.

Given the infrequent occurrence of valid arguments and the effort required to master and maintain mastery of the predicate calculus, it is difficult to justify including the system in a text designed to provide techniques for the evaluation of everyday argument.

2.1.1.4 *Summary of Deficiencies.* The foregoing comments were made with a view to establishing the utility of the formal logic techniques found in Copi's text (and others like it) for the evaluation of inferences in everyday arguments. I conclude that they are of only marginal utility, for the following reasons:

1 The propositional and predicate deduction systems do not provide adequate decision procedures, since they cannot be used to demonstrate formal invalidity.
2 They are useful in only a minority of cases. Regarding the propositional calculus: most arguments do not contain a disjunction, a conditional, or a biconditional, so there is no point in testing them as written, since they are invalid in the first place. Regarding the predicate calculus: many arguments may be symbolized in the language, but most are probably enthymematic, and so invalid.[6]
3 The systems are difficult to master and maintaining mastery requires frequent practice.

2.1.2 *Traditional Texts: Deficiencies of Omission*

The deficiencies identified above have to do with the usefulness of the techniques provided in the traditional text for evaluating inferences in everyday arguments. In this section I wish to discuss some deficiencies in this kind of text that arise from what is not included. Three major deficiences can be noted: (1) no attention is given to premiss evaluation; (2) there is almost no discussion of inductive argument patterns; (3) materially deductively valid arguments are neglected; and (4) there is no overall evaluation procedure.

2.1.2.1 *Premiss Evaluation.* Anyone who turns to texts such as Copi's for guidance on whether or not particular arguments prove their conclusions will be surprised to find that these texts are concerned exclusively with only one facet of argument quality – inference quality. No attempt is made to reach judgments about whether one should accept the conclusions of the arguments examined. The sole question of interest is, Is the inference valid? Premiss quality is generally ignored completely, indeed in some such texts the authors come close to committing the error of equating inference evaluation with argument evaluation (Johnson 1987, 48). This exclusive concern with inference quality will be all the more puzzling to the novice who comes to realize that in evaluating premisses we must reach a judgment, based on the evidence we have at hand, of the value of $p(P)$. In doing this, we are deciding the extent to which we can validly infer P from such evidence. Thus, premiss evaluation, the other part of argument evaluation, also involves inference evaluation.

None of this will be surprising to the student of the history of logic, who can point out that logic as traditionally conceived from Aristotle's time is the science of identifying the principles of good inference. Applied logic is then the use of these principles to evaluate the inferences of particular arguments. Furthermore, the science of logic has always been conceived very narrowly by virtue of the espoused standard of what qualifies as a "good inference." Aristotle, the founder of the science, was a philosopher who believed that genuine knowledge arose from truths inferred deductively from other incorrigible truths. Like many since, he apparently was captivated by mathematics as a model for other sciences, although to give him his due, he also thought that non-demonstrative arguments deserved study (*Topics* 101a 25–38). In any case, he took valid syllogisms to be the paradigm of good inference.

Deductivism, as the Aristotelian view of inference quality has been called, is summed up, perhaps caricatured, in the view that inferences are either deductive or defective. This view is still with us, embodied in the standard textbooks. Thus, not only is logic confined to the discovery of principles of good inference, it is further limited to the discovery of deductively valid principles of inference that arise from logical form. This situation serves to explain the second major omission in the traditional texts.

2.1.2.2 *The Neglect of Inductive Argument.* The second major deficiency of the traditional texts is that they furnish almost no guidance for evaluating inductive inferences, despite the fact that there are a large number of such inference patterns in everyday use. They usually provide brief discussions of only two kinds of inductive patterns: enumerative induction and analogy.

Copi (1982, 389–92, 397–400), for example, spends seven pages describing what he calls the "argument by analogy" and furnishing six criteria for judging its inference quality. The information provided is fairly adequate, and his failure to discuss any other inductive pattern except enumerative induction (which is discussed in one page on the ground that it is "very similar to an argument by analogy, differing only in having a more general conclusion" (413)) is defended as follows: "Of these inductive arguments, perhaps the type most commonly used is the argument by analogy … Most of our own everyday inferences are by analogy … Analogy is at the basis of most of our ordinary reasonings from past experience to what the future will hold" (389–90).

While the third claim is plausible, the second – that most of our everyday inferences are by analogy – is not so plausible. Indeed, chapter 7 of this book provides evidence to the contrary.

The inadequate coverage of inductive patterns in the traditional logic text contrasts with the coverage found in another textual genre: the rhetoric and debating texts. Most of them cover at least half a dozen of the more fundamental inductive patterns. This difference is explained in good measure by the fact that many traditional logic textbook writers are deductive chauvinists, people who believe the Aristotelian view just discussed, that arguments are "deductive or defective." There are a good many arguments, however, that are considered acceptable by rational people but lack deductively valid inferences. In this section I wish to identify some examples and defend their acceptability, to show that deductive chauvinism is misguided.

The arguments that we can regard as inductively valid have a common feature: they can be conceived as presumptively valid, or defeasibly valid. In the absence of what Toulmin calls "rebuttal conditions" (see chapter 4, below), which we are to understand are normally absent for arguments of these patterns, the inferences are adequate as a basis for belief and action.

Toulmin uses several examples to define the concept of presumptive validity. One is "Petersen is a Swede, so [presumably] he is a Protestant." The warrant for the inference claim is not the universal generalization "All Swedes are Protestant," as it would be for a deductively valid version. For, as Toulmin informs us, the proportion of Catholics in Sweden is less than 5 percent but more than 0 percent. Rather, the warrant must be either an explicitly qualified generalization such as "Nearly all Swedes are Protestant" or "More than 95 percent of Swedes are Protestant," or the unqualified generalization "Swedes are Protestant."

Arguments from effect to cause are a common form of inductive argument. As I write this, I notice the street is wet, whereas some time ago it was dry. I infer that it has begun to rain. I regard the argument as presumptively valid, in that I accept the conclusion without demur, in the absence of any reason to accept a rebuttal condition as operative. Thus, on the basis of my inference I would be willing to advise my wife to take an umbrella as she prepares to go out. The warrant for the inference can be expressed as a causal generalization: "Normally, rainfall causes streets to become wet." Backing the warrant itself are some laws of physics about the effects of water on surfaces.

The most important point here is that the causal laws associated with causal reasoning cannot adequately support warrants that are universal generalizations, so these inferences cannot be deductively valid. There are exceptional circumstances in which rainfall does not cause streets to become wet. One is when there is snow on the street. But there are others that we cannot anticipate. Since we cannot exhaustively list them, we cannot have deductively valid inferences in such arguments. Thus causal reasoning is inductive.

Inductive inferences are also commonly made in reasoning about rule-governed human conduct when the rules are customary, such as in matters of etiquette and morality. No official body or individual has enacted these rules. They have not normally been stipulated by any identifiable individual; they exist through community enforcement, legal and extralegal. For example, a friend is planning to build a device that will "unscramble" the cable television signal of one of the movie channels for which there is an extra charge. I argue, "Watching their movies without paying is theft, so you must not do it." The warrant for the inference might be worded, "Normally one must not commit theft." This warrant can be seen as backed by the claim "Normally theft is wrong," which in turn is backed by the explanation why theft is wrong: theft is the obtaining of a benefit to which one is not morally entitled.

The uses of "normally" in stating the warrant and its backing is necessary because moral rule claims are only prima facie, or presumptive. The example just given has the form "X is Y, so one must not do X." However, circumstances may make it permissible to do X. Eating human flesh is prohibited in many societies, but people have done so when survival makes it necessary, for example, after ship sinkings at sea, after air crashes in remote areas. No moral fault is found with those who survive such ordeals, because they have adequate excuses.

Customary rules, then, are defeasible. There are rebuttal conditions associated with them, but these conditions cannot be exhaustively stated, since we cannot anticipate all the circumstances that embody them. This point is important because it means that warrants supported by such rules are not unqualified universal generalizations, which in turn means that the arguments can only be inductively valid, not deductively valid.

Arguments like those just discussed can, as we all know, be adequate enough to be relied on in choosing a course of action. It is regrettable that the traditional textbooks do not explore the many inductive patterns that are embodied in everyday argumentation. I regard this as the major deficiency of such texts.

2.1.2.3 *The Neglect of Materially Valid Arguments.* Stressing techniques for identifying formally valid inferences, the traditional texts ignore the need to evaluate inferences that are deductively valid but not formally valid. This is probably due to a failure to recognize that there are arguments that have this property. And this failure is explained by the fact that logicians often equate deductive validity with formal validity.[7]

Arguments that are materially deductively valid have inference warrants that are necessarily true because they are entailed by the existence of rules. The argument "Sam is a typical bachelor, so Sam has never been married" has a deductively valid inference. The warrant, "If anyone is a typical bachelor, then that person has never been married," is entailed by the definition of "bachelor." And because the definition represents a semantic rule, the warrant is a necessary truth. Thus, it is not possible for P to be true and C to be false. In other words, the inference is deductively valid, even though not formally valid. To be sure, this is a trivial example, but some of these arguments are not.

Arguments having materially deductively valid inferences have this property by virtue of the existence of two kinds of rules: constitutive and regulative ones. These are logically quite different, however. The constitutive/regulative distinction has been brought to the fore by John Rawls and John Searle. Searle explains the distinction as follows: "regulative rules regulate antecedently or independently existing forms of behavior … But constitutive rules do not merely regulate, they create or define new forms of behavior … Regulative rules characteristically have the form … "Do X" or "If Y do X." Within systems of constitutive rules, some will have this form, but some will have the form "*X* counts as *Y*," or "*X* counts as *Y* in context *C*" (1969, 33–5).

First, consider arguments that are deductively (but not formally) valid by virtue of having warrants that represent regulative rules. A sign by the curb at a shopping mall reads, "NO PARKING: FIRE LANE." This represents a regulative rule expressible as "Do not park here." Now suppose a person is before a judge in the jurisdiction in which this sign occurs, and she says, "You parked in an area designated as a fire lane, so you are guilty of violating Highway Code Section 27.34." If this is a strict liability offence (that is, there are no legally acceptable excuses), the argument is deductively valid. The judge is able to move from a "physical" fact to a legal one, with truth preservation, by virtue of a warrant, that is, "If anyone parks in an area designated as a fire zone, that person is guilty of violating Highway Code Section 27.34." This warrant is true by virtue of the regulative rule specified in that section, which might begin, "Parking in an area designated as a fire zone is an offence."

Providing that there are no exceptions under the legal rule, the warrant is a necessary truth, although it is only contingent on the existence of the rule. We might say the warrant is true in every possible world in which the rule exists. This is parallel to the argument about Sam. In that case we could say the warrant is true in every possible world in which the relevant linguistic rules exist. That the use of a particular word is governed by the rules associated with it is a contingent fact too. Such materially deductively valid arguments arise because there are rule-based systems in place that allow people acting as legislators to enact regulative rules operative within the jurisdiction of the system.

Inferences warranted by constitutive rules, such as the one about Sam, are somewhat different. As Searle stresses, such rules, having been agreed upon by those would participate in an activity, make such an activity possible. In the game of chess, the piece that can move any number of squares in any direction counts as the queen. Without the queen and the other pieces there could be no games of chess.

Athletic games are also based on constitutive rules, and in some cases the rules are exceptionless, permitting deductively valid inferences to be made from player behaviour. Providing play is in progress, for example, providing that baseball is being played, arguments like this one given by an umpire are deductively valid: "The baserunner was tagged with the ball when not on a base, so he's out." The warrant here can be stated as "If a baserunner is tagged with the ball when not touching a base, that person is out." The warrant is true because of a constitutive rule to the effect that being tagged when not touching a base counts as being out. In such a situation there is no point in anyone challenging the decision if they accept the premiss. Disagreement about such arguments in baseball can only be about the truth value of the premiss. To disagree with the inference claim is (by *modus tollens*) to disagree with the warrant, which in turn is to call the rule into question. But to raise such an issue is not conceptually possible within a game of baseball; it is to dispute the rules rather than their application to a particular situation.

Inferences relying on stipulative definitions can also be deductively valid. A simple example is "The platypus is a mammal, since it suckles its young," which is a deductively valid argument in zoology because its inference is backed by a stipulative definition of "mammal."

To summarize, in this section I have argued that there are arguments that are not formally valid, but they are deductively valid anyway, because they have warrants that are necessarily true. By providing only techniques that can identify formally valid inferences, the traditional texts provide no method of testing inferences for material validity.

2.1.2.4 *Evaluation Procedures.* The fourth major omission in the traditional texts is the failure to provide an overall evaluation procedure leading to a degree-of-proof judgment or something equivalent to it. The inference-evaluation techniques provided are not integrated into an overall evaluation procedure. This deficiency can be explained as a consequence of the conception of logic as the study of inference principles, rather than as the study of argument-evaluation techniques. In this respect the traditional logic texts contrast very unfavourably with the informal logic texts.

2.2 THE NEW APPROACH: INFORMAL LOGIC

The traditional view of argumentation as exemplified in Copi's *Introduction to Logic* and its clones published by rival publishers can be said, in light of the foregoing deficiencies, to represent an attempt to utilize mathematical logic for inference evaluation of nonmathematical reasoning. While the Copi-style text continues to be in common use, a growing number of texts are appearing that are quite different in their curriculum philosophy. Because these are sufficiently different from each other, one must resist labelling them as a type, but they represent a shift from a mathematical logic orientation to a "critical thinking" or "informal logic" orientation.[8] "Critical thinking" does not have the same denotation for all authors of critical thinking texts, and the same can be said for "informal logic." Nor do individual authors accept that these two labels denote the same subject matter, although the authors of one text are on record as claiming that they do (Little, Groarke, and Tindale 1989). I shall not attempt a conceptual analysis of these labels. My interest here is merely to examine the argument-evaluation procedures found in some of the better-received texts in the genre(s).

2.2.1 Origins of the New Approach

It appears that the term "informal logic" was first put into circulation by Gilbert Ryle when he used it as the title for one of his Tanner Lectures (1954). While his talk itself is interesting and provocative, the choice of "informal" instead of "non-formal" was probably unfortunate, suggesting as it does that such logic is non-rigorous or even slap-dash. In any event, the selection of the term as the title for a journal means that those labouring in this particular academic vineyard are pretty well stuck with "informal logic" as the name for their specialty.

In their brief history of the development of informal logic, Blair and Johnson note that beginning about 1970 textbooks differing from the Copi model began appearing: "Over the past decade something new has been emerging in logic ... The outlook we refer to is characterized by two interrelated features. First, there has been a turn in the direction of actual ... arguments in their native habitat ... Second, there has been a growing disenchantment with the capacity of formal logic to provide standards of good reasoning that illuminate the argumentation of ordinary discourse" (1980, 4–5). Among the better-known early texts embodying this new outlook are Howard Kahane's *Logic and Contemporary Rhetoric* (1971), Stephen Thomas' *Practical Reasoning in Natural Language* (1973), Michael Scriven's *Reasoning* (1976), and Johnson and Blair's *Logical Self-Defence* (1977).

None of these texts include syllogistic or the propositional and predicate calculi as inference-evaluation tools. None devote time to Mill's methods or other facets of scientific reasoning. They overlap with the traditional text only in devoting space to fallacies and problems of meaning. They are all focused on the evaluation of natural argumentation as it is found in the modern media, so that they are faced with the challenge of identifying the components and structure of the arguments they deal with. (This challenge did not arise for the traditional texts since they relied on neatly contrived passages of argumentation containing only one inference.) Furthermore, they are all concerned with argument evaluation, rather than just inference evaluation.

Since these texts were published and marketed there has been a steady stream of texts appearing, each representing their author's conception of a better informal logic text. The new-style texts, as the above comments suggest, represent a vast improvement over the standard type. Most conspicuously, they are all concerned with the complete task of argument evaluation, not just with inference evaluation. Nevertheless, in my opinion, they can be improved upon in several respects.[9] I shall highlight these areas for improvement by discussing their approaches to what I take to be the main elements in an argument-evaluation system.

2.2.2 *The Elements of an Argument-Evaluation System*

An argument-evaluation system for dealing with natural argumentation must involve the following elements, minimally: (1) a method of depicting argument structure, (2) strategies for evaluating inferences, (3) strategies for premiss evaluation, (4) a strategy for arriving at an overall judgment of argument quality, and (5) a formal procedure that incorporates these strategies.

2.2.2.1 *Depicting Argument Structure.* A distinguishing feature of the informal logic texts is that they wish to deal with everyday arguments, some of which may be relatively complex and most of which are unclear, to some degree, in the formulation of their propositions and the relationships among them. They tend not to be "sanitized" in the way the contrived examples of the traditional texts are.

Probably the best way of depicting the logical structure of natural arguments containing three or more propositions is to use a diagram format of some kind. Various formats are possible. Of the four texts mentioned above, three of them use diagrams for depicting structure. Only Kahane does not, and his text would be better if he had used them. The other three provide good advice to the student for constructing diagrams. Thomas is particularly strong in this respect.

In chapter 4 I shall evaluate the formats that various authors have presented and argue the superiority of a particular type.

2.2.2.2 *Inference-Evaluation Strategies.* All four texts mentioned above are concerned primarily with inductive arguments and the evaluation of their inferences. Two approaches seem to be exemplified. Both Kahane and Johnson and Blair proceed on the assumption that if we are adept at identifying the most common fallacies found in everyday argument, we will be able to identify good arguments more or less reliably. In its crudest form, the principle relied on is that if an inference is not an instance of one of the fallacies covered in the text, then it is likely to be a good one.

This approach has the advantage of enabling the writers to draw on extensive research that has been done on the fallacies, going back to

Aristotle. It can also serve to help students avoid fallacious reasoning, insofar as it takes these forms, by making them aware that such reasoning actually is fallacious. On the other hand, this approach essentially stresses the pathology of argument. I have found from teaching experience that students tend to become pessimistic about the use of argument for persuasion. They unconsciously come to believe that every argument proffered to them has a serious flaw. When faced in a test situation with arguments to evaluate, some of which are acceptable and some not, they frequently allege that the acceptable ones commit fallacies.

The fallacy approach, I think, tends to create the presumption that any given argument is defective and that it is to be accepted only after we fail to spot a defect. The view that inductive arguments are presumptively defective is supported by the inclusion in these two texts and many others of the alleged fallacy of hasty conclusion. If one has deductivist prejudices it is easy to believe that all inductive arguments commit this fallacy, since none guarantees the truth of its conclusion.

Johnson and Blair are aware of this problem with the fallacy approach. They respond by making four "observations": (1) knowledge of fallacies is useful to prevent being taken in by defective arguments; (2) negativity can be offset by applying this knowledge to one's own arguments; (3) textbook writers can combat negativity by including good arguments among those the student evaluates; and (4) exercising discrimination in evaluation reduces the chance of excessively negative judgments (1983, 33).

Point (1) is undoubtedly true and represents a compensating benefit of the approach. Point (2) does not seem to have much force, as it may amount to saying that being unfair to others' arguments is justified by being unfair to one's own. Point (3) can help prevent errors of appraisal, but in my experience this strategy is not very effective. Point (4) is not very helpful, as it amounts to saying that there is more to argument evaluation than just identifying fallacies, without stating what that is.

Using something like a fallacy "checklist" to identify acceptable inductive inferences is not very practical as an inference evaluation strategy, even if our checklist is exhaustive. If an argument does involve an inference fallacy and we are quite familiar with the fallacy forms, we will be able to reliably decide that the inference is defective, because we can "see" that our argument is an instance of a particular fallacy. But if it does not clearly correspond to any of the patterns, ought we to say the inference is acceptable? Each fallacious pattern has variants; the presentation of the argument may obscure its identity as an actual fallacy, or we may simply be unfamiliar with the fallacious pattern that the argument in fact exemplifies.

The texts by Thomas and Scriven take a more neutral view as regarding presumption of validity or invalidity. Both present a general strategy for evaluation, that of counterexampling against the universal generalization form of the warrant: "Criticism strategy involves the key move of 'counterexampling.' It applies to many types of premiss and all types of inference ... To counterexample an inference, treat it like a one-way generalization ... if the statement A is supposed to imply statement B, try to think of cases where A would be true but B would be either definitely false or unlikely" (Scriven 1976, 44). According to Thomas, "to decide whether an argument is valid, one need only ask the following question: If the statements expressing the reasons were true, would it be possible or likely for the conclusion to be false?" (Thomas 1973, 71–2).

While the counterexampling strategy for inference evaluation is logically sound, these writers do not develop it to make it really useful. This is probably explained by their belief that applying it in practice "is an exercise in imagination" (Scriven 1976, 44) and cannot be made into a mechanical procedure because we are evaluating content rather than form.

This deficiency prompts Johnson to complain about *Reasoning* that "the theory of criticism is not well developed. Scriven wants to avoid fallacy theory, but it is not clear what he wishes to put in its place" (Johnson 1981, 135).[10] One response to this challenge is suggested by this complaint by Tomko: "The most glaring weakness in informal logic texts as a whole is the lack of attention given to non-deductive arguments" (1979, 358). I will discuss such arguments in chapter 7.

Setting aside Johnson's complaint for now, the actual use of the counterexampling strategy for arriving at inference quality judgments is quite intuitive in the hands of both Thomas and Scriven. Thomas uses a set of grading terms to obtain some precision in inference judgments, but he operates intuitively in arriving at such judgments. Given the argument "It took over a year to finish the post office building; the plaster began to crack after it was completed; the heating system broke down; therefore, somebody was taking graft," he has this to say: "This argument is quite weak. Although the reasons provide some evidence in favour of the conclusion, they fall far short of establishing it. Applying the criterion of validity stated above, this is shown clearly. To the proper question, 'Could the reasons be true and yet the conclusion be false?' the answer, obviously, is 'Yes, it is quite possible.' There are many imaginable ways in which the statements given as reasons could all be true without anyone's having taken graft. For example, perhaps the workmen were incompetent" (1973, 73).

This is fairly good inference evaluation, but quite intuitive. There is obviously a connection between the likelihood of the counterexample case and the likelihood of the conclusion, given the premises, and a judgment of the former is being made to arrive at one for the latter. The first judgment is made intuitively, the relationship is intuitive, and the inference rating is based on these two intuitions. It would be better if an intuitive judgment of the likelihood of the counterexample being true could lead us by some principle or formula to a definite rating for the inference, thereby eliminating one intuitive step that might give rise to different judgments by different evaluators.

It seems clear that, because of the intuitive nature of the procedure, the student using Thomas' text will acquire the ability to evaluate inferences accurately only by studying his examples of actual evaluations. This is typical of almost all texts in this genre. Relative to simple arguments, those containing a single inference, it is a "rough and ready" but workable procedure. But it is not likely to be reliable when applied to extended arguments.

2.2.2.3 *Premiss Evaluation.* As for premiss evaluation, the four texts represent two distinct approaches. Kahane and Johnson and Blair use a fallacy approach. Kahane discusses eight premiss fallacies. The same philosophy is relied on as for inference evaluation: the inability to detect a fallacy is considered to be a good ground for accepting a premiss.

Thomas and Scriven follow the approach of traditional texts (in practice if not in theory), which is to regard premiss evaluation as outside the scope of logic. Thomas provides no strategies for premiss evaluation. He follows the traditional texts in his preoccupation with inference quality. Scriven sprinkles advice on premiss evaluation throughout his text, rather than providing extended coverage. This approach is probably explained by his observation that "it's a good general principle that the main function of argument analysis is to concentrate on errors of logic rather than errors of fact" (Scriven 1976, 73).

With the exception of Thomas, these texts provide some useful information on premiss evaluation. They all recognize a place for it in argument evaluation, and in this respect they are superior to the traditional text. On the other hand, they are not very systematic. They do not attempt to identify the logically different kinds of assertions that might serve as premisses and to isolate the truth conditions associated with each so that an evaluator can have a sense of what is relevant in judging particular premisses.

2.2.2.4 *Overall Appraisals of Argument Quality.* Ideally, the goal of argument evaluation is to arrive at an accurate judgment of how probable the premises of an argument make the conclusion, based on the information we have. The traditional texts do not make such judgments so, understandably, they provide no guidance for making them. The new breed make these judgments but, except for Scriven, do not stress the need to do so, nor do they provide a methodical way of basing them on inference and premiss judgments.

Kahane makes summative judgments in various forms; he says, for example, "The main defect in this article is that it begs all the interesting questions" (1971, 122). He does not stress the need to make them, however. The same can be said of Thomas and of Blair and Johnson. Scriven goes further, including an "overall evaluation" step in his formal procedure. His advice is, "Now, make your final judgment on the argument. Grade it, in several dimensions if you like, but then give yourself an overall grade. It's a cop-out not to. You must decide whether it does have force, and how much, for you" (1976, 45).

This exhortation is admirable, so far as it goes. But no specific guidance is given on what grade to give when we have judged inferences and premisses. No grading vocabulary is provided either.

2.2.2.5 *Formal Evaluation Procedures.* Of the four texts, only Scriven presents a procedure that is explicit and intended to be followed in evaluating all the arguments contained in the book. I believe that his text may have been the first informal logic text to introduce an explicit procedure, and I shall describe and comment on it in the next chapter when I propose my own version.

Kahane and Thomas evidently intend the student to absorb their procedures by following their evaluations. Blair and Johnson provide a well-articulated procedure late in their text, as a means of dealing with extended arguments. It is as well-developed as Scriven's, but its value in the text is diminished because of their decision not to employ it in dealing with the fallacies, which take up the first half of the text.

2.2.3 Summary

Perhaps enough has been said to convey certain impressions about the "new wave" texts to the reader not familiar with them:

1 In contrast to the traditional Copi-style text, they direct their attention to argumentation found in everyday life.
2 In contrast to the Copi-style text, they are concerned with argument evaluation, not just inference evaluation.
3 They deal with inductive argumentation, since most natural argument is of this kind, but they do not deal with specific common

forms of inductive arguments that people use on a regular basis. This deficiency has not been addressed in later texts, other than in my *Argument Evaluation* (1984). Most writers are still under the influence of Copi in this respect.

4 They provide useful guidance for identifying and portraying argument structure, but not very satisfactory guidance for inference and premiss evaluation.[11]

5 They are not very methodical, and there is too much reliance on intuition. (Perhaps this is just a way of saying that they are *too* informal.)

In the chapters that follow, I intend to present and argue for a system of argument evaluation that is more systematic and explicit in its evaluative judgments. Such a system is better able to arrive at an accurate judgment of argument quality when extended arguments have to be evaluated.

3 An Argument-Evaluation System

In the last chapter a number of deficiencies were identified in texts of both the traditional and informal logic types. Although the latter type must be considered a vast improvement in usefulness for evaluating everyday argument, there were deficiencies noted that could be summarized in the complaint that the informal logic texts are unnecessarily informal.

I believe that the informal logic approach can be more systematic in arriving at judgments about argument quality, more precise in stating these judgments, and if I am right about this, more accurate in its appraisals.

3.1 OUTLINE OF A THEORY OF ARGUMENT EVALUATION

An adequate argument-evaluation procedure must be based on two things: (1) an adequate concept of an argument, and (2) an adequate conception of what counts as a good argument. I have argued that the concept of argument appropriate to evaluating an argument logically is that of a propositional complex. Here I wish to say what I take a good argument to be.

In terms of meeting the appropriate standards of goodness, an ideal argument has a true premiss and a true inference claim. I will argue in the next chapter that most arguments encountered in everyday life are not ideal in this sense. They are said to be inductive, rather than deductive. But some are regarded as good arguments in the sense that we are persuaded by them to accept their conclusions with enough confidence to act on them. And many provide appreciable, if not adequate, support for their conclusions. To do justice to inductive arguments when we evaluate them I will take my cue from Skyrms: "Many people know that logic has to do with correct reasoning and framing compelling arguments. Many also know that there are two basic branches of logic: inductive logic and deductive logic. Fewer people know that inductive logic is somehow tied up with the concept of probability" (1986, 1).

I have already said that an arguer – and by innocuous extension, an argument – makes three claims: (1) "P" is true; (2) "If P then C" is true; and (3) "C" is true. Now the probability of C, given the argument, is the joint probability of "P" and "If P then C." That is,

$$p(C) = p[P \& (\text{If } P \text{ then } C)].$$

An axiom of probability states that

$$p(A \& B) = p(A) \times p(B/A).$$

Now we can write

$$p(C) = p(P) \times p[(\text{If } P \text{ then } C)/P].$$

The term "$p(B/A)$" in the axiom takes account of cases in which A is relevant to B. When it is not, $p(B/A) = p(B)$. The concept of a conditional is such that if we are ignorant of P and trying to decide how probable the conditional is, the discovery that P was true would have no relevance to our deliberation. Thus,

$$p[(\text{If } P \text{ then } C)/P] = p(\text{If } P \text{ then } C).$$

We can now write

$$p(C) = p(P) \times p(\text{If } P \text{ then } C).$$

Later (section 3.2.5.1) I will argue that the probability of the conditional is the conditional probability $p(C/P)$. (This might seem self-evident, but those who interpret ordinary conditionals as the material implication of formal logic oppose this interpretation.) Finally, we can write

$$p(C) = p(P) \times p(C/P)$$

A measure of argument goodness, then, is obtained by assigning a probability to P, getting a value of $p(C/P)$, and obtaining their mathematical product.[1] This formula is the basis of the evaluation procedure to be presented in this book.

Perhaps some clarification of what $p(C)$ represents is desirable. In effect, when an evaluator arrives at a $p(C)$ value for an argument, s/he is expressing how good P alone is as a means of proving C. No other evidence for C is to play a role in the evaluation. Two kinds of information can be relied on, however: information relevant to P and information relevant to the inference claim. It follows that $p(C)$ is independent of the prior probability that the evaluator might have assigned to C. Thus, it may be the case that H considers C as true following evaluation of the argument, even though H does not regard P as proving C. This is explained by the possibility that H already had assigned a fairly high prior probability to C on the basis of other information, and P supplements that other evidence. Obviously, P may be more or less important in helping a particular person judge C, depending on how high the prior probability of C is, and how good P is as evidence for C. However, I will not be concerned with the question of the role P has in persuading H that C.[2] I will be solely concerned with techniques and procedures for deciding how much support arguments give their conclusions.

One final point: $p(C)$ represents argument support for C, not the support that P provides if it is true. People frequently treat $p(C/P)$ as a measure of the support that P gives C, but in doing so they are relying on what Skyrms calls the certainty model of epistemic probability: "The certainty model lives up to its name in assigning epistemic probability of one to each [premiss]" (1986, 18). In contrast, in using the above formula for $p(C)$, we are operating with what he calls the "fallibility model" (19). With this model, $p(P)$ can have a value less than one. Skyrms regards the fallibility model as more realistic, and I agree.

3.2 AN ARGUMENT RATING SCHEME

The key to being more systematic is to use a well-developed evaluation procedure. Precision, I shall argue, is enhanced by using rating schemes for expressing premiss, inference, and conclusion judgments. Accuracy of conclusion judgment depends upon the rating schemes and upon the strategies used for arriving at premiss and inference ratings. These strategies will be discussed in later chapters. In this chapter I wish to propose and defend a set of rating schemes and an evaluation procedure.

In the next three sections I shall develop a numerical rating scheme and a translation guide for rating premisses, inferences, and conclusions. But before doing so I wish to provide a response to those writers of informal logic texts who have not adopted an argument rating system and want some reasons for so doing.

3.2.1 *The Need for a Rating Scheme*

Informal logic and critical thinking texts allow the evaluator to express argument-quality judgments in whatever natural language vocabulary they deem appropriate, while at the same time illustrating part of the correct vocabulary by means of evaluating examples. If the learner conscientiously emulates the language used by the authors of the text, there is some likelihood of felicitousness in their inference-quality judgments, but experience indicates that there will be a fairly high incidence of infelicitous terminology (for example, "true inferences," "false arguments"). This is probably due to a tendency of the novice to confuse inference and premiss evaluation.

There will also be a fair bit of disagreement as to argument quality in the absence of standard terminology. Consider for a moment the relatively ideal case in which (1) two persons have the same information; (2) each attributes the same persuasive force to it; and (3) there is no standardized terminology for expressing their judgment. In this situation different terminology will often be used, which can easily create the impression, for them and others, that the parties are disagreeing. If such situations occur too frequently it will give novice users of an evaluation scheme the impression that "it is all subjective," which may lead to the conviction that argument quality cannot be rationally discussed.

Consider, on the other hand, the case in which (1) and (2) apply, but people do share a common set of "grading labels." Chances are that if they associate similar standards with each label, they will arrive at the same judgment.

Of course people will sometimes disagree in using a standardized terminology, since they have different kinds and amounts of information and may also "see" the same information as having different degrees of persuasive force. But experience in teaching a system of evaluation that uses a standardized ratings scheme (Grennan 1984) has convinced me that even a large group can often come to agree on a rating once all relevant information has been exposed and evaluated. When a group experiences such a consensus, it strengthens the conviction that argument evaluation is a rational and objective process.

One reason, then, for using a rating scheme with formally specified evaluative terms is that it can reduce interpersonal differences in argument appraisals. A more important reason to adopt a scheme of the kind I will advocate is that it promotes accuracy in overall argument ratings by enabling us to avoid the conjunction fallacy, which I will describe shortly. This fallacy has the effect of leading us to judge arguments too favourably.

In most logic texts argument quality is said to be a matter of soundness. If an argument is "sound," it proves its conclusion. Soundness is often defined as

Soundness = true premises + (deductively) valid inference.

This definition of a good argument is unfortunate in a number of ways, and I have advocated a more adequate definition:

$$p(C) = p(P) \times p(\text{If } P \text{ then } C).$$

One important advantage of the probabilistic definition is that it reflects the fact that conclusion probability involves a product relation, whereas the traditional version obscures this, thereby inviting the student to infer that the relationship is somehow additive. And by their practice of arriving at judgments of conclusion support intuitively (based on premiss and inference quality judgments, of course), informal logic text authors fail to clarify the relationship. Indeed, there is reason to suppose that they themselves do not accurately make conclusion-support judgments, since there is good scientific evidence that people who do not rely explicitly on the rules of probability tend to use an algorithm for deriving $p(C)$ from $P(P)$ and $p(C/P)$ that is incorrect. Cognitive psychologists call this the "conjunction fallacy," for reasons that will be made clear.

Users of the traditional texts did not commonly commit the conjunction fallacy, simply because they were not given the opportunity of assigning a conclusion-support rating based on premiss and inferential support ratings. They were not given the opportunity, since they were concerned only with inferential support and perhaps even identified inference evaluation and argument evaluation.[3] However, when complete argument evaluation is the task, as it is in the newer informal logic texts, the two ratings must be properly combined to obtain an accurate conclusion-support rating, and there is research data that shows that we may accurately judge inferential and premiss support separately, yet reach a too-favourable conclusion-support judgment because of the intuitive algorithm we rely on.

A detailed study with good methodological credentials was conducted by Wyer and Goldberg (1970). They investigated, among other things, whether subjective probability judgments obey the mathematical relationship $p(A\&B) = p(A) \times p(B/A)$. (Here $p(A\&B)$ corresponds to $p(C)$ in $p(C) = p(P) \times p(C/P)$.) They describe their method as follows: "Fifteen pairs of statements were selected ... five pieces of information were required for each pair of statements A and B: $p(A)$, $p(B)$, $p(B/A)$, $p(A\&B)$, and $p(A$ or $B)$. A 75-item questionnaire, therefore, was constructed in which subjects were asked to estimate the likelihood that appropriate statements or combinations of statements were true ... A total of 40 introductory college students, mostly freshmen, participated in the study. Few had any background in probability theory" (1970, 103).

The results were reported, in part, as follows: "the values of the quantities $p(A) \times p(B/A)$, $p(A) \times p(B)$, and $p(A\&B)$ were determined for each subject for each set of statements. These values were then averaged over subjects ... the predicted value $[p(A) \times p(B/A)]$ was substantially less than the obtained value [for $p(A\&B)$]" (104).

This tendency has been well documented by others: "Previous studies of the subjective probability of conjunctions focused primarily on the multiplicative rule $p(A\&B) = p(B) \times p(A/B)$ ... The results showed that people generally overestimate the probability of conjunctions in the sense that $p(A\&B) > p(B) \times p(A/B)$" (Tversky and Khaneman 1983, 311).

Wyer and Goldberg go on to perform a statistical analysis of their data that suggests to them that "in fact subjects' estimates of the conjunctive are much closer to the simple average of $p(A)$ and $p(B)$" (1970, 104).

In sum, the authors found that subjects tend to use an intuitive algorithm for judging $p(A\&B)$ that yields systematically over-optimistic results. In the context of judging $p(P\&C)$ for an argument, we can expect that, even given values for premiss probability $(p(P))$ and inferential support $(p(C/P))$, naive evaluators without guidance will arrive at a value for $p(P\&C)$ (which is written as "$p(C)$" throughout this work) that is significantly higher than it would be if they relied on the product rule, because their intuitive algorithm involves (roughly) averaging the two support values.

Thus, it might seem that if we are to impart an ability to accurately arrive at a conclusion-support judgment, subjects must be trained to avoid the conjunction fallacy. However, this is easier said than done. As with other inborn dispositions to commit reasoning errors, it is not effective in the long run to simply call people's attention to the error when they commit it. A new context or different propositional content or different logical structure may evoke the error again.

One way of ensuring compliance with the product rule is to use a ratings system in which the conclusion-support rating is predetermined

Table 1
The Thomas Rating Scheme

Status of Reasons	*Degree of Validity* *(Degree of Confirmation of Inference)*					
	Deductively Valid	*Strong*	*Can't Tell*	*Moderate*	*Weak*	*Nil*
Definitely true	S	S	CS	U	U	U
Probably true	PS	M	CS	U	U	U
Uncertain	CS	CS	CS	U	U	U
Probably false	PU	PU	PU	U	U	U
Definitely false	U	U	U	U	U	U

according to an appropriate rule by the selection of premiss and inference ratings. That is, the system is such that the evaluator makes the latter two decisions and consults a table or formula to find the proper conclusion-support rating.

3.2.2 *Two Extant Rating Schemes*

There are, to my knowledge, only two complete rating systems found in the informal logic literature.[4] One is contained in *Argument Evaluation* (Grennan 1984); the other was developed by Stephen Thomas. I will evaluate each of these, beginning with the Thomas system.

Thomas's rating system is shown in Table 1. It was presented at the 1990 ISSA (International Society for the Study of Argumentation) conference in Amsterdam but did not appear in the proceedings. It is an extension of the inference rating system found in his text (1973, 79). Thomas presents a matrix containing argument-soundness judgments (my "conclusion-support" judgments).

The symbols in the matrix are defined as follows:

S: The reasoning is sound and reliable.
PS: The reasoning is probably sound and reliable.
M: The reasoning is marginal; it is close to being sound and reliable, but it is not quite certain, or totally reliable beyond a reasonable doubt.
CS: We cannot say whether the reasoning is sound or unsound (and so, we should not rely on it).
PU: The reasoning is probably unsound and unreliable.
U: The reasoning is unsound and unreliable.

Table 2
Grennan's (1984) Rating Scheme

Rating	Probability Range
√	75–100%
?	50–75%
x	0–50%

The soundness ratings that occur in the matrix suggest to me that the matrix is based on the product rule, although no explicit statement of this rationale is given. Thus, in using the matrix, an evaluator who decides that the only premiss is probably true and that the degree of validity is strong, would consult the matrix and find that the soundness verdict is M. That is, the reasoning is marginal.

This rating system is, overall, quite satisfactory within its limitations, but one of its limitations is serious: it is usable only for arguments whose conclusions have only one premiss. This is obscured by Thomas' presentation, as all of the examples he evaluates are one-premiss arguments. But in everyday argumentation people tend to present all the items of evidence in their possession in trying to support their conclusion. Frequently there is more than one item.

The only alternative (non-numerical) rating system I am aware of is presented in *Argument Evaluation* (Grennan 1984). It has the advantage of being usable for multipremiss arguments, although this advantage is not pointed out in the text itself. The scheme uses a rating "vocabulary" of three symbols: "√", "?", and "x". Each was to have three roles, serving to rate premisses, inferences, and conclusions. It might be thought that this triple ambiguity would be confusing to those learning the system, but in practice it has not proved to be.

Symbols like these require definitions to specify their meanings within the system of evaluation, and I chose probability-range definitions, which made it possible to construct a matrix like Thomas's that would conform to the product rule. The definitions are shown in Table 2.

The matrix was constructed by taking the mean value for each symbol and calculating the conclusion value by the product rule. For example, given a premiss rating of "√" (mean value = $7/8$) and an inference rating of "?" (mean value = $5/8$), we calculate that $p(C) = 35/64 = 0.55$. Thus, I chose to enter the conclusion rating in the matrix as "?" since the calculated value fell within the 50–75% range. Similarly, with both inference and premiss rated "?", the calculated value

Premise Inference	√	?	x
√	√	?	x
?	?	x	x
x	x	x	x

Fig. 1.   Conclusion-rating matrix (Grennan 1984, 44)

for $p(C) = 5/8 \times 5/8 = 0.39$. Therefore, I entered "x" in the matrix for this combination.

Using this approach to determine matrix values, I developed the conclusion-rating matrix shown in Figure 1. Like Thomas's matrix, this one appears to work only with arguments having one premise per conclusion, but actually it can be reinterpreted to deal with multipremiss arguments. Consider a two-premiss, one-inference argument. The premisses are P_1 and P_2, the conclusion C. The conclusion-support value is $p(C) = p(P_1) \times p(P_2) \times p(C/P_1 \& P_2)$. Now since the matrix is a device for following the product rule, we can obtain a rating for the premiss set simply by regarding it as dealing with P_1 and P_2 rather than "premiss" and "inference." So if P_1 is rated "√", say, and P_2 is rated "?", we can find the rating for the premiss set to be "?". Having done this, we can take the premiss set rating and the inference rating and find the rating for conclusion support. If we had had three premisses we would take the joint rating for the first two and the rating for the third, and find the rating in the matrix that would represent the rating for the set of three premisses. This rating system can, therefore, deal with multi-premiss arguments. This is an essential feature of any adequate rating system.

Each of the rating systems discussed above has advantages. Thomas's use of ordinary language for a rating vocabulary restricts him to dealing with single-premiss arguments. He could, however, add a second matrix containing only premiss rating terminology so that he could perform the premiss-set rating that I described for my system. But even with this feature, both of these systems are somewhat clumsy to use in dealing with multipremiss arguments, since they require the repetitive use of matrices as described above.

3.2.3 Developing a New Rating Scheme

Numerical probability values are easier to use than the systems just discussed. We simply assign values to each premiss and the inference, and then calculate the product of the values. No matrices are needed, and more precision ought to be possible, because we are not working with rating terms that are defined by probability ranges. On the other hand, as I noted before, people are not in the habit of making probability judgments in numerical terms. This fact may make the system more difficult to operate.

To overcome this difficulty we can design the procedure so that evaluators form their judgments from a standard verbal set (one set for premises and one for inferences) and then use a translation table to obtain the numerical equivalent of each rating. To construct such a table, we ought to operate on the principle that the rating is a numerical "synonym" for the standardized verbal judgment. It would undermine the credibility of a rating system if its numerical ratings did not closely reflect the meanings of the standardized verbal rating expressions. Ideally then, we would want people who had not been exposed to the rating system to be able to assign, on request, a numerical synonym to any verbal expression in the system such that that numerical value was the same as the value in the translation guide.

In settling on a set of expressions, three criteria are important: (1) the expressions should have minimal vagueness; (2) the scheme must allow us to make the finest distinctions that represent genuine differences; and (3) the scheme must cover the probability range from 0 to 1. Criterion (3) is easily met, but (2) raises difficulties. How many different ratings do we need for a practical ratings scheme? To arrive at an answer, I will first canvass answers that can be found in the literature.

We judge the simplest complete argument to be acceptable when we regard the premiss as true and the inference as valid (that is, the inference claim is true). The traditional texts use this formula in conjunction with, in effect, two-value rating schemes. Premises are to be judged as true or false, inferences as valid or invalid, and conclusions as proved or unproved.

This rating system is far too crude. While we wish to adhere to the law of the excluded middle and maintain that every proposition is either true or false, the actual truth value of a proposition may be obscured for us by a lack of information. The evidence for the premiss may be inconclusive, so that rationality requires us to say, for example, that "this premiss is probably true," or "likely false." In the interests of accuracy, then, the two-value rating scheme is unacceptable.

Furthermore, a two-value inference-rating scheme is too crude for judging most inferences. Most arguments we encounter are inductive rather than deductive. Once one is willing to recognize that not just deductively valid arguments are good arguments, several important implications must be accepted, one of which is that inference validity in inductive arguments is a matter of degree. This means that their inferences must be evaluated in probabilistic terms, either verbal or numerical.

Now if premiss and inference grading terms must be probabilistic, conclusion support ratings must also, since they are based on the others. What is the relationship between conclusion support and the other two parameters? As I argued in section 3.1, any argument can be conceived as the conjunction of the actual premiss set, the implicit inference claim, and the entailed conclusion. Since the truth of the premiss- and inference-claim conjunction entails the truth of the conclusion, the probability of the conclusion, $p(C)$, will be the joint probability of the parts of the conjunction, whose value will be $p(P) \times p(\text{if } P \text{ then } C)$.

The three-value scheme presented in *Argument Evaluation* represents an improvement over the traditional two-value one because it accommodates probabilistic judgments. However, experience in using this scheme and observing students using it has convinced me that it is too "coarse-grained." Occasions have frequently arisen when we have felt that we could make more precise judgments. But how many ratings are needed to express the finest discriminations? Thomas, in the rating scheme presented above, uses five values in his premiss rating scheme: "definitely true," "probably true," "don't know or uncertain," "probably false," and "definitely false." This arrangement gives more precision than the three-value system, but can we have even more? This is best answered by turning our attention to the other side of our translation table – the numerical column.

The decision to use a numerical rating scheme itself provides some guidance. First of all, it forces us to choose between decimal and fraction formats. A decimal format is preferable because in using the rating system, we are required to multiply ratings, and this is much easier with a decimal format. Having chosen a decimal format, we can see that it would be inappropriate to use a format with more than one decimal place. It is simply not justifiable to claim that a premiss should be rated, say, 0.66 rather than 0.65. Thus, the numerical ratings will have to be chosen from among this set of values: 0.0, 0.1, 0.2, 0.3, 0.4, 0.5, 0.6, 0.7, 0.8, 0.9, and 1.0.

Clearly, it is desirable to be able to express the judgment that a premiss is true, so we will want 1.0 as a rating. It is also desirable to be able to express a judgment that the premiss is false, which would be represented by a rating of 0.0. By adopting these values we can meet criterion (3), that the scheme must span the probability range from zero to one.

It is also desirable to have the value 0.5 as a rating. It is a threshold value in the sense that if a claim is rated above 0.5, a rational betting person would assent to it if forced to choose between saying it is true or false. Conversely, if that person rated it lower than 0.5, s/he would choose to say it is false.

If we include 0.0, 0.5, and 1.0, how many of the other eight values should be incorporated? This can be established only by testing rating schemes in the course of evaluating actual arguments. My experience leads me to believe that the most "fine-grained" scheme that we can meaningfully use is an eleven-point scale, using all the numerical values given above.

3.2.4 A Premiss Rating Scheme

Given the eleven numerical values, we must choose a set of verbal synonyms for premiss evaluation. We could proceed by stipulating synonyms based upon our individual semantic intuitions. This was how I proceeded in *Argument Evaluation* and apparently how Thomas did too, in his text and in the extended scheme described above. But this approach has an element of subjectivity that ought to be avoided if possible. It would be better to use data obtained from a larger number of rating users.

Some data of this kind is available. Several psychologists have conducted studies in which they asked subjects to give numerical "definitions" of particular probabilistic expressions. They have found that there is some vagueness and some confusion about the terms, but the vagueness does not make them unusable as argument ratings. For example, one team found that "likely" had a median value of 0.75; two thirds of the respondents gave a value between 0.64 and 0.86 (Lichtenstein and Newman 1967, 564). Another study found that it was given a median value of 0.70, and half the responses were between 0.65 and 0.79 (Behn and Vaupel 1982, 76).

To minimize vagueness, a rating scheme ought to rely on the root expression that has the least vagueness. The findings indicate that expressions containing the root term "likely" have less vagueness than ones containing "probable" or "possible." In one study (Lichtenstein and Newman 1967, 564)), the range for two thirds (those within one standard deviation of the mean) of the responses for these three terms was "likely": 0.64–0.86; "probable": 0.58–0.92; "possible": 0.26–0.72. These figures show that "possible" is too vague as a probabilistic term. Since the estimate dispersion for "likely" is the narrowest, I will present a premiss rating scheme that relies on it.

In presenting the rating scheme (Table 3), I have included the median values obtained from the two studies, when available. It will be

Table 3
Premiss Rating Scheme

Verbal Rating	Assigned Rating	Lichtenstein and Newman	Behn and Vaupel
P is true	1.0	–	–
P is very likely	0.9	0.90	–
P is quite likely	0.8	0.80	–
P is likely	0.7	0.75	0.70
P is somewhat likely	0.6	0.60	–
P is as likely as not	0.5	–	–
P is more likely false than true	0.4	–	–
P is somewhat unlikely	0.3	0.33	–
P is unlikely	0.2	0.16	0.20
P is very unlikely	0.1	0.10	0.10
P is false	0.0	–	–

noted that the actual numerical definitions given by subjects result in a certain asymmetry. For example, in the Lichtenstein and Newman study "likely" is 0.75, whereas "unlikely" is 0.16, and in the Behn and Vaupel study the values are 0.70 and 0.20 respectively. There may be a problem of consistency here, which we might address by stipulating appropriate numerical values for the various expressions. However, I have chosen to take a descriptivist view by choosing verbal expressions to match numerical values, based on the testimony. There are two exceptions: (a) no suitable expression was given a value of 0.4 by subjects, so I have relied on my own intuition to adopt "more likely false than true" as a suitable verbal equivalent; (b) no expression containing "likely" was given a value of 0.5, so I have provided one ("P is as likely as not") that I am confident would be replicated in a poll. The former definition, on the other hand, may prove on investigation to be slightly in error.

3.2.5 Developing an Inference Rating Scheme

In section 3.1 I claimed that argument quality, the degree of support that an argument gives its conclusion ($p(C)$) is the product of the joint probability of the premisses ($p(P)$) and the probability of the inference claim (p(If P then C)). I also said that inference-claim probability can be equated with the conditional probability of C, given P ($p(C/P)$). This interpretation has been challenged, so before I discuss the terminology of an inference rating scheme, I will defend it.

3.2.5.1 *Inference-Claim Probability.* The analysis of inference-claim probability depends upon how one analyzes the meaning of the conditional itself. To deal with this issue of interpretation correctly, we must begin by recognizing that "If X then Y" can express different kinds of connections. Irving Copi provides a useful classification of these. He begins by giving examples of four different conditionals, "each of which seems to assert a different type of implication, and to each of which corresponds a different sense of 'if-then'" (1982, 291):

A If all humans are mortal and Socrates is a human, then Socrates is mortal.
B If Leslie is a bachelor, then Leslie is unmarried.
C If blue litmus paper is placed in acid, then the litmus paper will turn red.
D If State loses the Homecoming Game, then I'll eat my hat.

He later comments on this set of examples as follows: "Every conditional statement means to deny that its antecedent is true and its consequent false, but this need not be the whole of its meaning. A conditional such as A also asserts a logical connection between its antecedent and consequent, one like B asserts a definitional connection, C a causal connection, D a decisional connection" (280).

Several issues can be raised about the foregoing passage. First, is it appropriate to conceive of each example as involving a different sense of "if-then"? Neither Copi nor anyone else is disposed to say that conjunctions containing different kinds of conjuncts involve different senses of "and." But Copi seems to think that since the facts that ensure the truth of his examples are of different types, "if-then" must have different meanings in each case.

This view indicates that he is operating with a truth-conditions theory of meaning. But although (A) and (B) can be said to have different meaning by virtue of different associated truth conditions, this does not show that conditionals have no common meaning elements contributed by their "if-then" components. It shows only that the content of the antecedent and consequent contribute to the meaning of the conditional. Indeed, Copi recognizes that conditionals do have a common meaning component: the denial that both the antecedent is true and the consequent is false. Let us consider this thesis.

Should we agree that "If X then Y" is synonymous with "It is not the case that both X is true and Y is false"? This commits us to accepting the material implication (to be represented here by "$X \supset Y$") definition of "If X then Y," and this definition does not square with the

Table 4
Truth Table Definition
of Material Conditional

X	Y	$X \supset Y$
T	T	T
T	F	F
F	T	T
F	F	T

properties that many ordinary conditionals have. That definition can be expressed in a truth table as shown in Table 4.

There are a number of fatal deficiencies in defining "If X then Y" in this fashion. The main one is that ordinary conditionals are not truth functional; they do not satisfy the definition for material implication. Consider line 1 of the table. "If the moon is a geological satellite of Earth, then it is smaller than Earth" corresponds to it. But "If the moon is a geological satellite of Earth, then men have been there" contains true propositions but is false, because there is no basis for asserting a connection between these facts. That is, one cannot infer that a conditional is true from simply knowing that its antecedent and consequent are true.

Consider line 3. "If Earth is a satellite of the moon, then the two move relative to each other" corresponds to the values for X and Y on this line. But unfortunately so does this example: "If Earth is a satellite of the moon, then Earth is heavier than the moon," which is a false claim because of certain principles of physics. Consider also line 4. "If Earth is a satellite of the moon then Earth is lighter than the moon" is true by the same principles of physics. On the other hand, "If Earth is a satellite of the moon, then the moon is the centre of our solar system" is false by virtue of some astronomical facts.

The preceding examples make the point that ordinary conditionals do not conform to the material implication definition, except at line 2 of that definition. Thus, the formula "It is not the case that both X and not-Y" either does not capture enough of the meaning of "If X then Y," or does not capture any of it. I do not think the latter alternative is correct, however. Those who utter conditionals are committed to maintaining "It is not the case that both X and not-Y," even though it is not an adequate definition for "If X then Y." The explanation for this state of affairs is that "It is not the case that both X and not-Y" is entailed by "If X then Y," whatever expressions are synonymous with it.

One definition that can be considered for "If X then Y" is "The truth of X (when true) guarantees the truth of Y." This is probably not the only expression that might be seen as synonymous with "if-then." Pollock, for instance, suggests "the truth of X makes Y true" or "the truth of X brings about the truth of Y" (1975, 51). All of these formulations imply a connection between X and Y that is affirmed independently of the truth values of the connected propositions.

If we accept "The truth of X (when true) guarantees the truth of Y" (to be symbolized as "$X \Rightarrow Y$") as a definition of "If X then Y," we find that the conditional entails the material implication definition, since the expression "Both X and not-Y" cannot be true when "$X \Rightarrow Y$" is true. On the other hand "$X \supset Y$" can be true, given certain values for X and Y, when X and Y are not connected, i.e., when "$X \Rightarrow Y$" is false. Coincidental events and states provide good examples. Consider "If the CN Tower is in Toronto then the Taj Mahal is in India." Now if we "translate" the assertion as "The truth of 'The CN Tower is in Toronto' guarantees the truth of 'The Taj Mahal is in India,'" its logical oddness is apparent. (The stylistic oddness is irrelevant.) Most of us would go further and say that it is false, there being no connection between the two phenomena. On the other hand, if it was legitimate to translate the conditional into "It is not the case that both the CN Tower is in Toronto and the Taj Mahal is not in India," we would have to say that it is true.

I have tried to show that the logical component of an ordinary conditional assertion can be expressed by "The truth of X (when true) guarantees the truth of Y ($X \Rightarrow Y$)" and that this form entails material implication ($X \supset Y$) but is not entailed by it. In other words, material implication is part of the meaning of ordinary conditionals, but not all of it.

Returning now to Copi's treatment of the four conditionals he proffered as examples of the diversity of such assertions, it should be obvious that the meaning of anyone uttering any of these could be adequately expressed in the form "The truth of X (when true) guarantees the truth of Y." Thus, I conclude that this form represents an adequate synonym for the everyday "if-then," whether it is factual (like examples A and B) or counterfactual like C.

It is now time to discuss how p(If P then C) is to be determined. Obviously, when an inference is deductively valid, the value of p(If P then C) is 1. However, in inductive arguments, the truth of P does not guarantee the truth of C, but only makes it probable. Therefore, we can say that p(If P then C) is less than 1. But how do we determine the actual value?

There are basically two theories of how the probability of a conditional is to be determined. One position is that the probability of a conditional is some sort of conditional probability. This is the position advocated by Adams, who maintains that "the probability of an indicative conditional of the form 'if A is the case then B is' is a conditional probability … that should equal the ratio of the probability of 'A and B' to the probability of A" (1975, 3). This definition arises from the probability axiom that

$$p(A\&B) = p(A) \times p(B/A).$$

On this theory, "$p(\text{if } P \text{ then } C)$" can be defined as $p(C/P)$ within the probability calculus.

The only other account given attention is the view of Copi and most other logicians, i.e., that the relationship is expressible as the probability of the conditional rendered as material implication. But, as I have already pointed out, the formulas "$P \Rightarrow C$" and "$P \supset C$" are not logically equivalent, so they cannot mean the same. This generates a suspicion that the probability of an ordinary conditional is $p(C/P)$, and not the probability of a material implication. I will now demonstrate that this is indeed so. The discussion can also be seen as further grounds for rejecting the material implication interpretation of "if-then."

The probability of the material implication conditional can be written

$$p(P \supset C) = p(-(P\&-C)).$$

Using some algebra and some probability axioms we can express this as

$$p(P \supset C) = 1 - p(P) + p(P\&C).$$

The analysis reveals two major problems with the material implication interpretation. First, and most important, it makes conditional probability a function of $p(P)$. This is highly counterintuitive. The ordinary concept of a conditional is taken to express a relationship between two propositions, one that can be judged to be true or false regardless of the truth values of the constituent propositions. My judgment that the proposition "If Diego Maradona is a father then he has begat a child" is true, does not wait upon any investigation of Maradona's personal life.

Secondly, the probability values obtained by determining $p(P \supset C)$ are at odds with actual cases. Consider this simple case. A die is rolled, and without seeing the number rolled, I say "If it's under 4 then it's odd." Intuitively, we would think that there are three values under 4 and that 2 are odd, so the initial probability of the conditional is 2/3.

Using the formula for $p(C/P)$, $p(P\&C)/p(P)$, we can determine that $p(P\&C) = 1/3$ because 2 values out of 6 are both under 4 and odd (i.e., 1 and 3). There are 3 values out of 6 that are odd, so $p(P) = 1/2$. Thus, we calculate that $p(C/P) = (1/3)/(1/2) = 2/3$. This corresponds to the intuitive value.

I will calculate the value for $p(P \supset C)$ using the formula "$1 - p(P\&$ $-C)$." There is one favourable case of $P\&-C$, that is, when the number is both odd and not under 4, i.e., 5. Thus $p(P \supset C)$ has the value $5/6$. This value is, of course, incorrect, and, unfortunately, too high.

It can be shown that, with one exception, $p(P \supset C)$ will always be higher than $p(C/P)$. To do this we express it as a function of $p(C/P)$ by substituting $p(C/P) \times p(P)$ for $p(P\&C)$ in the equation for $p(P \supset C)$. We get

$$p(P \supset C) = 1 - p(P)(1 - p(C/P)).$$

How do the two parameters compare in magnitude? Suppose we assign an arbitrary value N to $p(C/P)$. We now have

$$p(P \supset C) = 1 - p(P)(1 - N).$$

Now suppose we vary $p(P)$ from 0 to 1. With $p(P) = 0$, $p(P \supset C) = 1$. As $p(P)$ increases, $p(P \supset C)$ drops, until at $p(P) = 1$ it reaches N. Thus, $p(P \supset C)$ is always higher than $p(C/P)$, except when $p(P) = 1$. For example, when $p(C/P) = 0.5$, we find that $p(P \supset C)$ has a value between 0.5 with $p(P) = 1$, and 1.0 with $p(P) = 1$.

On the above grounds I reject the material implication interpretation of "$p(\text{if } P \text{ then } C)$." It results in values of "$p(\text{if } P \text{ then } C)$" that are too high and which depend on $p(P)$. The $p(C/P)$ interpretation, on the other hand, yields the correct answers.

3.2.5.2 *An Inference Rating Scheme.* Having adopted a premiss rating scheme and interpreted "$p(\text{if } P \text{ then } C)$" as "$p(C/P)$," I must now develop a rating scheme for inferences. Unfortunately, I have not been able to find any research data correlating inference evaluative expressions, per se, with numerical values. However, we should remember that inference-quality judgments are, implicitly, judgments about the probability of conditional claims. Consequently, it is appropriate to use the same 11-value numerical scale as for premiss rating. The fact that we are making judgments about hypothetical claims rather than categorical ones should make no difference in terms of how precise the judgments can be. The problem is, what linguistic expressions do we associate with each numerical value?

We can work around the absence of data by adopting a modified version of the premiss rating scheme. One way of adapting that scheme is to use the form "Given (only) P, C is Q," where Q stands for the expressions used in the premiss scheme. This formulation is neutral as to whether P is true, which is essential for inference-quality judgments. However, we must keep in mind that the argument evaluation exercise is one performed in isolation: other items of evidence, favorable and unfavorable, are to be set aside in judging the evidential force of the premisses with respect to the conclusion. This amounts to regarding the prior probability of C as 0.5 (there is no evidence either way). An example will enforce this point.

Suppose we are presented with this argument: "The horizon on the ocean looks flat, so Earth is flat." An informal evaluation of this argument could proceed as follows. "The premiss is true. As for the inference: given only the premiss, the conclusion is quite likely but not guaranteed, since there could be a curvature of the horizon that we cannot see. So, given only this argument, the conclusion is quite likely true."

The above evaluation is a brief but fairly adequate one. Whether the evaluator takes it to be the case that it is "quite likely" that Earth is flat depends, of course, on whatever other evidence s/he has. If the premiss of this argument is the only evidence (favourable or unfavourable) that the person has, it would be reasonable to accept the conclusion until other evidence becomes known.

By adapting the premiss rating table, we get the inference rating scheme shown in Table 5. One important difference from the premiss rating table is that the scheme covers cases in which P is irrelevant (0.5) and relevant, but unfavourable. Normally, we will encounter arguments for claims, and the arguer will have the sense to select favourably relevant premisses. Thus, most of the time we will be choosing a rating above 0.5. Theoretically, it is possible that an arguer uses as a premiss a proposition that s/he thinks is favourable but that the evaluator takes to be irrelevant (e.g., an arguer commits a relevance fallacy) or unfavourable evidence.

3.2.6 *A Conclusion-Support Rating Scheme*

Once we obtain a numerical rating value for the final conclusion we have, in effect, arrived at our overall judgment of the argument. For a number of reasons, it would be desirable to express this judgment verbally. Most people need to "reenter" the verbal world to fully appreciate how good they have found the argument to be. They have no ready-made verbal synonym for the numerical ratings, so the ratings

Table 5
Inference Rating Scheme

Verbal Rating	Assigned Rating	
If P is true,		
C is true	1.0	⎫
C is very likely	0.9	
C is quite likely	0.8	⎬ P is favourably relevant to C
C is likely	0.7	
C is be somewhat likely	0.6	⎭
C is as likely as not	0.5	⎬ P is irrelevant to C
C is more likely false than true	0.4	⎫
C is somewhat unlikely	0.3	
C is unlikely	0.2	⎬ P is unfavourably relevant to C
C is very unlikely	0.1	
C is false	0.0	⎭

are not very meaningful for them. Such people are in a predicament analogous to the American who asked me how cold it gets in Nova Scotia. I replied that it occasionally drops to about −20 degrees Celsius. He then asked me how cold that was! He could not correlate the temperature I had cited with his own experience, which was correlated with Fahrenheit values.

The American's plight differs in one way from that of the argument evaluator. I can convey my information to him by "translating" the −20-degree-Celsius value into Fahrenheit. When he learns that the temperature occasionally drops to −4 degrees Fahrenheit, he can then associate this level of coldness with his own experience: cold enough to require an overcoat, cold enough to make outside activities unpleasant, and soon. The argument evaluator, on the other hand, cannot have the 0.8 value correlated with another numerical value that is correlated in his or her mind with some evaluative description. There is no such value. S/he is in a position analogous to someone who is unfamiliar with all temperature scales.

This analogy tends to overstate the difficulty the argument evaluator is in. Most people would be disposed to judge an argument with a conclusion rating of 0.8 as fairly good, since the argument is seen as making the conclusion 80 percent likely. What is needed is a translation schema that provides a specific verbal synonym for the numerical rating values.

Table 6
Conclusion-Support Ratings

Rating	Conclusion Support
	Given only this argument, the conclusion is
1.0	true
0.9	very likely
0.8	quite likely
0.7	likely
0.6	somewhat likely
0.5	
0.4	
0.3	given no support
0.2	
0.1	
0.0	

As is the case for inference-quality judgments, there is no data on overall argument-quality judgments, so the premiss rating scheme will be relied on here too. The conclusion-support scheme is shown in Table 6. Since we are evaluating arguments in isolation (i.e., assuming for evaluation purposes that the prior probability of the conclusion is 0.5), the conclusion-support table differs again from the other two in that an argument will have no logical value if it does not raise the value of $p(C)$ in the evaluator's mind to something greater than 0.5. That is, if $p(C)$ is calculated to be 0.5 or less, the argument has not gone anywhere toward proving C, so we can say that it gives C no support.

3.3 THE EVALUATION PROCEDURE

Before presenting the evaluation procedure I advocate, I shall discuss several of the more satisfactory ones found in the texts.

3.3.1 Scriven's Procedure

Scriven's procedure was something of a pioneering effort in informal logic texts. It contains seven steps (1976, 39):

1 Clarification of meaning (of the argument and of its components);
2 Identification of conclusions (stated and unstated);

3 Portrayal of structure;
4 Formulation of (unstated) assumptions;
5 Criticism of
   (a) the premisses (given and "missing"),
   (b) the inferences;
6 Introduction of other relevant arguments;
7 Overall Evaluation of this argument in the light of 1 through 6.

Step 1 can be seen as involving the expression of each of the propositions in the argument in the clearest possible way. This will require, in some cases, decisions about what is extraneous in the argumentation passage. Step 2 might be better included under "portrayal of structure," since it is one aspect of identifying each proposition as a premiss or conclusion. One reason for having a separate step is that the key step in understanding any argument is to identify the final conclusion, which is normally the main influence on the form and content of the argument.

Step 3 involves the construction of a diagram containing the propositions represented as circles, identified by numbers, and connected by lines when one proposition is a premiss for another. I discuss diagramming in the next chapter, but here I want to comment that Scriven's diagramming format, or something similar to it, is the best method of depicting argument structure. I believe he was the first to use this method in a logic text, although Beardsley used a diagramming technique as far back as his (1950). The need for a diagrammatic approach arose when writers decided to turn their attention to extended arguments, ones with at least two inference steps. The writers of the traditional texts did not feel any pressure to express arguments in a nonverbal way, since they normally discussed contrived arguments containing only one conclusion.

Step 4 is, as Scriven says, "the most difficult part of reconstructing an argument" (1976, 43). In chapter 9 I discuss the need for it and the strategies proposed by various writers (including Scriven) for formulating missing premisses. I argue that if we adopt the inductive inference-evaluation approach I advocate, we seldom need to consider adding propositions to stated arguments.

The appropriateness of adding premisses is determined to some extent by what one takes to be the ultimate goal in initiating the argumentation. If the goal is to determine the actual truth value of S's conclusion and if it is possible for S and H to enter into a dialogue, then it would serve the interests of both for H to propose any additional premisses s/he thinks are needed to make the argumentation for C acceptable. This might even include mentioning additional evidence, although new evidence cannot strictly count as part of the original argument. When interaction between S and H is not possible, such as when S's argument is uttered in a book or in some other impersonal medium such as radio or television, the enterprise can still be seen as cooperative by H. H can still propose missing premises for S's argument, but it will not be possible to get S's input on the suitability of these premises. If the context is a formal or informal debate or a courtroom case, interaction is possible, but the relationship is adversarial. In such situations H's orientation will involve the criticism of S's argument, but no overall judgment of its persuasive force is necessary for H, since what S and H say is intended to persuade a third party. The third party must make the overall judgment.

If, on the other hand, H's aim is to decide on the truth value of C when interaction with S is not possible, H will take the evidence contained in S's argument, conjoin it with the relevant information H already has, and then decide whether C is true. Scriven's step 6 suggests that this is the scenario he envisages in dealing with arguments. If so, step 4 is an appropriate one to include if furnishing missing premises is intended to enable S's argument to exert its optimum persuasive force. My procedure, which is attuned to evaluating the argument as uttered, makes room for the addition of grounds when these are missing, as described in chapter 9.

Step 5, criticism of the premises and inferences, is the heart of Scriven's procedure: the previous steps are preliminaries to the evaluation of an argument. (In referring to "premises" here, Scriven is obviously referring to the uninferred premises.) Any argument evaluation procedure that pretends to be adequate must include the equivalent of step (5). In my version I formulate inference criticism and uninferred-premiss criticism as separate steps to impress upon the student that these are radically different activities.

The inclusion of step 6, introduction of other relevant arguments, is, in an important sense, not a step in argument evaluation. Scriven justifies its inclusion by saying, "If you stopped after step 5, you'd have a thorough critique and sometimes that is all that's called for, but you wouldn't know what to think yourself" (1976, 44). I accept that when an issue is personally important to us, an argument directed to it deserves an accurate evaluation, and then we should take this further step. However, I question the location of the step in the sequence. There are reasons to place it after step 7, the overall evaluation.

Scriven justifies its inclusion at this juncture in connection with step 7. At step 7 Scriven says, "Go back to your criticisms. How devastating are they?" In the course of giving some more specific advice on reaching an overall verdict he suggests, "Look at the results of step 6 ...

they ... may help you to see what the original argument was after" (1976, 45). Study of Scriven's treatment of examples shows that there is some value to this advice, but my own experience in using his text leads me to believe that students become confused about what the actual criticisms of the argument are. Put succinctly, I think Scriven's injection of step 6 into the argument-evaluation procedure produces a tendency to equate claim evaluation with argument-evaluation. For this reason I do not think that other arguments should be examined before we make an overall judgment of the argument at hand.

This presentation and discussion of Scriven's procedure has enabled me to bring to the reader's attention some of the more controversial issues in argument-evaluation procedures. I chose to present Scriven's procedure because it was used as a model by text writers in the 1980s. For instance, David Hitchcock's text uses a similar procedure, and he explicitly says that his procedure "is a variant of that found in Michael Scriven's *Reasoning*" (Hitchcock 1983, xi). He also includes a step corresponding to Scriven's step 6, prior to requiring an overall judgment of the argument. And he adds an additional requirement, not labelled as such, that follows the overall appraisal: "You should support this judgment in a critique that sets out the results of your investigation ... You should make your critique as understandable as possible to someone who has not learned any of the terminology of this book" (220).

I think this additional step is a desirable one when there is a need to respond to the argument, so I shall include it as the final step in my own procedure.

3.3.2 *The Proposed Argument-Evaluation Procedure*

The procedure set out below is designed to lead the evaluator of an argument to an accurate judgment of the extent to which the argument proves its conclusion. In effect, this is a judgment of the adequacy of the reasons for the conclusion. The procedure is narrow in focus in that it is not designed to lead the evaluator H to the truth about the conclusion. This is a different task that would involve H in considering all the information available to H that is relevant to the conclusion. Of course an evaluation of S's argument has a bearing on this bigger task, since it enables H to discover the proper "weight" of S's reasons.

In presenting the procedure I will deal with a relatively simple two-inference argument of transparent structure. On my way to work one morning my passenger and I notice a gray-haired man putting out things for garbage collection. One item is a disposable diaper box. My passenger says, "He's putting out a diaper box, so there's been a baby at his house; therefore, he is a grandfather."

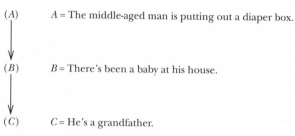

(A)   A = The middle-aged man is putting out a diaper box.

(B)   B = There's been a baby at his house.

(C)   C = He's a grandfather.

Fig. 2.   A simple two-inference argument

Step 1. Construct an argument diagram. The evaluation of arguments of any complexity can be made much easier by depicting their logical structure in diagram form. Diagrams enable us to "see" the structure all at once, whereas in a verbal presentation the propositions are presented sequentially. In the next chapter I shall discuss the various formats in which arguments might be diagrammed, but I shall use the format I advocate here, in illustrating the evaluation procedure.

Since the outcome of this step is a clear and accurate representation of the argument, it necessarily involves any clarification of meaning that is required, including uncovering and eliminating ambiguities, reducing vagueness, and other cognate activities. The argument given above has the form "*A* so *B*, therefore *C*." The argument indicator-words show that there are two inferences made, beginning from one uninferred premiss. It will be diagrammed as in Figure 2.

Step 2. Evaluate and rate inferences. It is useful to distinguish the process from the product when trying to arrive at an inference rating. Evaluation is the process of reflectively utilizing appropriate strategies to arrive at a judgment of inference validity formulated in the standardized verbal terminology of the translation table. Rating is the step of selecting the verbal judgment and entering the corresponding probability rating on the diagram. Strategies for evaluating inferences will be described and examined in chapter 5 (deductive inferences) and chapter 6 (inductive inferences).

The practice of entering ratings on the argument diagram was found to be convenient in *Argument Evaluation* (Grennan 1984). When inference and uninferred-premiss ratings have been placed on the diagram, we do not have to scan the text of steps 2 and 3 looking for the ratings when we calculate conclusion ratings. They are "before our eyes." The argument in the example has two inferences to evaluate. I judge that if *A* is true, it is very likely that *B* is true, so I assign a 0.9 rating to the inference and enter this on the diagram on a horizontal line

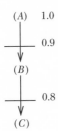

Fig. 3.   Inference and premiss ratings

drawn between premiss and conclusion. The warrant information I have is that almost invariably empty diaper boxes are the effect of diaper use in a home.

In evaluating the second inference, from *B* to *C*, I ask myself, given that there has been a baby in this middle-aged man's house, how likely is it that he is a grandfather? This is an effect-to-cause inference pattern (see chapter 7), so that validity depends on whether there are any other plausible explanations of *B*, other than *C*. Only one possibility comes to mind: this man is a new father. I judge this alternative explanation to be much less likely in the part of the world where I live. It is much more common for middle-aged men here to be new grandfathers rather than new fathers. Therefore, I decide that if *B* is true, it is "quite likely" that *C* is, so I enter 0.8 on the diagram in the appropriate place.

Step 3. Evaluate and rate uninferred premisses. Strategies for evaluating uninferred premisses are discussed in chapter 8. The approach there is to classify the various types by content and logical structure and identify the kinds of evidence relevant to each. In the example, the uninferred premiss is an observation-claim corroborated by me, the evaluator. In the circumstances, I judge that there is less than 1 chance in 20 that the claim is false, so I rate it 1.0 and enter the rating near *A* on the diagram. The diagram now looks like Figure 3.

Step 4. Rate conclusions. In proper argument evaluation the degree of proof of the conclusion is determined solely by premiss and inference ratings. Conclusions are not evaluated as isolated claims. The degree of support is calculated by multiplying the premiss and inference ratings, beginning with the first inference steps of course, since the rating of the final conclusion depends on the ratings of the intermediate ones.

In the example considered here, we calculate the rating of *B* as $1.0 \times 0.9 = 0.9$, and enter this value beside *B* on the diagram. To get

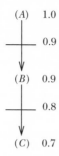

Fig. 4.   Argument completely rated

the rating for the final conclusion, C, we first calculate $0.9 \times 0.8 = 0.72$, and then round this to the nearest tenth to get the final conclusion rating, 0.7.

Completely rated, the argument diagram now looks like Figure 4 (of course, in an actual evaluation the diagram is drawn only once).

Step 5. Formulate response. First we consult the conclusion-support translation table to find the standardized verbal equivalent of the numerical rating. According to the Table 6 we judge that the conclusion is "somewhat likely." Thus, my response to S could be, "Your argument does not quite adequately prove your conclusion, as there is a slight possibility that this man is a new father himself."

This completes the preview of the evaluation system, showing how the rating scheme is integrated into the procedure. Evaluation strategies for steps 2 and 3 will be discussed in following chapters. The rating scheme has been covered in this chapter. The next chapter will deal with step 1.

3.3.3 *Variations*

Readers who have taught informal logic courses might at this point feel that the procedure being advocated is not sufficiently "user friendly" to be taught to students. The inference-evaluation procedure, in particular, is complicated; the rating scheme requires relatively fine discriminations.

The eleven-value scheme gives optimum precision, but at a price: even highly competent evaluators can disagree about what rating to assign an inference or premiss. Such disagreements will be exacerbated when people in a group have different amounts and kinds of information. This situation arises in a classroom context. Since it is pedagogically counterproductive to engage in extended disputes over whether, for example, an inference warrants a 0.7 or a 0.8 rating, we should adopt a more coarse-grained rating scheme. The simplest one would be the traditional two-value one (true-false, valid-invalid, proved-not proved). However, this scheme is too imprecise. We are often in a position in real life argument evaluation in which reflection makes us reluctant to choose either of these values: there is evidence to support both values. It is logically better, then, to add a third value, 0.5, to create a three-value scheme.

I have used this scheme in teaching the evaluation procedure and found that unanimity in ratings can usually be obtained, sometimes only after some discussion, which is itself a valuable part of the learning process. In my experience, as classes become more proficient at evaluation, the need for a finer-grained scheme increases. Depending on the class, one can either begin with the three-value scheme and move to a five-value one (for example, 0, 1/4, 1/2, 3/4, and 1) or begin with the five-value one.

Beginning with a five-value scheme can be pedagogically risky. It can place students in a situation in which they cannot decide which of two adjacent ratings to assign, perhaps because they are not clear about the "weight" of the evidence they have. In real-life situations, the evaluator can discover more evidence to tip the balance one way or the other, but in a course context there is a limited amount of time to investigate an argument topic, and it is generally desirable for the teacher to have students work on a great variety of arguments. The procedure presented, with its eleven-rating scheme, should be seen as a version to be used by those trained in argument evaluation.

As regards the inference evaluation procedure, I have found that having students operate at a more intuitive level at first is the best policy. As I teach it, I have them identify the three most plausible rebuttal factors (see chapter 6) they can think of, then set aside ones that are relatively less plausible than the most plausible one. Then they choose a rating for the inference in light of the remaining rebuttal factors. In using these beginner's systems the five steps are followed. The only difference is that the argument rating might not be as accurate as it could be.

3.3.4 A Difficulty for the Rating System

The system proposed can lead to unrealistic overall evaluations in certain circumstances, regardless of which ratings scheme we use. I presented an illustration of the problem in my text, *Argument Evaluation* (1984, 44–5).[5]

In the example, we suppose that someone utters this argument about students at Podunk U: "Students at Podunk study very little.

Most students at Podunk have part-time jobs. So Podunk students don't learn a lot in college." Suppose the argument has a convergent pattern (see chapter 4), each premiss being put forward as independent evidence for the conclusion.

Now suppose an evaluator discovers that Podunk U is in a small town where few jobs are available. This evaluator might well regard the second premiss as false. As a result, if we follow the product rule, we end up with the conclusion rated 0 too. But the evaluator might regard the first premiss as adequate proof for the conclusion. That is, if the arguer had not been given the second premiss, s/he might have rated the first premiss 1, the inference from it to the conclusion as 1, and thereby rated the conclusion as 1. Thus, evaluating the whole argument, the system dictates that we rate the argument 0, but if a premiss was left out, we would regard the conclusion as proved. This result is unfortunate and, to some extent, unintuitive: we would not expect an argument to become *less* persuasive if we add a premiss.

Elsewhere (Grennan 1986) I presented one solution to this paradox. It involved evaluating each "sub-argument," each argument produced by pairing each premiss with the conclusion separately, and seeing which sub-argument has the highest rating. That rating would be taken as the whole argument rating. Obviously, this is a cumbersome approach, one unsuitable to evaluating argument in everyday contexts.

Another approach seems to be more rough-and-ready but avoids the paradox. We begin our evaluation by evaluating and rating the un-inferred premisses. Then we *set aside any premiss not rated higher than 0.5.* (This 0.5 threshold-level was chosen because it prevents $p(C)$ from exceeding 0.5, the maximum value at which we would say that the argument is totally unpersuasive. At $p(C) = 0.6$, the argument has to be regarded as making the conclusion more likely than not, and therefore as modestly successful.) Having identified such premisses, we then evaluate the argument without these premisses and take the resulting final conclusion-rating as our overall rating of the original argument.

This approach has the obvious advantage of making evaluation easier. In the Podunk example, we need only to evaluate the inference from the first premiss to the conclusion. In a serial form of argument such as "*A*, so *B*, therefore *C*," if we judge *A* to be false, we have only one inference, not two, to evaluate. This approach may also have the advantage of corresponding to the thought processes that evaluators actually follow in such circumstances. I suspect people just ignore premisses they cannot accept, because they do not qualify as conclusion-evidence for them. But this opinion is based only on personal introspection and informal enquiry. I have not found any research studies to confirm it.

Does the premiss-rejection approach also have the advantage of giving an intuitively satisfactory result? It seems to, although there is the worry whether the argument actually evaluated is really the arguer's argument. I do not intend to pursue this matter further here. Obviously, this paradox of evaluation warrants further study.

4 Diagramming Arguments

The system of argument evaluation presented in this work relies on depicting the structure of arguments in diagrammatic form. However, in the broader context of argumentation studies the value of diagrammatic representations of arguments has been questioned. Charles Willard has raised a number of objections which, in the end, seem to amount to the complaint that no diagram can "serve as a structural representation of human cognitive processes given the complexity of those processes" (1976, 311). From the perspective of the two types of diagrams to be examined here, Willard has constructed a straw man. These diagrams do not aspire to serve the function he identifies. They have a more modest role – depicting relationships among the propositions that constitute arguments conceived as propositional complexes.

Willard also has another, more relevant, argument against constructing diagrams:

a group of propositions [sentences?] on a sheet of paper might rightly be called "argument" in one sense, that of literature, but they have nothing to do with actual interactions among people ... the form of an argument in a speech text may have little or no clear relationship to the propositional relationships envisioned by both source and receiver ... In sum, the argumentation theorist or rhetorical critic who diagrams the contents of speech texts is doing nothing more significant than drawing pictures of lines on sheets of paper. (1976, 313)

The weakness of this argument is that the correct illocutionary effect does occur most of the time, and can occur only because H can discern

S's communication intention (message) from the text. And this depends on there normally being a clear relationship between the sentences in the text and the "propositional relationships envisioned by both source and receiver." As Kneupper observes in his detailed critique of Willard's paper, "The analyst and critic can understand the meaning of the speech text because language is a traditional, conventional, cultural resource" (1978, 184).

Given the failure of arguments against diagramming, what advantages do diagrams provide? As part of an argument-evaluation procedure, the creation of a logically correct diagram helps ensure that the elements to be rated are recognized for what they are, so that the proper sort of evaluation strategy is selected for each. This is a highly important consideration because those untutored in argument evaluation are disposed to regard a passage containing an argument as a mere collection of assertions. Perhaps the most obvious manifestation of this attitude is the inclination to counterargue against the perceived conclusion, thereby ignoring the assertions that are provided to support it. There is also a tendency to confuse premiss criticism and inference criticism, which results in an inability to recognize the logical significance of the criticisms one produces.

To be adequate, any diagram format must be able to depict the different elements in an argument, and to depict them differently. The propositional-complex model found in the traditional logic texts such as Copi's *Introduction to Logic* makes only one distinction between propositions, that between premisses and conclusions: "An argument is not a mere collection of propositions, but has a structure. In describing this structure, the terms 'premiss' and 'conclusion' are usually employed. The conclusion of an argument is that proposition which is affirmed on the basis of the other propositions of the argument, and these other propositions which are affirmed as providing support or reasons for accepting the conclusion are the premisses of that argument" (1982, 6–7). Obviously, Copi is thinking of arguments with one inference step. Where arguments with two inference steps (e.g., of the form "*A*, so *B*, therefore *C*") are discussed, writers might distinguish between inferred and uninferred premisses or between intermediate and final conclusions.

In analyzing an argument on this model, we simply distinguish between conclusions and their premisses. But from a theoretical standpoint this is too simple. To make this clear let us consider two examples

1 The wind has backed from southwest to southeast. The barometric pressure is dropping fast. So a storm is coming.
2 Elvis is a man. All men are mortal. Therefore Elvis is mortal.

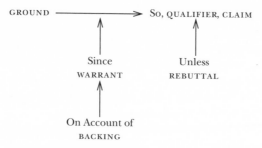

Fig. 5. Model T

In argument 1 we can easily identify two premisses and a conclusion, and from the content we can discern that the two premisses each represent evidence for the conclusion. Moreover, they are independent of each other as items of evidence. In any diagram format we adopt, it would be desirable to connect each of these premisses to the conclusion separately, and essential to connect them in the same way.

But what about argument 2? Here the first premiss seems to be evidence for the conclusion, but the second one does not. It is not about Elvis in any straightforward way, as the first one is. Yet it clearly plays a role in the argument. What this suggests is that premisses are not all the same in being direct evidence for their conclusions. And if this is so, a good diagram format ought to reflect this.

4.1 TOULMIN'S MODEL OF ARGUMENT

Stephen Toulmin has developed a model that recognizes, in a certain way, the difference between the premisses in the Elvis argument and, indeed, in any valid syllogism.[1] First presented in *The Uses of Argument*, published in 1958, it has undergone some changes in terminology since, and I shall present the version given in *An Introduction to Reasoning*, published in 1984. In the former work he used the term "datum" in place of the more traditional "premiss," and in the latter he replaced "datum" with "ground." In what follows I will retain the original term in quoting from *The Uses of Argument* but use "ground" when discussing his model.

The Toulmin diagram is actually a graphic model illustrating the relationship between the different logical roles that Toulmin thinks the components of an argument have. As such, it is a theory of what constitutes an argument, or a conceptual scheme for individuating the components of an uttered argument. The most refined version, which I call "Model T," is shown in Figure 5.

Each capitalized term, except "QUALIFIER," stands for a proposition (with one important exception, as we shall see) that has a different status within an argument. "QUALIFIER" stands for an expression qualifying the claim, such as "presumably" (Toulmin 1958, 102), "almost certainly" (109), and so on. The two most fundamental components are the "GROUND" and the "CLAIM," which correspond to "premiss" and "conclusion" in most logicians' usage. REBUTTALS are "conditions … indicating circumstances in which the general authority of the warrant would have to be set aside" (101). The BACKING for the WARRANT will be putative facts that support the WARRANT (105).

The most novel concept in the model is that of a warrant. At first sight, a logician might assume that warrants are propositions, the products of assertions, as grounds and claims and backings are. This interpretation is given credence by several passages: for example, "[warrants] may normally be written very briefly (in the form 'if P then C')" (Toulmin 1958, 98). Such language is common in *The Uses of Argument*. At one point he says that the argument "Harry's hair is red, so it is not black" has a valid inference, "on account of the warrant 'if anything is red, it will not also be black'" (98). This so-called warrant is an ordinary conditional proposition. Consider another example: "Harry was born in Bermuda. So, presumably, Harry is a British subject." According to Toulmin the warrant that supports this can be cast as a generalized conditional, "if a man was born in a British colony then he may be presumed to be British" (105), or as a generalization: "a man born in Bermuda will generally be a British subject" (105).

Toulmin's treatment of these examples suggests that in the Elvis example, "All men are mortal" can be conceived as a warrant within the argument. However, in spite of these examples and ways of speaking of warrants, Toulmin's fundamental conception of a warrant is that it is a rule or inference-license authorizing one to infer the claim from the ground. While he may sometimes call warrants propositions, he is clear that, if they are, they are propositions of a special kind. At one point he refers to them as "propositions of a rather different kind: rules, principles, inference licenses." And the completion of the last quote is telling: "[Warrants] may normally be written very briefly (in the form 'If D then C') but, for candour's sake, they can profitably be expanded and made more explicit: 'Data such as D entitle one to draw conclusions, or to make claims, such as C,' or alternatively 'Given data D, one may take it that C'" (1958, 98). On the same page he says that warrants "act as bridges, and authorize the sort of step to which our particular argument commits us," that is, inferring the claim from the ground. From this account, the warrant for the Elvis argument would be something like "Given that a thing is a man, we are entitled to infer that it is mortal."

It seems clear, then, that Toulmin's model is not homogeneous in the sense that it represents a set of propositions arising from an uttered argument. Rather, the ground and claim are propositions, and the arrow running between them represents the mental act of making an inference. We are entitled to perform this act when we have an authorization, that is, a correct warrant. Warrant backing, on the other hand, is propositional in that it is supposed to be factual: "the backing for warrants can be expressed in the form of categorical statements of fact quite as well as can the data" (1958, 105). Of course, this difference between warrants and backing may generate a difficulty in describing the status of the line running from backing (a proposition) to warrant (a rule, license, or authorization), but I will not try to sort this out. My interest in putting Toulmin's model forward is to see how it can be adapted to provide a model that qualifies as a propositional complex. His model does not quite serve this aim, as it is not fully homogeneous. That is, it contains one element (the warrant) that does not represent a proposition.

Nevertheless, even though Toulmin might prefer the inference-license interpretation of the warrant, it is open to us to adopt the propositional interpretation if we seek a homogeneous propositional-complex model. In the next section I will adopt this interpretation in an attempt to develop a model that improves on Model T.

4.2 THE "T2" MODEL OF AN ARGUMENT

Whichever interpretation of "warrant" we choose, it is clear that Toulmin thinks of warrants as supporting a link between ground and claim. What interpretation should we give to the arrow from P to C in a purely propositional model?

The simplest argument we can utter has the form "P, so (therefore, etc.) C." In making such an utterance S is committed to three claims: (1) P is true; (2) C logically follows from P, which amounts to claiming that "If P then C" is true; and (3) C is true by virtue of claims (1) and (2). I shall call claim (2) the "inference claim," routinely formulate it as "If P then C," and label it "I."[2]

An acceptable model of an argument as a propositional complex must contain a representation of each of the three claims and depict how they are logically related. Clearly, the premiss and conclusion can be depicted by words or other symbols, as in Toulmin's model, since they are explicitly asserted in a completely stated argument. How do we depict the inference claim?

The first point to note is that the inference claim for any particular argument is necessarily implicit in the stated argument.[3] To see why inference claims have this peculiar feature, consider an argument utterance symbolized as "*A*, so *B*." By definition, the inference claim is "If *A* then *B*." Now suppose we add "If *A* then *B*" to the original argument, in an attempt to make the inference claim explicit. The argument form is now "*A*; if *A* then *B*; so *B*." But the inference claim for the revised argument is "If *A* and if *A* then *B*, then *B*." If we now add this, we change the stated argument again, generating a new inference claim. Thus, an infinite regress begins when we try to make it explicit in the argument.[4]

The reader can now see, I hope, that inference claims cannot be part of the utterance complex, because they express a relationship between the uttered premises and the conclusion. Thus, *ex hypothesi*, they are not themselves uttered. Their existence is marked by the explicit presence in the uttered argument of argument-indicator terms such as "so," "therefore," "because," and so on, which serve to convey the illocutionary force of the utterance complex (van Eemeren and Grootendorst 1983, 31).

Now since inference-indicator words are intended to express a certain link between premises and conclusion, we might well want to emulate Toulmin's practice of drawing an arrow between premises and conclusion. However, in a propositional-complex model, the arrow will not depict a mental act of inferring, as it does in the Toulmin model. Rather, the arrow can be seen as representing the inference claim. This is especially felicitous because it reminds us that the inference claim is not expressible in words, whereas the other two propositions are.

We can, then, adequately represent a single-premiss argument using "*P*" and "*C*" by connecting them with a vertical, downward-pointing arrow. The arrow represents the inference claim. (This will be the case only when there is one premiss. Example (1), given at the beginning of this chapter, will have two arrows, one going to the conclusion from each premiss. We must say, therefore, that each arrow represents an evidential-support relation and, sometimes, conclusive evidential support.) It appears that this format was first presented by Monroe Beardsley in *Practical Logic* (1950), but its acceptance in recent years is probably due to the popularity of Michael Scriven's text *Reasoning* (1976). Thus, I will refer to these diagrams as "Scriven-type" diagrams.

There are some differences between authors on the details of depiction. One controversial issue with practical implications is how assertions are to be represented. (This question has no logical importance, of course.) Some texts present the assertions in written form (see

Thomas 1973; Beardsley 1950). One problem with this practice is its clumsiness in presenting complex arguments. A more serious problem is that the process of arriving at an acceptable version of a diagram often requires the construction of draft or preliminary versions. On tests I have frequently found that my students will have drawn three or even more versions before settling on one. If they were required to write out all the assertions each time, a considerable amount of time would be wasted. The use of symbols standing for the assertions is more efficient. Most texts using symbols use numbers inside circles or boxes for assertions.[5] The other alternative is to use letters.

It seems desirable to depict logical structure in as much detail as is practically feasible. To this end it is better to enclose each assertion in a circle or box, but have individual letters or numbers stand for propositions rather than assertions. This enables us to write conditionals as, for example, "If A then B" (or "If 1 then 2"), and alternations as, for example, "Either A or B" (or "Either 1 or 2"), rather than writing each as simply "A." In this context letters have one advantage over numbers: logicians have traditionally used letters in "translating" arguments into propositional-logic "language." In arguments containing logically compound assertions (conditionals, biconditionals, and disjunctions), we can comply with this convention if we have, say, the letter sequence A, B, C, etc., stand for propositions that are (1) assertions not representing conditionals, biconditionals, or alternations, and (2) those propositions logically connected within an assertion of one of these three kinds. It will not be necessary to worry about conjunctions, since their parts can be deemed to be assertions themselves. As such, they ought to be in separate circles to facilitate evaluation.

In everyday argument most assertions qualify as simple propositions, so that in many cases making the letters stand for assertions or propositions results in the same diagram. But if the letters stand for propositions rather than assertions, we can see more of the logical structure of some arguments when we diagram them. For instance, consider this example. A couple comes home from the movies to find that their house has been burglarized. They wonder how the burglar gained entry. They recall that all the ground-floor windows are normally locked, except the living room window. One of them says, "The only unlocked window is in the living room, so if the burglar entered through a window, then there are tracks in the flower bed under the living room window. But there are no tracks there, so he didn't enter through a window. Therefore we must have left the back door unlocked." If we substitute letters for each distinct proposition and retain the other language, the semisymbolic version would be written as follows: "A, so if B then C. But not C, so not B. Therefore D." On the other hand, if letters

(A)

(B)

Fig. 6.   Single-premiss argument

were used to stand for assertions, we would have this semisymbolic version: "*A*, so *B*. But *C*, so *D*." This is much more logically opaque, and the second inference would not be seen to be formally valid.

In the format to be advocated here, we can carry the symbolization one stage further by adopting the symbols for logical connectives used in the propositional calculus (including one for "not"). Thus, we can depict such arguments at the "microstructure" level, as well as at the "macrostructure" level (Freeman 1991, xi).

4.2.1 *One-Premiss Arguments*

The simplest case is that in which the conclusion (claim) has one premiss serving as its ground, for example, "The premier directs the civil service to award lucrative contracts to his supporters, so the premier practices political patronage." The semisymbolic version is "*A*, so *B*." The diagram is shown in Figure 6.

4.2.2 *Convergent Arguments*

One of the most common structures for a three-assertion argument is called the "convergent" pattern, the appropriate pattern when there are two independent grounds given for a claim. Example (1), given at the beginning of this chapter, is such a case. The semisymbolic version is "*A*; *B*; so *C*." *A* and *B* provide independent support for *C*, in the sense that "each separate reason still would support the conclusion just as well even if the other (separate, independent) reason(s) were false" (Thomas 1973, 39). Given that the arrow in the format signifies "logically supports," it is appropriate to connect each of these premisses directly to their conclusion. Thus, we diagram the argument as shown in Figure 7.

4.2.3 *Linked-Premiss Arguments*

According to James Freeman, "The central problem confronting the standard [Scriven-type] approach to argument diagramming is making clear the distinction between convergent and linked structure" (1991, 9). The problem arises because some arguments contain

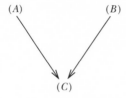

Fig. 7.   Convergent-premisses argument

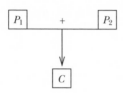

Fig. 8.   Dependent-premisses argument

assertions that have a bearing on conclusion support but are not direct evidence for the conclusion. Most of the modern informal logic texts try to come to terms with this problem.

Consider, for example, the following argument: "The crime was committed by someone who is very strong. But George is a weakling, so he cannot be the culprit" (Little, Groarke, and Tindale 1989, 17). The authors comment that "the two premisses in the argument work together to establish the conclusion. In a diagram, we capture this aspect of the argument by placing a plus (+) sign between the premiss boxes, drawing a line between them, and using a single arrow to join them to the conclusion." The diagram they give is shown in Figure 8.

Here P_1 seems to be a warrant for inferring C from P_2, since P_2 is a (putative) fact about George that is favourably relevant to C, another assertion about George.

Some other authors follow a similar convention. Freeman (1988, 175) diagrams "(1)Sam's car uses too much gas since (2)it is a 1968 model car and (3)such cars are far less fuel efficient than later models" as shown in Figure 9.

Here 2 is an assertion about Sam's car put forward as evidence for 1, a further assertion about it; 3 is a warrant.

Johnson and Blair (1983, 16) diagram the following argument in an analogous way (Figure 10): "(1)Textbooks don't usually contain jokes. (2)Don't expect jokes in this book. (3)This is a textbook."

Here 1 is a warrant for inferring 2 from 3. Other authors adopt a similar format.[6] Most of them provide the same sort of justification for depicting their arguments in a way that makes both premisses appear

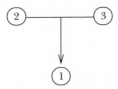

Fig. 9.   Freeman's linked-premiss example

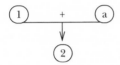

Fig. 10.   Johnson and Blair's linked-premiss example

to have the same role in the argument. Freeman (1991) gives the most detailed justification, so I propose to challenge his.

Freeman expounds his approach by imagining that an arguer has stated a one-premiss argument. If an arguee asked the arguer to explain why the stated premiss is a reason for the stated conclusion, "she would be asking Toulmin's warrant generating question – How do you get from your proffered reason to your initial claim as conclusion? This means that the premise, as stated, is somehow incomplete" (1991, 93).

The word "incomplete" in this context is unfortunate. In what way is the premise incomplete? Even if the warrant is then proffered, does this *complete* the premise? The premiss as originally stated will presumably be an item of evidence that is such by virtue of the truth of the inference warrant. The relationship is internal to the argument as a propositional complex. The *stating* of the warrant cannot change the evidential status of the premiss. It can only make the arguee aware of what is being relied on as warrant. At best, we can only say that the argument is incomplete for the arguee, in the sense that she does not appreciate, so far, its logical force.

Freeman elaborates on his "incompleteness theory" by means of (a later version of) his example:

For example, if the proponent supports his claim that Jones's car uses too much gas with the premiss that it is a 1968 model, our challenger may not see why that premise is relevant to the conclusion at all. A proper answer, then, will remedy this incompleteness by explaining the relevance … For example, our proponent could offer 'Cars made around 1968 are far less fuel efficient than other models and if a car is less fuel efficient than some other models, it uses too much gas.' (1991, 94)

Freeman diagrams the example with the added premiss as shown in Figure 9. He comments on this case,

Notice that here we do not have a new, further reason to support our conclusion, some new fact or some new data, but a completion of the original reason. In effect, we still have just one reason for the conclusion, but a reason divided, broken over, expressed by two statements … The proponent intends his answer to the relevance question to be taken together with his answer to the "Why?" question as one reason for his original claim. Structurally, these statements link together to constitute a reason for the conclusion. (1991, 94)

It seems clear that the kind of incompleteness at issue here is incompleteness of knowledge. The arguee cannot appreciate the logical force of the original argument because s/he lacks information, that is, knowledge of the warrant. But this is not *logical* incompleteness. Had the arguee been aware of the inefficiency of 1968 cars, would the original argument have been complete? Specifically, does the fact that makes a reason a good one constitute part of that reason? The fact that we can not only distinguish the two but separate them as well suggests otherwise.

While each of the texts discussed above uses a slightly different format, they all have in common two things: they have a single arrow going to the conclusion, and they all portray both premisses the same way. This feature can be called the "symmetry treatment." Formats that give the symmetry treatment to arguments of the kind being discussed cannot serve as fully accurate models of those arguments, because they do not depict the different logical roles of the premisses. As noted in the comments on each example, one premiss is direct evidence for the conclusion, but the other premiss is a proposition whose truth makes the former premiss evidence for the conclusion. That is, it is the warrant for the argument consisting of the former premiss and the conclusion.

So how should the so-called "linked" arguments that contain warrants be diagrammed? Return again to the Elvis argument, presented at the beginning of this chapter. Intuitively, "All men are mortal," taken by itself, does not seem to be relevant to "Elvis is mortal." This is probably because it is not explicitly about Elvis. The evidence given for saying that a thing has a particular property is usually the fact that it has some other property, or the fact that some causally related state of affairs or event exists or occurs.

It might be suggested that someone might say "All men are mortal, so Elvis is mortal" in a particular context, and the arguee might become convinced that Elvis is mortal, as a result. Should we say in such contexts that the generalization functioned as evidence? No. In such cases the arguer is relying on the arguee knowing that Elvis is a man. In face-to-face contexts, this could be depended upon, at least in the western world. But it makes more sense in such cases to say that the arguee consciously (or unconsciously) added the unstated premiss in the course of reaching the conclusion. If the arguee believed that "Elvis" is the name of a newly discovered planet, for example, s/he would be mystified, rather than persuaded, by the argument.

I conclude that the minor premiss and the major premiss of a syllogism have different logical roles. Whereas the minor premiss serves as independent evidence or support for the conclusion, the major premiss does not. If the roles of the two premisses of a syllogism like the Elvis example differ and the minor premiss can be seen as evidence or support for the conclusion, what then is the role of the major premiss? To identify this role, we must view the syllogism from a logical point of view.

From a logical point of view, the form of the "Barbara" syllogism can be written as "All S is M, and all M is P, so all S is P." The major premiss is the second one. In the Elvis example this premiss is "All men are mortal." Now "All M is P" is logically equivalent to (or at least entails) the conditional "If a thing is M, then it is P." This in turn entails "If this particular thing is M, then this particular thing is P." (This step relies on what is called the rule of "universal instantiation" in most versions of the predicate calculus.) Thus, in our example "All men are mortal" is logically equivalent to "If a thing is a man, then that thing is mortal." This in turn entails "If Elvis is a man, then Elvis is mortal." But this last proposition represents the inference claim of the enthymematic version of the argument (the version containing only the minor premiss as a premiss). Thus, the major premiss entails the inference claim of the enthymeme. That is to say, it provides (if true) conclusive evidence or support for that inference claim. And this being so, it cannot be conclusive evidence or support for the conclusion itself, since "If P, then C" is not logically equivalent to C, nor does it entail C.

We now have the answer to how to accommodate the major premisses of Barbara syllogisms in our model. They cannot be represented as "P_2" in the convergent diagram. But since they support the inference claim of the enthymeme, which is represented by the arrow from P to C, it is appropriate to draw an arrow from the major premiss, W, to the arrow between P and C, as shown in Figure 11 as Model T2. This model for diagramming supposedly linked arguments containing warrants has the virtue of showing the different roles of ground and warrant. It shows the ground as providing direct evidence for the claim, which is a convention already adopted. It does not require us to treat a ground (the minor

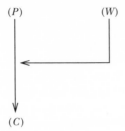

(P)   (W)

(C)

Fig. 11.   Model T2

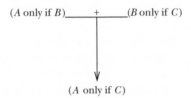

(A only if B)_____ + _____(B only if C)

(A only if C)

Fig. 12.   Linked-premiss argument

premiss in the syllogism) differently from the way it is depicted in the convergent-argument case. And it adequately depicts the relationship between the warrant and the remainder of the argument.

I have argued in this section that arguments containing warrants are not properly diagrammed as linked in the way most authors advocate. In a sense, this amounts to saying that such arguments are not linked arguments. But this is not to say that no arguments can be diagrammed in the linked format. In particular, arguments that contain conditional and disjunctive premisses should be diagrammed in this way. Consider this example: "One is eligible for a driver's licence only if one is old enough. One is old enough only if one is sixteen. So one is eligible for a driver's licence only if one is sixteen." The semisymbolic version is "A only if B; B only if C; so A only if C."

Here neither premiss represents direct evidential support for the conclusion. Such evidence would take the form of a citation of a legislative act stipulating that the earliest age for eligibility is sixteen. Nor is one of the premisses a warrant. Thus, neither the divergent nor the T2 format is appropriate. A linked-premiss format is required, as shown in Figure 12, which indicates that, jointly, the premisses support the conclusion, but since neither provides independent support, neither is directly connected to the conclusion.

Returning now to the matter of how to diagram arguments containing warrants, it must be acknowledged that there are a number of practical problems arising from adopting this format for diagramming syllogisms and other arguments in which warrants are stated. Most importantly, there is the question of whether or not we can distinguish grounds and warrants in such arguments.

4.3 DISTINGUISHING WARRANTS FROM GROUNDS

Several writers have challenged the warrant/ground distinction by arguing that it is difficult or impossible to make in concrete cases.

4.3.1 *The Van Eemeren Challenge*

Van Eemeren et al. give this argument: "Toulmin emphasizes that the difference in function between the data [ground] and the warrant is the main distinction. But even in combination with other criteria it is often difficult in practice to establish, using this functional distinction, exactly which statements are the data and which statement serves as the warrant" (van Eemeren, Grootendorst, and Kruiger 1984, 205). They try to make their case by altering an example of Toulmin's (discussed in sec. 4.1, above), in which he identified the claim as "Harry is a British subject," the datum (ground) as "Harry was born in Bermuda," and the warrant as "A man born in Bermuda is a British subject." They present a case in which the claim is made and the role of the other two statements seems to be switched. That is, the defender of the claim answers the challenger's question "What have you got to go on?" (this is Toulmin's question that supposedly leads to the citing of the ground) by saying, "A man born in Bermuda is a British subject," because he assumes that the "challenger" knows that Harry was born in Bermuda. But then the challenger asks "How do you get there?" (this is Toulmin's question for eliciting a warrant) to which the defender responds, "Harry was born in Bermuda." This dialogue shows that the arguer's assumption was mistaken, and it is supposed to show that the last claim "functions as a bridge between [the first two]" (van Eemeren, Grootendorst, and Kruiger 1984, 205), and that it thereby qualifies as a warrant.

I do not find the reasoning here persuasive. A warrant is supposed to be a logical bridge, which is to say it is supposed to entail or support an inference claim. It is absurd to say that "Harry was born in Bermuda" supports "If a man born in Bermuda is a British subject, then Harry is a British subject." Furthermore, "A man born in Bermuda is a British subject" is not evidence for the claim. To be evidence it ought to be about Harry, explicitly. On the other hand, the general claim does entail "If Harry was born in Bermuda, then Harry is a British subject," so it can serve as the warrant. Perhaps it might be said that "Harry was born in Bermuda" serves as an "epistemic bridge" between the other two for the arguee, but this bridge is a quite different kind of thing.

To distinguish datum (ground) from warrant, we rely on content, rather than the context of argument utterance, because datum and warrant are logical concepts. Sequence of presentation has no bearing, no matter how appropriate the questions "What have you got to go on?" and "How did you get there?" seem to be. Perhaps these questions are a bit ambiguous, but the former seems to me to be a request for evidence. In the example, only one proposition seems to fit the bill.

What the arguer has done is provide the wrong answer to the "What have you got to go on?" question. This would give the example force only if it is assumed that the ground is what the arguer says it is. But we need not and, indeed, must not assume this in argument evaluation. Ordinary arguers are not as aware of the difference between grounds and warrants as informal logicians are, so they can be expected to confuse them sometimes in contexts such as that of the example.

4.3.2 *Freeman's Challenge*

The most sustained case against depicting warrants and grounds differently in our argument diagrams has been made by Freeman (1991). His conclusion is that "It is our contention that although Toulmin's notion of warrant is straightforwardly applicable to arguments as process, its application to arguments as products … is highly problematic. It is so problematic in fact that we conclude the concept of warrant is an inappropriate category for analyzing arguments as products" (50).

The concept is applicable to arguments as process because in live dialectical exchanges that proceed on the model of proper dialectical exchanges as Freeman specifies them, the "What have you got to go on?" and the "How did you get there?" questions are asked. The answer given by the arguer to the first is (supposedly) the ground; the answer to the second is (supposedly) the warrant. If we are present at the exchange, we hear what each is (Freeman 1991, 50). The situation is different for arguments as products, or propositional complexes: "The problem is that when confronted with an argument as product, an argumentative text, we do not know what generating questions have been asked. This we must imaginatively construct, to the best of our ability, from the evidence the argument itself provides. Will the argument as product give us unambiguous indications for reconstructing these questions?" (50–1).

Freeman tries to make his case for a negative answer to this question by reviewing some examples. We might, he thinks, encounter arguments such as this: "John will not come to the party, because if Mary is coming, John won't." He asks (rhetorically), "Doesn't the question 'How do you get from stated hypothetical premise to conclusion?' arise for this argument? And wouldn't we expect the answer to be 'Mary is coming to the party'?" He concludes from this expectation, "So in the argument 'John will not come to the party, because if Mary is coming, John won't and Mary is coming to the party' how do we know which statement presents the data and which is the warrant?" (1991, 51).

Freeman's case rests on the assumption that grounds and warrants in arguments are determined by the arguer's answers to our two questions. But this assumption is not an authoritative criterion. Warrants are identified by their role in the argument (conceived as a propositional complex). As I have argued, they are the premises that entail or support the inference claim. As such, the example is infelicitous, because the conditional represents the inference claim of the single-premiss argument "John will not come to the party, because Mary is coming to the party." However, the point remains that we can easily identify the ground in the two-premiss argument, and we can also recognize that in the original one-premiss version no ground was given. In such a case, the stated premiss is irrelevant to the conclusion. This should be obvious, because ordinary language conditionals do not permit us to infer any categorical propositions from them.

My interpretation of Freeman's example, then, is this: the arguer originally used a premiss (the conditional) that could not serve as a ground for the conclusion being argued for. Nonetheless, this was the arguer's stated premiss, and it would have been improper to replace it with a premiss that can serve as a ground, because we would not have been diagramming the uttered argument. But the arguer is not the final authority on whether the stated premiss is a ground or warrant: that question is a matter of propositional content. Specifically, to qualify as a ground, a proposition has to provide evidence for the conclusion (in an inductive argument), and to qualify as a warrant, a proposition has to support the inference claim generated by the premiss and conclusion.

At first blush, it seems a bit odd to take the view, as Freeman does, that warrants occur in the dialectical process but are not to be included in the propositional-complex model, especially since ground, claim, modal qualifier, and rebuttal get to be included in both. Freeman seems to take this view because he chooses to stay with Toulmin's interpretation of a warrant as an inference rule. This decision leads him to infer from Toulmin's work that "if a statement is of conditional form, [one should] take it as the warrant" (1991, 71). But then he rejects Toulmin's analysis of what such conditionals are. According to Freeman, on Toulmin's interpretation warrant-expressing conditionals represent generalizations about observed instances, rather than "general categorical propositions [regarded] as descriptions involving inference, [that is] descriptive statements going beyond just what has been observed" (72). Freeman argues that as a result Toulmin's analysis makes warrants different from ordinary conditionals, which leads Freeman to reject the view that a generalized conditional can be a warrant. This, in turn, requires him to account for certain premises, such as generalizations in syllogisms, as described above. That is, what I would call the ground and the warrant are to be seen, according to Freeman, as parts of a single reason for the conclusion.

I find this treatment of warrants so bizarre that it qualifies the foregoing line of reasoning as a *reductio* argument. It would be better to take the view that Toulmin's warrants-as-inference-rules concept applies to arguments as processes and that the counterpart in arguments-as-products is a straightforward generalization.

Thus far, I have argued, in opposition to the writers cited, that warrants can be regarded as entailing or supporting inference claims. How successfully can this concept be applied? In what follows I make a case for saying that it can be applied to syllogisms, which can be seen as representing a good test case, especially since those critical of the warrant/ground distinction try to make their case using quasisyllogistic examples.

4.3.3 *Identifying Syllogism Warrants*

Until now I have considered only the syllogism about Elvis: "Elvis is a man. All men are mortal. So Elvis is mortal." As we have seen (sec. 4.2.3), this is of the form called "Barbara."[7] In such an example it is easy to see that the major premise is the warrant, because it is the only generalization. In its standard form, however, Barbara is written with two universal premises: "All M is P. All S is M. So all S is P." So consider a different example of this pattern: "All men are mortal. All players of Tottenham FC are men. So all players of Tottenham FC are mortal." Here we have two premises that are generalizations, not one. Which is the warrant, or is there no way to decide? This issue was not explicitly discussed by Toulmin.

The issue arises because the inference claim of a syllogism can be written in the form "If P_1 and P_2, then C," but the rule of exportation allows us to write this claim in two other forms: "If P_1, then (if P_2, then C)" and "If P_2, then (if P_1, then C)." Thus, each premiss can entail an inference claim. We cannot, then, distinguish warrants from grounds by relying only on entailment. One or more additional criteria must be used. The goal is to formulate criteria that enable us to distinguish the warrant and ground in every valid pattern.

There are 15 valid syllogistic patterns (Tapscott 1976, 411). They are formed from four types of generalization:

A-type: All x's are y.
E-type: No x's are y.
I-type: Some x's are y.
O-type: Some x's are not y.

Now when there is only one universal (A or E) premiss in a valid syllogism, we can regard that premiss as the warrant, since warrants are a level of generality above inference claims. For example, suppose we have the argument "All philosophers are intolerant of error. Some Canadians are philosophers. So some Canadians are intolerant of error." This argument has the valid pattern AII-1, and we can count the first premiss as the warrant because it is more general than the second premiss. It entails the inference claim "If some Canadians are philosophers, then some Canadians are intolerant of error." This level-of-generality criterion works for the ten patterns that have only one universal premiss. It also conforms with Toulmin's usage.

When both premisses are universal a different criterion is needed. Any E-type premiss (No x's are y) is logically equivalent to "All y is not x" and "All x's are not y," so that when both premisses are universal, they are equally general. There are only five such cases:

AAA-1: All M is P. All S is M. So all S is P.
EAE-1: No M is P. All S is M. So no S is P.
AEE-2: All P is M. No S is M. So no S is P.
EAE-2: No P is M. All S is M. So no S is P.
AEE-4: All P is M. No M is S. So no S is P.

As noted above, the E-type propositions can be written in the form "All x's ..." Thus, the last four on the list can have their conclusions written as "All S is not P." Now arguments whose conclusions are singular-referring (for example, their subject term is a proper name) can be valid syllogisms equivalent to any of the five patterns, because these assertions are equivalent to propositions of the form "All x's ..." For example, "Elvis is mortal" is equivalent to "All things that are Elvis are mortal." To use each of the five patterns to prove a claim about an individual, then, we need to rewrite each of the five:

AAA-1: All M is P. All S is M. So all S is P.
EAE-1: No M is P. All S is M. So all S is not P.
AEE-2: All P is M. All S is not M. So all S is not P.
EAE-2: No P is M. All S is M. So all S is not P.
AEE-4: All P is M. All S is not M. So all S is not P.

If we want syllogisms containing the proper name "N," we rewrite these as

AAA-1: All M is P. N is M. So N is P.
EAE-1: No M is P. N is M. So N is not P.
AEE-2: All P is M. N is not M. So N is not P.
EAE-2: No P is M. N is M. So N is not P.
AEE-4: All P is M. N is not M. So N is not P.

Note that in all cases (AEE-2 and AEE-4 are identical) the first premiss is always the generalization. Thus, when a single individual is referred to in the conclusion of a valid syllogism, the major premiss (the one not containing the subject-term of the conclusion) is always a generalization, and thereby serves as the warrant. So if the major premiss is the warrant in this special case, we can say that it is also the warrant when the subject-term of the conclusion denotes a class. Furthermore, referring back to the other 10 valid patterns, we find that the major premiss is the warrant in each of those cases as well.

Thus, using the criterion that the warrant must be the major premiss when the conclusion refers to a single individual, we have found that the warrant in a valid syllogism is the premiss that does not contain the referring expression of the conclusion. This finding accords with our ordinary concept of evidence in the sense that, given a claim and two propositions that might serve as evidence for it, the one that is explicitly about the referent of the claim is regarded as ground for the claim.

4.3.4 *Further Criteria for Individuating Warrants*

Having arrived at a specific criterion for distinguishing warrants and grounds in syllogisms, we must move on to deal with the issue of identifying warrants when the arguer does not provide them. Defining warrants as propositions that entail or support the inference claims of their arguments will not enable us to uniquely identify the warrants of such arguments. Consider again one of Toulmin's examples: "Harry was born in Bermuda. So, presumably, Harry is a British subject." Here the inference claim is "If Harry was born in Bermuda, then presumably Harry is a British subject." According to Toulmin, the warrant can be cast either as "if a man was born in a British colony, then he may be presumed to be British" or as "a man born in Bermuda will generally be a British subject" (1958, 105).

Aside from the fact that only the first alternative is expressed in inference-licence form, these two warrant candidates are not logically equivalent, since the first is about a larger class of individuals (i.e., men born in British colonies) than the latter (men born in Bermuda). This raises an issue of logic: is there a unique warrant for each inference claim? The example illustrates a problem, but it can also help to clarify the support relationship that holds between warrant and inference claim. There is a logical difference between the more general candidate and the more specific one: the latter is itself sufficient to entail the inference claim, whereas the former (when converted to propositional form) entails it only in conjunction with a second proposition, that is, "Bermuda is a British colony." This feature of more general propositions that back inference claims – that they do not by themselves entail inference claims – is an appropriate basis for rejecting them as warrant candidates.

Independent entailment, then, can be a criterion for warrant identification, but it may not be decisive in all cases. There could be candidates that meet this criterion but are more than sufficient to entail the inference claim. To rule out such candidates we can specify that warrants are minimally sufficient. This additional criterion has a welcome practical consequence. Normally, the minimally sufficient candidate is easier to defend, so that we are being fairer to the arguer if we attribute this one as the warrant being relied on. In the Toulmin example, then, the definition of "warrant" as "a proposition that is minimally sufficient by itself to entail the inference claim," enables us to prefer "A man born in Bermuda will generally be a British subject" as the correct warrant candidate.

The problem of identifying warrants just discussed deals with cases in which a warrant is not uttered in giving the argument. When an assertion is made that does supply support for the inference claim, we can diagram it as shown in Model T2.

4.3.5 *Warrants in Deductive Logic*

Matters are less complicated when we consider arguments cast in propositional or predicate calculi. In constructing derivations, each step

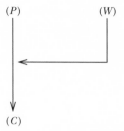

Fig. 13.   Argument containing stated warrant

represents a conclusion inferred from one or more premisses with the aid of an inference rule. For example,

(1) $A \& B$ Premise
(2) $A \supset C$ Premise / to prove: C
(3) A From 1 by simplification
(4) C From 2 and 3 by *modus ponens*

Line 3 is inferred, as noted, from line 1, relying on the simplification rule. Thus, line 1 is the ground for claim p, and the simplification rule, expressible as "$p\&q$, therefore p" is the warrant that authorizes the inference step. Similarly, *modus ponens* is the rule serving as the warrant for writing line 4. The same arrangement applies to the predicate calculus.[8]

4.3.6 *How Crucial Is the Ground/Warrant Distinction in Diagramming?*

If it is to be made in our diagrams, the distinction between warrants and grounds raises an issue in diagramming strategy. An evaluator needs to have a reasonably accurate diagram of an argument in order to focus the evaluation. For example, when there are two premisses, how critical is it to be sure that in choosing between the convergent pattern and the T2 pattern, one has chosen the correct diagram? Fortunately, accuracy in inference evaluation need not depend on a correct choice, as the following reasoning shows.

Suppose one premiss is a warrant, in which case it provides direct support for I, the inference claim. Thus, we can diagram the argument as in Figure 13. The following relationships apply:

(1) $p(C) = p(P) \times p(I)$
(2) $p(I) = p(W) \times p(I/W)$

(3) $p(C)$ $\quad = p(P) \times p(W) \times p(I/W)$, from (1) and (2)
(4) $p(I/W) = p(\text{if } W \text{ then } (\text{if } P \text{ then } C))$, by definition
(5) $p(I/W) = p(\text{if } (W \text{ and } P) \text{ then } C)$, from (4) by exportation
(6) $p(I/W) = p(C/W\&P)$, rewriting (5)
(7) $p(C)$ $\quad = p(P) \times p(W) \times p(C/W\&P)$, from (3) and (6)

The last equation represents the situation we would have if an argument consisted of two independent premises, P and W, and a conclusion, C. And since the original pattern is equivalent to it, in calculating $p(C)$, we can regard the first argument-pattern as equivalent to this convergent three-assertion argument for purposes of evaluation. Specifically, even though warrants are grounds for inference claims, we can treat them the same as premises that provide direct support for the conclusion when our goal is to obtain a value for $p(C)$. This means that in evaluating arguments, failure to identify warrants as such need not result in an incorrect argument rating.

This result is of practical importance, because most people who produce arguments are not clearly aware of the distinction between premises as direct support (grounds) and premises as warrants. As a result, the vocabulary used in expressing logical relationships in argumentation passages tends to be ambiguous. This example is typical: "Since mail is to be home-delivered to all houses in established neighbourhoods, we should be getting home delivery because we've moved into a well-established neighbourhood" (Little, Groarke, Tindale 1989, 18). The semisymbolic version is "Since A, B because C." Judging by assertion content, C is evidence for B, the conclusion. The term "because" shows this connection. On the other hand, the content of A is such that it qualifies as a warrant for the inference from C to B. That the utterer so conceives of it is suggested by "since," with some help from the comma.

This argument-passage is typical of cases in which both grounds and warrants are given, in the sense that most argument-indicator terms are used to introduce both grounds and warrants. But this practice ought to be expected, given the general public's lack of awareness of the distinction. No difficulty may arise in evaluation when we must second-guess the arguer's intentions, since (as demonstrated above) the error of identifying a warrant as a ground has no impact on the inference rating. However, this will not always be the case. In evaluating the argument in T2 form the steps are different in that there are two inferences to be considered, not one. It may be that in evaluating the argument in this form enables us to estimate inference quality better. Whether or not this is so would have to be checked by comparing results obtained by both approaches.

The convergent- and T2-diagram formats are the most common patterns for single-inference arguments containing three assertions. Each of the formats is convergent, in the sense that it "proceeds" from several premises to one conclusion. However, some argument utterances containing three assertions need to be interpreted as having two conclusions. These are called "divergent" arguments.

4.4 DIVERGENT ARGUMENTS

Thomas provides a good example of a so-called divergent argument: "It's going to rain, so we'll get wet and the game will be cancelled." He notes that "a divergent argument can also be treated as two separate arguments (having the same basic reason but leading to different conclusions)"(1973, 36). Freeman claims that there is "little at stake theoretically in whether we count so-called divergent arguments as one or several" (1991, 234).

I am not sure of the force of "theoretically" here, but from the standpoint of argument evaluation, and inference evaluation specifically, there are advantages to treating divergent arguments as separate arguments. For one thing, each inference has to be evaluated separately. Furthermore, in adopting the policy of separation, we can adopt two useful criteria for counting inferences and arguments: there are as many inferences as there are conclusions, and there are as many arguments as there are conclusions that do not serve as premises.[9] (I shall call conclusions that do not serve as premises "final conclusions." Some authors call them "main conclusions"; but "final conclusions" contrasts with "intermediate conclusions," any conclusions that serve as a premises for other conclusions.)

4.5 SERIAL ARGUMENTS

The fourth type of diagram structure for three-assertion arguments is the "chain" or "serial" form, appropriate when an argument has one uninferred premiss serving as ground for an intermediate conclusion, which in turn is a ground for the final conclusion. It is shown in Figure 14.

4.6 DEPICTION OF MODAL QUALIFIERS
IN DIAGRAMS

If our diagram conventions are to be complete, they must include a depiction of each of the elements that commonly appear in arguments. Since careful arguers frequently qualify their conclusions (using "probably," "nearly certain," and the like) so as to express what they take to

Fig. 14.   Serial argument

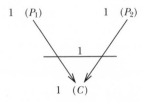

Fig. 15.   Argument with implicit modal qualifiers shown

be a lack of support, our diagrams would be importantly incomplete if we neglected to represent such qualifiers when they appear in the argument utterance.

How is this representation to be done? One approach is based on the fact that the arguer can be thought of as producing an argument product with implicit ratings. When there is no modal qualifier uttered, we can take the arguer to implicitly have rated each uninferred premiss as 1, and each inference as 1. For example, the arguee can view a one-inference convergent argument as coming from the arguer with the ratings shown in Figure 15. Here, the arguee can think of these implicit ratings as ones that s/he is invited to accept. Whether or not s/he does accept them is a matter of completing the argument-evaluation process.

On the other hand, the arguer might be diffident about the adequacy of her or his evidence and use a qualifier: "P_1 and P_2, so probably C." We could depict this version by selecting a probability value that gives a correct numerical definition for "probably" and entering it as the arguer's inference rating. Then calculating the conclusion rating by taking the product of the three ratings gives us a rating equal in value to the inference rating, as shown in Figure 16. The "0.7" in front of the conclusion is supposed to represent "probably C" in the utterance. Again, the arguer could be said to be inviting the arguee to accept his or her rating of the argument, which, in this case, is a qualified one.

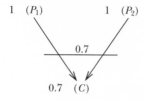

Fig. 16.   Argument with evaluator's ratings

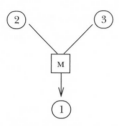

Fig. 17.   Freeman's mode of depiction for qualifiers

This approach can also accommodate premiss qualifiers. If, for example, in the last case the arguer had said "P_1 and probably P_2, so probably C," we would have had a "0.7" in front of P_2, a "1" for the inference, and a "0.7" for the conclusion.

When evaluating these arguments, the arguee would begin by entering the arguer's implicit ratings. Then, the argument would be evaluated while ignoring them (see sec. 6.1.2 for details). Based on the evaluations, the arguee would choose to accept or reject the implicit ratings. For example, it might be decided that the conclusion rating should be slightly lower, so that the arguer is entitled to say only, "It is somewhat probable that C." Obviously, this way of depicting qualifiers is easy to integrate into an argument-evaluation system of the kind advocated in this book.

Freeman presents a different mode of depiction that is suitable in the absence of numerical ratings. He depicts the modal qualifier M for a two-premiss convergent argument as shown in Figure 17 (1991, 127). Obviously, this is a way of depicting the qualification of inference quality. Presumably, the presence of a premiss qualifier would be shown by having a block containing the qualifier word in front of the premiss. Ordinarily, a logically competent arguer would realize that a premiss qualifier dictates the need for a conclusion qualifier, so there would also be a block containing a qualifier next to the conclusion.

If one is using verbal ratings, Freeman's approach to qualifier depiction ought to be satisfactory. It makes the evaluator aware that the

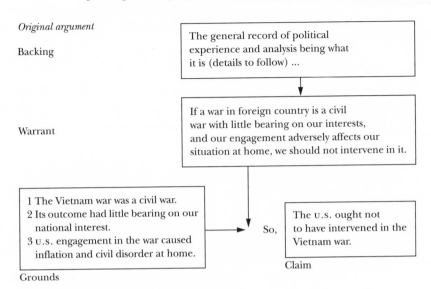

Original argument

Backing

The general record of political
experience and analysis being what
it is (details to follow) ...

Warrant

If a war in foreign country is a civil
war with little bearing on our interests,
and our engagement adversely affects our
situation at home, we should not intervene in it.

1 The Vietnam war was a civil war.
2 Its outcome had little bearing on our
national interest.
3 U.S. engagement in the war caused
inflation and civil disorder at home.

So,

The U.S. ought not
to have intervened in the
Vietnam war.

Claim

Grounds

Fig. 18.   Toulmin's diagrammatic interpretation

arguer has qualified some component of the argument, so that it needs to be evaluated in that light.

4.7 COMPARISON OF DIAGRAM FORMATS

In previous sections we have seen how arguments of various kinds can be diagrammed using the Scriven-type format. Toulmin's format was also presented. Which type of diagram is most useful when argument analysis is a prelude to argument evaluation? One important consideration is this: the format adopted must be capable of depicting arguments clearly, regardless of their complexity.

Let us compare the two approaches using an example from Toulmin, Rieke, and Janik (1984, 75). They suppose someone to claim that the United States ought never to have intervened in the Viet Nam war and to support this claim by saying, "Let's face it, the war was a civil war in the first place; its outcome had little bearing on our national interests overseas; and America's involvement only caused inflation and civil disorder at home." Their diagram is shown in Figure 18. Figure 19 shows the argument diagrammed in the other format. The "code" used in Figure 19 is as follows:

A = The Viet Nam war was a civil war.
B = Its outcome had little bearing on our national interests.

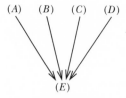

Fig. 19.   The Scriven interpretation

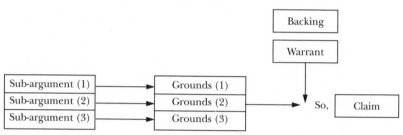

Fig. 20.   Toulmin's expanded version

C = U.S. involvement caused inflation at home.
D = U.S. involvement caused civil disorder at home.
E = The U.S. ought not to have intervened in the Vietnam war.

Here the premisses independently support E, the conclusion. The third premiss mentioned by the arguer is a conjunction, so I have divided it into two (C and D) because different sorts of evidence are relevant to the two parts.

The diagrams shown in Figures 18 and 19 reflect two different approaches. Figure 18 identifies the warrant being relied on, and its backing; Figure 19 includes only what was asserted. At this level of complexity there is little to choose between the two types as starting points for argument evaluation. However, Toulmin, Rieke, and Janik then suppose that each ground is supported by reasons and produce three "sub-arguments" for each ground, each as complex as the original. To represent how they tie into the original, they present the version shown in Figure 20 (1984, 77, fig. 7-5).

Figure 20 masks considerable complexity, since each sub-argument is as complex as the original argument, which consists of the three grounds, the claim, and its associated warrant and backing. The other type of diagram, on the other hand, can be extended upward to incorporate the reasons given for those grounds, as shown in Figure 21.

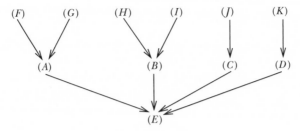

Fig. 21.   Scriven's version expanded

The code for the extra items in Figure 21 is as follows:

F = North Vietnam was not acting as a puppet for another nation.
G = The vast majority of the fighters on both sides were Vietnamese.
H = Vietnam does not contain natural resources vital to the U.S.
I = Vietnam's becoming communist need not upset the balance of power in the world.
J = The Vietnam war was financed by printing money.
K = The Vietnam war provoked protest movements, often violent.

This type of diagram has the advantage of indefinite extension, as the example shows. Consequently, it permits us to depict an entire argument in one diagram.

Another important advantage of the Scriven-type format is that it does not require the inclusion of unstated warrants and warrant backing. Although trying to identify warrants, in particular, can lead to increased understanding of how the arguer intends the argument to work, this benefit would accrue only if we identify the warrants correctly. This identification is not as easy as it may sound, as the earlier discussion of warrant individuation implies. In any case, as a preliminary to argument evaluation, we need not, and probably should not, try to identify arguer's warrants.

The standard approach to inference evaluation involves reviewing the information one has that counts for and against the inference. In effect, this approach amounts to evaluating the inference warrant. If the inference strikes the evaluator as satisfactory, his or her judgment is likely to be based on an accepted generalization that represents the arguer's warrant for that inference. When the judgment is more negative, the evidence given in support of the judgment will amount to a rejection of the arguer's warrant. In adopting the Scriven-type format, then, one will be indirectly taking account of warrants in the course of inference evaluation.

4.8 CONCLUSION

I have argued for the superiority of the Scriven-type format for depicting argument structure. It does not require us to differentiate between grounds and warrants among the assertions in the arguments, but I have argued that this level of analysis is not required for argument evaluation since conventional inference evaluation indirectly deals with arguer's warrants when unstated. When they are stated, they are diagrammed as support for the evidential link between ground and claim. Furthermore, even if the evaluator misidentifies a warrant as a ground, this will not necessarily result in an inaccurate evaluation.

5 Evaluation of Deductive Inference

In this chapter I will assess the strengths and weaknesses of currently available techniques for testing inferences for deductive validity, both formal and material, including some techniques that have not been given the attention they deserve.

5.1 TESTING FOR FORMAL VALIDITY

In the area of inference-evaluation technique, modern-day logicians have devoted almost all their attention to developing logical systems that can be used to test inferences for deductive validity arising from logical form. When an argument is formally valid the warrant supporting its inference claim is a formal tautology. I will examine techniques that have been developed for evaluating arguments involving propositional reasoning and for arguments involving class reasoning.

5.1.1 *Evaluating Propositional Reasoning*

The techniques to be evaluated in this section are methods for evaluating inferences in arguments that can be cast in the "language" of the propositional calculus. When we are faced with an argument symbolized in this language, the first point to note is that the propositional calculus has the potential for testing validity only if it contains at least one disjunction (or logical equivalent, such as $-(-p\&-q)$), or one conditional (or logical equivalent, such as $-p \vee q$), or one biconditional (or logical equivalent). (Arguments containing a conjunction as a premise can be regarded as cases in which the conjuncted proposition represents two separate asserted propositions, so arguments containing conjunctions do not, on that account, have the potential of testing valid.) The assertions of arguments lacking all three of these connectives can be symbolized as single letters, and no such arguments can be deductively valid within the system ("p therefore q" is invalid, as is "p and q therefore r," and "p and q and r therefore s").

One drawback common to all the techniques that cast arguments in the language of the propositional calculus is that they are not totally reliable, since certain inference patterns that are not intuitively acceptable will test valid. The problem cases for the propositional calculus arise from the definition of "if p then q" as material implication. One well-known kind of case involves question-begging arguments, which qualify as valid because the pattern "$(p \ \& \ q) \supset p$" is formally valid. With true premises, such arguments are sound but do not prove their conclusions. There are other examples. This pattern qualifies as valid: "p, so if q then p." This pattern is said to be one of the paradoxes of material implication, but it would seem to be simply a formal fallacy not identified as such by the propositional calculus. The following is a counterexample to the claim that the pattern is valid:

> The person writing this material is a philosopher, so if the moon is made of cheddar then the person writing this material is a philosopher.

Here the premiss is true but, since the antecedent of the conclusion is irrelevant to the consequent, the conclusion is false. That is to say, $p(C/P) = 0$. Any argument in which q is irrelevant to p can serve as a counterexample to the claim that the pattern is deductively valid. It tests valid in the propositional calculus by virtue of defining the conditional as material implication, but is deductively invalid because there are arguments that show that it is possible for the premiss to be true while the conclusion is false. Another basic pattern that is incorrectly deemed valid is this: "not-p, so if p then q." This error is also caused by defining the conditional as material implication. A counterexample is "The moon is not made of cheddar, so if the moon is made of cheddar, then the person writing this material is a philosopher."

Two other basic forms that test valid as a result of the conditional definition are also intuitively invalid: "not-p and not-q, so if p then q," and "p and q, so if p then q." The latter form seems to exemplify indirectly the fallacy of *post hoc ergo propter hoc*.

Each of the foregoing cases appears to be valid when tested using the propositional calculus, yet counterexamples show each to be invalid. The error arises from symbolizing "if p then q" as material implication, that is, as "$p \supset q$." Supporters of the material implication interpretation of the indicative conditional downplay these errors and others arising from the same cause as the negative side of a trade-off between utility and accuracy. The calculus, they say, correctly tests many valid patterns, which makes it a very useful inference evaluation device (Bedell 1976, 228).

From a theoretical point of view this utility argument is not very satisfactory, but from the point of view of practical evaluation it has force, especially when we consider that the examples given above appear to be invalid by intuition. That is, given a good grasp of the logical concepts they involve, especially the concept of an indicative conditional, we can "see" that they are invalid patterns without constructing counterexamples. Thus, when we encounter an argument having one of these patterns we can decide that its inference is invalid without using a propositional calculus test. In such cases we are protected from making errors of judgment to which the calculus would lead us.

However, not all cases of invalid arguments that test valid can be recognized intuitively as invalid. Consider this example: "If I will have eternal life if I believe in God, then God must exist. I do not believe in God. Therefore, God exists" (Pospesel 1974, 190; quoted in Bedell 1976). Now if we exercise our intuitions on the original version we will observe a certain paradoxical air about it, but it is difficult to be confident of invalidity because of the complexity. At this point we can choose either to test it by constructing a good counterexample or by using the propositional calculus. Because of the complexity, we may anticipate difficulty in adopting the former course. So suppose we adopt the latter. Substituting letters for the propositions, the argument can be written as "If A if B, then C; not B; therefore, C." When we translate this into the language of propositional logic we get "$(b \supset a) \supset c \, / -b \, // \, c$." This is a valid pattern. The reason is that, to show invalidity, "c" must be false and "$-b$" true. But since "b" must then be false, "$b \supset a$" is true, which means that the first premiss is false. So it is impossible to get all premisses true and the conclusion false at the same time.

Having come this far, atheists who have complete faith in the propositional calculus may feel their atheism being eroded! They will accept the second premiss but may feel that the first premiss has plausibility. That is, if belief in God entails eternal life, it might seem to follow that God must exist, to ensure this result. Here I can come to the atheist's aid by providing an example to show the argument pattern is invalid: "If the internal angles of St Peter's Square total 360 degrees if it is square-shaped, then square figures have internal angles totalling 360 degrees. St Peter's Square is not square-shaped. Therefore, square figures do not have internal angles totalling 360 degrees." Such logically complex cases as the God argument make both the discernment of invalidity and the construction of counterexamples difficult.

One supporter of the use of the propositional calculus has this response to the God argument: "(1) Anomalous arguments such as the 'God' inference are extremely rare. (2) Every such argument I have ever encountered was invented by some logician to illustrate a defect in propositional logic" (Pospesel 1974, 192). His observations, if true, can be explained in terms of our disposition to construct only arguments that are simple enough for us to judge their validity intuitively. Even to the trained mind, the God example is slightly too complex. The untrained mind, that is, the mind lacking an adequate grasp of the conditional concept, is disposed to go astray at a simpler level, as the occurrence of the common formal fallacies shows.

It seems, then, that from the practical standpoint of argument evaluation, the possibility of getting a wrong answer when an inference is invalid is not such a serious problem. Those with an adequate grasp of the concept of a conditional can identify invalidity intuitively in simpler cases, and these cases make up the majority of the ones we encounter. Those who do not have an adequate grasp of conditionals can rely on propositional logic (or better, a truth table approach – see the following sections) even in the simpler cases, even though they will sometimes get the wrong answer, because, on balance, they will be correct more often.

Now, when an argument is not simple and is actually valid, is there a corresponding possibility that the propositional calculus may show it to be invalid? The obvious, and correct, answer is "no," since deduction techniques are not decision procedures. We may fail to show validity because we lack the skill required to construct a proof. But are there cases in which the argument pattern becomes invalid when translated into propositional logic terms? The most likely way in which this can occur is through the substitution of material implication (to be symbolized throughout as "$\supset$") for ordinary conditionals, that is, through substituting "$p \supset q$" for "if p then q."

Now suppose we have an argument of the form "If A then B; C; therefore D." Substituting variables for the propositions and revising the format, we have this argument form: "$p \Rightarrow q / r // s$." Here "if ... then" is symbolized by "$\Rightarrow$" – and will be from now on. If this is a valid pattern, we will not be able to make the first premiss true when (a proposition substituted for) "s" is false and "r" is true. If we substitute "$p \supset q$" for "$p \Rightarrow q$" will the pattern remain valid? Well, if the former entailed the latter, it would, because the falsity of "$p \Rightarrow q$" would entail the falsity of "$p \supset q$." But unfortunately, "$p \supset q$" does not entail "$p \Rightarrow q$," as we can see by substitutions for "p" and "q" such as "the CN Tower is in Toronto" and "the Taj Mahal is in India." So this approach to showing that arguments remain valid when the material implication replaces conditionals fails. A better attempt, using induction, has been made by Copi.

According to Copi, "valid arguments containing conditional statements remain valid when those conditionals are interpreted as asserting material implications only" (1982, 296). As evidence, he shows that *modus ponens, modus tollens,* and the hypothetical syllogism remain valid by the truth table test. These are all valid in the sense that no counterexamples can be constructed when they are expressed using an ordinary conditional. All the same, this is only an inductive defence of the validity-preserving thesis, not a deductive demonstration.

The best defence of the validity-preserving thesis, to my mind, is supplied by A.J. Dale (1974, 91–5). He presents a set of twelve schemata that are valid when expressed using the ordinary conditional concept, then observes that if we substitute the material implication concept in each case, we can deduce the Hilbert-Bernays axioms (Kneale and Kneale 1962, 527). Any system of logic that entails this axiom set is complete, in the sense that any valid argument consisting of well-formed formulae can be shown to be valid. Barring any unforeseen hitches in Dale's case, it appears that any argument that is valid when expressed in everyday language and that can be symbolized in propositional logic will be valid when tested by deduction or truth table method.

5.1.1.1 *The Propositional-Deduction Method.* The deduction system found in modern texts is a variant of a system first developed by Gentzen (1934). He called his system "natural deduction" because the rules of inference in the system supposedly correspond to ones that ordinary people use. A serious disadvantage of these deduction systems is that they are not decision procedures: they are only proof procedures. That is, they can show that some arguments cast in their "language" are formally valid but cannot demonstrate that invalid ones are invalid. For example, there are rules and axioms that allow us to discover that an argument expressed semisymbolically as "If A then B, and if B then C, therefore if A then C" is formally valid in the propositional calculus. But there are no such rules to demonstrate that "If A then B, and if C then B, therefore if A then C" is formally invalid. The best that can be done is to infer, from failures to construct a proof, that the argument is formally invalid. This, of course, would be an inductive inference.

Given that inference evaluation normally begins in a state of uncertainty about the quality of the inference, axiomatic deductive systems

Table 7
Truth Table Definitions of the Logical Connectives

not-*p*	if *p* then *q*	either *p* or *q*	both *p* and *q*	*p* if and only if *q*
− *p*	*p* ⊃ *q*	*p* ∨ *q*	*p* & *q*	*p* ↔ *q*
F T	T T T	T T T	T T T	T T T
T F	T F F	T T F	T F F	T F F
	F T T	F T T	F F T	F F T
	F T F	F F F	F F F	F T F

such as the propositional and predicate calculi are limited in their practical use for testing inferences in everyday arguments. A further practical disadvantage of these deduction systems is that they are not easy to learn, and once they are learned, it is possible to retain one's skill only by continual use. Anyone who has more or less mastered such a system can attest to both these facts. More seriously, the experience of those of us who have taught these systems indicates that only a minority can master them.

5.1.1.2 *The Truth Table Method.* The truth table method relies on the definitions of the logical connectives (including "not") symbolized in the propositional and predicate calculi. These definitions are truth functional: a value for a proposition created by connecting two others is given for each pair of values that the simple variables can have, as shown in Table 7.

The truth table method is, unlike the deduction systems, a decision procedure of sorts. In testing an inference pattern we determine the truth values of all premiss forms and of the conclusion form, for all combinations of variable (*p, q, r,* etc.) truth values. The inference pattern is deemed valid if and only if there is no combination of variable values that yields a T for all premisses and F for the conclusion. Consider the inference pattern "*p ⊃ q / q ⊃ r // p ⊃ r.*" We perform a test by constructing a truth table for each assertion form, as shown in Table 8. The pattern is found valid because there is no line where "*p ⊃ q*" is T, "*q ⊃ r*" is T, and "*p ⊃ r*" is F. Given the definitions, that is, it is impossible for an argument of this form to have true premisses and a false conclusion. On the other hand the pattern "*p ⊃ q / r ⊃ q // p ⊃ r*" is invalid, as Table 9 shows. This pattern is deemed invalid by virtue of line (2), which shows that with "*p*" and "*q*" being true and "*r*" false, we would have an argument with true premisses and a false conclusion. That is, the logical form of the pattern does not guarantee the truth of the

Table 8
Test of a Valid Inference Pattern

p	q	r	$p \supset q$	$q \supset r$	$p \supset r$
T	T	T	T	T	T
T	T	F	T	F	F
T	F	T	F	T	T
T	F	F	F	T	F
F	T	T	T	T	T
F	T	F	T	F	T
F	F	T	T	T	T
F	F	F	T	T	T

Table 9
Test of an Invalid Inference Pattern

p	q	r	$p \supset q$	$r \supset q$	$p \supset r$
T	T	T	T	T	T
T	T	F	T	T	F
T	F	T	F	F	T
T	F	F	F	T	F
F	T	T	T	T	T
F	T	F	T	T	T
F	F	T	T	F	T
F	F	F	T	T	T

conclusion, given the truth of the premises, but for formal validity there must be no exceptions.

The truth table test is a mechanical decision procedure that tells us whether or not it would be possible to construct an argument with true premises and a false conclusion that corresponds to the form of the particular argument we are evaluating. Such a counterexample would show formal invalidity itself. For example, the last test tells me that one can be created, and what truth values its propositions must have. Here is one: "If Garfield is a cat then Garfield is an animal. If Garfield is a dog then Garfield is an animal. Therefore if Garfield is a cat then Garfield is a dog." It is unnecessary, practically speaking, to actually create a counterexample. An indefinite number of arguments can be created and with a little imagination we can always find one. With these safe assumptions we can claim that the truth table test itself shows invalidity.

The truth table method is simpler than the propositional calculus to use and learn, and is an adequate decision procedure for testing the argument patterns encountered in life that contain conditionals, bi-conditionals, and disjunctions. Of course, it is tedious to use when patterns contain more than three variables because the number of table lines doubles for each variable added. With three variables, eight lines are needed to cover all combinations. With four, sixteen lines would be required, and with five, thirty-two would be required. Fortunately, most inferences we might have occasion to test by this method usually have no more than four distinct simple propositions. This is not to say that it cannot deal with arguments containing more simple propositions. Most relatively complex everyday arguments containing more than three simple propositions have more than one inference step, but usually only two or three propositions are involved at each step. Since we test only one inference at a time, the procedure can deal with this complexity.

5.1.1.3 *The Reverse Truth Table Method.* A more efficient approach is one often described in logic texts. It is introduced to deal with invalid arguments. It too relies on the truth table definitions of the connectives and also relies on the same principle for testing validity. This method is referred to variously as the "abbreviated truth table method" (Tapscott 1976, 140), the "method of assigning truth values" (Copi 1982, 345), and the "trial and error method" (Tapscott 1976, 140). This last description reflects a misconception among text authors about the method and no doubt accounts for the small space that most of them devote to it. They seem to think that it cannot be mechanical in the way that the standard truth table method is. In what follows I shall develop it sufficiently to show that it can indeed be quite mechanical in its own way. I shall refer to the more developed version as the "reverse truth table method" (RTT, for short). This name is appropriate because the RTT method involves deriving variable values from assigned premiss and conclusion truth values, the reverse of what is done using the truth table method.

Essentially, the aim of the RTT method is to identify a line in the truth table for an inference pattern on which all premisses are true and the conclusion is false. Such a line, if it exists, shows invalidity. In the weaker version of the method, only whole premisses or conclusions are subject to truth value assignments. Premisses are assigned T and conclusions F. Following an initial assignment, we rely on the truth table definitions of the connectives to infer truth values for parts of

Table 10
Test of a Valid Pattern by the RTT Method

$p \supset q$			$r \supset q$			$p \supset r$		
T	T	T	F	T	T	T	F	F
4	6	7	5	9	8	2	1	3

whole assertion forms. Each step is numbered because only certain sequences are logically permissible, and this numbering enables us to check for a correct sequence. We proceed until either (a) the inferred variable values make a premiss F or the conclusion T, in which case the pattern is valid, or (b) the inferred variable values result in all premisses being T and the conclusion F, in which case the pattern is invalid. An example will clarify.

Suppose the argument we are testing has this logical form: "$p \supset q$ / $r \supset q$ // $p \supset r$." The test is recorded as shown in Table 10. Each step is justified as described below.

Step 1 We are entitled to assign F to the conclusion or T to a premiss at any time provided that values already entered do not permit us to infer its value. To show that it is an assigned value we underline it.

Step 2 Line 2 of the definition for "$\supset$" is the only line on which the conditional is F, so we can infer that the antecedent is T.

Step 3 For the same reason we can infer that the consequent is F.

Step 4 Justified by step 2. At any time we can enter a known variable value.

Step 5 Justified by step 3.

Step 6 No more values can be inferred, so we assign a value of T to the first premiss to enable us to make further inferences. Note that we cannot infer a value for the premiss from knowing its antecedent is T. Referring back to the definition for "$\supset$," there are two lines on which the antecedent is T, lines 1 and 2. On line 1 the conditional is T but on line 2 it is F. Thus, the premiss value is not determined by step 4, so we are free to assign T to it. To indicate that the value is assigned, we underline it.

Step 7 From steps 4 and 6 we can infer that q is T. This inference is authorized by the fact that the antecedent is T and the conditional is T only on line 1 of the definition. So the consequent must be true.

Step 8 Authorized by step 7.

Table 11
RTT Test Requiring Value Choice

$p \supset q$	$q \supset r$	$p \supset r$
T	F	T F F
4	5	2 1 3

Step 9 Authorized by the conditional definition. This represents the completion of line 3.

We have been able to arrange to have both premisses T and the conclusion F, so the pattern is invalid. In effect we have identified line 2 of the complete truth table for the pattern. Note that several other sequences were possible. For example, step 2 could have been step 3 and vice versa. And we could have inferred T for the second premiss solely from the fact that "r" was F; this is because, even though there are two lines in the definition that have the antecedent F (lines 3 and 4), the conditional as a whole is T on both of them. This stresses the point that we can sometimes infer a value for a proposition or variable whenever it has a single truth value.

The method requires that every complex proposition or part thereof have only one main connective under which we write its truth value. This is normally the case in propositional logic, but not always. Since, for example, "$p \& q \& r$" is logically equivalent to "$(p \& q) \& r$" and "$p \& (q \& r)$," all are well-formed formulae. When we are using the RTT method, however, the first is not well-formed. We must choose one of the others so that only one connective is outside parentheses. The negation sign serves as the main connective when it is the only one outside parentheses, but to limit the number of parentheses, a convention is used that allows negation signs to be outside parentheses when one other connective is outside also. Thus, instead of writing "$(-p) \supset (q \vee r)$," we write a simpler version: "$-p \supset (q \vee r)$." Readers are to understand that in such cases the true connective is the main connective.

Let us test one more pattern, the other one tested using the truth table method. The test is shown in Table 11.

Step 1 The conclusion must be F if pattern is to be shown invalid, which is the goal of the procedure. This is allowable since its value cannot be inferred at this stage.

Step 2 Inferrable from line 2 of the definition.

Table 12
Completed RTT Test after Choice

$p \supset q$			$q \supset r$			$p \supset r$		
T	T	T	T	F	F	T	F	F
4	6	7	8	9	5	2	1	3

Table 13
Alternative Version of Test

$p \supset q$			$q \supset r$			$p \supset r$		
T	F	F	F	T	F	T	F	F
4	9	8	7	6	5	2	1	3

Step 3 Also inferrable from line 2.
Step 4 From step 2.
Step 5 From step 3.

At this point we cannot infer or enter any more values. We can proceed in two ways. Let us choose to assign T to the first premiss and complete the test as shown in Table 12.

Step 6 We assign T to the first premiss.
Step 7 Only line 1 of the definition is T-T, so we infer T for the antecedent.
Step 8 From step 7.
Step 9 Based on line 2 of the definition.

Notice that we were unable to arrange for the second premiss to be T. Our step 6 ensured that "q" is T, which ensures that the second premiss is F.

The other sequence we could follow after step 5 is to assign T to the second premiss instead of the first. The test could go as in Table 13. In this second version we end up with the first premiss being F as the ultimate result of making the second one T. Thus, no matter which way we proceed, we cannot have variable values that make both premisses T and the conclusion F. So the pattern is valid, as there is no line indicating invalidity in the full truth table.

The reader may wonder if we have to perform a further test if we cannot show invalidity the first time. If we use a trial-and-error

Table 14
RTT Test of an Invalid Pattern

$p \supset q$			$q \supset r$			$p \supset r$		
T	T	T	T	F	F	T	F	F
4	6	7	8	9	5	2	1	3

Table 15
Full Truth Table Version of RTT Method

Line no.	p	q	r	$p \supset q$	$q \supset r$	$p \supset r$	This line eliminated by entry no.
1	T	T	T	T	T	T	1
2	T	T	F	T	F	F	–
3	T	F	T	F	T	T	1
4	T	F	F	F	T	F	6
5	F	T	T	T	T	T	1
6	F	T	F	T	F	T	1
7	F	F	T	T	T	T	1
8	F	F	F	T	T	T	1

approach, as some texts recommend, we definitely should. But the RTT version does not require it in cases like the last example. I presented the second version to show that more than one sequence is usually possible. We can think of the procedure as one of elimination of full truth table lines as we complete the entries. Take, for example, the first attempt at showing invalidity, repeated here as Table 14 for convenience. Table 15 gives the full truth table and how lines were eliminated in the search for a line indicating invalidity. It can be seen from Table 15 that the RTT method simulates the search for a set of variable values indicating invalidity. Step 1 eliminates all such sets that make the conclusion T. When we make the first premiss T, we eliminate the line 4 set, and we arrive at line 2 in the end. But the line 2 set does not indicate invalidity either.

The test took all sets of variable values into account, so that even if invalidity was not shown, there would be no point in performing another test with a different sequence. The second version of the test would be the same, except that the variable set on line 2 would have been eliminated and our final set would have corresponded to line 4,

Table 16
Pattern Requiring Value Choice

$p \supset (q \vee r)$	$-(p \,\&\, q)$	r
F	F	
2	1	

Table 17
Completed Test after Value Choice

$p \supset (q \vee r)$	$-(p \,\&\, q)$	r
T T T T F	F T T T	F
3 4 6 5 2	10 7 9 8	1

so it too would have covered all variable sets in the search for the set indicating invalidity. By limiting the choice of value assignments and making only inferences from the connective definitions, we eliminate the need for more than one test in most cases. However, there are some that require an extra type of entry, as the one in Table 16 does.

After step 2 we cannot infer variable values by assigning T to the first premiss. We do not have a value for either its antecedent or its consequent. We cannot infer a value for "$q \vee r$" from step 2, because it could be either T or F (lines 2 and 4 of the definition of "$\vee$"). Assigning T to the second premiss does not help either. We could infer that "$p \,\&\, q$" is F, but we could infer no value for either variable, since this value is satisfied by lines 2,3, and 4 of the definition table.

The best remedy available is to have the power to assign a value to one variable. This has been found to be sufficient to make the system powerful enough to deal with every textbook example I have encountered. Selection of the variable, and the value assigned to it must be judicious in several respects, but the main criterion is that one should be able to infer a value for an additional variable, either directly or through assigning a value to a premiss or conclusion. In the example, I assign T to "p" in the first premiss and proceed as shown in Table 17.

Step 3   Variable value assigned.
Step 4   Premiss value assigned. There is no restriction on the number of premiss assignments one can make, except that an assignment cannot be made when the value is already inferrable.

Table 18
Full Truth Table Version

Line no.	p	q	r	p ⊃ (q ∨ r)	−(q & q)	r	This line eliminated by entry no.
1	T	T	T	T	F	T	1
2	T	T	F	T	F	F	–
3	T	F	T	T	T	T	1
4	T	F	F	F	T	F	4
5	F	T	T	T	T	T	1
6	F	T	F	T	T	F	3
7	F	F	T	T	T	T	1
8	F	F	F	T	T	F	3

Table 19
Test after Assigning Value

p ⊃ (q ∨ r)	−(p & q)	r
F T F	T F F	F
1 2	5 3 4	6

Step 5   The consequent of the conditional is T, from line 1 of its definition.

Step 6   From 2 and 5 and line 2 of the "∨" table.

Step 7   From step 3.

Step 8   From step 6.

Step 9   From 7 and 8 and line 1 of the "&" table.

Step 10   From 9 and line 1 of "−" table.

The value of the second premiss appears to indicate validity, but in
fact the test is not conclusive. To see why, consider the full truth table
for the pattern, shown in Table 18. Setting the conclusion (r) F eliminates legitimately all lines on which "r" is T. By assigning T to "p," we
eliminate lines 6 and 8 from consideration, but as the truth table
shows, each of these lines indicates invalidity. Because such possibilities arise when a value is assigned to a variable, failure to show invalidity after such an assignment requires that we retest with that variable
having the opposite truth value.

In the example, then, we must retest with "p" as F, as shown in
Table 19.

Step 1 Authorized by the previous test. We can infer that "p" must be F if the pattern is invalid.

Step 2 From step 1 and lines 2 and 3 of the "⊃" table.

Step 3 From step 1. (1 and 3 could have been entered in reverse order.)

Step 4 From step 3 and lines 3 and 4 of the "&" table.

Step 5 From step 4 and line 2 of the "−" table.

Step 6 Conclusion assigned F.

At step 6 we have found that, with "p" F and "r" F, the pattern is invalid, because of the entries for steps 1, 5, and 6. We have not established a value for "q," but this tells us that it can be either T or F, that is, that there are two lines indicating invalidity in the truth table: lines 6 and 8, the two not checked in the first test.

The last test shows that sometimes we reach a decision without making all entries. Indeed, it also shows that it is not possible in some cases to make all entries. This is not a drawback, however, because we are concerned only to obtain enough values of variables to show invalidity or to show that invalidity cannot be shown. Sometimes we find that before assigning a value to a variable we can infer a premiss value as F, or the conclusion value as T. When either of these situations occurs, we need proceed no further. It is not possible to show invalidity; the pattern is valid. If this occurs after we have been forced to assign a variable value, we must proceed to test with the opposite value for that variable.

Since assigning a value to a variable (other than when it represents a premiss or conclusion by itself) will require a second test when invalidity is not shown, it is more efficient not to make such an assignment until forced to. (Rarely, this may be at the very beginning.) We are not logically bound to follow this policy, however. Sometimes it is more efficient to make an astute variable assignment to get a quick decision. For example, if we had dealt with the last pattern by assigning "p" as F, we would have discovered invalidity in six steps! This sort of shortcut pays dividends only when the pattern is invalid. If it is valid we would have to test with the opposite variable value. All the same, the opportunity to assign a value to a variable (that is not a premiss or conclusion) has an important practical benefit: should the system user not see any further entry to be made, even if there is one or more, making a variable assignment enables him or her to resume inferring values.

Enough has been said, I hope, to show the value of the RTT as a method for evaluating inferences cast in the language of the propositional calculus. It is a true decision procedure, unlike deduction systems, but like the full truth table method. It is superior to the latter, however, in its brevity and elegance, regardless of argument complexity.

5.1.1.4 *The Truth Tree Method.* In the textbook "industry," the method to be described in this section first appeared in Richard Jeffrey's *Formal Logic: Its Scope and Limits,* published in 1967. He claims that "In contrast to the 'natural deduction' methods whose vogue in elementary logic texts began in 1950, the tree method is thrillingly easy to understand and to use" (1981, xi).

After using the truth tree method, I am disposed to agree with Jeffrey. Moreover, in terms of ease of understanding, the tree method seems to be better than the RTT method just described, and almost as easy to use. My description of the tree method will be extracted from Jeffrey's text.

In testing an argument-form cast in propositional logic, we list the premisses one under the other, followed by the denial of the conclusion. We then rely on seven deductive rules to infer the propositional variables or their denial. In doing so we create "trees" so that paths can be traced through the propositions of the test. A path is marked "closed" with an "x" when, having written down a variable (or its denial), we find that its denial (or affirmative) appears in the path we can trace back up the tree. This indicates that no set of variable truth-values occurs in this particular path, such that invalidity is demonstrated. When all paths of the completed tree are closed, the pattern is valid.[1]

For propositional logic, there are seven rules that occur in a test in these configurations:

1 Denied Denial

$$\frac{--p}{p}$$

2 Undenied Conjunction

$$\frac{(p\,\&\,q)}{\begin{array}{c}p\\q\end{array}}$$

3 Denied Conjunction

$$-(p\,\&\,q)$$

$$-p \qquad -q$$

4 Undenied Disjunction

$$(p \lor q)$$

p q

5 Denied Disjunction

$$-(p \lor q)$$
$$|$$
$$-p$$
$$|$$
$$-q$$

6 Undenied Conditional

$$p \supset q$$

$-p$ q

7 Denied Conditional

$$-(p \to q)$$
$$|$$
$$p$$
$$|$$
$$-q$$

Jeffrey also gives a rule for the biconditional, but I shall not present it here.

Rules 1, 2, 5, and 7 simply express the logical facts about what can be inferred from each proposition. Rules 3, 4, and 6 reflect a different situation. Consider 3, for example. The fork indicates that either one or the other (or both) of the conjuncts is false. That is, the second line can be viewed as expressing the equivalence "$-p \lor -q$." Since we are looking for a set of variable values that indicate invalidity, we need to consider a truth table line on which p is false and another on which q is false, to make sure we have checked all lines that might be invalidating.

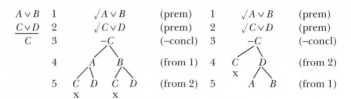

Fig. 22.   Jeffrey's example

In deriving values or forks from the premisses and the denied conclusion, we rely on the foregoing seven rules. When we arrive at a variable (or its denial) and find that its opposite appears in the path we can trace from it back up to the first line, we put an "x" under it, indicating that the path is closed. We then write another premiss (or the conclusion denial) in forked or unforked form beneath all variables (or their denials) that do not have an "x" under them, and break these down. Figure 22 shows an example given by Jeffrey (1981, 25).

This example shows that there is an element of choice in constructing trees. However, there is a principle that can be used to minimize complexity: below any variable, or string of them, standing alone, write a broken-down premiss (or denied conclusion) that will create a closed path right away. By this principle, the best premiss to select for line 4 is the one on line 2, since one branch will contain "C."

The left derivation illustrates the requirement to write a premiss under all variables that do not have "x" under them. At line 4 neither variable has an "x" under it, so the premiss must be entered twice at line 5. In the right version it only needs to be written once, since there is a "x" under the "C." The "x" is placed there because there is a "$-C$" in the path going up to line 1. This indicates that an invalidating set of variable values cannot be found on that path.

At line 5 of the right tree we find that all premisses and the denied conclusion have been broken down. This is indicated by following the practice of placing a check mark to the left of each premiss (or denied conclusion) when it has been broken down. At this point our tree tells us that there are two sets of variable values that show invalidity. The premisses are true and the conclusion false with (1) "A and D" true and "C" false, and (2) "B" and "D" true and "C" false. Thus, there are a total of three lines in the complete truth table that are invalidating.

This is a very brief exposition of the truth tree method, but even so it may enable the reader to utilize the method if s/he is able to test argument patterns using full truth tables. If more direction is needed, the reader is referred to Jeffrey (1981).

Table 20
RTT Test for Jeffrey's Example

$A \lor B$		$C \lor D$			C
T		F	T	T	F
5		2	3	4	1

The RTT method and the truth tree method are structurally analogous. The strategy is the same, that is, to test for validity by trying to derive an invalidating set of variable values. Pedagogically, both methods require an understanding of the propositional calculus up to the point of being able to understand how truth tables work. But beyond this point, the tree method seems to be easier to use: the student has to rely on only seven derivation rules. Of course the "rules" of RTT are simpler (for example, if the truth values given for parts of a complex proposition can only be found on a single line for the connective truth table, any other value on that line can be written in), but a greater variety of situations can arise in relying on the connective tables. Experience also shows that the format of the RTT method makes it difficult for beginners to keep the derivation sequence straight. The format for the tree method tends to prevent this sort of error.

On the other hand, the RTT method is usually more efficient for one who knows how to use both methods. For example, the RTT test for the pattern tested above (Figure 22) is as shown in Table 20. Here we begin by assigning "F" to the conclusion "C," entering step (2), assigning "T" at step (3) because the truth value of "$C \lor D$" is still undetermined after 2. Given 2 and 3, we can derive 4. Since "$A \lor B$" is undetermined at this point, we can assign it a "T". At this point we know that the pattern is invalid because we know that there are values for which both premises can be true while the conclusion is false. Thus, each method has advantages. The tree method can be learned more quickly, and perhaps therefore retained a bit longer. On the other hand, when mastered, the RTT method is less clumsy to use and, for this reason, quicker. But both methods are superior to the natural-deduction approach, for reasons given earlier.

5.1.2 *Evaluating Class Reasoning*

The traditional texts provide two conceptually and historically distinct techniques for evaluating class reasoning. Typically, they present classical syllogistic first, then the predicate version of deduction; the latter is portrayed as a more powerful system by virtue of the fact that it can show the validity of many patterns that the former cannot. In this section I will briefly assess these two approaches to evaluating class reasoning, and two approaches based on Venn diagrams.

5.1.2.1 *The Predicate Calculus*. Ironically, although the predicate calculus is more powerful in that it can demonstrate the validity of arguments involving any number of classes, it is weaker than the syllogistic in a crucial respect: as a deduction system (like the propositional calculus) it is a proof procedure but not a decision procedure. Thus, it cannot show that an invalid pattern is invalid. However, a supplementary procedure has been developed to test arguments cast in the predicate calculus for invalidity.

5.1.2.1.1 *The "Small Universe" Test*. Essentially, "an argument involving quantifiers is proved invalid if there is a possible universe or *model* containing at least one individual such that the argument's premises are true and its conclusion false *of that model*" (Copi 1982, 375). The method "translates" universally and existentially quantified propositions into instantiated equivalents. Assertions of the form "All S's are P," symbolized as "$(x)(S_x \supset P_x)$," is written as "$(S_a \supset P_a)$ & $(S_b \supset P_b)$ & ..." Assertions of the form "Some S's are P," symbolized as "$(\exists_x)(S_x \& P_x)$," are written as "$(S_a \& P_a) \lor (S_b \& P_b) \lor ...$"

Copi considers this argument: "All mercenaries are undependable. No guerrillas are mercenaries. Therefore no guerrillas are undependable" (1982, 375). This is symbolized in the predicate calculus as

$$(x)(M_x \supset U_x)$$
$$(x)(G_x \supset -M_x)$$
Therefore $(x)(G_x \supset -U_x)$.

If we consider a "universe" of one item, "a," this argument is logically equivalent to

$$M_a \supset U_a$$
$$G_a \supset -M_a$$
Therefore $G_a \supset -U_a$.

This pattern can be tested using either the RTT or the truth tree method. Using the RTT method, we find the inference to be invalid, as shown by Table 21.

There is one glitch in this approach. It is possible that an argument appears formally valid in a universe with one, or even two or three

Table 21
RTT Using "Small World" Approach

$M_a \supset U_a$		$G_a \supset -M_a$			$G_a \supset -U_a$		
T	T	T	T	TF	T	F	FT
5	5	6	8	910	2	1	34

members, but in a universe containing a larger number, it proves to be invalid. Copi gives this example to make the point: "All collies are affectionate. Some collies are watchdogs. Therefore all watchdogs are affectionate." In a one-member universe this is equivalent to

$$C_a \supset A_a$$
$$C_a \, \& \, W_a$$
Therefore $W_a \supset A_a$.

This pattern is valid, but if we test for a two-member universe, it is invalid (1978, 363). Thus, for any given argument, if it tests valid for a one-item universe, we must test with a two-item universe. What do we do if a two-item model tests valid? At what point do we stop? Copi provides no answer. Pragmatically, the best move at some point is to try to construct a proof using the rules of predicate calculus.

Thus, while the "small universe" approach can be useful, it has a limitation analogous to the proof procedure. With the latter, failure to derive the conclusion does not conclusively show invalidity. With the former, failure to show invalidity is not conclusive proof of validity. But using the two together can be effective. The main pragmatic difficulty with using the predicate calculus is cognitive: acquiring expertise in its use is even more difficult than for the propositional version, as the struggles of students in symbolic logic courses show. The other side of the coin is that acquired expertise cannot be maintained without constant use.

5.1.2.2 *Syllogistic.* For the reasons given above, syllogistic is a more practical system for evaluating arguments that can be cast in syllogism form, that is, arguments in which exactly three classes (terms) are mentioned with one term occurring in each premise but not in the conclusion (the "middle term"), and in which each assertion can be formulated in one of the following kinds of propositional form:

A-type: All x's are y's.
E-type: No x's are y's.

I-type: Some *x*'s are *y*'s.
O-type: Some *x*'s are not *y*'s.

The need to cast this sort of class reasoning in a standard form arises because the evaluation of a pattern is done through the use of a set of rules. In his version, Copi (1982, 227–35) has six rules:

1 A valid standard-form categorical syllogism must contain exactly three terms, each of which is used in the same sense throughout the argument.
2 In a valid standard-form categorical syllogism, the middle term must be distributed in at least one premiss. (A term is distributed in a proposition when it refers to all members of the class designated by the term; *x* is distributed in the A-type given above, *x* and *y* in the E-type, and *y* in the O-type.)
3 In a valid standard-form categorical syllogism, if either term is distributed in the conclusion, then it must be distributed in the premisses.
4 No standard-form categorical syllogism is valid which has two negative premisses (that is, E or O types).
5 If either premiss of a valid standard-form categorical syllogism is negative, the conclusion must be negative.
6 No valid standard-form syllogism with a particular conclusion can have two universal premisses.

Such a set of rules enables the user to identify valid and invalid syllogisms once the argument has been written as a standard-form categorical syllogism. However, in most natural languages there is much stylistic variation, allowing people to express categorical propositions in a number of different ways, the result being that one seldom encounters a standard syllogism in everyday argumentation. Normally one or more of the assertions has to be rewritten. This can be tricky. For instance, "Only *x*'s are *y*'s" is expressed in standard form as "All *y*'s are *x*'s." It is, I have found, difficult to get students to appreciate this intuitively implausible equivalency, and a number of others, without resorting to graphic representations such as the Venn diagram.

5.1.2.3 *Venn Diagrams.* Now if the Venn diagram is used as an aid one might as well use the Venn diagram method for testing syllogisms in the first place. Besides, it can be used to test inferences involving only two terms, such as the patterns associated with the traditional square of opposition (see Copi 1982, 188–9).

The Venn diagram method for syllogism testing utilizes a diagram format that enables us to graphically represent categorical syllogistic assertions, whether they are in standard form or not. The most common format is one having three overlapping circles (see Copi 1982, sec. 6.3). Copi provides a concise description of the method:

First, label the circles of a three-circle Venn diagram with the syllogism's three terms. Next, diagram both premises, diagramming the universal one first if there is one universal and one particular, being careful in diagramming a particular proposition to put the *x* on a line if the premises do not determine on which side of the line it should go. Finally, inspect the diagram to see whether or not the diagram of the premises contains the diagram of the conclusion: if it does, the syllogism is valid, if it does not, the syllogism is invalid. (Copi 1982, 223)

This procedure is relatively straightforward in its formulation. No technical terminology needs to be relied on, other than the concepts "universal" and "particular," which are easy to learn and remember. Diagramming premises is easy to learn. The main problem is in judging whether the "diagram of the premises contains the diagram of the conclusion." This is where most errors are made by novices, in my experience and according to other instructors I have consulted. And, of course, an error at this stage is fatal.

The most trouble seems to arise with syllogisms having at least one particular proposition. For example, consider this one discussed by Copi: "All great scientists are college graduates. Some professional athletes are college graduates. Therefore, some professional athletes are great scientists." The standard form of this argument is "All P's are M's; some S's are M's; therefore some S's are P's." Following the procedure we first diagram the first premiss by shading the area in which P's could be not-M's, to indicate that that pair of "cells" is empty. Next we diagram "Some S's are M's" by placing an "x" on the line running through the overlap between circles "S" and "M." This indicates that there is something in either one cell or the other, perhaps both. It would not be appropriate to place an "x" in each, or in just one, since we cannot infer such things from the premises. The diagram in Figure 23 shows the premises diagrammed.

Now, does the above diagram "contain" the diagram for the conclusion? According to Copi, the reasoning we use goes like this. Inspecting the diagram to see whether the conclusion of the syllogism appears in it, we find that it does not. For "Some S's are P's" to be diagrammed, an "x" would have to occur in the overlap between the circles for "professional athletes" and "great scientists." The upper part is empty, since it

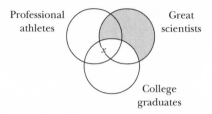

Fig. 23.   Venn diagram for Copi's example

is shaded. There is no "*x*" in the lower part either. The "*x*" on its edge does not guarantee there is something in it, since the "*x*" is appropriate when there is something only in the other part of the area marked with an "*x*". Obviously, the completion of the diagramming must be followed by a reasoning process, one that can be conducted in terms of diagram cells. It is not a difficult process, in most cases, and the foregoing example represents the most sophisticated level.

As an alternative to the "look to see if the conclusion has been diagrammed" approach,[2] we could look to see if the diagram of the contradictory of the conclusion can be added to that of the premises. In our example, the contradictory of the conclusion is "No professional athletes are great scientists." Symbolically, this is "No *S* is *P.*" Can this be diagrammed on the Venn diagram of our syllogism? Yes, because it is diagrammed by shading out the overlap between the "professional athletes" circle and the "great scientists" circle. When this is shaded out, there is still the possibility of something being in the cell common only to professional athletes and college graduates. That is, diagramming the contradictory of the conclusion is not incompatible with the two premises also being diagrammed.

5.1.2.4 *The Venn RTT Method.* An alternative way of using Venn diagrams has been developed (Grennan 1985). It has several advantages over the normal procedure. To use it, one needs only the standard Venn diagram (with its cells labelled), the ability to perform a truth table test of some kind, and the ability to convert syllogistic assertions into a propositional-logic form. To use this alternative method we label the cells in the diagram as shown in Figure 24 (or in some other way preferred).

The method requires us to write syllogistic assertions in terms of diagram cells. We have the cell names also stand for correlated propositions of the form "There is something in cell *A,*" for example. The Venn-equivalent of "All *S* is *P*" is "$-A$ & $-D$," that is, "It is not the case that there is something in cell *A,* and it is not the case that there is

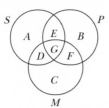

Fig. 24.   Venn RTT diagram

something in cell *D*." "No *S* is *P*" is written as "−*E* & −*G*"; "Some *S* is *P*" is written as "*E* ∨ *G*," that is, as "There is something in cell *E* or in cell *G* or in both" (an inclusive "or"). "Some *S* is not *P*" is written as "*A* ∨ *D*."

The last example discussed, a relatively tricky one for the traditional method, can serve to illustrate the Venn RTT method: "All great scientists are college graduates. Some professional athletes are college graduates. Therefore, some professional athletes are great scientists." The first step is to write the logical form of the argument. This does not require writing it in standard syllogistic form beforehand. All we need to do is replace the expressions denoting classes with "*S*," "*P*," or "*M*." In this case we have the following: "All *P*'s are *M*'s. Some *S*'s are *M*'s. Therefore, some *S*'s are *P*'s." To write the equivalent in propositional logic we simply express each assertion in terms of Venn diagram cell-contents. "All *P*'s are *M*'s" states that cells *B* and *E* are empty, that is, "−*B* & −*E*." "Some *S*'s are *M*'s" states that there is something in cell *D* or in cell *G*, perhaps in both, that is, "*D* ∨ *G*." "Some *S*'s are *P*'s" is written as "*E* ∨ *G*."

To test the argument we simply try to find values for the letters (treating them now as variables) that show invalidity. We can use either the full truth table method, the RTT method, or the truth tree method. Of course, the full truth table method is apt to be very laborious, since it may involve constructing a 16-line table, as the example does. The RTT method presented earlier is ideal for testing these patterns. Table 22 gives the result. The argument is invalid, and this has been shown without having to decide whether the conclusion diagram is contained in the joint-premiss diagram. As noted earlier, this process is a tricky one in some cases, this example being one such.

Basically, the alternative method is analogous to the traditional Venn method at the first stage. In the conventional procedure we diagram the premisses, and in the other one we write the propositional equivalent of what would be diagrammed. Of course, the new method does not require us to construct a diagram for each inference. Instead, we simply refer to a single preexisting one whose cells are labelled.

Which approach is better, the standard Venn method or the RTT version? Each is logically adequate. Each can be used with almost no

Table 22
RTT Venn-Equivalent Method for Syllogism Testing

−B & −E			D ∨ G			E ∨ G		
TF	T	TF	T	T	F	F	F	F
89	7	54	11	10	6	2	1	3

familiarity with syllogistic theory. This is an important advantage, since learning syllogistic theory is time-consuming. Copi, for instance devotes about forty-five pages of his text to it. In contrast, I cover syllogism testing based on the RTT method in eight pages, which can be taught in three classes (Grennan 1984, 220–8). Copi covers the conventional Venn approach in two sections (5.6 and 6.3), about fifteen pages.

If the user has had no exposure to a short truth table method or the truth tree method for testing inferences cast in propositional-logic form, the conventional Venn approach is the only usable one of the two. However, there is at least as much practical value in teaching a decision procedure for arguments that contain conditionals and disjunctions, as there is in teaching a procedure for syllogistic inference. Indeed, we may encounter more arguments of the former type. This suggests that the skilled evaluator should be equipped to use some version of the RTT or truth tree method, and would thus be equipped to learn the new method quite quickly.

As for reliability, my own experience suggests that the new method is better than the traditional version, if people can perform an RTT or truth tree test. One needs only to learn to write the syllogistic assertions in Venn-equivalent form, which is comparable to diagramming them. No further interpretation associated with the Venn diagram needs to be performed. Fewer errors occur in doing an RTT or truth tree test than in deciding whether a conclusion has been diagrammed in the course of diagramming two premises.

5.1.2.5 *Syllogistic with Existential Import.* The form of syllogistic invariably presented in current textbooks assumes that universal propositions (the A- and E-types) have no existential import. That is, if I assert "All Englishmen are brave," I am not committed to the proposition that there actually are Englishmen. In this respect my assertion is comparable to "All men of Atlantis are brave." This interpretation of A and E propositions was not espoused prior to the late nineteenth century. Before that, such propositions were considered to have existential import. On that interpretation, I would be committed to claiming the existence of Englishmen and men of Atlantis.

This interpretation seems to fit the ordinary person's concept of a universal generalization better than the modern version. It also is compatible with what speech act theory has to say about assertions: that an utterance having the form of an assertion does not count as one if there is reference failure. Thus if I say "All men of Atlantis are brave," I have failed to assert, so that no proposition has been asserted.

The change of position on this question came about when modern logic was developed. It became accepted that "All S is P" is to be analyzed as "For anything x, if x is S, then x is P," where "if ... then" is given the material-implication interpretation. When this interpretation is chosen, the universal proposition will be true when there are no x's that are S, because this makes the antecedent of the conditional false, which makes the conditional itself true. Thus, "All S is P" is true or false independent of whether there are any S's; that is, it has no existential import.

The classical tradition, on the other hand, interprets the A- and E-types as having existential import. Nine additional syllogistic patterns are valid once we adopt existential import for A- and E-type propositions. Five are subalterns, and as such are of little practical consequence. Several of the others are intuitively valid, so this is a welcome improvement. One such is the AAI-3 form, which is written symbolically as follows: "All M is P. All M is S. Therefore, some S is P."

As it happens, the Venn-RTT method can also be used to test syllogisms when existential import is accepted. Referring to the labelled Venn diagram (Figure 24), how do we write the first premiss in the above pattern? Part of it must include the claim that cells C and D are empty, because anything in these cells would be an M that is not a P. This is rendered as "$-C$ & $-D$." But this is not a complete formulation when there is existential import for A-type propositions. We also need to add that there is something in either cell F or cell G; otherwise we are allowing the possibility that the M circle is empty, in which case M would have no referent (C and D are already empty). Thus, we need to add "$F \vee G$." Given existential import, then "All M is P" is formulated as

$$(-C \, \& \, -D) \, \& \, (F \vee G).$$

By the same principles, "All M is S" is formulated as

$$(-C \, \& \, -F) \, \& \, (D \vee G).$$

The conclusion, "Some S is P," is formulated in the same way as before, since it always has existential import: "$E \vee G$." Our syllogism can be written in Venn-equivalent form as

$$(-C \& -D) \& (F \vee G) \: / \: (-C \& -F) \& (D \vee G) \: // \: E \vee G.$$

This pattern will be found to be valid when tested by the RTT method, or the propositional calculus. Indeed, all nine of the extra forms will test valid (Tapscott 1976, 412).[3]

Without existential import the pattern would be written as:

$$-C \& -D \: / \: -C \& -F \: // \: E \vee G.$$

This pattern will test invalid. The same will be found for the other eight added ones. They will be valid with existential import, and invalid without it.

It has been shown, then, that the Venn-RTT method can be applied to the classical syllogistic as well as to the modern version.

5.1.2.6 *Summary.* In summary, it has been argued that in several respects the traditional Venn diagram method for evaluating class reasoning is superior to the classical syllogistic approach: (1) it makes intuitive sense in application, whereas syllogistic is ad hoc; (2) it is broader in application, since it can be used to test inferences involving only two assertions and two terms, and ones with more than three terms; (3) it requires learning of fewer technical concepts.

It has also been argued that if evaluators are familiar with either the RTT or truth tree method, they will find that the alternative Venn method described above is more dependable. And since it is desirable to be able to test arguments cast in propositional logic form, the alternative Venn method is the most desirable means of evaluating class reasoning. The Venn-RTT method also has the advantage of being efficient if we adopt the existential-import version of syllogistic.

5.2 TESTING FOR MATERIAL VALIDITY

The foregoing sections have presented a review of the more effective systems for determining the presence of deductive validity arising from logical form, either in propositional or class reasoning. In both types of argument, validity occurs because the warrants for the inference claims are formal tautologies. The inference claims themselves are instances of valid patterns, the warrants.

In this section I shall discuss strategies for evaluating inferences in arguments that might be deductively valid by virtue of their propositional content. The traditional logic texts offer little guidance in this area, perhaps because they fail to note the frequency with which such arguments occur. This group of deductively valid arguments consists of arguments whose warrants are necessarily true because of either constitutive or regulative rules. That is, they are materially deductively valid, but not formally valid.

The existence of materially valid arguments was defended in chapter 2. Testing for validity amounts to deciding whether or not the warrant is necessarily true. In general, the conditions for validity depend on whether the warrant is based on constitutive or regulative rules.

5.2.1 *Constitutive Rule-Based Inferences*

Constitutive rules differ from regulative ones in that they make new kinds of action possible. The queen in chess is by stipulation defined as the piece that may move any number of squares in any direction. This specific freedom of movement constitutes being the queen and makes possible such manoeuvers in chess as checking, checkmating, and so on. Essentially, constitutive rules are expressed in definitions, which may be either stipulative or customary. An argument whose warrant is entailed by a correct stipulative definition is deductively valid. One that is backed by a customary definition will be valid only under certain conditions.

5.2.1.1 *Stipulated Constitutive Rule-Based Inferences.* Games provide examples of inference-making that relies on stipulated definitions. Consider a baseball game. Providing play is in progress, that is, that baseball is being played, arguments like this one given by an umpire are deductively valid: "The baserunner was tagged with the ball when not on the base, so he's out." The warrant here can be stated as "If a baserunner is tagged with the ball when not touching a base, that person is out." The warrant is true because of a constitutive rule to the effect that being tagged when not touching a base counts as being out. In such a situation there is no point in anyone challenging the decision if they accept the premiss. Disagreement about such arguments in baseball can only be about the truth value of the premiss. To disagree with the inference claim is (by *modus tollens*) to disagree with the warrant, which, in turn, is to call the rule into question. But to raise such an issue is not conceptually possible within a game of baseball; it is to dispute the rules rather than their application to a particular situation.

Stipulative definitions are part of activities that can be regarded as institutions, and they are legitimate when persons occupying appropriate offices or roles prescribe them. For example, in a legal system legislators are empowered to define offences such as murder. If "murder" is defined as "culpable homicide" in a particular legal jurisdiction, arguments such as this will be valid: "Dahmer committed culpable homicide, so he is guilty of murder." The warrant here, "If anyone committed culpable homicide, then s/he is guilty of murder," is entailed by the legal definition of "murder" in that jurisdiction.

Thus, in evaluating inferences that are supposedly based on legitimate stipulative definitions, we need to check the wording of the authoritative definitions. But there is frequently a complication arising from officially recognized exceptions. For example, in ice hockey, a goal is scored when the puck fully crosses the goal line, unless it was intentionally directed in by a high stick or by a player using something other than his stick. When all the official exceptions are denied, deductively valid arguments can be constructed: "X put the puck in the opponents' net and did not do it with a high stick and did not intentionally direct it in using something other than his stick, so X scored." When the premises of an argument relying on a stipulative definition do not deny the official exceptions, we can show invalidity when we find an exception condition operative.

5.2.1.2 *Customary Constitutive Rule-Based Arguments.* Not all arguments whose warrants are backed by constitutive rules can be deductively valid. Deductively valid arguments must have warrants that are necessarily true. This condition can frequently be met when the rules are stipulated, as we just saw. But the warrant can be open to counterexample when based on customary constitutive rules.

Inferences based on ordinary-language semantic rules are a case in point because, although such rules are conventional, they are also customary. That is, they exist as reflected in shared linguistic practices, not as a result of stipulation by some recognized authority. Because of this, they are, in Hart's terminology, "open textured" (1961, 124–5). They admit of exceptions that are not stipulated as such, that are often unanticipated when encountered. They also have the property of being projective too. That is, we are willing to apply the terms they govern to qualitatively new cases. For example, speakers can correctly apply and correctly withhold the expression "human being" with considerable uniformity to almost everything they encounter, but the current abortion debate can be seen as partly a matter of dealing with a qualitatively new (for most speakers) case: at what stage of development does a human fetus count as a human being? And to take a hypothetical case, would beings from another world having our DNA "fingerprint" count as human beings?

Another way of characterizing customary constitutive rule-based claims is to say that they admit of borderline cases. Since "human being" seems to have borderline cases, for example, the following argument may not be deductively valid at this time: "E has the DNA 'fingerprint' of a human being, so E is human." To be deductively valid this argument must rely on the warrant "If anyone has the DNA fingerprint of a human being, then that individual is human." But current linguistic practice may involve having ones forebears originating from Earth as a necessary condition for "humanhood," and it is conceivable that there are beings elsewhere in the universe that have DNA fingerprints like ours.

The main point for purposes at hand is that, regardless of how many borderline cases have been dealt with, ordinary language concepts are not such that further borderline cases can be ruled out. Thus, warrants in arguments that rely on customary constitutive rules cannot be necessarily true, which means that inferences are not deductively valid unless they contain certain qualifications.

Nevertheless, deductively valid arguments can be constructed if arguments are properly formulated. Proper formulation requires the restriction that non-borderline cases are being considered. For example, "Myrtle is a non-borderline case of a woman who has never been married, so Myrtle is a spinster." The semantic rules governing "spinster" are such that "All non-borderline cases of women who have never been married are cases of spinsters" is necessarily true. Any putative counter-example of a woman who has never been married but might not be a spinster will necessarily count as a non-case or a borderline case of a woman who has never been married. For example, if it is said that Martha has never been married, but is not a spinster, because she cohabits with a man, she can be set aside as a counterexample because she is at best a borderline case of someone who has never been married, since her current arrangement is marriage in fact, if not in law.

Therefore, even when the rules backing a warrant are custom-based, they can entail that the warrant is necessarily true if the expressions "non-borderline" or "typical" are used in a premiss to block counterexamples that can arise from the open texture of concepts established by customary conventional usage. In evaluating inferences based on customary rules, then, we need to establish whether the warrant is vulnerable to counterexample. The inclusion of an appropriate qualifier may secure validity.

5.2.2 *Regulative Rule-Based Inferences*

Now let us consider arguments that may be deductively (but not formally) valid by virtue of having warrants that represent regulative rules. The distinction between stipulated and customary rules applies to regulative rules also. I will discuss the two kinds separately.

5.2.2.1 *Stipulated Regulative Rule-Based Inferences.* Stipulated regulative rules can be the basis for warrants that are necessarily true. Here is an example that was discussed earlier in a different context. A sign by the curb at a shopping mall reads "NO PARKING: FIRE LANE." This represents a regulative rule expressible as "Do not park here." Now suppose a person is before a judge in the jurisdiction in which this sign occurs and she says, "You parked in an area designated as a fire lane, so you violated Highway Code Section 27.34." If this is a strict liability offence (that is, there are no legally acceptable excuses), the argument is deductively valid. The judge is able to move from a "physical" fact to a legal one, with truth preservation, by virtue of a warrant, that is, "If anyone parks in an area designated as a fire zone, then that individual commits an offence under Highway Code Section 27.34." This warrant is true by virtue of the regulative rule specified in that section, which might begin, "Parking in an area designated as a fire zone is an offence."

As in the case of stipulated constitutive rules, the existence of official exceptions must be taken into account. If each of them is denied as part of the premisses, the conclusion follows deductively. Otherwise, when an exception applies, the inference will be invalid.

5.2.2.2 *Customary Regulative Rule-Based Inferences.* Customary regulative rules as warrant-backing raise the same sort of difficulty noted for customary constitutive rules. There are several paradigmatic types of such rules, including moral rules and rules of etiquette. I shall use moral cases for discussion.

Moral rules can take the form "E did X, so E committed an offence under rule R," but the possibility of deductive validity is limited because moral rules are open textured, admitting of recognized (but not official) exceptions and unrecognized (because unencountered) exceptions. To be capable of deductive validity, the pattern must be modified to include reference to circumstances: "E did X in circumstance C, so E committed an offence under rule R." The associated warrant now has the form "All cases of doing X in C are cases of committing an offence under rule R." Providing that an exhaustive specification of C does not mention an excusing condition, the warrant will be true.

Theoretically, specification of C would mention all morally relevant physical and psychological facts about the agent E, about the persons affected by E's action, the characteristics of the act itself, and the physical setting in which the act occurs. However, most people have a good ability for identifying excuses, so that in practice it is often easy to see that no excusing conditions obtain.

It should be apparent that the general procedure given for warrants backed by constitutive rules, modified slightly, can be used to evaluate inferences in arguments with warrants backed by regulative rules. We formulate the warrant, then check to see if it is entailed by the rules. For exceptions to be taken into account their denials must be mentioned in the premises, which means that they must also must be present in the warrant.

5.2.3 *Hitchcock's Approach to Material Validity*

In several papers David Hitchcock has presented a somewhat more economical method of checking for deductive validity. Instead of formulating a warrant and scrutinizing its backing, he recommends writing the logical form of the argument by making certain variable substitutions, then seeing if we can find values that yield true premises and a false conclusion: "Consider the argument 'Cows are herbivores, so they are not predators.' This argument meets our substitutional necessary condition for validity, in that no substitution on 'cows' produces a counterexample. This substitutional condition is equivalent to the condition that no instance of the form or schema 'F's are herbivorous, so F's are not predators' has a true premiss and a false conclusion" (Hitchcock 1989, 5).

To create a sufficient condition for validity Hitchcock extends the substitutional requirement to include hypothetical instances. He introduces this extension using this example: "Cattle are monstrously inefficient. Even in good areas they convert only 5% of the potential food in the grass into meat." He comments, "it is not enough that all actual animals which convert only 5% of the potential food in grass into meat are monstrously inefficient; it must also be the case that any hypothetical animal which did so would be monstrously inefficient" (1989, 5–6). Earlier, Hitchcock warns that the range of substitutions must be limited to intracategorial ones, so as to rule out spurious counterexamples.

The application of Hitchcock's theory of validity to inference evaluation is fairly straightforward in theory. The evaluator writes a schematic version of the argument, replacing, it would seem, all occurrences of the referring expression in the conclusion with a variable. For example, we write the schema for the last argument as "X's are monstrously inefficient. Even in good areas X's convert only 5% of the potential food in the grass into meat." Next, the evaluator attempts to identify a value for "X" that (a) is a species of the same genus as cattle and (b) produces an argument that has a true premise and a false conclusion; that is, X is identified as an animal that in good areas converts only 5% of the potential food in the grass into meat, but that is not considered monstrously inefficient. As already noted, this approach is economical in the sense that we do not have to formulate the inference warrant, then think up a counterexample. Should an appropriate substitution be found, the argument can be declared deductively invalid forthwith.

One difficulty in using the strategy is in deciding which expression is to be replaced by the variable.[4] In the formulation given above, it was said to be the referring expression in the conclusion. But consider this example of Hitchcock's: "You shouldn't tell this patient he has terminal cancer, because you will feel awful if you do." According to the above formulation we would write the argument schema as "X shouldn't tell this cancer patient he has terminal cancer, because X will feel awful if X does." Should we try to find someone who will feel awful but should tell the patient? This does not seem to be the correct direction to take. It seems more appropriate to write the schema as "You shouldn't do X, because you will feel awful if you do X." On the other hand, perhaps the schema should be "You shouldn't tell E that P, because you will feel awful if you do," or even "Y shouldn't tell E that P, because Y will feel awful if Y does."

Perhaps it helps to note that argument schemas are inherently general, so that not just the referring expression of the original argument must be replaced, but also the predicate expression, if it ascribes a particular quality or property. In this example, it happens that what is ascribed is particular because it involves a particular act (telling this patient that he has cancer). Thus, we can say that the schema should contain a symbol that stands for a kind of act: telling patients that they have cancer. On the principle that a schema must not contain any terms specifying particulars, perhaps this is the appropriate one: "X shouldn't do A, because X will feel awful if X does A." Here we have generalized the referring expression and the predicates as well. Moreover, this qualifies as the minimally generalized version. It is desirable to generalize no more than necessary because the usefulness of the method depends on being able to regard the generalization as backing for the inference claim that the argument, and arguer, must rely on. A higher level generalization may not always be said to relied on.[5]

The last example points to a practical problem, and perhaps a logical one as well. In using the method, arriving at the correct schema will sometimes be tricky, because of the generalizing problem. At bottom, the procedure amounts to counterexampling by parallel case, and perhaps the difficulty is intrinsic to such a strategy. One way of dealing with such a problem is to choose another inference-evaluation strategy that does not involve generalizing from the inference claim. The "rebuttal factor" method presented in the next chapter can be applied to materially valid arguments and is, I would contend, better, because it does not require such generalizing.

6 Inductive Inference Evaluation

The strategies discussed in the last chapter were developed to identify deductively valid inferences, either ones that are formally valid by virtue of having formal tautologies as warrants or ones that are materially valid by virtue of having necessarily true warrants. Any argument that is found to be deductively valid in either of these ways can be given the highest possible inference rating. But how are we to deal with ones that are found not to be deductively valid?

A "deductive chauvinist" would have no difficulty with this question: we should regard the arguments as logically worthless, ignore them! But as I argued in chapter 2, this is a totally unsatisfactory view, inasmuch as many arguments that are deductively invalid have relatively high values of $p(C/P)$, high enough to entitle us to accept their conclusions if the premises are acceptable.

6.1 EVALUATING INDUCTIVE INFERENCES

In this section I will present a revised version of a popular inductive-inference evaluation technique and a procedure to deal with inductive arguments containing modalities. The textbooks I am acquainted with do not offer very adequate guidance for dealing with such arguments, although some recognize the importance of modalities in inductive argumentation.[1]

6.1.1 *Evaluating Inferences with No Qualifiers*

When conclusions are not qualified, a technique commonly recommended in the textbooks is that of counterexampling. We formulate the warrant, which would be a universal generalization, then try to adduce at least one clear counterexample to refute it. Failure to adduce a counterexample entitles us to declare the warrant true and the inference valid. If a counterexample is identified, we declare the warrant false and the inference invalid.

This approach has a number of deficiencies. First, it may not do justice to an inference when it is not materially valid. The actual value of $p(C/P)$ $(p(I))$ may be fairly high, yet the warrant in the form of a universal generalization may be false, by virtue of a counterexample. And if the warrant is false, $p(C/P)$ supposedly is zero. This value would vastly underrate the inference in some arguments. For instance, given "Harry was born in Bermuda, so he is a British citizen," the categorical form of the warrant is "All men born in Bermuda are British citizens." Identifying one man who was born in Bermuda but who is not a British citizen serves to show the warrant (as formulated) is false, which supposedly shows that $p(C/P) = 0$. But yet, the premiss is good grounds for the conclusion.

This particular deficiency can be overcome by expressing the warrant in hypothetical form. For the example, it would be "If any man is born in Bermuda, then that man is a British citizen." The value for $p(W)$ (the probability of the warrant) will be the probability that any particular man is a British citizen, given that he was born in Bermuda. The facts of the case are such that $p(W)$ may deserve a rating of 0.8 or even higher. Whatever value is assigned is also the inference rating (I), since $p(I/W) = 1.0$, and $p(I) = p(I/W) \times p(W)$.

I will call the procedure described here the "warrant-evaluation" procedure for inference evaluation. It involves three steps:

1 Write out the inference claim (e.g., "If Harry was born in Bermuda, then Harry is a British citizen").
2 From the inference claim derive the hypothetical version of the warrant (e.g., "If any man was born in Bermuda, then that man is a British citizen").
3 Based on the information one has that is relevant (favourably and unfavourably), assign a probability value to the warrant using the inference rating table (Table 5) in chapter 3. The inference rating equals the warrant rating. (For example, in my opinion, if it were true that a man was born in Bermuda, it would be "adequately proved for most purposes" that he is British. The corresponding rating is 0.8.)

This procedure is feasible, but it involves the problem of correctly formulating the warrant, raised earlier (section 5.2.3) in discussing Hitchcock's approach to identifying material validity.

Before turning to the problem of evaluating inferences in arguments containing qualified assertions, I ought to point out that the warrant-backing approach can be used in the course of evaluating inferences that are materially deductively valid. In such cases the backing will be rules, semantic or otherwise. We will find that we can judge the consequent of the warrant to be certainly true, given the antecedent, so the inference would be rated 1.0.

In light of this, the sections on material deductive validity in the last chapter are not to be regarded as presenting a special procedure for dealing with arguments having a special property but as an attempt to show that arguments can be deductively valid without being formally valid. Those sections were necessary because the existence of materially deductively valid arguments is not commonly recognized by logicians and others who engage in argument evaluation. They will have served their purpose if the reader is now aware that particular inferences may deserve being assigned a $p(C/P)$ value of exactly 1 even though they are not formally valid.

6.1.2 *Evaluating Inferences with Qualified Assertions*

It is not commonly appreciated that almost any inductive argument can be logically satisfactory if modal qualifiers are used to accomodate the relevant facts that have a bearing on the inference claim, for instance, the argument "Harry was born in Bermuda, so it is highly likely that Harry is a British citizen." Given that, say, 90% of those born in Bermuda are British citizens, this argument is logically satisfactory. On the other hand, "Harry was born in Bermuda, so he is a British citizen" is not as satisfactory, given this fact.

Restricting the discussion to one-premiss arguments for expositional convenience, there are two ways in which modal terms can be used in inductive arguments.[2] First, arguments can have the form "P, so $(Qc) C$." (Here "Qc" stands for a modal expression preceding C.) In such a case the speaker S is expressing a judgment that P is not sufficient to warrant outright acceptance of C. That is, S is rating $p(C/P)$ as distinctly less than 1. Second, arguments can be doubly qualified: "$(Qp)P$, so $(Qc) C$." (Here "Qp" is a modal expression preceding P.) In this case there are two bases for C being qualified: (a) S is expressing a reservation about P, but considers the inference to be satisfactory, so that Qc is determined solely by Qp; (b) S has reservations about both P and the inference.

Since the use of modal terms by arguers reflects their evaluations of grounds and inferences, one way we can evaluate arguments containing modal terms is to set aside the arguers' evaluations that these terms reflect, obtain values for $p(P)$ and $p(C/P)$, then comment on the argument in terms of whether the argument's modalities are logically appropriate. That is, are the assertions qualified too much, or too little? When P is not qualified, we simply make a judgment about it as before.

Consider the simplest case first: only the conclusion is qualified. For example, someone says "The official opposition will win the next provincial election, so there is a good chance that university grants will be increased then." In using this method, we first evaluate the argument without the modality, using the procedure outlined in section 3.3.2 of chapter 3. The argument is, "The official opposition will win the next provincial election, so university grants will be increased then."

At step two, inference evaluation, I consider several facts: the opposition has been regularly condemning the government for its stinginess toward the universities; on the other hand, the opposition is on record as opposing any new taxes, but has been claiming that the government has not been trying hard enough to balance its budget. On this basis, I judge that the inference rating is 0.5 – it is just as likely that a change in government will not result in grant increases, as that it will.

At step three, uninferred premiss evaluation, I take several things into account: the government is less popular at this time than the opposition party; on the other hand, the polls show that the government is gaining in popularity and may overtake the opposition by election time. I judge the latter result to be distinctly possible, so I rate P as 0.4.

At step four I calculate $p(C)$ to be 0.2. So the conclusion rating for the unqualified version of the argument is 0.2.

Step five differs, in these cases, from the original version. It involves several sub-steps:

(a) We must compare the premiss-modality in the original argument with one that correlates with our premiss rating. We can use the premiss rating table (Table 3) from chapter 3 to obtain a verbal rating. In this case, the verbal rating is "More likely false than true." There was no modality in the original argument.

(b) We must compare the conclusion-modality in the original argument with one that corresponds to our conclusion-support rating. There is an incommensurability situation here, in that conclusion-modalities are normally propositional modalities, not conclusion-support modalities. However, we can deal with this by thinking of conclusion support as a matter of how probable P makes C. This enables us to use the premiss rating table to get a verbal rating that can be compared with the one in the original argument. For the example, a 0.2 rating corresponds to "highly unlikely," whereas the argument-conclusion modality is "there is a good chance that." This is quite a bit higher than my rating.

(c) I am now in a position to formulate a response, which could begin like this: "Your argument does not show that there is a good chance that university grants will be increased after the next election. Indeed, it remains highly unlikely. First, it is more likely false than true that the opposition will win the next election because ... [cite evidence from step two here]. Secondly, even if the opposition does win, the facts [cite evidence from step two] suggest that there is only a 50–50 chance that grants will be increased."

The same amended procedure can be used to deal with cases in which there is also a premiss modality, since the above version represents just the special case in which the premiss is unqualified.

An interesting question arises in these cases: if we evaluate the unqualified version of an argument and decide that the qualifiers are logically appropriate, what do we say about the original argument? That it proves its conclusion? If we regard the modalities as parts of the premiss and conclusion, it would seem that we must. For in such a case the inference claim, which has the form "If $(Qp)P$ then $(Qc)C$," would have to be regarded as true by the evaluator.

This issue has been addressed by Allen, who advocates what he calls "the inference-claim criterion"[3] for evaluating inferences: "An argument's inference is sound if and only if the argument's inference claim is true" (1988, 59). Allen is using "sound" in a special way, since he distinguishes it from "valid": "a valid argument being one whose conclusion must be true if its premisses are true" (1989, 57). (He regards modalities as external to their premisses and conclusions, as do I.)

Allen's adoption of "sound" as an evaluative term for inferences may not be the best choice, because it has an established use in logic: an argument is sound when its premisses are true and its inference valid (see, for example, Copi 1982, 62). Perhaps the term "correct" can be used to good effect in making judgments about arguments containing modalities. We might say that when the inference claim is regarded as true, the inference is correct, and when the premiss modality is appropriate, we might say that the antecedent of the inference claim (premiss plus its modality) is correct. We might also say that the argument is correct when these two conditions are met. The use of the term "correct" (or some cognate term) in these ways is necessary if we distinguish propositions from their modalities.

There is also a case to be made for regarding premises and conclusions as qualified propositions. That is, the propositions themselves are not "*P*" and "*C*," they are only a part of them. The main disadvantage in adopting this approach is that we would have to regard all correct (in the sense given above) arguments as good arguments, even if the conclusion modality was an extremely weak one. For example, the arguer might recognize that the asserted premiss, though acceptable, entitles her or him to conclude only that "there is some evidence that C." In some commonly used sense, this argument would not be a good argument, because it would do little to persuade *H* that *C*. It seems to be this pragmatic notion of goodness of argument that makes locutions such as "Your premises prove that there is a slight possibility that ..." seem paradoxical or anomalous, at best.

It might be objected that an arguer who deemed it logically appropriate to use such a conclusion modality would not bother to utter the argument, so that my complaint is "merely theoretical." But such arguments do get uttered, typically in desperate situations in which we want to maintain hope of a positive outcome, for example, "It did not drop below freezing overnight, so there is a possibility that we will find them alive." Furthermore, it is desirable to have adequate conceptual resources to cover all cases, even rare and unusual ones. Thus, it seems preferable to regard modalities as modifying premises and conclusions, and to adopt something like the correctness terminology.

Henceforth, I will revert to discussing inductive arguments that lack modalities. Since the procedure advocated for dealing with ones that do contain modalities involves evaluating them without the modalities, whatever is relevant to the latter will be relevant to the former also.

6.2 THE REBUTTAL-FACTOR APPROACH TO INFERENCE EVALUATION

The reader will recall that in chapter 4 I presented and analyzed Toulmin's model of an argument. One component of the model is the warrant, a proposition that, when true, entitles us to infer a claim from a ground offered as evidence for it. Toulmin's discussion is especially noteworthy because he recognized that many (or most) acceptable everyday argument patterns are only presumptively valid. That is, an argument that follows an acceptable pattern has an acceptable inference only in the absence of "circumstances in which the general authority of the warrant would have to be set aside" (1958, 101). Toulmin calls these circumstances "conditions of rebuttal." I call them "rebuttal factors." Thus, the pattern "*X* was born in Bermuda, so *X* is a British subject" is presumptively valid because most substitutions for *X* (such as "Harry") will create a good argument if the ground (premiss) is true. However, Toulmin observes that "the argument is not by itself conclusive in the absence of assurances about his parentage and about his not having changed his nationality since birth."

Since Toulmin first wrote about presumptively valid argument patterns, others have also called attention to this feature. John Pollock, in particular, has advocated the concept. In one of his most recent works Pollock explains his views in terms of the statistical syllogism, which he formulates as follows: "Most A's are B's. This is an A. Therefore this is a B."

The premisses of the statistical syllogism can at most create a presumption in favor of the conclusion, and that presumption can be defeated by contrary information. In other words, the inference licensed by this rule must be a defeasible inference ... Our knowledge of the world cannot be reconstructed in terms of logically conclusive reasons. It is now generally granted in epistemology that there are two kinds of reasons – defeasible and nondefeasible ... Defeasible reasons are what I have called "prima facie reasons" ... Considerations making it unreasonable to accept the conclusion of a prima facie reason are defeaters ... undercutting defeaters ... attack the connection between the prima facie reason and its conclusion ... For example, if I know that x is illuminated by red lights and such illumination often makes things look red when they are not, then I cannot be justified in believing that x is red on the basis of it looking red to me. What I know about the illumination constitutes an undercutting defeater for my prima facie reason. (Pollock 1990, 78–9)

It should be clear that Toulmin and Pollock are talking about the same concept of defeasible reasoning. Pollock's "defeaters" are rebuttal factors. We have here the conceptual basis for an inductive-inference evaluation strategy.

6.2.1 *Derivation of the Rebuttal-Factor Approach*

When considering defeasible reasoning, we can write the inference claim as "If P then C, unless ..." What follow "unless" are rebuttal factors, so we can be more explicit and express the situation as "(If P then C) unless (R_1 or R_2 or ...)." The term "unless" here is logically equivalent to "or," but it is what logicians call the "exclusive 'or.'" When the "or" in a true proposition of the form "X or Y" is an exclusive "or," X is true or Y is true, but not both. This is how the above proposition works: if "If P then C" is true, the other part is false, and vice versa. We can now write the formula as

(If P then C) exclusive-or (R_1 or R_2 or ...).

This formula, however, entails

If P then $(C$ exclusive-or $(R_1$ or R_2 or $...))$.

This last one will be true of arguments that are not presumptively valid, as well as ones that are. Some examples will show this.

Suppose that it is October in Nova Scotia, where this book is being written. Someone says, "It's sunny this morning, so it will be warm this afternoon." Now there are only occasional warm days in October here, so the associated warrant cannot be prefaced by "generally" or any cognate expression. Nonetheless, we can claim something of the form "If it's sunny, then it will be warm this afternoon or the high pressure area over us will keep the air cool." The argument moves from one phenomenon to another that could be an effect of it. Consider a case in which we try to infer the cause of a given phenomenon. A professor enters the college library early in the new term and notes more students are there using the facilities than there would have been a few years ago. He thinks, "There are more students using the library this year, so students are more conscientious than they used to be." In this case too we are reluctant to say that the inference is presumptively valid. But this claim may be true: "If there are more students using the library this year, then either students are more conscientious than they used to be or there are more students enrolled than there used to be." Here the rebuttal factor is a different and competing explanation of the premiss. Any doubt about the truth of this claim will arise from the feeling that not all of the plausible rebuttal factors (explanations) have been included.

These examples suggest that something of the form of our last formula will be true so long as (a) P is relevant to C,[4] and (b) all rebuttal factors are enumerated. In probability terms, anyone who accepts the last formula regards it as having a probability of 1, so we can write

$p[($ if P then $(C$ exclusive-or $(R_1$ or R_2 or $...)))] = 1$.

Since the proposition in the square brackets is a conditional, we can rewrite it as

$p[(C$ exclusive-or $(R_1$ or R_2 or $...)) / P] = 1$.

The probability axiom "$p(X$ exclusive-or $Y) = p(X) + p(Y)$" allows us to write

$[p(C/P) + p((R_1$ or R_2 or $...) / P)] = 1$.

We can now express the probability of the inference claim in terms of the rebuttal factor probabilities:

$$p(C/P) = 1 - p((R_1 \text{ or } R_2 \text{ or } ...) / P).$$

Now the "or" in $(R_1$ or R_2 or ...) is ambiguous. In some cases, it functions as an inclusive "or." When an inclusive "or" appears in a true proposition of the form "X or Y," either X is true or Y is true, and both can also be true. When more than one rebuttal factor can be present, $(R_1$ or R_2 or ...) must be formulated using the inclusive "or" because it is possible for more than one rebuttal factor to be present at a time. (This is true in the argument about Harry. It may turn out that neither of his parents is a British subject, and that he has taken citizenship elsewhere.)

Suppose that there are only two rebuttal factors and they are inclusive. We would then calculate $p(C/P)$ using this formula:

$$p(C/P) = 1 - p((R_1 \text{ inclusive-or } R_2) / P).$$

This can be written as

$$p(C/P) = 1 - [p(R_1/P) + p(R_2/P) - p((R_1 \text{ \& } R_2) / P)].$$

Dropping the square brackets, we can write

$$p(C/P) = 1 - p(R_1/P) - p(R_2/P) + p((R_1 \text{ \& } R_2)/P).$$

Now $p((R_1 \text{ \& } R_2) / P) = p(R_1/P) \times p(R_2/R_1/P)$. And if the rebuttal factors are logically independent, as they usually are, $p(R_2/R_1/P) = p(R_2/P)$, so we can write

$$p(C/P) = 1 - p(R_1/P) - p(R_2/P) + (p(R_1) \times p(R_2)).$$

As it happens, this formula can be written as

$$p(C/P) = (1 - p(R_1/P)) \times (1 - p(R_2/P)).$$

Furthermore, this can be generalized to any number of rebuttal factors, so when the rebuttal factors are inclusive we use "Formula 1":

$$p(C/P) = (1 - p(R_1/P)) \times (1 - p(R_2/P)) \times (1 - p(R_3/P)) \times ...$$

Turning now to the case in which the rebuttal factors are exclusive, things are simpler. Our original formula was

$$p(C/P) = 1 - p((R_1 \text{ or } R_2 \text{ or } R_3 \ldots) \, / \, P).$$

We rewrite this formula as

$$p(C/P) = 1 - p((R_1 \text{ exclusive-or } R_2 \text{ exclusive-or } R_3 \ldots) \, / \, P).$$

As already noted, a probability axiom allows us to write

$$p(C/P) = 1 - [p(R_1/P) + p(R_2/P) + p(R_3/P) + \ldots].$$

Dropping the square brackets, the formula for $p(C/P)$ when the rebuttal factors are exclusive ("Formula E") is

$$p(C/P) = 1 - p(R_1/P) - p(R_2/P) - p(R_3/P) - \ldots$$

Thus, since the value for $p(C/P)$ is different using these two formulas, it seems that, for maximum accuracy, after identifying the plausible rebuttal factors, we must determine whether they are inclusive or exclusive, so that we can select the correct formula.

There are a number of reasons for not accepting this approach. First, it would be simpler if we could use only one formula. That way we would not have to make the inclusive-exclusive judgment after identifying plausible rebuttal factors.

Second, a serious problem can arise in using Formula E. An example can be used to uncover it. A homeowner notes a small round hole in his picture-window that has a circular concave shape. He infers that someone has fired a BB gun at his window. His argument is "There is a small round hole in my window, so someone has fired a BB gun at it." Relevant background information includes these facts: (a) the house is the normal distance from the street; (b) the street is paved; (c) the hole may have been there for some time.

Inference evaluation of arguments of this kind by the rebuttal factor method involves the identification of other plausible explanations for the premiss, as rebuttal factors. These are normally exclusive. What other plausible explanations are there for a small round hole in a window in this context? The following possibilities come to mind:

1 The hole was made by a pellet from a pellet gun.
2 The hole was made by a small stone thrown off by a passing vehicle.
3 The hole was made by a stone thrown by someone.
4 The hole was made by a small stone thrown by a lawnmower.

To determine the inference rating in the most accurate way, I need to assign $p(R/P)$ values to each of these four rebuttal factors. The best way to do this is to make some guesses about the relative frequencies of causes for holes of this kind. Given the background information and other knowledge that is relevant to such matters, I consider that 1 is R_1, the best alternative explanation. I am under the impression that there are quite a few pellet guns around the area. I decide that $p(R_1/P) = 0.6$. The next best I judge to be 4, but it is much less likely because of the shape of the hole: $p(R_2/P) = 0.2$. The other two factors are individually even less likely because, given the distance a small stone would travel from the street, it is not very likely to make a hole. For simplicity, let 2 and 3 count as "other factors" and label this R_3, giving it a value of 0.2.

I am now in a position to calculate $p(C/P)$, using Formula E:

$$p(C/P) = 1 - 0.6 - 0.2 - 0.2 = 0.0.$$

This calculation entails that the inference is totally invalid, but it cannot be correct. There are probably as many BB guns around as there are pellet guns.

What has happened? Basically, I have fallen victim to an unfortunate human propensity that is well documented by cognitive psychology research. In one study (Robinson and Hastie 1985) people were asked to assign probability values to a number of exclusive hypotheses (explanations), A, B, and C, about who committed a murder in a mystery story. The subjects assigned values to $p(A)$, $p(B)$, and $p(C)$ that totalled to a value greater than one. The only way to avoid this error in assigning values to exclusive rebuttal factors is to assign them at the same time, keeping in mind that the sum of the rebuttal factor values plus $p(C/P)$ must equal 1 when all significant rebuttal factors have been identified. Applying this approach to the example can be done as follows.

Starting with the assumptions that it is equally likely that a BB gun or a pellet gun caused the hole and that either is fairly likely, I assign a value of 0.5 to each. But this commits me to claiming that the other factors are negligible, and I do not want to say this. Therefore, I reduce these values to 0.4 and assign 0.1 to each of the other two ("stone from his lawnmower" and "other factors"). This brings the sum to 1.0, as required. But notice that the frequency value of each cause requires me to take account of the frequency of BB guns as a cause. That is, in getting values for the rebuttal factor probabilities, I need to make a judgment of $p(C/P)$ also. Thus, I am not really relying on independent judgments of each rebuttal factor to get $p(C/P)$, which ideally I ought to do. Therefore, using Formula E has two drawbacks: we may vastly underrate $p(C/P)$ by a propensity to overrate the $p(R/P)$ values; and in trying to avoid overrating $p(R/P)$, we must assign a value to $p(C/P)$ in the course of rating the rebuttal factors, which defeats the purpose of relying on rebuttal factor values to get a value for $p(C/P)$.

Using Formula I is a different story. It has the form

$$p(C/P) = (1 - p(R_1/P)) \times (1 - p(R_2/P)) \times (1 - p(R_3/P)) \times \dots$$

This equation can, of course, yield the correct value for $p(C/P)$ when the rebuttal factors are inclusive, as in the argument about Harry. Here, even the sum of rebuttal factor probabilities can exceed one. Suppose there are only two rebuttal factors and I judge each separately. Suppose I assign a value of 0.6 to each. This yields a value of 0.16 for $p(C/P)$, which is a rating of 0.2. The point to note is that Formula I never gives a zero or negative value for $p(C/P)$ as Formula E can.

Let us apply Formula I to the last example, using the initial values I assigned to the rebuttal factors:

$$p(C/P) = (1 - 0.6) \times (1 - 0.2) \times (1 - 0.2) = 0.256.$$

This value corresponds to an inference rating of 0.3, which is lower than what I considered to be the correct value, but only one level lower. This shows that, by using Formula I instead of Formula E when the rebuttal factors are exclusive, we protect ourselves quite well from the tendency to overrate rebuttal factor probabilities. Of course, this tendency is also bound to be at work when the rebuttal factors are inclusive, so it is necessary to look at the impact of overrating when this is the case. I will discuss it using the "Harry" example.

One version of the argument was "Harry was born in Bermuda, so Harry is a British citizen." There were two rebuttal factors: (1) neither of his parents is British, and (2) he has become a naturalized citizen of another country.

Suppose I must evaluate the inference, and have identified the two rebuttal factors but have little extra information about Harry other than that I know that P is true. I do have an impression that it is uncommon for children born in Bermuda to have non-British parents, that Harry has lived in Canada for some time, and that British citizens do not commonly change their citizenship.

On the basis of these impressions, I then decide that $p(R_1/P) = 0.2$, and $p(R_2/P) = 0.3$. I can now calculate that

$$p(C/P) = (1 - 0.2) \times (1 - 0.3) = 0.56.$$

This is an inference rating of 0.6. But suppose I then do some research and find that only 10% of children born in Bermuda have non-British parents, and that 80% (not 70%) of those born British who leave British territory do not become citizens of other countries. The revised values for $p(R_1/P)$ and $p(R_2/P)$ are 0.1 and 0.2. The revised value of $p(C/P)$ is

$$p(C/P) = (1 - 0.1) \times (1 - 0.2) = 0.72.$$

This is an inference rating of 0.7. I now think the inference is slightly better than I did. But even though I initially overrated both rebuttal factors, this only resulted in underrating the inference by one level.

Substituting a variety of initial (overrated) and final (accurate) values for the rebuttal factors in Formula I reveals that even if we overrate by 40%, the rating error is only two levels. For example, suppose there are two rebuttal factors and both are initially rated 0.7, then suppose the final ratings are each 0.5. This is a very large overrating, but the initial inference rating is 0.1, and the final one is 0.3. Therefore, it seems that using Formula I has the distinct advantage of minimizing the inference rating error when the rebuttal factors are inclusive. Formula E does not have this effect when exclusive rebuttal factors are overrated. This suggests that we would be better off using Formula I even when we know that the rebuttal factors are exclusive.

Of course, one consideration in deciding to use Formula I in all cases is accuracy. It may be that the majority of presumptively valid arguments have mutually exclusive rebuttal factors. Most of the argument patterns presented in chapter 7 have associated rebuttal factors that are exclusive. For example, arguments that have an effect-to-cause pattern are very common. The rebuttal factors for them are alternative explanations for the event or state reported in the premiss, such that the correctness of one of them excludes the others as explanations. On the other hand, some of the patterns have rebuttal factors that may be inclusive. The cause-to-effect pattern to be described later often has ones like this. While the pattern is not used as frequently as effect-to-cause, it is by no means rare.

How inaccurate will we be in using Formula I to calculate inference ratings when rebuttal factors are exclusive? When the "or" is inclusive, "$p(X$ or $Y)$" equals "$p(X) + p(Y) - p(X \& Y)$." But when "X" and "Y" are exclusive, it equals "$p(X) + p(Y)$" as already noted. This means that if we treat the "or" as inclusive in all cases, the calculated value for "$p(C/P)$" will be slightly high when the "or" is exclusive. The inaccuracy involved here is not great, because "$p(X \& Y)$" equals "$p(X) \times p(Y)$." The value of this product involves the multiplication of two values less than one, so that the parameter always has a value less than either "$p(X)$" or "$p(Y)$." Furthermore, in an argument with a reasonably good inference, the values for "$p(R_1)$," "$p(R_2)$," etc., will be well below 1.0, so the "$p(X \& Y)$" value will be small. An example will show how these considerations favour treating the rebuttal factors as inclusive, for practical purposes.

Returning to the damaged window example, it will be recalled that I settled on the following values for the rebuttal factors: $p(R_1/P) = 0.4$; $p(R_2/P) = 0.1$; and $p(R_3/P) = 0.1$. Using the correct formula, Formula E, $p(C/P) = 0.4$. Using Formula I, we get

$$p(C/P) = (1 - 0.4) \times (1 - 0.1) \times (1 - 0.1) = 0.486.$$

The inference rating using Formula I is 0.5, one level above the correct rating for these rebuttal factor ratings. But this is not a big error when we remember that the practice of assigning rebuttal factor probabilities is a rough-and-ready one anyway.

With all of these considerations in mind, I conclude that we can use Formula I in determining $p(C/P)$, even when the rebuttal factors are exclusive. While this will result in overrating the inference slightly in this case, the tendency to overrate rebuttal factors themselves is best combatted by using Formula I, even when the rebuttal factors are exclusive.

Formula I shows that, in theory, we can determine an inference rating by assigning probability values to each of the rebuttal factors we can identify. However, there are several difficulties that must still be addressed. First of all, a critic might suggest that there are an indefinite, or at least a very large, number of rebuttal factors associated with any argument. Since each of these has some finite probability if it is an empirical consideration, it looks as if $p(C/P)$ will normally have a low value.

This argument has some prima facie plausibility. Some of it may come from the idea that if there are an indefinite number of rebuttal factors and each has a probability greater than zero, $p(C/P)$ will tend to zero even if their probabilities are quite small. One might think, "If (R_{n+1}) reduces $p(C/P)_n$ by some amount however small, and there are a very large number of rebuttal factors, $p(C/P)$ must keep getting smaller, so that if there is an indefinite number, it must drop to zero." But this need not be so. In fact, even with an infinity of rebuttal factors, it need not go to zero.

Consider an entirely artificial case in which there are actually an infinity of rebuttal factors, where $p(R_1) = 0.5$, and each succeeding one is half the value of its predecessor. Here the value of $p(C/P)$, taking into account all rebuttal factors, is

$$p(C/P) = (1 - 1/2) \times (1 - 1/4) \times (1 - 1/8) \times \ldots$$

Table 23
Petersen's Possible Religion

Rebuttal Factor	Religious Affiliation
R_1	Petersen is Roman Catholic
R_2	Petersen is an unbeliever
R_3	Petersen is a Jew
R_4	Petersen is Islamic
R_5	Petersen is a Hindu
R_6	Petersen is a Zoroastrian

Now the right-hand side has an infinity of terms, which is to say that there is no last term in the above product. Yet, surprisingly, $p(C/P)$ tends to a limiting value of about 0.28.[5] Thus, the existence of an infinite number of rebuttal factors in a given case does not by itself allow us to infer that $p(C/P)$ is asymptotic to zero. This applies to some real cases because the formula for $p(C/P)$ shares the property of the above series: it is convergent, rather than linear. That is, since each new rebuttal factor is smaller than its predecessor, its impact is less.

Consider one of Toulmin's examples: "Petersen is a Swede, so he is a Protestant." Even given the information that no more than 5% of Swedes are non-Protestant and most of those are Roman Catholic, and given some general knowledge about Swedes and the world at large, someone raising this difficulty might identify the items in Table 23 as rebuttal factors, since all of them have $p(R)$ values greater than zero. Since there are an enormous number of religions and affiliation with any particular one is logically possible, it might seem that $p(C/P)$ cannot be very high. But let us see how it goes. Of necessity, I will be relying on estimates in judging values for $p(R)$ in what follows. My figures need only be realistic to make my case.

About 4% of Swedes are Roman Catholic, so $p(R_1) = 0.04$. This leaves 1% of the population to be accounted for, about 90,000 persons. If about 60,000 are unbelievers, $p(R_2) = 0.007$. If about 30,000 of the remainder are Jewish, $p(R_3) = 0.0035$. If there are about one half as many Islamics as Jews, $p(R_4) = 0.00175$. Suppose there are about a similar number of Hindus, so $p(R_5) = 0.00175$. As for Zoroastrians, we might suppose there are 100 in Sweden, so that $p(R_6) = 0.0000111$. Now suppose we calculate $p(C/P)_n$, where "n" is the number of rebuttal factors included in the calculation of $p(C/P)$ (see Table 24).

These values for $p(C/P)$ are based only on personal estimates of rebuttal factor probabilities (except for the first), but they convey the

Table 24
Probabilities of Petersen's Adherence

n	$p(C/P)_n$
1	0.960
2	0.953
3	0.950
4	0.948
5	0.94662
6	0.94661

impression that even if we extend our rebuttal factor list to cover every religion that has ever been identified, it would be appropriate to rate the inference of the argument 0.9. In effect, there comes a point at which including more rebuttal factors does not alter the value in the first decimal position, so that adding more does not change the rating. The example and discussion shows, I think, that the form of Formula 1 does not result in values for $p(C/P)$ normally tending to zero when there are an indefinite number of rebuttal factors, as may be the case in real situations. As the example of the mathematical series shows, this impression can be an illusion generated by the form of the formula.

A second difficulty, of a practical nature, stems from the fact that there can be a large number of rebuttal factors in particular cases. That is, calculating $p(C/P)$ appears to be too laborious to be useful. In view of this practical drawback, it might be asked, why not get an inference rating by just assigning a value to $p(C/P)$, ignoring rebuttal factors altogether? This would represent a trade-off between usefulness and accuracy. Analysis of people's performance in doing it this way shows that we do not get very accurate ratings using this approach. Specifically, we tend to assign a rating that is too high. Taking rebuttal factors into account tends to yield a more accurate inference rating.

Another reason in favour of identifying rebuttal factors in inference evaluation is that we must provide some justification for claiming that an inference is not satisfactory (when it is not). One good way of doing this is to cite plausible rebuttal factors, since the higher their probability, the poorer the inference. Therefore, it is desirable to identify and rely on the associated rebuttal factors of an argument if we are to accurately and fairly judge the quality of its inference. But how is this to be done conveniently?

We could simply identify rebuttal factors, decide roughly how plausible each is without actually assigning a probability value to it, then simply take them into account intuitively in assigning a value to $p(C/P)$. This approach is better than not identifying them systematically, but assigning values and relying on the formula should be even more accurate. To reduce the labour involved in the calculation, we could adopt the principle that only plausible rebuttal factors are to be considered, where "plausible" means $p(R/P)$ is greater than or equal to, say, 0.1. However, this might not reduce our calculation labours, since there might be four or more rebuttal factors that are more probable than this in a given case.

An inspection of Formula 1 suggests that it might be worth examining how the less probable rebuttal factors affect the inference rating based upon it. In the Petersen example we could have ignored all rebuttal factors except the first, which would have led us to rate the inference 1.0. In so doing, we would have rated it only one level too high. In most cases we are not likely going to be able to ignore all but the first rebuttal factor, but it is worth seeing at what point we could ignore them.

Assuming all of the rebuttal factors associated with an inference are identified, how many of them must be included in the $p(C/P)$ calculation to ensure that the inference rating will not change by the addition of another one? In other words, how small must $p(R_n)$ be to qualify as the lowest rebuttal factor to be included? At some point, the rounded-off value for $p(C/P)$ will not be changed by including a factor in the calculation. For example, if $p(R_1) = 0.5$, $p(R_2) = 0.2$, and $p(R_3) = 0.1$, then $p(C/P) = 0.36$, so the inference rating is 0.4. If we include only the first two rebuttal factors, $p(C/P) = 0.40$, so the inference rating is again 0.4. But if we test with a different set ($p(R_1) = 0.5$, $p(R_2) = 0.4$, and $p(R_3) = 0.3$) the rating is 0.2 when all are included, but 0.3 when R_3 is set aside.

To determine how many rebuttal factors must be included to get an accurate inference rating, I identified all of the combinations of rebuttal factor ratings, given three rebuttal factors, for the set of values 0.1, 0.2, 0.3, 0.4, 0.5, 0.6, 0.7, 0.8, 0.9. The possible ratings combinations for four rebuttal factors were examined, and the value for $p(C/P)$ for each combination was calculated according to the above equation. In any combination two or more values could be the same, but since we label them "R_1," "R_2," "R_3," etc., in decreasing magnitude, a value R_n can equal but not exceed the value for R_{n-1}. There were 495 such combinations. The same was done for combinations of three rebuttal factor values, which corresponds to the case in which there is no fourth rebuttal factor. There were 165 combinations. With two rebuttal factors there were 45, and with one there were only nine.

Table 25
Formula Accuracy

Number of Rebuttal Factors	Total Combinations	Number within +/– 0.1	
4	495	484	
3	165	155	
2	45	44	
1	9	9	
Total	714	692	(96.9%)

Then, by trial and error I examined some simple algorithms that might be used to get accurate values of $p(C/P)$ without using the above product formula. The best fit was obtained for

Inference rating = 1.0 – R_1 rating – (0.1 × N),

where N = total number of rebuttal factors rated 0.3 or higher, including R_1. Using this formula, I calculated the inference ratings for each combination and compared these values with the ratings based on rounding off the values for $p(C/P)$ calculated using the product formula. The algorithm was quite accurate. As Table 25 shows, it gave a value within one level of the correct value in 96.9% of all cases.

The algorithm can be the basis for the rebuttal-factor inference rating scheme. It is particularly useful, because we exclude those rebuttal factors that qualify as "very unlikely" (given P) according to the premiss rating table (see Table 3, chapter 3) and those that are even more improbable. Those deserving a rating of 0.3 and above I shall call "plausible rebuttal factors." We do not need to actually rate the plausible ones, except in the case of R_1, the one we judge to be most plausible. If we find that there are two, or even three, most plausible ones, we simply use the rating that they merit as the value for R_1. They are all counted in arriving at our value for "N," except when none are rated above 0.2. In this case we still assign a rating to R_1, but N is zero.

In practice, it is desirable to try to identify two or three rebuttal factors, for thoroughness. If we were to think up only one, it is very possible that we would not have identified the most plausible one. By thinking up three candidates for the label "R_1," we improve our chances of finding the right one. This is important because accuracy depends on it. If we choose a less probable rebuttal factor, we will end up rating the inference too highly. Of course, there may not be three plausible ones, because the argument may have a good inference. Indeed, if it has a very good inference there will not be *any* plausible rebuttal factors. But this is something we can discover only by trying to identify one.

6.2.2 *Inference Evaluation by Rebuttal-Factor Method*

The original procedure requires only changes to step two, inference evaluation (sec. 3.3.2), to accomodate the rebuttal-factor approach.

2(a) Identify all the plausible ($p(R/P)$ = at least 0.3) rebuttal factors. The total number is N.

2(b) Identify the most plausible one. This is R_1. Assign it a rating.

2(c) Determine the inference rating by applying the formula "$I = 1.0 - R_1$ rating $- (0.1 \times N)$." A handy way to apply it is to start with a rating of 1.0, subtract the number of levels corresponding to the rating of R_1, then lower this value one level for each plausible rebuttal factor (including R_1).

To illustrate the use of the procedure, I will evaluate a nautical argument. Someone says to me as we drive to the boat for a day's sailing, "The wind is light out of the northwest, so it will be difficult sailing into the marina this afternoon." He says this because our planned trip will be such that on the way back, the marina will be to the northwest. Sailboats cannot sail directly into the wind, although well-designed ones can sail to within forty-five degrees of it.

2(a) I have several items of background information. I have heard the morning weather forecast, which predicts a hot day and the approach of a low-pressure system from New England in the evening, which would cause the wind to back toward the west. I also know that on hot days a seabreeze builds in the afternoon, which tends to neutralize any wind from the land. This information provides me with two plausible rebuttal factors: (1) a seabreeze will neutralize the northwest wind; (2) the low pressure system will cause the wind to swing toward the west.

2(b) I conclude that 1 is the most plausible rebuttal factor, partly because the forecast indicates that the low will not make its presence felt until evening, after we have returned to the marina. I decide that $p(R_1/P) = 0.7$.

2(c) Calculate the inference rating:
$I = 1.0 - 0.7 - (0.1 \times 2) = 0.1$

Thus, I deem my companion's argument to have very little logical merit. The current wind conditions are not much evidence for his claim that it will be difficult sailing into the marina in the afternoon.

Parenthetically, relying on Formula 1 and assuming that there are no other rebuttal factors and that R_2 has a rating of 0.3, the value for $p(C/P) = (1 - 0.7) \times (1 - 0.3) = 0.21$. This represents an inference rating of 0.2. In theory our result from the simpler formula is one level too low, but this result depended on the value assignment for R_2. Had I estimated it as 0.4, both results would have been the same.

6.2.3 *Interim Summary*

I have presented a technique for evaluating inductive inferences based on Toulmin's concept of a rebuttal factor. I have argued that the most accurate way of determining $p(C/P)$ is to rely on Formula 1:

$$p(C/P) = (1 - p(R_1/P)) \times (1 - p(R_2/P)) \times \ldots$$

Some examination of the behaviour of Formula 1, indicated that we can approximate its results using another formula that requires us to establish the total number of plausible rebuttal factors (N), but it requires us only to assign a specific value to $p(R_1/P)$:

Inference rating = $1.0 - R_1$ rating $- (0.1 \times N)$.

One interesting feature of the method is that in using it, we are complying with the "principle of discrimination", that is, the principle that criticism should be directed primarily against the significant flaws in an argument (Johnson and Blair 1985, 187). We comply with it in the course of identifying the most plausible rebuttal factors.

6.2.4 *The Rebuttal-Factor Method vs Counterexampling*

The rebuttal-factor method contrasts favourably with the counterexampling approach in a crucial respect. As already described, the latter involves formulating the warrant, then attempting to refute it by counterexample. For example, the inference claim for the sailing argument is "If the wind is light out of the northwest this morning, then it will be difficult sailing into the marina this afternoon." The warrant is "Whenever the wind is light out of the northwest in the morning, it will be difficult sailing into the marina in the afternoon." The counterexampling approach would have us recall occasions on which the wind was light northwest in the morning, but there was no difficulty sailing into the marina in the afternoon. Since there is no qualifier in the inference claim, the warrant is a universal generalization. Thus, the identification of even one occasion that is a clear counterexample shows that $p(W) = 0$. Since $p(I) = p(W) \times p(I/W)$, $p(I) = 0$ in this case.

It should be obvious that this approach is not entirely satisfactory. For one thing, the inference claim has a probability greater than zero. For another, the evidence brought forward is essentially statistical: on some (many, a few, etc.) occasions the one event did not follow the other. By contrast, the rebuttal-factor method invites the evaluator to cite factors that would explain the nonoccurrence of the anticipated event: a sea-breeze counteracts the wind in the afternoon. As a justification for saying that the inference is not fully valid, this response is more intellectually satisfying, because more logically fundamental. Expressing one's misgivings by saying that sometimes it is not difficult sailing into the marina even though there is a light northwest wind in the morning may not satisfy the arguer, who may grant the point but request an explanation for it.

Another relative advantage of the rebuttal-factor method over the counterexampling approach is that it channels one's search for evidence against the inference claim more narrowly. In identifying rebuttal factors, we automatically rely on the particular argument and its context. In the example, for instance, information about the particular day and time of year are relied on. In finding counterexamples, on the other hand, we focus on a generalization, leaving open the possibility that the counterexamples are irrelevant to the particular argument. We might, for instance, mention that last week we could sail into the marina without difficulty, even though the wind was like this in the morning but the weather situation was quite different. Or, even further from the mark, we might mention a day last winter.

Careful use of the counterexampling approach will help ensure that clear cases are adduced, but since it focuses on the refutation of a generalization, the possibility of producing irrelevant ones is always there. It needs to be stressed that in evaluating arguments, we are primarily concerned with how probable *this* premise makes *this* conclusion, not with how premises referring to things of this kind support conclusions referring to things of some other kind. The rebuttal-factor approach takes this point seriously.

6.2.5 *The Rebuttal-Factor Method vs The Bayesian Method*

Bayes' Theorem can be stated as

$$p(H/D) = B / (B + 1), \text{ where}$$
$$B = (p(D/H) \times p(H)) / (p(D/-H) \times p(-H)).$$

The parameter "$p(H/D)$" can be seen as the probability of "If D then H," where this conditional represents the warrant for the inference claim of the argument. The value "$p(H)$" represents the "prior probability [of H], meaning the probability before D is known" (Baron 1988, 190). Since "If D then H," the warrant, entails "If P then C," $p(H/D) = p(C/P)$ for the argument. Therefore, if we obtain values for $p(D/H)$, $p(D/-H)$, and $p(H)$, we can calculate $p(C/P)$. (The value for $p(-H) = 1 - p(H)$.)

A simple example will serve to indicate that the exact calculation of $p(C/P)$ by the rebuttal-factor approach yields the same result as using Bayes' formula. Suppose a die is rolled and I cannot see it but am told by an unimpeachable source that the number is under 4. I reason, "It's under 4, so it's odd." The parameter $p(D/H)$ is the probability that the number is under 4, given that it is odd. The total possibilities are 1, 3, and 5. The favourable ones are those under 4, that is, 1 and 3. Thus, $p(D/H) = 2/3$. The parameter $p(D/-H)$ is the probability that the number is under 4, given that it is not odd, that is, given that it is even. The possible cases are 2, 4, and 6. The favourable one is 2. Thus, $p(D/-H) = 1/3$. The prior probability of H (that it is odd) is $1/2$, so $p(-H)$ also equals $1/2$. Using the formula for B we calculate it as follows:

$$B = (p(D/H) \times p(H)) / (p(D/-H) \times p(-H));$$
$$B = (2/3 \times 1/2) / (1/3 \times 1/2) = (2/6) / (1/6) = 2.$$

Now we calculate $p(H/D)$:

$$p(H/D) = 2 / (2 + 1) = 2/3 = p(C/P).$$

Using the rebuttal factor method, we say, "If the die is under 4 then it's odd, unless it's 2." The value of $p(R/P)$ is the probability of the die showing 2, given that it shows a value under 4. Possible cases are 1, 2, and 3. The favourable case is 2, $p(R/P) = 1/3$. We calculate $p(C/P)$:

$$p(C/P) = 1 - p(R/P) = 1 - 1/3 = 2/3.$$

The Bayesian method may appear relatively complex in terms of this simple example, but in some cases it can ensure accuracy when we would otherwise go astray in intuitively assigning values to $p(R/P)$. Such cases arise in diagnostic contexts and when witness reliability is at issue. I will point this out in the next chapter when inferences from testimony are considered. An example presented there indicates that we can vastly overrate the value of $p(C/P)$ in such cases.

The main disadvantage of using the Bayes equation is that we must assign values to three parameters before calculating $p(C/P)$. This may well prove to be more difficult than simply assigning a value to $p(C/P)$

directly. For example, suppose two people see thunderclouds coming towards them and one says, "Thunderclouds are coming, so we are going to have a thunderstorm." To use the Bayes equation we need to determine

1 The probability of thunderclouds coming, given a thunderstorm;
2 The probability of thunderclouds coming, given the nonoccurrence of a thunderstorm;
3 The prior probability of thunderstorms at this time of year or on this date each year.

To use the rebuttal-factor method, I would judge that there is only one plausible rebuttal factor: the clouds will not be "mature" enough to give us a thunderstorm, given that they are coming. Without research, an evaluator may be better prepared to assign a probability value to this rebuttal factor than to either 2 or 3, although 1 can be confidently assigned a value of 1.0. The meteorology people could supply accurate data for 3, but it seems that an accurate judgment for 2 would be as difficult to make as the rebuttal-factor judgment.

7 An Inductive Argument Typology

In the previous chapter I introduced the rebuttal-factor approach for evaluating the inferences of inductive arguments. Prior to that I discussed the warrant-backing method, which requires us to judge $p(C/P)$ after reviewing the warrant backing that is relevant to the inference. Neither of these approaches by itself provides specific strategies for inference evaluation, but of course, since we are dealing with arguments whose warrants are dependent on argument content itself, we cannot expect the procedures to be both specific and universal.

Specific advice for inference evaluation must be given in terms of particular inductive argument patterns, if it is to be useful. Perhaps recognition of this truth has been responsible for logicians' despair over inductive logic as a worthwhile academic research specialty. Perhaps it is thought that there are as many argument patterns as there are potential arguments, so that it is hopeless to try to provide criteria of inference validity. This way of thinking may have led some logicians to ignore inductive logic, but one has only to look at the work being done in fallacy theory to see how we can proceed. Fallacy theorists attempt to analyze the logical flaws in arguments of identifiably similar patterns. To do this, they first attempt to name and describe the fallacious pattern. And given the amount that has been written about such fallacies as *ad hominem*, *ad verecundiam*, and so on, it seems clear that that tradition proves the possibility of identifying recurring patterns of inference.

Now, as I have argued elsewhere (Grennan 1991), if patterns of intrinsically defective inductive arguments can be identified and classified, it would seem that the same can be done for arguments that have presumptive (prima facie) validity. And, indeed, while logicians have not attempted this, rhetoric scholars have done so with considerable success. Scholars with other backgrounds in argumentation studies are also disposed to confirm the feasibility of the project too: "All argumentation which appears in practice, may be seen as specific content for a certain argumentation scheme" (van Eemeren and Kruiger 1987, 71). They go on to discuss three types of schemes that I present in section 7.2.1.

7.1 ARGUMENT-PATTERN TYPOLOGIES

We might ask at this point, What practical purposes would be served by-developing an adequate argument-pattern typology? Why is a typology more desirable than a mere compendium of patterns? One reason that comes to mind is that an adequate typology might simplify the problem of utilizing inference-evaluation strategies. If we are acquainted with a collection of the most common patterns having presumptive validity and their associated inference-evaluation strategies, we can evaluate the inference of a particular argument we encounter like this: (a) identify the pattern embodied in the argument; (b) recall the associated inference evaluation principles; (c) apply them to the argument to arrive at a judgment of inference quality.

As those of us who try to teach "fallacy spotting" know only too well, human memory limitations inhibit the effectiveness of this procedure. The same limitations arise for presumptively valid inductive argument patterns also. The first challenge is access to the patterns stored in memory. The greater the number differentiated, the more difficult it is to recall the full set, and therefore the more difficult it will be to successfully complete step (a). If we are successful at step (a), we must still recall the evaluation principles associated with the pattern. An understanding of the pattern will help us recall these principles, but there is still the possibility of mixing up the patterns and evaluation principles.

Now if we can develop an adequate typology of patterns based on some combination of content and structure, we might find that there are only a few pattern types, with relatively general principles of evaluation. This would lower the demands on the memory and thereby promote more accurate inference evaluation.

7.1.1 *The Perelman and Olbrechts-Tyteca Typology*

Logicians have been developing argument-pattern typologies since the time of Aristotle.[1] In recent years perhaps the most famous typology was presented by Perelman and Olbrechts-Tyteca in *The New Rhetoric* (1969). They classify about 100 argument patterns. Their main distinction is between argumentation by "association" and by "dissociation." According to Kienpointner, this corresponds roughly to a distinction between justification and refutation (1987, 283). But it seems that the same patterns can occur as means of association and dissociation, so that the structure of their typology can be described by considering only the association category.

"Associative" patterns are of three kinds: (1) "quasilogical" patterns (for example, argument from definition, division of whole into parts), (2) patterns "based on the structure of reality" (for example, means-end arguments, arguments from authority), and (3) patterns that "establish the structure of reality" (for example, arguments from example to generalization).

I will not examine the Perelman classification[2] further, as I share the view of van Eemeren, Grootendorst, and Kruiger: "The defective demarcation of the various sorts of argumentational schema and the shortcomings in the typology's systematics together make it difficult to answer the question of whether this is to any degree a realistic survey of the argumentational schemata which are in practice influential in the acquisition of approval for theses" (1984, 256).

Given that I am engaged in a normative enterprise, that is, the formulation of the conditions of logical adequacy for particular argument patterns, the cataloguing and classifying of patterns found in *The New Rhetoric* can only be a starting point for my enterprise, since theirs is an essentially descriptive enterprise: "We seek, first of all, to characterize the different argumentative structures" (Perelman and Olbrechts-Tyteca 1969, 9). Elsewhere they declare that "our interests are ... those of logicians desirous of understanding the mechanism of thought" (6). Unfortunately, the work is not a very advanced starting point because the authors "don't describe the internal structure of their argumentative schemes, in spite of their explicit intention to do so" (Kienpointner 1987, 284; see Perelman and Olbrechts-Tyteca 1969, 187).

7.1.2 *Argument Fields*

Several other principles of classification can be found in the rhetoric literature. One principle is to classify by argument field, an approach used by Toulmin, who presented this criterion for field differentiation: "Two arguments will be said to belong to the same field when the data [grounds] and conclusions in each of the two arguments are, respectively, of the same logical type: they will be said to come from different fields when the backing or the conclusions in each of the two arguments are not of the same logical type" (Toulmin 1958, 14). In his textbook he identifies law, medicine, science, aesthetics, sports writing, and politics as fields (Toulmin, Reike, and Janik 1984, 271), apparently on the ground that "each of these enterprises has its own basic goals, and the procedures of argumentation developed to further those goals vary correspondingly from one enterprise to another" (1984, 271).

Now while we can perhaps distinguish fields by goals and procedures of argumentation, can we expect each field to have unique patterns of argument indigenous to it? Surely not: as Benoit and Lindsey put it, "we should not expect each field to have its own logical type (distinct argument form); rather, argument fields may posess a constellation of argumentative forms which are found individually in other fields, but not in that particular configuration" (1987, 216). They support this claim by providing an argument-pattern typology based on six kinds of warrants and examining the frequency of their occurrence in the fields of law (the courts), policy debate, and religion. No field was found to rely on a single pattern.

Another objection to classifying patterns by fields is raised by Zarefsky: "Most instances of argumentation do not occur within the confines of any academic discipline. They involve personal and public matters on which the arguers lack the specialized expertise associated with an academic discipline ... One could define public and personal arguments as fields in their own right, but doing so would confound our attempt to define fields by the subject-matter content of arguments" (1982, 196).

It appears, then, that fields cannot be individuated by identifying unique argument patterns associated with them, nor can every occurrence of a pattern be seen as occurring within some field, at least if we think of fields as professions or academic disciplines. Thus, it is more appropriate to classify argument patterns by some other organizing principle.

7.2 THE EHNINGER AND BROCKREIDE TYPOLOGY

In developing a typology of presumptively valid argument patterns here I shall rely on the work of Ehninger and Brockreide, presented in their *Decision by Debate* (1963). Their typology is comprehensive, if not exhaustive, and relies heavily on Toulmin's model. Specifically, they classify by warrant type, and within type by conclusion type.

7.2.1 *Warrant Classification*

Ehninger and Brockreide identify nine generic types of inductive arguments distinguished by the warrants relied on:

1 "Cause," in which validity depends on the truth of a causal generalization. Two different patterns are included here, reasoning from cause to effect, and from effect to cause.[3]

2 "Sign," in which validity depends on the premiss reporting a causally related symptom of the phenomenon reported in the conclusion (for example, clouds building is a sign of future rain), or in which the "sign" is a conventionally associated phenomenon (for example, the sound of a dinner bell enabling us to infer that dinner is about to be served).

3 "Generalization," in which the premiss reports that the members of a sample have some attribute and in the conclusion it is inferred that the population as a whole has that attribute. For example: "Most of the racing drivers here today are men, so most racing drivers are men." I shall label this category "sample-to-population," a more descriptive term.

4 "Parallel case," in which the premiss reports that an instance has an attribute and it is inferred that another instance of the same kind of thing has the same attribute.[4] For example: "Nova Scotia reduced its highway fatality rate by better enforcement of its seat belt law, so Ontario could reduce its fatality rate by doing the same."

5 "Analogy," in which the premiss reports a relationship between two items, the warrant states that an alleged relationship between a second pair of items is similar to that between the first pair, and it is concluded that the alleged relationship between the second pair does exist.

6 "Classification," in which the premiss is a generalization about the members of a class, the warrant states that what is true of the members is also true of a hitherto unexamined member, and it is concluded that the generalization applies to the unexamined one. I shall label this kind of warrant "population-to-sample."

7 "Statistics" denotes a category of patterns that rely on statistical warrants.[5] Ehninger and Brockreide identify warrants correlated with three statistical activities:

   (a) "Counting and measuring," in which the premiss reports raw data about the sample, the warrant is a formula for determining the value of some parameter of interest, and it is concluded that the sample has a particular value of that parameter of interest.

For example: "Students *A*, *B*, and *C* are male; students *D*, *E*, *F*, and *G* are female, so more than 50% of students in the sample are female." The warrant here is the formula for calculating the parameter "percentage female."

(b) "Comparisons," in which the premiss reports raw data about two comparable samples in terms of some parameter of interest, the warrant is a formula for determining the value of the parameter, and it is concluded that one of the two samples exceeds the other by some magnitude in terms of that parameter. For example: "The lowest three students scored 30 and the highest three scored 60, so the highest scored twice as high as the lowest." The warrant is the formula "high score/low score."

(c) "Central tendencies," in which the premiss reports the value of some chosen parameter for each member of the sample and the warrant is a formula or instruction for calculating an average, from which it is concluded that the average value for the sample is such-and-such. For example: the premiss includes the ages of the students in a class, and it is concluded that the median age is 19 years, 3 months. The warrant is the formula "The median age is that age at which half the students are younger and half are older."

8 Authority, in which the premiss is a report that a person (or organization, etc.) states a claim, the warrant states that that source is reliable, and it is concluded that the claim is true. For example: "The bookmakers say that the Oakland Athletics will win the 1990 World Series, so the Oakland Athletics will win the Series."

Ehninger and Brockreide also identify another type of pattern they call "motivational": "The warrant states a motive for accepting the claim" (1963, 163). Their first example uses the premiss "Continued testing of nuclear weapons is needed for u.s. military security"; the warrant is "The u.s. is motivated by a desire to maintain … military security"; and it is concluded that "continued testing of nuclear weapons is probably desirable for the u.s."

The authors regard examples like this as cases of the emotional mode of proof, a category of proof distinct from the logical mode. Apparently, such examples are supposed to rely on motives rather than reasons in authorizing the inference from premiss to conclusion. The argument pattern might be formulated like this: (*P*) Doing *A* brings about/maintains *G*, so (*C*) doing *A* is desirable for person (group) *S*, since (*W*) *S* wants to bring about/maintain *G*. With the argument written this way, we can think of *P* and *W* jointly proving *C*, but there is an anomaly in the structure: *W* contains a reference to *S*, but the premiss is cast as a generalization. Thus, the pattern does not conform to Toulmin's model. Yet our authors think it does.

The second example involves the same anomaly. Its conclusion is a prescriptive claim rather than an evaluative one, but the same anomaly occurs in its pattern: (P) Doing A brings about/maintains G, so (C) S should do A, since (W) S wants to bring about/maintain G.

Conformity with the Toulmin model can be secured in both cases by switching premiss and warrant, so that we have (1) (P) S wants to bring about/maintain G, so (C) doing A is desirable for S, since (W) doing A brings about or maintains G; and (2) (P) S wants to bring about/maintain G, so (C) S should do A, since (W) doing A brings about/maintains G. Here the warrants are a generalization about means and ends that support the inference claim of the arguments by linking A and G in the proper way.

It should be clear that each of these two patterns is exemplified in everyday argumentation and that each has the presumptive validity feature of the Toulmin model. Furthermore, although there is reference to possible motives in the warrants, the warrants themselves provide reasons for inferring conclusions from premisses. Thus, they can be regarded as patterns in the "logical mode" rather than the "emotional mode." Accordingly, I shall include them in my enumeration of inductive patterns as "motivational" patterns in place of the two patterns given by Ehninger and Brockreide, but they will be called "ends-means" patterns.

To summarize, I have identified the following kinds of argument patterns, based on the analysis provided by Ehninger and Brockreide:

1 Cause to effect: The phenomenon mentioned in P produces the one in C.

2 Effect to cause: The phenomenon mentioned in P is best explained by C.

3 Sign: The phenomenon mentioned in P is symptomatic (naturally or conventionally) of one reported in C.

4 Sample to population: What is true of a sample of X is also true of other X's.

5 Parallel case: What is true of the referent of P is also true of the referent of C by virtue of their similarity.

6 Analogy: B_1 is to B_2 in C as A_1 is to A_2 in P.

7 Population to sample: What is true of known X's is also true of this X.

8 Authority: S (the assertor of C) is a reliable source.

9 Ends-means: The action mentioned in C generally achieves the end mentioned in P.

I will not discuss the statistics category, as it appears to be a class of reasoning patterns, rather than a single pattern, and in any case it is essentially mathematical.

7.2.2 *The Ehninger and Brockriede Claim Classification*

The Ehninger and Brockreide typology individuates generic argument patterns by warrant type, and within each type by the kind of conclusion to be proved. Their view is that there are four main kinds of assertion or claim: "designative," "definitive," "evaluative," and "actuative." In what follows I shall examine their accounts of these kinds and revise and extend them where it is deemed necessary.

7.2.2.1 *Actuative Claims.* As the name implies, these are claims advocating action, either the adoption of a policy for action of a certain kind in a recurring situation or the adoption of a specific course of action in a situation in which it appears appropriate to make some response. A more important distinction drawn among these claims is whether or not the action is being advocated as a matter of conformity to a rule. In such cases the claim is most appropriately phrased in the form "S must A," where "S" stands for a person, a group, or organization, and "A" stands for the action or refraining from action that is advocated. Here are some examples: "Sam must apologize"; "Sam must not insult his neighbors"; "Fathers must act as good role models for their sons"; "Canada must compensate Japanese-Canadians for their incarceration during World War Two"; "Players must leave the playing field after being called out"; "People who cannot keep an appointment must inform the other parties as soon as they know they are unable to meet."

As the examples show, the behaviour may be advocated on the basis of rules of law, games, morality, or etiquette. Whatever the case, the claim implies that there is no choice for those who are properly subject to the rules. I shall refer to actuative claims like this as "obligation claims."

The other class of actuative claims consists of two distinct kinds. Both can be expressed as "S ought to A." One kind is used when A is a supererogatory act, an act of good samaritanism. In such cases the claim is made when it is in the interest of another that X should do (or refrain from doing) A, yet X has no rule-created obligation to do A. I will call actuative claims of this kind "supererogatory actuative claims," or simply supererogatory claims.

The other kind is the prudential recommendation "X ought to do A because A is seen as being in the interest of X." (This does not exclude the possibility that others may benefit from X's doing A, however.

When the physician tells Sam that he ought to walk for a half hour each day, Sam's acting on the recommendation may make him feel better, and those who have contact with him will enjoy his extra congeniality.) I will call these claims "prudential actuative claims," or prudential claims, for short.

These two subclasses of actuative claims contrast with the rule-conforming ones in that they advocate acts that are optional. We ought to give money to certain charities, but no rules compel it. We ought to see Australia, but we can go elsewhere if we choose.

7.2.2.2 *Evaluative Claims.* Evaluative claims express our judgments about the goodness of things as things of a particular kind. They are of three distinct forms: grading claims, ranking claims, and comparison claims.

1 Grading claims: "This is a good cantaloupe," and the label "Grade A" found on turkeys in the supermarket are grading judgments arrived at by comparing the item to relevant standards of goodness.
2 Ranking claims: "Steffi Graf is the best female tennis player at this time" is an example. When we rank something we compare it with all other things of the same kind, given a set of standards. By contrast, in grading we ignore other things of the same kind, for example, when we say, "Graf is a great tennis player."
3 Comparison claims: An example is "Gretzky is a better hockey player than Howe was." Whereas in ranking we locate a thing on a spectrum of goodness with all the other things of the same kind, in making comparisons we simply compare things within a class, in terms of a set of standards.

7.2.2.3 *Designative Claims.* Ehninger and Brockreide say that designative claims have to do with "whether something is" (1963, 102). Philosophers have labelled these claims "factual," although this label is not meant in the sense of "truthful"; rather, it means something like "empirical." It will be helpful to classify further in view of the logically different kinds of support that different claims of this broad type have.

The most basic distinction to be made is between "brute facts" and "institutional facts." This distinction was advertised and relied on by Searle in *Speech Acts* (1969). The paradigms of brute facts, he says,

vary enormously – they range from "This stone is next to that stone" to "Bodies attract with a force inversely proportional to the square of the distance between and directly proportional to the product of their mass" to "I have a pain," but they share the feature that the concepts which make up the knowledge are essentially physical, or, in its dualistic version, either physical or mental ... the basis for all knowledge of this kind is generally supposed to be simple empirical observations recording sense experiences. (50)

As Searle notes, claims in the brute fact category are verified by observation. They can, however, be divided into claims about physical and about mental phenomena. The most basic claims about physical phenomena are observations of perceivables, such as "The sun is setting," "That's a police car," "That man has purple hair."

The most basic claims about mental phenomena are reports of mental states based on observation of behaviour: "He's upset"; "She believes he's faithful"; "I have a headache." The best evidence for such claims about others is confirmation by the individual referred to. Provided that we regard the person as trustworthy, there will normally be no evidence of other kinds that can change our judgment when it is based on such confirmation. When such claims are in the first person to begin with, they will be subject to doubt by H only to the extent that H doubts S's sincerity. Since the evidence relations for claims ascribing mental predicates are different from claims about observable phenomena, I shall call the former "mental-world claims" and the latter "physical-world claims."[6]

After describing and identifying brute fact claims Searle goes on to note that

large tracts of apparently fact-stating language do not consist of concepts which are part of this picture ... there are many kinds of facts, and facts which obviously are objective facts ... which are hard, if not impossible, to assimilate to this picture. Any newspaper records facts of the following sorts: Mr. Smith married Miss Jones; the Dodgers beat the Giants three to two in eleven innings; Green was convicted of larceny; and Congress passed the Appropriations Bill ... Such facts as are recorded in my above group of statements I propose to call institutional facts. (1969, 50–1)

I shall follow Searle in calling these claims "institutional" claims. Their existence is made possible by the existence of human activities that arise from constitutive rules. For example, "The Dodgers beat the Giants three to two in eleven innings" is a meaningful claim because of constitutive rules that make it possible for baseball teams to exist and score runs.

We can think of the rules making it possible for someone to make performative utterances such as "I now pronounce you husband and wife" and thereby cause a couple to be married, as power-conveying constitutive rules. The performative utterance itself does not constitute an assertion, since it lacks truth value, but reports based on it such as "Mr. Smith married Miss Jones" are assertions, ones that are verified by establishing that the person who made the performative utterance had the appropriate powers.

Now even though institutional claims presuppose the existence of explicit or implicit constitutive and regulative rules, they are verified by observation, by anyone familiar with the rules. In this sense they are like physical claims, which are verified by observation by anyone familiar with the semantic rules applicable to the sentence. For this reason, I will treat institutional claims as physical-world claims.

7.2.2.4 *Definitive Claims.* Ehninger and Brockreide associate definitive claims with the question of what a thing is. "For example ... whether a certain extent of genetic and somatic radiation damage can be defined as extensive radiation harm, or whether Jones' action constitutes burglary are ... questions of definition to be established in proofs as definitive claims" (1963, 52). Elsewhere they cite a further example: "In this election, majority should be defined as a majority of members present and voting" (1963, 141). The examples have something in common. All can be cast in the form "X counts as/constitutes Y":

1 R roentgens counts as extensive radiation harm.
2 A majority of members present and voting counts as a majority in this election.
3 Jones' action counts as burglary.

It may be this common feature that led Ehninger and Brockreide to regard 3 as a definition, but it obviously is not. As a conclusion in an argument it would rely on a definition for a warrant, but it is not one itself: "Jones broke into the house and removed the VCR without the owner's consent, so Jones' action counts as burglary, since (W) 'burglary' is defined as 'theft from a building after trespass.'" Example 3 is best regarded as a physical-world claim and better phrased simply as "Jones committed burglary" if it is being based on his behaviour. If based on knowledge that Jones had been found guilty of burglary, it would be an institutional claim by virtue of being a legal fact.

Definitive claims can often be cast in the form "(definition) constitutes/counts as (term defined)," but this criterion would make the category narrower than it should be. For instance, it would exclude "Bachelors are men." But this claim is true by virtue of a constitutive rule that defines the word "bachelor." It is, then, a conceptual truth even though it is not a definition.

There are other conceptual claims that are best included in this category: formal tautologies such as "If either A or B, and not-A, then B," and physical tautologies such as "Solid iron does not float in water." All of these have the feature of being necessarily true, if true, by virtue of the concepts used in stating them. For example, anything that floated could not (logically) count as iron. For this reason I shall change the name of claims in this category from "definitive" claims to "constitutive rule" claims.

Thus far, by relying on the Ehninger and Brockreide typology, I have identified the following kinds of claims:

1 Obligation claims: X must do A;
2 Supererogatory actuative claims: X ought to do A;
3 Prudential actuative claims: X ought to do A;
4 Evaluative claims, of which there are three kinds: grading, rating, and comparison;
5 Physical-world claims, which include both physical brute facts and institutional facts;
6 Mental-world claims, which ascribe mental phenomena;
7 Constitutive-rule claims, which are based on definitions and other necessary truths and falsehoods; and
8 Regulative-rule claims, which express obligations and prohibitions.

The eighth category was not found as part of the Ehninger and Brockreide typology. Whereas claims expressing constitutive rules are conceptual claims, under the above classification claims expressing regulative rules do not seem to be easy to classify. Accordingly, I have made a special category for them. Regulative-rule claims are expressible in the form "X is obligatory" or "X is prohibited": "Driving on the right is obligatory"; "Possession of any automatic-firing weapon is prohibited"; "Insulting people is prohibited"; "Saving someone's life when there is no risk to your own is obligatory"; "Entry to the restaurant while wearing golf shoes is prohibited." As these examples indicate, the utterances that express regulative rules have truth value. For example, we can meaningfully ask "Is it true that driving on the right is obligatory?" Thus, they must be counted as assertions.

Regulative rules can be of various kinds, as determined by the logical grounds for asserting them. The first two rules given above are legal, the third and fourth are moral, and the last is a rule of an organization. A broader classification that will be useful distinguishes between enacted and unenacted regulative rules. Unenacted rules reflect the existence of commands emanating from a group and addressed to each individual in the group. But the behaviour has not been declared as required or prohibited by an agent acting on authority based on formal rules. Such rules can commonly be said to be customary. Enacted rules owe their origin to the existence of institutions that endow an agent with the power to enact rules. Legal rules thus emanate from a legislative body, and club rules about the wearing of golf shoes emanate from the golf club.

7.3 A REVISED TYPOLOGY

Ehninger and Brockreide identify argument patterns by identifying the types of warrants and the types of claims that could serve as conclusions and then deciding which types of claims could be inferred using the various kinds of warrants. Of 30 combinations of conclusions and warrants, they settle on 20 acceptable patterns.

Here I wish to follow a somewhat different procedure, one that might be more comprehensive. Since I have distinguished 8 claim-types, there are 64 combinations of claim-pairs that might represent presumptively valid inference patterns. Whether or not a particular claim-pair does represent a valid pattern is determined by whether or not the warrant derivable from the pair corresponds to one of the eight legitimate warrant types. It appears that Ehninger and Brockreide relied on their logical intuitions to discriminate between acceptable and unacceptable patterns. I agree that this must be the basis for adequacy. It is difficult to see what could replace this criterion. Certainly not the logical calculi, since *ex hypothesi*, we are dealing with deductively invalid arguments.

The ideal for any typology is to include all and only those items that count as genuine cases. In justifying a claim that a typology is exhaustive, one must maintain that one has an exhaustive classification of both warrants and claims. I do not wish to claim that in what follows I identify all the logically legitimate inductive inference patterns. For one thing, I am concerned only with patterns that can be conceived as having one premiss (ground), and we often provide two or more premisses in support of our conclusions.[7] Of course, some logicians regard most of the patterns I discuss as two-premiss arguments, because they consider warrants to be premisses. However, in chapter 9 I argue that we need not count warrants as premisses for conclusions (they are, rather, premisses for inference claims), so I regard the patterns presented here as structurally complete.

The task of scrutinizing 64×8 (512) possibilities in search of presumptively valid patterns is not as formidable as it might seem, for several reasons. There are general restrictions that reduce the number of useful patterns, patterns that can be used in persuading H to accept a particular claim. First, of course, there is the logical requirement that P must be relevant to C. Some patterns can be rejected on this basis.

Second, a useful pattern is one that, in its normal employment, has a premiss that is more acceptable to H than the conclusion, prior to the utterance of the argument. To put it another way, P is regarded a priori as more probable than C. This condition is implied by the concept of an argument as a linguistic device intended by S to persuade H that C. Such persuasion occurs only when H regards P as more confirmed than C.

An example of an argument that is unacceptable on this basis is this one relying on a parallel-case warrant to prove an obligation claim: "Your neighbour, who also served in Viet Nam, must turn in his old service rifle, so you must turn yours in." If we are trying to persuade a person to turn in his weapon, we are not likely to do so using this argument. He will regard the premiss as being as doubtful as the conclusion, for the same reasons. This is not to say that no parallel-case argument is useful. It just happens that ones involving obligation claims are normally not useful.

Furthermore, a judicious sorting of the warrant types can save effort. It will be recalled that some of the warrants had a special feature: the property predicated of the premiss referent was also predicated of the conclusion referent. The patterns (discussed in sec. 7.2.1) are, we recall, sample to population, in which what is true of a sample of X is also true of other X's; parallel case, in which what is true of the referent of P is also true of the referent of C by virtue of their similarity; and population to sample, in which what is true of known X's is also true of this X. Now the only claim-pairs that might rely on these warrants are ones in which each claim is of the same type. When the pairs are mixed, we need not check for presumptively valid patterns that rely on these three warrants. Thus, there are only 8×3 (24) possibilities that have to be checked for these warrants.

To further simplify, the authority pattern (in which the warrant is "S [the assertor of C] is a reliable source") can be dealt with separately because its premiss is always a physical-world claim, that is, a claim that someone has asserted something. It is discussed in section 7.4. Furthermore, the ends-means pattern (in which the warrant is "The action mentioned in C generally achieves the end mentioned in P") uses only a mental-world claim as premiss ("P wants W") and either a prudential-actuative claim as conclusion ("P ought to do A"), or an evaluative claim ("A is desirable for P"). Thus, there are really only two claim-pairs that can rely on the means-end warrant to produce presumptively valid arguments. These will be discussed in section 7.3.3.2. And finally, the analogical pattern (in which the warrant is "B_1 is to B_2 in C as A_1 is to A_2 in P") merits separate discussion because it is logically unique. It is discussed in section 7.5.

We are left, then, with three patterns: effect to cause, cause to effect, and sign. In theory, each claim-pair might rely on one of these warrants, so there are 64 × 3 (192) possibilities that need to be checked. In what follows I will present only sketches of the argument patterns that seem to be presumptively valid and useful for proving their conclusions, based on the above considerations. I regard these as sketches because each deserves a fuller analysis than there is space for here. Their appearance here is intended to represent an invitation to other logicians to study the patterns to the extent that they deserve. They may deserve considerable study if the effort put into the study of the classical fallacies is any indication. I cannot refrain from noting here, though, that from the perspective of this book, the massive effort devoted to the study of *invalid* argument patterns, at the expense of the more useful patterns to be presented here, strikes me as extraordinarily perverse.

The format I have chosen includes propositional forms for premisses and conclusions, the forms that warrant backing would have, and the most important rebuttal factors that have to be accounted for in evaluating inferences in arguments instantiating the pattern. Obviously, the pattern description and evaluation information can be presented in various ways. In the literature, the format most similar to mine is that of Schellens (1987, 36). He presents the evaluative criteria in question form but does not distinguish the criteria relevant to inferences from those relevant to premisses. I regard this as an important, but correctible, deficiency.

7.3.1 *Arguments for Obligation Claims*

Arguments for obligation claims are expressible in the form "*S* must (must not) do *A*," although in writings on ethical theory the word "ought" is commonly used instead of "must." I do not find "ought" to be as felicitous in this context, since it seems (to me at least) that "*S* ought to do *A*" implies that doing *A* is optional for *S*, rather than compulsory. Alan White shares this view:

philosophers, and particularly moral philosophers, have assimilated "must" and "ought" ... The notion expressed by "must" is, however, quite different from that expressed by "ought" ... What ought to be is in the situation the appropriate, perhaps because the right or the best, thing; what must be is the only thing ... "must" indicates ... that because of a particular requirement, whether legal, economic, prudential, or moral, the features of the situation are such that the agent has only one course open to him ... "Ought," by contrast, indicates that in the situation one of several courses open is the right or the best course. (1975, 158–9)

Besides this conceptual support for preferring "must," there is also clear etymological support: "'Deontological' comes from the Greek for what one must do" (Williams 1985, 16).

7.3.1.1 *Arguments with Obligation Premisses.* The patterns for arguments with obligation premisses are the following.

Sample-to-Population Version

Premiss Form: $N\%$ of x's must do A.

Conclusion Form: $N\%$ of X's must do A.

Example: "Seventy percent of the 100 15-year-olds polled in Halifax must be home by 10:00 P.M. on weekday nights. Therefore, 70% of Canadian 15-year-olds must be home by 10:00 P.M. on weekday nights."

Warrant Backing: x is representative of X's.

Rebuttal Factors: (1) The sample is too small; (2) there is systematic bias in the sample selection. In the example it is plausible to think that a systematic bias results from conducting the poll in a small geographic area.

Population-to-Group/Individual Version

Premiss Form: $N\%$ of X's observed must do (refrain from doing) A.

Conclusion Form: $N\%$ of group x (things of kind X) must do (refrain from doing) A.

Comment: This pattern is not the best way to prove such claims. The best way is to cite an appropriate regulative rule. But in the absence of the oportunity to do so, this pattern can provide grounds for the claim.

Example: "Most professors in Canada must teach three courses each term. Therefore, professors at Saint Mary's University must (that is, are obligated to) teach three courses each term."

Warrant Backing: The members of group X are typical of X's generally.

Rebuttal Factor: The group X is untypical in some relevant respect. In the example, the inference would be undermined by facts such as that the Saint Mary's faculty have a strong union that has negotiated a lesser teaching load.

Parallel-Case Version

Premiss Form: Person x_1 must do (refrain from doing) A.

Conclusion Form: This other person (x_2) must do (refrain from doing) A.

Comment: This is not a useful pattern, since P will not normally be better known to H than C is. Both claims normally rest on the same regulative rule, which is that *A* is prohibited or required of people in a particular category.

Obligation-Premiss Version

Premiss Form: *S* must (must not) do *A*.

Conclusion Form: *S* must (must not) do *B*.

Example: "Sam must allow the security guard to inspect his luggage, so he must unlock his suitcase."

Comment: This pattern can be conceived as an effect-to-cause pattern, since doing (refraining from doing) *B* can be seen as bringing about *A*.

Warrant Backing: *B* is the only means of fulfilling the obligation to do (refrain from doing) *A*.

Rebuttal Factors: There are other ways of fulfilling the duty to do (refrain from doing) *A*.

7.3.1.2 *Obligation Claims With Other Kinds of Premisses.* The patterns for obligation claims with other kinds of premisses are the following.

Supererogatory-Premiss Version

Premiss Form: *S* ought to do *A*.

Conclusion Form: *S* must do *A*.

Comment: This is not a valid pattern. Obligatory acts cannot be inferred from ones that are desirable only in the interests of others.

Prudential-Premiss Version

Premiss Form: *S* ought to do (refrain from doing) *A*.

Conclusion Form: *S* must do (refrain from doing) *A*.

Comment: This is not a valid pattern. Obligatory acts cannot be inferred from optional ones that are in one's own interest.

Evaluative-Premiss Version

Premiss Form: *x* is a *G(A)*. (*G* is an evaluative term such as "good").

Conclusion Form: *S* must (must not) do *A*.

Warrant Backing: *S* must do whatever is *G(A)*. This is a cause-to-effect pattern, in the sense that the obligation to do *A* is "created" by *P*, when accepted.

Rebuttal factor: There is a consideration that overrides doing *A*, such as "*A* is immoral," or "*A* is not in *S*'s long-term interest."

Example 1: "In this chess situation, Q-KB7 is the best move, so you must make this move." Here the warrant backing is "One must try to win." Trying to win requires making the best (in the long term) moves one can.

Example 2: Teacher to pupil: "The word 'ain't' is a vulgar synonym for 'isn't,' so you must not use it in place of 'isn't.'" Warrant backing: One must speak proper English.

Physical-World Premiss Version

These assertions are about either institutional or purely physical activities or states. In both cases, observation can be used to verify or falsify them.

Premiss Form: *P* (any claim about brute facts or any institutional claim).

Conclusion: *S* must (must not) *A*.

Warrant Backing: The warrant backing is a function of the content of *P.*

Rebuttal Factor: There is an excuse that relieves *S* of the obligation, or there is a justification in the form of a morally more important duty.[8]

Example 1: "Sam promised his wife that he would baby-sit the children tonight, so he must try to be home from work before she has to go out." Here the warrant backing is "We must do whatever is within our power to fulfill our promises." The premiss is an institutional claim, since promising is a contract-making action.

Example 2: "The streets are very icy, so Sam must not take his daughter to the movies." Here the warrant backing is "Drivers must not endanger the life and health of their passengers unnecessarily." The premiss is a brute-fact claim.

Example 3: This is the ancient moral dilemma example, updated. Sam is given a pistol by Irwin for safe-keeping, promising to return it when Irwin wanted it. Irwin appears one evening, very angry, asking for his pistol. He says his wife is having an affair. Sam is afraid he might harm her, so he is reluctant to give it back, but Irwin argues, "You promised to give it back to me when I wanted it, so you must give it back." A rebuttal factor is operative here: Sam is justified in refusing to return the pistol, because he has a duty to prevent loss of life, a duty that ranks higher than the duty to keep this particular promise. The inference is invalid.

Mental-World Premiss Version

These premisses involve the ascription of mental attributes to individual persons or groups of persons, and in some cases to "lower animals."

VERSION ONE

Here the person with the obligation is the person who has the mental state.

Premiss Form: *S* is *M*.

Conclusion Form: *S* must (must not) do *A*.

Warrant Backing: Mental attributes can create duties. Here there is a cause-to-effect pattern; the truth of the premiss gives rise to the obligation.

Rebuttal Factor: There is an excusing condition, or a justification, for not fulfilling the duty.

Example: "Sam is already convinced that Jones is guilty, so he must not accept a place on the jury."

VERSION TWO

Here the person who is supposed to have the obligation is different from the person with the mental attribute.

Premiss Form: *S* is *M*.

Conclusion Form: *P* must (must not) do *A*.

Warrant Backing: One person's mental attribute can create a duty for another to act in a way appropriate to the presence of the attribute.

Rebuttal Factor: *P* is unaware, through no fault of *P*, that *S* is *M*.

Example: "Sam is already convinced that Jones is guilty, so the defence attorney must not recommend him for his client's jury."

Constitutive-Rule Premiss Version

Premiss Form: *D*'s count as *W*'s.

Conclusion: *S* must do (refrain from doing) *A*.

Comment: This is not a valid pattern; the premiss is irrelevant to conclusion.

Regulative-Rule Premiss Version

These premisses can be expressed as prohibitions or obligatory acts reflecting the existence of rules. This is the most effective pattern for proving the existence of obligations that are not self-incurred by contract making.

Premiss Form: *A* is prohibited (obligatory).

Conclusion Form: *S* must not (must) do *A*.

Warrant Backing: One must not (must) do what is prohibited (obligatory).

Rebuttal Factor: *S* has an adequate excuse, or an overriding duty.

Example 1: In the firearm example, Irwin might have said, "Breaking a promise is prohibited, so you must not break your promise." Here Sam could claim an overriding duty to prevent Irwin's wife from being put at risk.

Example 2: John is taking his wife to the hospital to give birth, perhaps within the hour. Her mother is accompanying them for "moral support." He is driving rather fast so the mother-in-law says, "Exceeding the speed limit is legally prohibited, so you must slow down." Here John could offer an adequate excuse: "Except when there is a medical emergency."

7.3.1.3 *Summary: Proving Obligation Claims.* Claims that can be written in the form "$N\%$ of all X's must (must not) do A" can be proved (in the sense of being made epistemically acceptable to rational persons) by claims of the form "$N\%$ of X's in this sample of X's must (must not) do A." These arguments commonly involve verbal qualifiers such as "all," "most," and so on. Claims of the form "$N\%$ of the X's in this group must (must not) do A" can be proved by ones of the form "$N\%$ of heretofore-observed X's must (must not) do A." Claims of the form "S must (must not) do a" ("a" stands for an act of kind A) can be proved by premises of these forms:

Obligation: S must (must not) do b (b brings about a).
Evaluative: a is a $G(A)$ ("G" is an evaluative expression).
Physical-World: x is F (F is a physical-world property).
Mental-World (1): S is M (M is a mental-world property).
Mental-World (2): S_2 is M (S_2 is a person other than S).
Regulative-Rule: A is obligatory (prohibited).

7.3.2 *Arguments for Supererogatory Claims*

Supererogatory claims can always be phrased in the form "S ought to do A." They express the judgment that it is in the interest of someone other than S for S to do A. Normally such acts involve a degree of sacrifice for S, and this is why people are praised for performing such "good Samaritan" acts.[9]

7.3.2.1 *Arguments with Supererogatory Premisses.* The patterns for arguments with supererogatory premisses are the following.

Sample-to-Population Version
Premiss Form: $N\%$ of X's ought to do (refrain from doing) A.
Conclusion Form: $N\%$ of X's ought to do (refrain from doing) A.
Example: "Ninety percent of the households in Bedford ought to contribute to the United Way charity. Therefore, 90% of Canadians ought to contribute."
Comment: This is not a useful pattern. Anyone doubting C is just as likely to doubt P. As discussed later, superogatory claims are best proved by claims describing the needs of those who would benefit from the act.

Population-to-Group/Individual Version
Premiss Form: $N\%$ of X's ought to do (refrain from doing) A.
Conclusion Form: $N\%$ of x's ought to do A.
Comment: This is not a useful pattern. Anyone who doubts C is also
   likely to doubt P. This is because of the universal nature of supererogatory claims. Any two individuals who are typical of a class will
   be equally expected to do a good deed. Thus, even if x's are typical
   of X's, we cannot expect P to prove C.

Parallel-Case Version
Premiss Form: x_1 ought to do A.
Conclusion Form: x_2 ought to do A.
Comment: This is not a useful pattern, since normally the reason for
   any two people or groups to act as good Samaritans in the same con-
   text will be the same. P is not better known than C.

Supererogatory-Premiss Version
Premiss Form: S ought to do A.
Conclusion: S ought to do B.
Warrant Backing: Doing B is, for most people, an effective means of
   doing A.
Rebuttal Factor: Doing B is not a means of bringing about A that S can
   employ.
Example 1: "I ought to help the needy in this area, so I ought to make
   a generous contribution to the United Way campaign."
Example 2: Geraldine has defective kidneys requiring more and more
   hours of kidney dialysis. Someone says to her twin brother Gerald,
   "You ought to do whatever you can to help your sister live, so you
   ought to give her one of your kidneys." If Gerald's kidneys are beginning to malfunction, he could insist that this is an inappropriate way
   for him to help his sister.

7.3.2.2 *Supererogatory Claims with Other Kinds of Premisses.* The patterns
for arguments making supererogatory claims with other kinds of premisses are the following.

Obligation Premisses
Premiss Form: S must (must not) do A.
Conclusion Form: S ought (ought not) to do A.
Comment: This is not a valid pattern. Obligation assertions and
   supererogatory claims are essentially incompatible, since in
   the latter, acting (refraining) is optional, but in the former it
   is not.

Prudential Premisses

Premiss Form: S ought to do (refrain from doing) A.

Conclusion Form: S ought to do (refrain from doing) B.

Comment: This is not a valid pattern. A recommendation to act in one's own interest is not relevant to whether one acts in the interests of another. These are competing reasons.

Evaluative Premisses

Premiss Form: x is a $G(X)$.

Conclusion Form: S ought to do A.

Warrant Backing: Doing A is in the interests of X's that are G.

Rebuttal Factor: S is not in a position to do A.

Example 1: "The eagle is a majestic bird, so we ought to ensure that it is protected from hunters."

Example 2: Mary's high school science teacher believes that she has exceptional talent in physics. She tells the parents, "Mary is an excellent physics Ph D prospect, so you ought to enroll her at MIT when she graduates." The parents might respond that they cannot afford to send Mary there.

Physical-World Premisses

Premiss Form: S is F.

Conclusion Form: S ought to do A.

Warrant Backing: A person with S's characteristic F ought to do A.

Rebuttal Factor: Doing A will/might require too great a sacrifice by S.

Example: A group on a hiking trip have been caught in a sudden storm that has washed out the bridge they need to use to get back to camp. However, there is an old pedestrian suspension bridge that the other bridge replaced. No one has used it for years, though. One of the group says, "Sam is the lightest one here, so he ought to try to cross the old bridge to get help." On examining the old bridge, Sam might respond by saying "There's a better than 50-50 chance that it will break, and I would drown."

Mental-World Premisses

Premiss Form: S is M.

Conclusion Form: P ought to do A.

Warrant Backing: P's doing A is in S's interest.

Rebuttal Factor: Doing A is not appropriate for P.

Example: Robin is in love with his female colleague Marian, and she is aware of this. A female friend of hers knows they are going to the same conference and says to Marian, "Robin is in love with you, so you ought to share a room with him at the conference." If she is married she could respond that loyalty to her husband makes this inappropriate.

Constitutive-Rule Premisses
Premiss Form: *D* counts as *W.*
Conclusion Form: *S* ought to do (refrain from doing) *A.*
Comment: This is not a valid pattern. Conceptual claims have no relevance to possible action.

Regulative-Rule Premisses
Premiss Form: *A* is obligatory (prohibited).
Conclusion Form: *S* ought to do (refrain from doing) *A.*
Comment: This is not a valid pattern, unless "ought to" is given the sense of "must." But then we no longer have a supererogatory conclusion.

7.3.2.3 *Summary: Proving Supererogatory Claims.* Claims that can be written in the form "*S* ought (ought not) to do *a*" (where *a* is an act of kind *A*) can be proved by claims of the following forms.

Supererogatory: *S* ought (ought not) to do *b* (*b* brings about *a*).
Evaluative: *a* is a *G(A)* ("*G*" is an evaluative expression).
Physical-World: *S* is *F* (*F* is a physical property of *S*).
Mental-World: S_2 is *M* (*M* is a mental state of another).

7.3.3 *Arguments for Prudential Claims*

Arguments for prudential claims can be expressed in the form "*S* ought (ought not) to do *A*."[10] They can have the negative form, because sometimes it is appropriate to recommend that not doing something is in a person's interests.

7.3.3.1 *Arguments with Prudential Premisses.* The patterns for arguments with prudential premisses are the following.

Prudential Premisses
Premiss Form: *S* ought (ought not) to do *A.*
Conclusion Form: *S* ought (ought not) to do *B.*
Warrant Backing: *B* is an effective way of bringing about *A.*
Rebuttal Factor: Because of some characteristic of *S* or some aspect of *S*'s circumstances, *B* is not an appropriate way for *S* to bring about *A.*
Example 1: "Canadians ought to avoid heart disease, so they ought to eat less animal fat."
Example 2: Sam says to his overweight grandfather, "You ought to lose weight, so you ought to take up jogging." The grandfather might want to respond that that would not be an effective way for him to lose weight, since he has a heart condition.

Sample-to-Population Version
Premiss Form: *N*% of *x*'s ought (ought not) to do *A*.
Conclusion Form: *N*% of *X*'s ought (ought not) to do *A*.
Example: "Thirty percent of the students at this college ought to cut back on the hours they work at part-time jobs. Therefore, 30% of Canadian college students ought to cut back."
Comment: This is not a useful pattern. Someone doubting *C* would not be persuaded by being given *P*. S/he would want to hear how some goal of the students is being undermined by part-time work. As discussed later, the best evidence for prudential claims is a true claim about a goal that someone has, one that will be served by the recommended behaviour.

Population-to-Group/Individual Version
Premiss Form: *N*% of *X*'s ought (ought not) to do *A*.
Conclusion Form: *N*% of *x*'s ought (ought not) to do *A*.
Example: "Almost all students in Canada ought to complete high school. Therefore, almost all students in my town ought to complete high school."
Comment: This is not a useful pattern, since anyone who doubted *C* would doubt *P*. Indeed, since *P* is about a larger group than *C*, it may be more difficult to prove than *C*.

Parallel-Case Version
Premiss Form: S_1 ought (ought not) to do *A*.
Conclusion Form: S_2 ought (ought not) to do *A*.
Comment: this is not a useful pattern, since normally the support for the premiss also would be the best support for the conclusion. The support in each case would take the form: "*x* wants to satisfy *W*."

7.3.3.2 *Prudential Claims with Other Kinds of Premisses.* The patterns for prudential claims with other kinds of premisses are the following.

Obligation Premisses
Premiss Form: *S* must (must not) do *A*.
Conclusion Form: *S* ought (ought not) to do *B*.
Warrant Backing: Doing (not doing) *B* will help make it possible for *S* to meet the obligation to do (not to do) *A*.
Rebuttal Factor: Circumstances or something true of *S* means that doing (not doing) *B* is not an appropriate course of action in meeting the obligation.
Example 1: "Sam must allow the airport security people to search his luggage, so he ought to allow extra time for boarding his flight."

Example 2: "Sam must ensure that his elderly mother is cared for, so he ought to move her in with him." The conclusion would not follow if Sam had no room for her.

Supererogatory Premisses
Premiss Form: *S* ought to do *A*.
Conclusion Form: *S* ought (ought not) to do *B*.
Warrant Backing: Doing *B* is a way of bringing about *A*.
Rebuttal Factor: *B* is not appropriate for *S* because of some characteristic of *S* or some circumstance.
Example: "Physicians ought to treat injured people at the scene of a traffic accident, so they ought to carry their medical bag in their car."

Evaluative Premisses
Premiss Form: *x* is a $G(X)$.
Conclusion Form: *S* ought (ought not) to do *A*.
Warrant Backing: It is in a person's interest to choose things that are rated "G."
Rebuttal Factors: (1) There is a better *X* to be had under the same conditions; (2) *x* is an inappropriate choice for *S*.
Example 1: "Honda Accords are excellent medium-priced sedans, so you ought to buy one of those."
Example 2: "The Lexus is considered the best sedan on the road right now, so you ought to buy one of those." You might want to say that it doesn't follow in your case, as you cannot afford a Lexus.

Physical-World Premisses
Premiss Form: *X* is *F*.
Conclusion Form: *S* ought (ought not) to do *A*.
Warrant Backing: It depends on the content.
Rebuttal Factor: It depends on the content.
Example: "Zsa Zsa Gabor was convicted of assaulting a policeman, so she ought to be more cooperative when dealing with them in future."

Mental-World Premisses
Premiss Form: *S* is *M*.
Conclusion Form: *P* ought (ought not) to do *A*.
Warrant Backing: Doing (not doing) *A* is a desirable response to *S*.
Rebuttal Factor: *A* is not appropriate given *P*'s situation or characteristics.
Example: At a dinner party one man says to another, "Your wife is annoyed at you for not giving her any attention, so you ought to talk to her at dinner."

Mental-World Premisses (Ends-Means)
Premiss Form: *S* wants *E*.
Conclusion Form: *S* ought (ought not) to do *A*.
Warrant Backing: *A* is the most effective means to achieve *E*.
Rebuttal Factors: (1) *A* is not a means available to *S*; (2) doing *A* conflicts with the pursuit of other interests of *S*.
Example: "Sam wants a reliable car, so he ought to buy a Mercedes." While the Mercedes has the best reliability record, Sam may not be able to afford one.

Constitutive-Rule Premisses
Premiss Form: *D* counts as *W*.
Conclusion Form: *S* ought (ought not) to do *A*.
Warrant Backing: It is in one's interest to use the term "*W*" when referring to things/attributes that are *D*.
Rebuttal Factor: *S* wishes to create a special impression in speaking to another.
Example: "Adult human females count as women, so men ought not to refer to adult human females as girls." In a particular case, a man may intentionally want to offend a woman.

Regulative-Rule Premisses
Premiss Form: *A* is obligatory (prohibited).
Conclusion Form: *S* ought (ought not) to do *A*.
Warrant Backing: It is in one's interest to comply with the rules.
Rebuttal Factor: The rule does not apply to *S* at all, or there are special circumstances.
Example: "Parking in a 'No Parking' area is prohibited, so you ought not to park here." The conclusion might not follow if the person addressed has diplomatic immunity or the car has broken down.

7.3.3.3 *Summary: Proving Prudential Claims.* Claims of the form "*S* ought (ought not) to do *a*" can be proved by claims of these forms:

Prudential: *S* ought (ought not) to do *b* (*b* brings about *a*).
Obligation: *S* must do (not do) *b* (*a* makes doing *b* possible).
Supererogatory: *S* ought to do *b* (*a* makes doing *b* possible).
Evaluative: *x* is a *G*(*X*) ("*G*" is an evaluative term).
Physical-World: *x* is *F* (*F* is physical quality; *x* may be *S*).
Mental-World: S_2 is *M* (S_2 is someone else).
Mental-World (Ends-Means): *S* wants *E* (*E* is in the interest of *S*).
Constitutive-Rule: "*W*" means the same as "*D*" (*D* is the definition of "*W*").
Regulative-Rule: *A* is obligatory (prohibited).

7.3.4 *Arguments for Evaluative Claims*

There are three sorts of evaluative claims[11] that can serve as conclusions: grading claims (x is a $G(X)$), ranking claims (x is an $R(X)$), and comparison claims (x_1 is a $B(X)$ than x_2, where "B" is a comparative expression such as "better").

7.3.4.1 *Evaluative-Premiss Versions.* Many of the valid patterns for proving evaluative claims involve evaluative premisses as well. In this section I will canvass the possibilities to identify them.

7.3.4.1.1 *Conclusions Involving Grading.* The patterns for arguments whose conclusions involve grading are the following.

Sample-to-Population Version
Premiss Form: $N\%$ of x's are $G(X)$.
Conclusion Form: $N\%$ of X's are G.
Warrant Backing: The sample is representative of the total population.
Rebuttal Factor: There is a systematic bias in sample selection, or the sample is accidentally unrepresentative because too small.
Example: "Thirty percent of the apples in this box are Grade A. Therefore, 30% of our crop is Grade A." The most plausible rebuttal factor for the example is that the apples were picked from a single tree that is untypically good.

Population-to-Group/Individual Version
Premiss Form: $N\%$ of observed X's are $G(X)$.
Conclusion Form: $N\%$ of x's are $G(X)$.
Warrant Backing: x's are normal/typical X's.
Rebuttal Factor: x's are unusual in some relevant respect.
Example: "Most policemen in Canada are good marksmen. Therefore, most policemen in my town are good marksmen." Here the inference would be undermined if it was discovered that the policemen in my town have no opportunity for target practice.

Parallel-Case Versions
Premiss Form: x_1 is a $G(X)$.
Conclusion Form: x_2 is a $G(X)$.
Warrant Backing: x_1 and x_2 are alike in all relevant respects.
Rebuttal Factor: x_2 is different in some crucial respect.
Example: "The peach I just ate was delicious, so this peach from the same basket will be delicious." Here it is possible that although the two peaches came from the same basket, they did not come from the same tree.

Evaluative-Premiss Version
Premiss Form: x is a $G_1(X)$.
Conclusion Form: x is a $G_2(Y)$.
Warrant Backing: A $G_1(X)$ is generally a $G_2(Y)$.
Rebuttal Factor: There is something unusual about x as an X.
Example: "Lendl is a great tennis player, so he is a good athlete."

7.3.4.1.2 *Conclusions Involving Ranking.* The patterns for arguments whose conclusions involve ranking are the following.

Sample-to-Population Version
Premiss Form: x, an individual/sample of X's, is an $R(Y)$.
Conclusion Form: X's are $R(Y)$.
Warrant Backing: x is representative of X's.
Rebuttal Factor: x is unrepresentative because of a sample-selection bias.
Example: "These peaches from tree 79 are the best we have sampled, so the peaches on tree 79 are the best in the orchard." It may be that whoever picked from tree 79 picked from a part of the tree that receives more sun than the rest of it.

Population-to-Group/Individual Version
Premiss Form: Observed X's are $R(Y)$.
Conclusion Form: x is $R(Y)$.
Warrant Backing: x is typical/representative of X's.
Rebuttal Factor: x differs from the typical X in some crucial respect.
Example: A university admissions officer says, "Freshmen from that high school are, on average, the best we get. So the ones coming from there next year will be the best."

Parallel-Case Version
Premiss Form: x_1, an X, is an $R(Y)$.
Conclusion Form: x_2, an X also, is an $R(Y)$.
Warrant Backing: x_2 is like x_1 in relevant respects. Validity depends on the proportion of those in category X that have the attribute $R(Y)$.
Rebuttal Factor: x_2 differs from x_1 in a crucial respect.
Example: "Lendl, who is eligible to enter any of the top tennis tournaments, is one of the ten best players in the world. So MacInroe, who is also eligible, is one of the ten best players in the world." Here we need to ask what proportion of those eligible to enter any tournament are in the top ten. The rebuttal factor here is "More than the top ten are invited to all tournaments."

Evaluative-Premiss Version
Premiss Form: x is a $G_1(X_1)$, a $G_2(X_2)$, a $G_3(X_3)$, etc.

Conclusion Form: x is an $R(X)$.

Warrant Backing: The gradings mentioned in the premiss are sufficient to qualify x as an $R(X)$.

Rebuttal Factor: x is deficient in some respect X_n.

Example: "Gretzky is a superb playmaker, an excellent shooter, and a good penalty killer. So he is the best hockey player in the world."

7.3.4.1.3 *Conclusions Involving Comparisons.* Whereas in ranking we locate a thing on a spectrum of goodness with all the other things of the same kind, in making comparisons we simply compare one thing of a class of things to another in that class, in terms of a set of standards.

Sample-to-Population Version

Premiss Form: x_1 is a $C(X)$ than x_0.

Conclusion Form: X_1's are $C(X)$ than X_0's.

Warrant Backing: x_1 is representative of X_1's, and x_0 is representative of X_0's.

Rebuttal Factor: Because of sample-selection bias or small samples, either x_1 is not representative of X_1's, or x_0 is not representative of X_0's, or both.

Example: "The students in introductory psychology at Ivy College are more intelligent (on average) than the ones taking it at Enormous State University (ESU), so students at Ivy College are more intelligent (on average) than those at ESU." Depending on the magnitude of the difference and the test used to measure intelligence, it may be that the Ivy College people are simply better educated than the ESU people, enabling them to score a bit higher.

Population-to-Group/Individual Version

Premiss Form: Observed X_1's are $C(X)$ than observed X_0's.

Conclusion Form: x_1 is a $C(X)$ than x_0.

Warrant Backing: x_1 is similar to observed X_1's in relevant respects, and x_0 is similar to observed X_0's in relevant respects.

Rebuttal Factor: Either x_1 differs from observed X_1's in a crucial respect, or x_2 differs from observed X_2's in a crucial respect, or both.

Example: "Observed bear cubs raised in the wild are better equipped to survive in the wild than ones raised in captivity. So that one living with its mother in the wild will be better equipped than the orphaned one we are raising here at the zoo."

Parallel-Case Version

Premiss Form: x_1 is a $C(X)$ than x_0.

Conclusion Form: x_2 is a $C(X)$ than x_0.

Warrant Backing: x_2 is like x_1 in relevant respects.

Rebuttal Factor: x_2 differs from x_1 in a crucial respect.

Example: "The peach from the red basket was tastier than the one from the blue basket, so this one from the red basket will be tastier than the one from the blue basket." Here it may be plausible to suppose that the two from the red basket were picked from different trees or at different stages of ripeness.

Comparative Premiss Version

Premiss Form: x_1 is a $C_1(X_1)$ than x_2; x_1 is a $C_2(X_2)$ than x_2; etc.

Conclusion Form: x_1 is a $C(X)$ than x_2.

Warrant Backing: The respects in which one thing of kind X is superior to another, as mentioned in the premiss, are jointly sufficient to make it a $C(X)$ than the other.

Rebuttal Factor: x_1 is inferior to x_2 in some crucial respect.

Example: "University A has more programs than university B; it has a lower student-teacher ratio and larger library holdings. So A is a better university than B."

7.3.4.2 *Nonevaluative-Premiss Versions.* There will be a set of patterns for each kind of evaluative claim.

7.3.4.2.1 *Conclusions Involving Grading.* The patterns for arguments whose conclusions involve grading are the following.

Obligation-Premiss Version

Premiss Form: S must (must not) do A.

Conclusion Form: S, a member of the class of X's, is a $G(X)$.

Comment: An invalid pattern. Obligations are not evidence for evaluative claims.

Supererogatory-Premiss Version

Premiss Form: S ought (ought not) to do A.

Conclusion Form: S, a member of the class of X's, is a $G(X)$.

Comment: This is an invalid pattern. Recommendations to do a good deed are not relevant to evaluative claims.

Prudential-Premiss Version

Premiss Form: S ought (ought not) to do A.

Conclusion Form: S, a member of the class of X's, is a $G(X)$.

Comment: This is an invalid pattern. Advice that something is in one's interest is irrelevant to evaluative claims.

Physical-World Premiss Version

Premiss Form: x has good-making attributes $g_1, g_2 \ldots g_n$ of things of kind X. ("Good-making" implies that a thing is a good one of its kind if it has enough such characteristics.)

Conclusion Form: x is a $G(X)$.[12]

Warrant Backing: Things with $g_1, g_2 \ldots g_n$ qualify as $G(X)$.

Rebuttal Factor: x has deficiencies b_1, b_2, etc.

Example 1: "Wayne Gretzky holds more than 80 scoring records in the NHL, so he is a great player."

Example 2: "The Jaguar accelerates and decelerates quickly, has good cornering power, and is very comfortable. So it is a great luxury sedan." Most owners might admit that this does not qualify it as "great," because in the past it has been seriously unreliable.

Mental-World Premiss Version

Premiss Form: S has valuable attributes $g_1, g_2 \ldots g_n$ of things of kind X.

Conclusion Form: S is a $G(X)$.

Warrant Backing: Persons with $g_1, g_2 \ldots g_n$ qualify as $G(X)$.

Rebuttal Factor: S has deficiencies b_1, b_2, etc.

Example: Sally's friend Zoe tries to persuade her that Sam would make a good husband: "Sam is sensitive, he likes women as people, and he wants to settle down. So he is good marriage material." Sally says that, on the other hand, he wouldn't be much of a companion because he plays golf all weekend.

Constitutive-Rule Premiss Version

Premiss Form: D counts as W.

Conclusion Form: D's are $G(X)$.

Warrant Backing: Whatever is a W is a $G(X)$.

Rebuttal Factor: This W is not $G(X)$.

Example: "Exceeding the posted speed limit counts as speeding. So exceeding the posted speed limit is an illegal act."

Regulative-Rule Premiss Version

Premiss Form: A is obligatory (prohibited).

Conclusion Form: A is $G(X)$.

Warrant Backing: Whatever is obligatory (prohibited) is $G(X)$.

Rebuttal Factor: A is a special case.

Example: "Exceeding 50 kph past my house is legally prohibited. So exceeding 50 kph is an irresponsible act." It may be that exceeding 50 kph by a small amount does not represent any significant increase in risks.

7.3.4.2.2 *Conclusions Involving Ranking*. The patterns for arguments whose conclusions involve ranking are the following.

Obligation-Premiss Version
Premiss Form: S must (must not) do A.
Conclusion Form: A is an R act.
Comment: This is not a useful pattern, even though P may entail C. Normally, P is more controversial than C.

Supererogatory-Premiss Version
Premiss Form: S ought (ought not) to do A.
Conclusion Form: A is an R act.
Comment: This is not a useful pattern. P may entail C, but normally P is as controversial as C. This is why C is commonly used to prove or argue for P.

Prudential-Premiss Version
Premiss Form: S ought (ought not) to do A.
Conclusion Form: A is an R act.
Comment: Here R takes the values "wise," "sensible," and so forth. This is not a useful pattern. Although P may entail C, C normally is used to prove P.

Physical-World Premiss Version
Premiss Form: Among X's, x ranks mth in good-making attribute g_1, nth in attribute g_2 ...
Conclusion Form: x is an $R(X)$.
Warrant Backing: The attributes mentioned are jointly sufficient to qualify x for the ranking.
Rebuttal Factor: x lacks an attribute necessary to qualify for the ranking.
Example: "In the luxury performance car category, the Jaguar sedan is second best in acceleration, third in braking power, and first in cornering power. So it is one of the top three sedans in performance."

Mental-World Premiss Version
Premiss Form: Among X's, x ranks mth in valuable attribute g_1, nth in attribute g_2 ...
Conclusion Form: x is an $R(X)$.
Comment: Here g_1, g_2, etc., are mental attributes of x.
Warrant Backing: The rankings mentioned in the premiss are sufficient to entail that x is an $R(X)$.

Rebuttal Factor: A ranking necessary to qualify for the ranking has not been mentioned in the premiss.

Example: "Mr. Gorbachev is one of the shrewdest and best educated people and one of the people most knowledgeable about the West to be found in his country. So he is one of the best leaders the USSR could have at this time."

Constitutive-Rule Premiss Version
Premiss Form: W is D; "W" means the same as "D."
Conclusion Form: W's are $R(X)$.
Comment: This is not a valid pattern. Conceptual truths are not evidence for rankings.

Regulative-Rule Premiss Versions
Premiss Form: A is obligatory (prohibited).
Conclusion Form: A is an R act.
Comment: The existence of a requirement cannot by itself be a basis for a ranking, although it may entail a grading proposition. For example, "Murder is legally prohibited" does not serve as evidence for "Murder is the worst crime."

7.3.4.2.3 *Conclusions Involving Comparisons.* The patterns for arguments whose conclusions involve comparisons are the following.

Obligation-Premiss Version
Premiss Form: Members of this community must (must not) do A rather than B.
Conclusion Form: A is a C act than B.
Example: "People must lie rather than put someone's life at risk. So lying is morally less wrong than putting someone's life at risk."
Comment: This is not a useful pattern. Although P may entail C, C is usually better evidence for P than vice versa.

Supererogatory-Premiss Version
Premiss Form: S ought (ought not) to do A rather than B.
Conclusion Form: A is a C act than B.
Example: "One ought to give money to the Salvation Army to help vagrants rather than to vagrants on the street. So giving money to the Salvation Army to help vagrants is a better form of charity than giving it to the vagrants themselves."
Comment: As the example suggests, P may entail C, but generally C is regarded as better evidence for P than vice versa. This is not a useful pattern.

Prudential-Premiss Version
Premiss Form: S ought (ought not) to do A rather than B.
Conclusion Form: A is a wiser/more sensible/more beneficial act than B.
Comment: The comment is the same as for the last pattern.

Physical-World Premiss Version
Premiss Form: Consists of a set of observations of respects in which x_1
   is superior to x_2, but these are not grading judgments.
Conclusion Form: x_1 is a $C(X)$ than x_2.
Warrant Backing: The respects in which one thing of kind X is superior
   to another, as mentioned in the premiss, are jointly sufficient to
   make it an $R(X)$ than the other.
Rebuttal Factor: There is at least one unmentioned respect in which x_1
   must be superior to x_2 to merit the rating in C.
Example: "Graf has beaten Navratilova in most of their matches in the
   past year, so Graf is a better tennis player than Navratilova."

Mental-World Premiss Version
Premiss Form: Consists of a set of mental attributes in which it is
   claimed that x_1 is superior to x_2.
Conclusion Form: x_1 is a $R(X)$ than x_2.
Warrant Backing: The respects in which one thing of kind X is superior
   to another, as mentioned in the premiss, are jointly sufficient to
   make it an $R(X)$ than the other.
Rebuttal Factor: There is at least one unmentioned respect in which x_1
   must be superior to x_2 to merit the rating in C.
Example: "Sam is more astute than Marvin; he is a clearer thinker and
   knows more about the company's product line. So he is a better candidate for the promotion than Marvin."

Constitutive-Rule Premiss Version
Comment: There is no pattern. Definitions are not evidence for evaluative claims.

Regulative-Rule Premiss Version
Comment: There is no pattern. The premiss would involve claiming
   something like "x_1 is more obligatory than x_2," but this claim is non-
   sensical.

7.3.4.3 *Summary: Proving Evaluative Claims.* Since there are three
distinct kinds of evaluative claims, they will be discussed separately.

7.3.4.3.1 *Proving Grading Claims.* Claims of the form "$N\%$ of all X's are
$G(X)$" can be proved by

$N\%$ of X's in this sample are $G(X)$.

Claims of the form "$N\%$ of these X's are $G(X)$" can be proved by

$N\%$ of heretofore observed X's are $G(X)$.

Claims of the form "This X is a $G(X)$" can be proved by

Parallel Case: That X is a $G(X)$.
Evaluative: This X is a $G_2(Y)$ (X is a species of Y).
Physical World: This X has good-making attributes g_1, g_2, etc., of X's.
Mental World: This S has good-making attributes g_1, g_2, etc., of persons of kind S.
Constitutive Rule: D's count (semantically) as W's.
Regulative Rule: Acts of kind X are obligatory (prohibited).

7.3.4.3.2 *Proving Ranking Claims.* Claims of the form "$N\%$ of all X's are $R(Y)$" (where X's are members of the class of Y's) can be proved by

$N\%$ of X's in this sample are $R(Y)$.

Claims of the form "$N\%$ of the X's in this group are $R(Y)$" can be proved by

$N\%$ of heretofore observed X's are $R(Y)$.

Claims of the form "This X is an $R(Y)$" can be proved by

Parallel Case: That X is an $R(Y)$.
Grading Claim: This X is a $G_1(X_1)$, a $G_2(X_2)$, etc.
Physical World: Among X's, this X ranks mth in good-making attribute g_1, nth in good-making attribute g_2, etc. (The g's are physical features.)
Mental World: Among X's, this X ranks mth in good-making attribute g_1, nth in good-making attribute g_2, etc. (The g's are mental features.)

7.3.4.3.3 *Proving Comparison Claims.* Claims of the form "$N\%$ of all X_1's are $C(X)$ than X_0's" can be proved by

$N\%$ of these X_1's are $C(X)$ than those X_2's.

Claims of the form "$N\%$ of these X_1's are $C(X)$ than those X_0's" can be proved by

$N\%$ of heretofore observed X_1's are $C(X)$ than heretofore observed X_0's.

Claims of the form "This X is $C(X)$ than that X" can be proved by

Physical World: This X is superior to that X in relevant respects F_1, F_2, etc. (F's are physical attributes.)

Mental World: This X is superior to that X in relevant respects F_1, F_2, etc. (F's are mental attributes.)

7.3.5 *Arguments for Physical-World Claims*

As noted already, these physical-world claims are of two kinds: claims about brute facts and claims about institutional facts. The use of the term "fact" is not intended to preclude the possibility that such claims can be false. It is used because the expression "brute fact" has currency in the literature.

7.3.5.1 *Physical-World Premiss Versions.* The patterns for arguments involving premises about the physical world are the following.

Sample-to-Population Version
Premiss Form: $N\%$ of x's are F.
Conclusion Form: $N\%$ of X's are F.
Warrant Backing: x is representative of X's.
Rebuttal Factor: There is a systematic sample-selection bias, or the sample is unrepresentative by accident, because it is small.
Example: "Ten percent of those in this class (of 150) are left-handed. Therefore, 10% of the human population are left-handed." The most plausible rebuttal factor is a selection bias arising from the small geographical area from which the sample is drawn, that is, there is a race-related (or other) genetic factor common to most people in the sample that makes them untypical of humanity as a whole.

Population-to-Group/Individual Version
Premiss Form: $N\%$ of observed X's are F.
Conclusion Form: $N\%$ of x's are F.
Warrant Backing: x's are like the observed X's in other relevant respects.
Rebuttal Factor: x is in some relevant way not representative of X's.
Example: "About 10% of the human population is left-handed. Therefore, 10% of the students in my logic class are left-handed." Here the inference is presumptively valid unless the class is quite small (under 20?) or if there is a selection bias, for example, if the argu-

ment is about a society in which people are made to learn to use their right hand as the favoured hand.

Parallel-Case Version
Premiss Form: x_1 (an X) is F.
Conclusion Form: x_2 (also an X) is F.
Warrant Backing: x_1 and x_2 are similar in other relevant respects.
Rebuttal Factor: There is a crucial difference between x_1 and x_2.
Example: "Arsenal, currently near the top of the English First Division, is a high-scoring team. Therefore, Tottenham, also near the top, is a high-scoring team." Here, there is the distinct possibility that Tottenham may be a defensive-minded team.

Physical-World Premiss: Cause-to-Effect Version
Premiss Form: P.
Conclusion Form: C.
Warrant Backing: Generally, events/states like P cause events/states like C.
Rebuttal Factor: Something intervenes to prevent C when P occurs.
Example: "The fog is thickening, so there will be flight delays and cancellations." A rebuttal factor here is that the fog is low-level and below the elevation of the airport.

Physical-World Premiss: Argument-from-Sign Version
Premiss Form: P.
Conclusion Form: C.
Warrant Backing: P is generally a sign or symptom of C.
Rebuttal Factor: An intervening factor prevents C from occurring.
Example: "Susie has started to sneeze, so she will have a cold tomorrow."

Physical-World Premiss: Effect-to-Cause Version
Premiss Form: P.
Conclusion Form: C.
Warrant Backing: The event/state reported by C is the best explanation for the event/state reported by P.
Rebuttal Factor: Some other event/state is the best explanation of P.
Example: "Gasoline prices have just gone up again, so the oil companies have increased their profit margins." A rebuttal factor here is that the government has increased its tax on gasoline.

7.3.5.2 *Physical-World Claims with Other Kinds of Premisses.* The patterns for physical-world claims involving other kinds of premisses are the following.

Obligation Premiss

Premiss Form: *S* must (must not) do *A*.

Conclusion Form: *S* is *F.*

Comment: Obligations are not ordinarily evidence for physical attributes, but even when they are relevant, the conclusion is normally easier to establish than the premiss. This is not a useful pattern.

Supererogatory Premiss

Premiss Form: *S* ought (ought not) to do *A*.

Conclusion: *S* is *F.*

Comment: This is not a useful pattern. Even though the premiss can sometimes entail the conclusion, such premisses are normally more difficult to prove than the conclusions.

Prudential Premiss

Premiss Form: *S* ought (ought not) to do *A*.

Conclusion Form: *S* is *F.*

Comment: The comment is the same as for the last pattern.

Evaluative Premiss

Premiss Form: A grading, ranking, or comparison claim.

Conclusion: *X* is *F.*

Example: "Sam is a good gridiron football player, so he is big."

Comment: The comment is the same as for the supererogatory-premiss pattern. In the example the premiss given would be harder to prove than the conclusion.

Mental-World Premiss: Causal Version

Premiss Form: *S* is *M*.

Conclusion Form: *S* is *F.*

Comment: Here *M* is a mental predicate and *F* is a physical one. *M* produces *F* in *S.*

Warrant Backing: Generally, this mental state/event results in behavioural event/state *F.*

Rebuttal Factor: Something intervenes to prevent the result that *S* is *F.*

Example: "Sam has a toothache, so he won't be very good company at dinner tonight."

Mental-World Premiss, Effect

Premiss Form: *S* is *M*.

Conclusion Form: *S* is *F.*

Warrant Backing: The conclusion is generally the best explanation for the premiss.

Rebuttal Factor: Some other physical-world fact is the correct explanation of the premiss.

Example: "Susie is sad, so she didn't get the job she was interviewed for."

Mental-World Premiss, Sign
Premiss Form: S is M.
Conclusion Form: X is F.
Warrant Backing: Events/states of the kind mentioned in the premiss are signs or symptoms of ones in the conclusion.
Rebuttal Factor: Some factor intervenes to prevent the occurrence of C.
Example: "People are fed up with the prime minister, so his party will lose the next election."

Constitutive-Rule Premiss
Premiss Form: D counts as W.
Conclusion Form: W's are F.
Example: "A woman who has never married counts as a spinster, so spinsters are women."
Comment: As the example suggests, this is a deductive pattern.

Regulative-Rule Premiss
Premiss Form: A is obligatory (prohibited).
Conclusion: A is F.
Comment: This is not a valid pattern. The citing of a rule is not normally evidence for a claim about the physical world.

7.3.5.3 *Proving Physical-World Claims.* Claims of the form "$N\%$ of all X's are F" can be proved by

$N\%$ of this sample of X's are F.

Claims of the form "$N\%$ of these X's are F" can be proved by

$N\%$ of heretofore observed X's are F.

Claims of the form "This X is F" are proved by

Parallel Case: That X is F.
Physical World, Cause to Effect: P. (P reports an event or state that causes X to be F.)
Physical World, Sign: P. (P mentions a sign or symptom of X being F.)
Physical World, Effect to Cause: P. (P reports a phenomenon that is explained by C.)

Mental World, Cause: *S* is *M*. (*M* is a mental state that provides a motive for *S* to bring it about that *X* is *F*. *X* may be *S*.)

Mental World, Effect: *S* is *M*. (That *X* is *F* explains the fact that *S* is *M*.)

Mental World, Sign: *S* is *M*. (*S*'s being *M* is a sign that *X* is *F*. *X* may be *S*.)

7.3.6 *Arguments for Mental-World Claims*

Mental-world claims can be written as "*S* is *M*," where "*S*" refers to a sentient entity and "*M*" ascribes a mental property to *S*. Included among such properties are intentions, motives, attitudes, beliefs, and sensations. In general, because the existence or presence of mental phenomena are unobservable except in our own case, inferring that they exist is hazardous. Of course, we make such inferences all the time and with a surprising degree of success.

Strictly speaking, the phenomena "nearest" the mental states or events of others are their own mental states or events. Of course, proving mental claims from these states or events requires knowledge of their existence. At one remove inferentially, we can rely on claims about their behaviour, especially their verbal behaviour. At a further remove we can infer mental claims from various other kinds, although strictly speaking these inferences require an intermediate conclusion that states that the person believes the premiss claim.

7.3.6.1 *Mental-World Premiss Versions.* The patterns for arguments involving premisses about the mental world are the following.

Sample-to-Population Versions
Premiss Form: *N*% of *x*'s are *M*.
Conclusion Form: *N*% of *X*'s are *M*.
Warrant Backing: *x*'s are a representative sample of *X*.
Rebuttal Factors: (1) There is a systematic bias in the sample selection; (2) the sample is so small that it is accidentally unrepresentative.
Example: "Most of the players I talked to are unhappy about the coach's firing. Therefore, most players on the team are unhappy about it." It is possible that the speaker talked to too few players, and they might well have been the only ones unhappy to see the coach go.

Population-to-Group/Individual Version
Premiss Form: *N*% of observed *X*'s are *M*.
Conclusion Form: *N*% of these *X*'s are *M*.

Warrant Backing: These X's are, in relevant respects, similar to the previously observed X's.

Rebuttal Factor: These X's differ from the previously observed ones in some crucially relevant respect.

Example: "Most Canadian first-year college students feel insecure. Therefore, most first-year students in my logic course feel insecure." The most plausible rebuttal factor would be some cultural peculiarity of my region that makes my students untypical.

Parallel Case Version

Premiss Form: P_1 is M.

Conclusion Form: P_2 (in the same designated class) is M.

Warrant Backing: The class is relatively homogeneous. Often, the broader the class, the more likely that things in the class are dissimilar in crucial (for the argument) respects.

Rebuttal Factor: P_2 differs in some crucially relevant respect, other than in being M.

Example: "Jill, Sue's mother, is upset with her. So Jack, her father, is upset with her too." Here Jill and Jack belong to the same class, that is, the class of parents. On the other hand, if the conclusion referred to Bill, Sue's brother, the class would be that of Sue's family. This might involve some dissimilarities that undermine the inference. For example, behaviour that upsets a parent may not upset a sibling.

7.3.6.2 *Mental-World Claims with Other Premisses.* The patterns for mental-world claims involving other kinds of premisses are the following.

Obligation Premiss

Premiss Form: S must (must not) do A.

Conclusion Form: S is M.

Warrant Backing: People who must (must not) do A are M.

Rebuttal Factor: S does not recognize the duty to do (refrain from doing) A.

Example: "Sam must apologize to Sue tonight, so he is apprehensive about going to the dinner party."

Supererogatory Premiss

Premiss Form: S ought to do (refrain from doing) A.

Conclusion Form: S is M.

Comment: This is not a valid pattern. Advice to act for another's benefit is not normally evidence for mental states.

Prudential Premiss
Premiss Form: S ought to do (refrain from doing) A.
Conclusion Form: S is M.
Comment: This is not a valid pattern. Advice on how to gain a benefit is not normally relevant to the question of the existence of a mental state.

Evaluative Premiss, Cause
Premiss Form: A grading, ranking, or comparison claim about S.
Conclusion Form: S is M.
Warrant Backing: Evaluative judgments of this kind produce mental phenomenon M.
Rebuttal Factor: S is unaware of, or disagrees with, the evaluation.
Example: "Sam had a good round of golf today, so he will be in a good mood tonight."

Evaluative Premiss, Effect
Premiss Form: An evaluative claim.
Conclusion Form: S is M.
Warrant Backing: S's being M is the best explanation of P.
Rebuttal Factor: P is explained by another mental attribute of S.
Example: "Sam is playing well today, so he is concentrating more than usual."

Physical-World Premiss, Cause
Premiss Form: P.
Conclusion Form: S is M.
Comment: The premiss here is some event or state in the physical world that might be expected to have a mental impact on S. That is, P is a cause of C.
Warrant Backing: Events/states of the kind reported in P generally produce mental events/states of the kind reported in C.
Rebuttal Factor: Something "blocks" the occurrence of the event/state C.
Example: "Sam burned the steaks, so his wife will be angry."

Physical-World Premiss, Sign
Premiss Form: S is F.
Conclusion Form: S is M.
Warrant Backing: The occurrence of the sign/symptom reported in P is generally correlated with the mental event/state M.
Rebuttal Factor: S is trying to mislead others about her/his mental state.

Example: "Sam is furrowing his brow, so he is becoming irritated with his wife's nagging."

Physical-World Premiss, Effect
Premiss Form: *P.*
Conclusion Form: *S* is *M.*
Comment: Here the mental state/event *M* is conceived as producing the event/state *P.*
Warrant Backing: *C* is the best explanation for *P.*
Rebuttal Factor: Something else is a good explanation of *P.*
Example: "The Israelis continue to settle people on the occupied West Bank of the Jordan, so they do not intend to allow it to be a Palestinian homeland."

Constitutive-Rule Premiss
Premiss Form: *D* counts as *W.*
Conclusion Form: *S* is *M.*
Comment: This pattern is invalid. Definitional truths are not evidence for the presence of mental states.

Regulative-Rule Premiss, Version One
Premiss Form: *A* is obligatory (prohibited).
Conclusion Form: *S* believes that s/he must do (refrain from doing) *A.*
Warrant Backing: People generally accept the rules of the community.
Rebuttal Factor: *S* does not regard the rule as legitimate.
Example: "Wearing a veil in public is obligatory for women in Iran. So Mrs Khomeni believes that she must wear a veil."
Comment: This kind of argument is really only useful in making inferences about persons who are members of, but outside, the community in which the rule is operative. We find ourselves making such inferences when, on our "home ground," we meet people from other cultures.

Regulative-Rule Premiss, Version Two
Premiss Form: *A* is obligatory (prohibited) in society *S.*
Conclusion Form: Members of *S* believe that *A* is desirable (undesirable) conduct.
Warrant Backing: *C* is the best explanation of *P.*
Rebuttal Factor: The rule is enforced even though the majority lack the conviction that *A* is desirable (undesirable) conduct.
Example: "Caring for elderly parents is obligatory here, so people here believe that it is desirable to care for one's elderly parents."

7.3.6.3 *Proving Mental-World Claims.* Claims of the form "*N*% of all *S*'s are *M*" can be proved by

N% of this sample of *S*'s are *M*.

Claims of the form "*N*% of these *S*'s are *M*" can be proved by

N% of heretofore observed *S*'s are *M*.

Claims of the form "*S* is *M*" are proved by premisses of these kinds:

Parallel Case: S_2 is *M*. (S_2 is another individual in the same designated class as *S*.)

Obligation: *S* must (must not) do *a*.

Evaluative: *P*. (*P* is a grading, ranking, or comparison claim.)

Physical World, Cause: *P*. (*P* is a physical-world claim whose truth can produce the mental state *M* in *S*.)

Physical World, Sign: *P*. (The occurrence of the sign or symptom mentioned in *P* can produce *M* in *S*.)

Physical World, Effect: *P*. (*P* is best explained by *S*'s being *M*.)

Regulative Rule (1): *A* is obligatory (prohibited). (With this premiss, "*M*" is equivalent to "believes s/he must do (not do) *A*.")

Regulative Rule (2): *A* is obligatory (prohibited) in *S*'s society. (With this premiss, "*S*" is equivalent to "members of this society," and "*M*" is equivalent to "believe that *A* is desirable (undesirable) conduct.")

7.3.7 *Arguments for Constitutive-Rule Claims*

Constitutive-rule claims can have several forms. When they are enacted definitions, as in definitions of particular offences in criminal law or in rule books for games, they can have the forms "*W* is *D*" (murder is culpabable homicide) or "*W* when *D*" (a goal is scored when the ball has completely entered the net). In each case, we can express the rule in the form "*D* counts as *W*."

When the rule expresses an unenacted definition, as in ordinary language definitions, we commonly use the form "The word '*W*' means '*D*,'" where the claim is true when the expression "*D*" is synonymous with "*W*." But since this form unnecessarily encourages us to infer that there are entities called "meanings," I shall use a safer form: "The word/expression '*W*' means the same as the word/expression '*D*.'"

7.3.7.1 *Constitutive-Rule Premiss Versions.* There are no useful patterns for arguments with constitutive-rule premisses.

Sample-to-Population Versions
Comment: There is no useful pattern. Semantic claims are either necessarily true or necessarily false. Percentage and proportion terms cannot sensibly occur in such claims.

Population-to-Group/Individual Version
Comment: For the reasons discussed in conjunction with sample-to-population inferences, there is no such pattern.

Parallel-Case Version
Comment: This is not a valid pattern. Normally, a definition of one word is no evidence for the truth of a definition of another one.

7.3.7.2 *Constitutive Claims with Other Kinds of Premisses.* The patterns for constitutive claims involving other kinds of premisses are the following.

Obligation Premiss
Premiss Form: *S* must (must not) *A*.
Conclusion Form: *D* counts as *W*.
Comment: This is not a valid pattern. Obligations are not evidence for the correctness of definitions.

Supererogatory Premiss
Premiss Form: *S* ought (ought not) to do *A*.
Conclusion Form: *D* counts as *W*.
Comment: This is not a valid pattern. Recommendations to act in the interests of others are not relevant to the correctness of definitions.

Prudential Premiss
Premiss Form: *S* ought (ought not) to do *A*.
Conclusion Form: *D* counts as *W*.
Comment: This pattern is not valid. Recommendations to act in one's own interest are not relevant to the correctness of definitions.

Evaluative Premiss
Premiss Form: An evaluative claim.
Conclusion Form: "*W*" means the same as "*D*."
Example: "A 1980 LaTour is an excellent Bordeaux, so the expression '1980 LaTour' means the same as 'excellent Bordeaux.'"
Comment: As the example suggests, this is not a valid form.

Physical-World Premiss, Version One
Premiss Form: A *W* is a *D.*
Conclusion Form: "*W*" means the same as "*D.*"
Warrant Backing: Whenever expressions are referentially coextensive, they are synonymous.
Rebuttal Factor: The warrant backing does not apply if the premiss is not a necessary truth.
Invalid Example: "A creature with a heart is a creature with a kidney, so 'creature with a heart' means the same as 'creature with a kidney.'" This example is invalid because the premiss is a contingent truth, not a necessary one.
Valid Example: "A person is called a spinster if and only if she is called a woman who has never married, so 'spinster' means the same as 'a woman who has never married.'"
Comment: This pattern does not rely on any of the warrant-backing principles identified by Ehninger and Brockreide.

Physical-World Premiss, Version Two
Where "*I*" stands for a rule-governed institution such as a game, or a club, or a legal system, we have the following pattern.
Premiss Form: In the official rulebook for *I*, it is stated that *D* counts as *W.*
Conclusion Form: *D* counts as *W.*
Warrant Backing: Official rulebooks correctly report the rules in force.
Rebuttal Factor: The warrant backing applies unless the rule has changed since the publication of the rule book.
Valid Example: "In the Criminal Code of Canada it is stated that culpable homicide counts as murder, so culpable homicide counts as murder."
Comment: Again, the warrant backing of the argument is not of a kind identified by Ehninger and Brockreide.

Mental-World Premiss
Premiss Form: Speakers of *L* believe that "*W*" means the same as "*D.*"
Conclusion Form: "*W*" means the same as "*D.*"
Warrant Backing: Speakers of a language are generally correct about word definitions in that language.
Rebuttal Factor: Speakers are able to use the word "*W*" in the correct physical and grammatical context without being correct about the nature of its referent or property.
Example: "Most speakers of English believe that 'livid' means the same as 'reddish', so 'livid' means the same as 'reddish.'" The conclusion does not follow: "livid" actually means the same as "bluish gray."

Regulative-Rule Premiss
Premiss Form: Using "W" to refer to D's is obligatory.
Conclusion Form: "W" means the same as "D."
Comment: This is not a useful pattern. Failure to comply with a linguistic rule simply amounts to not uttering the message we wish to
utter. There are no associated sanctions in everyday life. Thus, the
premiss is always false in these cases.

7.3.7.3 *Summary: Proving Constitutive-Rule Claims.* Constitutive-rule
claims of the form "'W' means the same as 'D'" can be proved by

Physical World (1): A W is a D.
Physical World (2): In the rule book for I, it is declared that D counts
as W. (I is the institution.)
Mental World: Speakers of L believe that "W" means the same as
"D." (L is the particular language.)

7.3.8 *Arguments for Regulative-Rule Claims*

Regulative rules can be expressed in the forms "A is prohibited" or "A
is obligatory." Since rules may be either enacted or unenacted (that is,
customary, in force by tacit agreement), certain patterns are useful for
proving the existence of one kind but not the other.

7.3.8.1 *Regulative-Rule Premiss Versions.* There is only one pattern for arguments with regulative-rule premisses.

Sample-to-Population Versions
There is no pattern. Statistical claims are logically inappropriate.

Population-to-Group/Individual Version
There is no pattern. Statistical claims are inappropriate.

Parallel-Case Versions
Premiss Form: A_1 is obligatory (prohibited).
Conclusion Form: A_2 is obligatory (prohibited).
Comment: Acts A_1 and A_2 are acts of ostensibly the same kind.
Warrant Backing: The acts are similar in other relevant respects.
Rebuttal Factor: A_2 differs from A_1 in some crucial respect.
Example: "Copying chapters of novels is prohibited, so copying chap-
ters of textbooks is prohibited." In the example, the narrowest
class to which novels and textbooks belong is the class of books.
The most plausible rebuttal factor is "Textbooks serve pedagogical

rather than entertainment purposes, so limited reproduction is permitted."

7.3.8.2 *Regulative-Rule Claims with Other Kinds of Premisses.* The patterns for regulative-rule claims involving other kinds of premisses are the following.

Obligation Premiss
Premiss Form: As one who is an X, S must (must not) do A.
Conclusion Form: A is obligatory for (prohibited to) X's.
Warrant Backing: Whatever X's must (must not) do is obligatory (prohibited).
Rebuttal Factor: S is a special case of X's.
Example: "Sam must remove his spiked golf shoes before entering the golf club bar, so removing one's spiked golf shoes before entering the bar is obligatory." This can be reworded as "As one who is wearing spiked golf shoes, Sam must remove them before entering the golf club bar, so removing one's spiked golf shoes before entering the bar is obligatory."

Supererogatory Premiss
Premiss Form: S ought (ought not) to do A.
Conclusion Form: A is obligatory (prohibited).
Comment: This is not a valid pattern. Recommendations/exhortations to act in the interests of another are not relevant to whether or not a rule is operative.

Prudential Premiss
Premiss Form: S ought (ought not) to do A.
Conclusion Form: A is obligatory (prohibited).
Comment: This is not a valid pattern. The premiss presupposes that A is optional conduct. It cannot be inferred from it that A is not optional.

Evaluative Premiss
Premiss Form: A is beneficial (harmful).
Conclusion Form: A is obligatory (prohibited).
Warrant Backing: Beneficial (harmful) acts are generally obligatory (prohibited).
Rebuttal Factor: A is not sufficiently beneficial (harmful) to warrant the imposition of a rule.
Comment: This pattern is not normally useful, because in most cases the conclusion is more easily established than the premiss. The premiss can serve as the explanation of the conclusion, however.

Physical-World Premiss and Enacted-Rule Conclusion (1)
Premiss Form: There is a statute/enactment declaring that doing (failing to do) *A* is an offence punishable by ...
Conclusion Form: *A* is prohibited (obligatory) for those within the jurisdiction of the enactment.
Warrant Backing: Those who produced the enactment are officially empowered to create such rules.
Rebuttal Factor: Procedural deficiencies make the enactment void.
Example: "Section 309(1) of the Criminal Code of Canada specifies that the possession of burglary tools in suspicious circumstances is an offence punishable on conviction by up to 14 years in prison. So possession of burglary tools in suspicious circumstances is prohibited in Canada."

Physical-World Premiss and Enacted-Rule Conclusion (2)
Premiss Form: Being declared guilty of doing (failing to do) *A* in jurisdiction *J* results in censure/sanctions.
Conclusion Form: Doing (refraining from doing) *A* in jurisdiction *J* is prohibited.
Warrant Backing: Generally, official censure/sanctions arise from rule violations.
Rebuttal Factor: The body/group inflicting censure/sanctions lacks official standing.
Example: "Being declared guilty of exceeding the posted speed limit in Nova Scotia results in the levying of a $62.50 fine. So exceeding the posted speed limit in Nova Scotia is prohibited."

Physical-World Premiss and Unenacted-Rule Conclusion (1)
Premiss Form: In society *S* people in situation *C* do (avoid) *A*.
Conclusion Form: In society *S*, doing *A* is obligatory (prohibited) in situation *C*.
Warrant Backing: People generally conform to the rules in their societies.
Rebuttal Factor: Doing (avoiding doing) *A* is merely habitual.
Example 1: "In Britain, people queue when waiting for buses. So in Britain, queueing for the bus is obligatory."
Example 2: "In Canada, people being introduced to someone commonly say 'How are you?' So in Canada etiquette requires that one ask about the health of those to whom one is being introduced." A rebuttal factor is operative here: saying "How are you?" is merely a conventional/habitual form of greeting.

Physical-World Premiss and Unenacted-Rule Conclusion (2)
Premiss Form: Members of *S* commonly censure/apply sanctions to fellow members when the latter do (fail to do) *A*.

Conclusion Form: *A* is prohibited (obligatory) in *S*.

Warrant Backing: Unenacted rules are generally enforced by the community.

Rebuttal Factor: None.

Example: "Local people clamoured for the laying of formal charges when a college student dropped a kitten out his fourth floor window for amusement. So harming animals for amusement is prohibited here."

Mental-World Premiss and Unenacted-Rule Conclusion

Premiss Form: Members of society/group *S* believe that *A* is obligatory (prohibited) in situation *C*.

Conclusion Form: *A* is obligatory (prohibited) in situation *C* in society/group *S*.

Warrant Backing: People are generally aware of the rules in their society/group.

Rebuttal Factor: Those who believe that *A* is obligatory (prohibited) are not typical of the membership of *S*.

Example: "Experienced golfers believe that one may not change balls during a hole. So changing balls during a hole is prohibited."

Constitutive-Rule Premiss

Premiss Form: *A* counts as *W*.

Conclusion Form: *A* is obligatory (prohibited).

Warrant Backing: Whatever counts as *W* is obligatory (prohibited).

Rebuttal Factor: *A* is a special case.

Example: "Culpable homicide counts as murder, so culpable homicide is prohibited."

7.3.8.3 *Summary: Proving Regulative-Rule Claims.* Claims of the form "*A* is obligatory (prohibited)" can be proved by claims of the form

Parallel Case: A_2 is obligatory (prohibited). (A_2 is relevantly similar to *A*.)

Obligation: *S* must (must not) do *A*.

Physical World (1): There is a statute/enactment declaring that failing to do (doing) *A* is a punishable offence.

Physical World (2): *S* has been punished for failing to do (doing) *A*.

Physical World (3): In society *S* people do (avoid doing) *A* in situation *C*.

Physical World (4): Members of *S* commonly informally punish fellow members of *S* when the latter fail to do (do) *A*.

Mental World: *S*'s believe that *A* is obligatory (prohibited).
Constitutive Rule: Failing to do (doing) *A* counts as a felony.

7.4 ARGUMENT FROM AUTHORITY

Ehninger and Brockreide call arguments from authority "authoritative arguments." They provide this description: "In authoritative arguments the data [grounds] consist of one or more factual reports or statements of opinion. The warrant affirms the reliability of the source from which these are derived. The claim reiterates the statement which appeared in the data, as now certified by the warrant" (1963, 51). This description seems to make the following report of *S*'s argument to persuade *H* appropriate: *R* utters "*A*, so *A*, because *S*, who affirms *A*, is a reliable source."

In the format I have been using, *R*'s argument can be written as

Premiss Form: *C*.
Conclusion Form: *C*.
Warrant Backing: *S* is a reliable source.

This pattern is clearly incomplete, in that *R*'s premiss is not *C*, but "*S* has affirmed that *C*," where *S* is the authority whom the arguer *R* is relying on to convince *H* that *C*. The correct argument form, then, is this:

Premiss Form: *S* affirms that *C*.
Conclusion Form: *C*.
Warrant Backing: *S* is a reliable source of information on the topic to which *C* belongs.

Arguments of this type are commonly encountered when someone chooses to use as a premiss a quotation from the news media, especially the print media such as newspapers and newsmagazines. To be convincing, the capable arguer will cite a quote or, more commonly, a paraphrase from an individual or organization that *S* believes has high epistemic credibility with *H*. In this scenario, the weakness of the argument normally resides in the inference claim. It is possible, of course, for *R* to have lied about what *S* said or to have incorrectly paraphrased it, but it is not difficult for *H* to confirm or disconfirm the premiss. *H* needs only to be given the reference for the quote and to consult the document. This will be more complicated when the quote was made in an electronic medium, and sometimes there will be no permanent record to consult. For this reason, premisses giving electronic media quotes have less prima facie credibility than premisses giving print media quotes.

7.4.1 *Inference Evaluation*

As was said, the weakness in arguments from authority is most commonly the inference. The evaluator's main task is to arrive at a value for $p(C / S$ asserts that $C)$. Some readers will realize that in accepting a claim on another's epistemic authority, we may be committing the classical fallacy of *ad Verecundiam*. The identification of this fallacy early in the history of logic has ensured that there is available a very useful body of analysis that identifies the conditions for committing it.[13] These conditions will serve as the basis for formulating the conditions that entitle us to judge the epistemic competence of the arguer, or what rhetoric theorists have traditionally called "ethos."

In the literature, two main kinds of epistemic competence have been noted. In one sort of case, the individual is in a position to know the truth value of the premiss by virtue of having observed the alleged event or state of affairs. Inferences relying on observation in this way are relying on what the courts call "eyewitness testimony." I shall call this sort of knowledge "observer knowledge." In the other sort of case, the individual is epistemically competent by virtue of being trained in a field or having extensive personal experience. I shall call this sort of knowledge "expert knowledge."

There are, then, two types of epistemically authoritative testimony that we may rely on: observer testimony and expert testimony. Each of these sources can be a basis for an evaluator to accept a claim, but only when certain conditions are met. These conditions will be outlined later.

Irrespective of which sort of authority is being relied on, arriving at an inference rating is done by obtaining a value for "$p(C / S$ affirms that $C)$." Obtaining an accurate value for this is not as straightforward as it appears. It is obviously a function of how good S's "track record" is on claims like C. But there is a well-documented possibility of fallacious reasoning when moving from a judgment of track record to a value for "$p(C / S$ affirms that $C)$." An example from the literature of cognitive psychology illustrates it. Tversky and Khaneman set the following problem for their research subjects:

A cab was involved in a hit-and-run accident at night. Two cab companies, the Green and the Blue, operate in the city. You are given the following data: (a) 85% of the cabs in the city are Green and 15% are Blue; (b) a witness iden-

Table 26
Cab Company Probabilities

	S affirms cab is Blue	S affirms cab is not Blue
Cab is Blue (0.15 × 100)	15 × 0.8 = 12	15 × 0.2 = 3
Cab is not Blue (0.85 × 100)	85 × 0.2 = 17	85 × 0.8 = 68

tified the cab as Blue. The court tested the reliability of the witness under the same circumstances that existed on the night of the accident and concluded that the witness correctly identified each one of the two colors 80% of the time and failed 20% of the time. What is the probability that the cab involved in the accident was Blue rather than Green? (1982, 156)

The argument the subjects have to deal with can be expressed as "The witness asserts that the cab involved in the accident was a Blue cab; so the cab involved in the accident was a Blue cab." Before reading on, readers are urged to make their own intuitive judgments of the probability of the inference claim. The correct answer will be given shortly.

Further research in the form of posttest interviews indicated that we have a strong tendency to regard $p(C\ /\ S$ affirms that $C)$ as a measure of S's track record. This was suggested by the fact that in the experiment many subjects gave a value of 80%, or nearly that, for the probability that the cab was Blue. In fact, the "hit-rate" parameter is $p(S$ affirms that $C\ /\ C)$. In the example, the witness' assertion about the cab colour is true in 80% of the cases observed. So, in effect, the subjects in the experiment might have been guilty of identifying $p(C\ /\ S$ affirms that $C)$, the inference rating, with $p(S$ affirms that $C\ /\ C)$, the hit-rate or reliability rating for S. And this error causes the evaluators to vastly overrate the argument, as we shall see.

But, if the 80% figure is not the value for "$p(C\ /\ S$ affirms that $C)$," how do we obtain it? The value we are looking for is $p(Cab$ is Blue $/\ S$ affirms cab is Blue). To get it we can proceed by thinking of the accident as occurring 100 times before the same witness and assuming that the 100-item sample is perfectly representative. The results can be presented in the grid shown in Table 26.

The upper row depicts the situation in which the cabs are Blue. There would be 15 of them because their base rate is 0.15. In 80% of the cases S will identify them correctly, and in 20%, S will misidentify them (shown in the left and right columns respectively). The lower

Table 27
Generalized Version of Cab Problem

	S affirms that C	S affirms that not C
$p(C)_i$	$p(C)_i \times (1 - E)$	$p(C)_i \times E$
$p(\text{not-}C)_i$	$(1 - p(C)_i) \times E$	$(1 - p(C)_i) \times (1 - E)$

row depicts the cases in which the cabs are Green (i.e., not Blue). In 20% of the cases, S will misidentify them, and in 80%, S will be correct (shown in the left and right columns respectively).

The value we want is p(Cab is Blue / S affirms it is Blue). To get this value, we want the proportion of cases in which the cab is Blue and S affirms it is Blue, out of the total cases in which S affirms it is Blue. The numerator will be the value (12) in the upper left-hand corner, and the denominator will be the sum of the values in the left-hand column (12 + 17). Thus,

p(Cab is Blue / S affirms cab is Blue) = 12 / (12 + 17) = 0.41.

Most subjects estimated that the cab was more likely Blue than Green, and many gave answers in the 70% or 80% range. But despite the witness's 80% reliability, the cab is more likely to have been Green than Blue. I will return to these findings later.

The table for the cab example can be seen as an instance of a generalized table (Table 27). On receipt of S's argument, H could judge how likely it is that S would be incorrect about the claim P. This likelihood would be E, expressed in decimal form. As in the cab example, we are only interested in favourable and unfavourable cases in which S affirms that C. Thus,

$$p(C / S \text{ affirms that } C) = [p(C)_i \times (1 - E)] / [(p(C)_i \times (1 - E)) + (E \times (1 - p(C)_i))].$$

This is, of course, one version of Bayes' Theorem, and it affords another explanation of why test subjects chose 0.8 as the value of $p(C / S$ affirms that $C)$. When $p(C)_i$ is 1/2, this value is always $1 - E$. Thus, we might hypothesize that subjects ignored the base rate by assuming that there was an equal chance, prior to testimony, that the cab was a Blue cab. They might think that since only two cab companies operate, there are only two possibilities, so that the prior probability of its being a Blue cab is 1/2. But in fact the possibilities are not equally likely.

Jonathan Cohen seems to be defending this reasoning pattern in an article in which he defends the judgments of the untutored subjects against charges of irrationality laid by Tversky, Kahneman, and others. He presents an example of an illness diagnosis that is structurally similar to the cab example, with base rate in favour of one of two alternative illnesses and test reliability of 80% for the other alternative. He then poses the question of what course of treatment (for disease A, which is 19 times as common as B, or for B) it would be rational for a particular patient to choose:

The test reports that you are suffering from disease B. Should you nevertheless opt for the treatment appropriate to A, on the supposition (reached by calculating as the experimenters did) that the probability of your suffering from A is $19/23$? Or do you opt for the treatment appropriate to B, on the supposition (reached by calculating as the subjects did) that the probability of your suffering from B is $4/5$? It is the former option that would be the irrational one for, qua patient, not the latter. (Cohen 1981, 329)

Cohen goes on to argue, "Admittedly, the standard statistical method would be to take the prior frequency into account here, and this would be absolutely right if what was wanted was a probability for any patient considered not as a concrete particular person, not even as a randomly selected particular person, but simply as an instance of a long run of patients." Despite this admission, Cohen argues further that any particular patient "needs to evaluate a propensity-type probability, not a frequency-type one ... the prior probabilities have to be appropriate ones, and there is no information about you personally that establishes a greater predisposition in your case to disease A than disease B. We have to suppose equal predispositions." Cohen then claims that "An analogous supposition has to be made about the cab colors" (1981, 329).

When he says we must assume equal predispositions, Cohen seems to be involved in the error of inferring that two alternatives are equiprobable, from the fact that they are the only two possibilities. I have occasionally tested for this error among my students by asking them questions such as "What is the probability that Christmas Day will fall on a Tuesday in the year 2023?" Before any instruction, I have found that about 20% will give $1/2$ as the answer, on the ground that it either will or will not fall on a Tuesday. But of course these alternatives are not equally probable, and the correct answer is $1/7$. Does Cohen make this mistake? Notice that he says "there is no information about you personally that establishes a greater predisposition in your case to disease A rather than disease B." But surely this would be true for most patients who contract *A* or *B*. In fact, there is a basis for inferring that the patient is more likely to have *A* than *B*: from Cohen's description, we have no reason to suppose that the patient is not a typical human being. And consequently the base rate can be used in determining the likelihood that the patient has *B*, given that the test indicates *B*.

Furthermore, Cohen seems to be guilty of inconsistency. If an individual can be truly described as "an instance of a long run of particular patients," which anyone could be, why would not the frequency concept apply? The fact that each of us is also "a concrete particular person" is neither here nor there. If a single individual is being referred to, why should a probability value change when we change our description? It seems preferable to take the view that one probability concept is defective.

Although Cohen would not raise this objection, people who find the 0.41 figure to be simply unbelievable in the cab example have been known to ask why they should accept Bayes' Theorem. The reason they should is simply that basic probability axioms entail Bayes' Theorem, so rejecting Bayes involves the rejection of at least one of these axioms. In fact, the four axioms form the basis of our probability calculus. These rules can be summarized as follows (Baron 1988, 182, 189):

1 If *A* and *B* are mutually exclusive,
  $p(A \text{ or } B) = p(A) + p(B)$.
2 $p(A) + p(\text{not-}A) = 1$.
3 If *A* and *B* are independent (neither is evidence for the other),
  $p(A \text{ and } B) = p(A) \times p(B)$.
4 The conditional probability of *A*, given *B* as true is
  $p(A/B) = p(A \text{ and } B) / p(B)$.

Since Bayes' Theorem can be derived from these four axioms and each of these rules can be recognized (with the aid of some simple examples) by most people as correct, we must accept the Bayes formula, because it is entailed by them. And, consequently, it would seem that we must accept the Bayesian answer to the cab problem.

However, diehards wishing to resist the unintuitive Bayesian result of 0.41 could still challenge that figure on other than mathematical grounds. The analysis presented in Table 26 assumes two things: (1) that the accident rate for the two cab companies is about the same, and (2) that probability is to be conceived as a relative frequency. I have already made a case for accepting the second assumption.

It seems clear that most subjects do not make use of the data concerning the relative numbers of Green and Blue cabs, which suggests that they do not make the first assumption. Should we conclude that people have a policy of ignoring base-rate data when more salient (to them) information is available? This conclusion would be hasty. It turns out that when the experiment was done without the witness testimony, "almost all subjects gave the base rate (0.15) as their answer" (Kahneman, Slovic, and Tversky 1982, 157). This finding suggests that in the absence of other information people do regard base rates as evidence.

However, this conclusion must be qualified. In yet another version of the experiment, the base-rate information that "85% of the cabs in the city are Green and 15% are Blue," was replaced with this item: "Although the two companies are roughly equal in size, 85% of cab accidents in the city involve Green cabs and 15% involve Blue cabs." In this version, the median answer was 0.60, which is roughly between the witness-reliability figure and the correct answer of 0.41. It has been hypothesized that this behaviour occurs because there is causal relevance in the latter version. Apparently it is easier for subjects to see, in fact, the relevance to such cases of causally relevant data than it is for them to see the relevance of mere statistical distribution. One way of putting this is to say that there is explanatory power in accident-rate data, but not in data concerning mere proportions. In the context of these examples, there is some sense in the distinction. After all, someone might say that s/he was not given any relevant information in being told that 85% of the cabs are Green and 15% Blue, that for all we know to the contrary, the Blue cabs might have a much higher accident rate than the Green cabs. But the more reasonable assumption is that this is not so.

One might suppose that subjects had trouble with the problem because the two facts relevant to the answer pointed in different directions. The proportion of Blue cabs in the city counted against the cab involved in the accident being Blue – statistically, it was much more likely that the cab was Green (not Blue). On the other hand, witness testimony strongly points to the cab being Blue.

However, other researchers have found that people are not accurate even when the items of evidence point in the *same* direction. In one experiment, subjects were told that the probability that any used car of a certain model year is in good condition is 0.9. They were also told that a particular judge of the condition of used cars was accurate in his judgments 60% of the time. They were then asked to estimate the probability that a particular car was in good condition, given that it was of the appropriate model year and that the judger says it is in good condition. In this task both items of evidence point in the same direction, so that their effect might be seen as cumulative. However, "Subjects typically give a value considerably lower than 0.9 under these circumstances" (Baron 1988, 215). The correct answer is 0.93.

The issue being a psychological one, I do not wish to pursue any further the possible explanations for subjects' behaviour in these different cases. Even if there is some defence for their ignoring the base rate in the first version, the fact that in the version in which accident rates were given, they did not correctly process the information when they saw that it was relevant suggests that people need to have their inference-evaluation skills upgraded for dealing with arguments from authority.

One way or another, improving one's accuracy in judging the inference quality of arguments from authority involves relying on Bayes' formula. But the complexity of the Bayesian formula makes it impracticable for everyday situations. On the other hand, it seems necessary, if we are to gain any accuracy in arriving at values of "$p(C / S$ affirms that $C)$," to rely on some formula or "recipe" that gives us results that approximate the Bayes results. We therefore face a trade-off between total accuracy (using Bayes) at one extreme, and ease of use (with some relative inaccuracy) at the other. In what follows I recommend a useful approach that embodies such a trade-off.

When using Bayes' Theorem in deciding whether to accept a premiss on the basis of testimony, there are two parameters that need to be given values: "error rate" (E) and "prior probability of C" $(p(C)_i)$. E equals 1 minus S's reliability as an authority (R) in such matters. We can assign a value to $p(C)_i$ by relying on whatever relevant information we might have at the time we evaluate an argument. In deciding on an error rate, we will seldom have track-record data to the degree that bookmakers have for sporting events, but there are guidelines that I will present below that will be helpful. Even though our estimates of the two parameters may only amount to guesses on some occasions, relying on Bayes' Theorem in conjunction with these guesses will bring us much closer to a correct value for "$p(C / S$ affirms that $C)$" than proceeding intuitively. The cab example should impress the reader on this point.

Let us begin by restating Bayes' Theorem:

$$p(C / S \text{ affirms that } C) = [p(C)_i \times (1 - E)] / [(p(C)_i \times (1 - E)) + (E \times (1 - p(C)_i)].$$

Since inference evaluation is the task, we are interested in guidance for those cases in which C is not already acceptable on the basis of other evidence, that is, for values of C under 0.8 or 0.7. We are also interested only in cases where E is significantly below $1/2$. (When we value E at $1/2$, we are saying that S's testimony provides no grounds for accepting C: S is as likely to be wrong as right.)

Looking at the formula, it is clear that the relationships between the parameters are not linear. Nevertheless, if we were looking for a simplified version, a linear one would be best. With a view to developing such a simplified formula that would give reasonably accurate results over the variable ranges specified above, I calculated values for $p(I)$ ($p(I)$ = p(If P then C)) with $p(C)_i$ taking the values 0.1, 0.2 ... 0.9 and with E taking values 0.1, 0.2 ... 0.4. There are 36 combinations of values. This formula gave reasonably good results (with a restriction applied):

$$p(I) = p(C)_i + 0.5 - E.$$

The restriction is that, since $p(I)$ cannot equal 1 (we are dealing with inductive inferences) or exceed 1, whenever the value of the right-hand side is greater than 1, we understand $p(I)$ to have a value "slightly less than 1," which allows us to give the inference a rating of "1." This will be the case when, for example, $p(C)_i = 0.7$ and $E = 0.1$.

The simplified formula is intuitively more attractive if we state it in terms of S's reliability (R). Since $R = 1 - E$, we get

$$p(I) = p(C)_i + (R - 0.5).$$

In this version, we can think of "$R - 0.5$" as representing "authority support" for C. Given that S has no credibility when $R = 0.5$, every improvement above that value provides more support for C. So if S's reliability is judged to be 0.9, $p(I) = p(C)_i + 0.4$. In such a case, S's testimony will provide adequate support for C when $p(C)_i$ is 0.6, or as low as 0.4. Described another way, this value "$R - 0.5$" is the answer to the question "How much extra support for C does S's affirming that C provide?"

The reader may be curious as to the accuracy of this relatively simple formula. Well, for the 36 value combinations of $p(C)_i$ and E, and rounding off values of $p(I)$ to one decimal place, the formula gave the correct result in 24 cases. It gave values that were high by 0.1 in 9 cases, and values that were low by 0.1 in 3 cases. Considering that our estimates for $p(C)_i$ and R are normally no more accurate than this, this formula, by virtue of its simplicity and relative accuracy, merits serious consideration for everyday use.

Applying the simple formula to the original cab example, we have $p(C)_i = 0.15$, and $R = 0.8$, so p(The cab is Blue / S affirms the cab is Blue) = $0.15 + (0.8 - 0.5) = 0.45$. The correct value, found using Bayes' formula, is 0.41. A subject who relied on this simple formula would, obviously, be close to correct, *providing* s/he recognized the base rate as 0.15. If s/he ignored it, as most did, that would amount to regarding the base rate as 0.5. In the absence of any data to the contrary, this assumption would be reasonable. But it happens to be otherwise in this case. If one (mistakenly) regards $p(C)_i$ as 0.5, the simple formula gives a value of 0.8, the value most subjects gave. The point here is that no formula can prevent people from making the error just described, which can be avoided only by making people aware of the role of base rates. That being admitted, the simple formula, by requiring us to "plug in" a value for initial probability, can help those who might otherwise not realize that it does play a role.

Applying the formula to the other example given above, the example of used car evaluation, we have the following data: (1) the probability that a car of a certain age is reliable is 0.9; (2) an "authority" on the condition of used cars is reliable 60% of the time. Using the simple formula, we get p(This car is reliable / S affirms that this car is reliable) = 0.9 + (0.6 − 0.5) = 1.0. As noted earlier, the "1.0" should not be regarded as indicating the claim is necessarily true or certain on some other basis. Rather, we should think of it as meaning, in this case, that the probability of the claim is greater than the initial probability but less than 1. The correct figure is 0.93. Recalling that subjects in this experiment gave a result somewhere between 0.6 and 0.9, we can see that having them use our simple formula would have resulted in an accurate estimate, because they would have been "forced" to add the two probabilities. That is, the simple formula has the highly desirable property of getting subjects to combine witness reliability and initial probability (base rate) in the correct way.

The simple formula has limitations. Specifically, when the initial probability is lower than 0.1 or S's reliability is greater than 0.9, the relationships are not sufficiently linear to allow its use. Cases of the first kind are ones in which persons, often portraying themselves as in a position to know, wish us to believe what, based on our prior knowledge, we find highly unlikely. That is, we are being expected to accept the claim based entirely on their say-so. Cases of the second kind are those in which we regard S as an expert or an otherwise unimpeachable source. Almost regardless of the initial probability of the claim, we infer its truth from S's testimony.

In such cases we must rely on Bayes' formula. What practical guidance can we get from it? One mathematical property of the formula is that, when $p(C)_i = E$, the inference claim has a probability of 1/2. This means that, however low $p(C)_i$ is, E must be significantly lower if we are to find the inference claim acceptable. How much lower? It turns out that when $p(C)_i$ is 0.1 or less, the Bayes formula can be simplified to the following form and yield a fairly accurate result:

$$p(I) = p(C)_i / (p(C)_i + E).$$

Using this formula, we can construct a table that shows the comparative error rates for different inference ratings (Table 28). The reader

Table 28
Error Rates Corresponding to Inference Ratings

Inference Rating	Error Rate
0.5	$p(C)_i$
0.6	$2/3\, p(C)_i$
0.7	$1/2\, p(C)_i$
0.8	$1/4\, p(C)_i$
0.9	$1/9\, p(C)_i$
1.0	$1/19\, p(C)_i$

should keep in mind that an inference rating of "1.0" means that $p(I)$ is 0.95 or greater. It does not mean that when $E = 1/19\, p(C)_i$, I is necessarily true. Or, to put it another way, it does not mean that the inference is deductively valid. If we are trying to decide whether or not to accept a highly implausible claim on the say-so of someone, Table 28 implies that we should do so only if we can justify regarding that person's error rate in the matter as, say, only $1/4$ as great as the likelihood of the claim, judged in terms of evidence we already have.

These figures have practical implications. One implication is that for claims that are exceedingly improbable, as judged by us, we should not accept them on anyone's say-so, since it is unlikely that anyone can be sufficiently reliable to offset the initial improbability of such claims. An example of this is testimony of the occurrence of a reputedly miraculous event. If we consider the likelihood of such an event to be low enough, we will not infer the occurrence of one from *anyone's* testimony, since the likelihood of observational error or lying on his or her part is comparatively greater.[14] The Bayes formula also tells us that when we regard a claim as having an unchanged probability after someone makes it, we are committed to assigning a 0.5 error rate to that person. That is to say, in this matter S's testimony has no value to us.

To summarize the foregoing discussion on inference evaluation in the case of argument from authority:

1 It was noted that inference quality is determined by Bayes' Theorem;
2 Given the complexity of the theorem, a more useful formula that yields fairly accurate results (when initial probability is 0.1 or higher and S's reliability is 0.9 or less) is

$p(C\, /\, S$ affirms that $C)$ = Initial probability of C +
$$(S\text{'s reliability} - 0.5).$$

3 The initial probability of C reflects the evaluator's information that is relevant to C, which could be called "evidence support" for C. The expression "S's reliability − 0.5" was earlier denoted "authority support" for C, so the formula can be written as

$$p(C / S \text{ affirms that } C) = \text{Evidence support for } C +$$
$$\text{Authority support for } C.$$

To use the simplified Bayesian formula, we must begin by assigning values to $p(C)_i$ and E. To obtain a value for $p(C)_i$ in a given case, we rely on any relevant information we already have that is not specific to the case at hand. Obtaining a value for E, however, requires relying on different considerations for observer testimony and expert testimony. I will now turn to a discussion of the guidelines that are appropriate for obtaining accurate estimates of error rates for the two kinds of cases.

7.4.2 *Observer Testimony*

In the matter of observer testimony, the following conditions must be met for reliability: [15]

1 The observer must have been in the appropriate place at the appropriate time. In the cab example, the witness would have to be at the scene when the accident occurred, and near enough to be able to distinguish a Blue cab from a Green cab.
2 The observer must have (or have had at the time) nondefective sensory modalities of the kind needed to observe the event/state. This is a matter of visual and aural acuity. Does the witness have normal visual acuity without corrective glasses? If not, was the witness wearing fully corrective glasses at the time? Is the witness's hearing normal, or if not, was a corrective device being used to ensure normal hearing? When physical events such as car accidents are witnessed, visual acuity is most crucial. When the testimony is about what was said, aural acuity is most crucial.
3 The observer must have attended to the event/state. When properly done, this would result in details being stored in memory. When the testimony reports verbal doings, it is important that the witness should recall the exact wording. When it is a physical event/state, a witness might conceptualize what is transpiring, or store it as a series of images.
4 Ideally, the testimony was made relatively soon after the observation. Consequently, when observers differ in their testimony, the testimony given earliest is to be deemed the most reliable, given that it

meets the first three requirements. (This condition is needed to deal with the possibility of memory failure over time.)

Each of the foregoing considerations is important for observer reliability, but studies have shown that humans are not as reliable as observers as once supposed. For those aware of such research, the claim "I saw it with my own eyes" no longer automatically gives testimony the credibility it once had. Because of this, an extra consideration needs to be added.

5 Was the situation one in which humans are prone to serious observational error? Unfortunately, two of the most common situations in which we would like to use observer testimony are ones in which we are especially prone to error: accidents and criminal acts. These tend to happen quickly and tend to be traumatic for victims and witnesses alike. This apparently interferes with cognitive processing of the event. For example, people who witness air crashes frequently report that the aircraft exploded before striking the ground, but air-accident investigations seldom find that this has occurred. That is, what really happened is that the aircraft disintegrated when it struck the ground. What explains the erroneous perception? It may be the fact that the sound of the crash reaches the observer later than the visual data. The latter, travelling at the speed of light, reaches the observer almost instantaneously. On the other hand, sound travels only about a third of a kilometre per second. So if a crash occurs a few kilometres away, visual data will precede aural data by a second or more. We apparently tend to correlate crash impact with sound, so that whenever a crash involves flames or visible explosion, naive observers interpret the flash as an explosion in the air, followed shortly by noise, which is assumed to be evidence of the crash. Humans are prone to this error because the light-sound discrepancy is not often experienced.

Thus, even when the first four conditions are met, it is important to know if the situation is one in which normal humans are subject to cognitive malfunction. The only way to know this is observation of repeated instances, either in experiments or by studying real-life cases. Of course, in a particular case, the most accurate approach is the one used in the cab example: establish the individual's personal error rate. But this is seldom a practical option.

7.4.3 Expert Testimony

Expert competence involves three main requirements. First, the person must have the appropriate epistemic credentials relative to the claim. The degree of knowledgeability required to qualify as an expert in relation to a particular claim depends upon how esoteric or arcane the claim is. Depending on the point of law at issue, for example, a police officer may qualify as sufficiently knowledgeable to qualify as an expert. On the other hand, if the point is more obscure, only a specialist lawyer or even a judge may be qualified.

Second, there is another component of the credibility of the source – trustworthiness. There should be no misgivings about S's "track record" in truth telling, nor should there be any suspicion of bias. These possibilities can be entertained by answering this question: "Does S have anything to gain in asserting C?" A positive answer does not, of course, automatically undermine S's credibility. S may well be telling the truth, but it is desirable to be aware of the possibility of lying or exaggeration. And when confronted with conflicting testimony, this principle may enable us to choose the correct claim.

Third, the general state of knowledge in the subject must be recognized: does C qualify as a controversial claim among accepted authorities? That is, do other authorities assign a different value to $p(C)$? In every field there are controversial issues at any given time, and in some fields some of these issues are of concern to the general public. In such cases the lack of consensus among experts ought to make us reluctant to conclude that any particular expert's opinion can be accepted.

7.4.4 Summary

Arguments from authority can be expressed in the form "S affirms that C, so C." Establishing $p(S$ affirms that $C)$ is a matter of access to S's testimony. Establishing a value for the inference $p(C / S$ affirms that $C)$ is a somewhat complex matter involving, for most people, the likelihood of serious error. The error resides in assuming that S's reliability is measured by $p(C / S$ affirms that $C)$, the inference rating value, whereas it is actually measured by the value $p(S$ affirms that $C / C)$.

To obtain the true inference rating we must use Bayes' Theorem, which expresses $p(C / S$ affirms that $C)$ as a function of reliability, $p(S$ affirms that $C / C)$, and of the prior probability of C, $p(C)_i$. Unfortunately, Bayes' Theorem, is a fairly complex equation, but simplifications can be made. When S's reliability is between 0.5 and 0.9, and $p(C)_i$ is greater than 0.1, a good approximation can be had using

$$p(C / S \text{ affirms that } C) = p(C)_i + (R - 0.5).$$

The first term on the right-hand side of the equation was called (sec. 7.4.1) "evidence support" for C; the second, "$R - 0.5$," was called "authority support." For the ranges given, the value of $p(C / S$ affirms that C) is the value of this calculation when the outcome is 1 or less. When the outcome is greater than 1, the inference rating is 1.0.

In obtaining inference ratings for arguments from authority, the main difference from patterns previously examined, is that the authority's error rate and the prior probability of C must be relied on. Evaluators commonly fail to factor in the prior probability. In effect, they are committed to saying that $p(C)_i = 0.5$, because with this value the Bayes' Theorem result is identical to S's reliability (R). But usually there will be a prior presumption for or against C, so that a Bayesian approach cannot be avoided. The formula developed in this section makes the Bayesian method practical.

7.5 ANALOGICAL ARGUMENTS

In the literature, two distinct kinds of analogical arguments have been identified. One relies on "predictive" analogies,[16] the other on what has been called "proportional" analogies.[17]

7.5.1 Arguments Relying on Predictive Analogies

Arguments relying on predictive analogies can be written in the form

$x_1, x_2, x_3 \dots x_{n-1}$, and x_n each have properties $F_1, F_2, F_3 \dots F_{n-1}$.
$x_1, x_2, x_3 \dots x_{n-1}$ also each have property F_n.
So x_n will be found to have property F_n.

A fundamental theoretical issue arises as soon as the pattern has been written: does this pattern really rely on analogy at all? Ehninger and Brockreide contrast this pattern with the proportion type by calling it "proof by a collection of parallel cases": "Proof by analogy is sometimes defined to include both the proof we are calling an analogy and the one we have labelled parallel case. We make a distinction between these types, because the proof by parallel case depends on a direct similarity between two cases, whereas an analogy involves a similarity in the relation which each of the two cases bears to something else" (1963, 142).

Support for their position is to be found in the fact that the inductive canon applies to arguments of this form.[18] This position is implicitly maintained by Copi, who, in a section called "Appraising Analogical Arguments" (1982, 397–400), provides criteria that constitute part of the inductive canon. Thus, it would seem that the predictive version of the argument from analogy is not really argument from analogy at all but a special form of inductive argument that, following Ehninger and Brockreide, we may call "proof by a collection of parallel cases" in its general form, and simply "proof by parallel case" when only two objects are involved.

7.5.2 *Proportional-Analogy Arguments*

Proportional-analogy arguments involve maintaining that the relationship between two different things is in some respect like the relationship between two other things. Perhaps these claims are called proportional analogies because they can be presented in the format of an arithmetical proportion. For example, we can write "A vw Golf is to a BMW 735 as a Chevy Cavalier is to a Cadillac" in the form

(vw Golf / BMW 735) = (Chevy Cavalier / Cadillac).

Analogical claims of this kind are efficient ways of conveying to someone that a thing has a set of characteristics by relating it to something already familiar to the hearer: they are efficient because we do not have to actually enumerate the characteristics. For example, if someone asks me to describe what my brother's dog Higgins looks like, I may be able to convey much of what is required by saying "He's a Kirby Puckett of the dog world." But I can be successful only if the hearer knows what the baseball player Kirby Puckett looks like (he is extremely stocky). This claim can be elaborated to correspond to the proportion format:

(Higgins / the typical dog) = (Kirby Puckett / the typical
baseball player).

These claims can occur in an argument pattern that can be written like this:

(P_1) $_xR_X$ (x is related to X in respects R_1, R_2 ... R_n).
(P_2) If $_xR_X$ then F_x.
(P_3) $_yR_Y = _xR_X$ (y is related to Y in the same way that x is related to X).
(C) F_y.

As stated, the pattern is deductively valid. In constructing analogues of y, an arguer will create a case (x) in which the analogue clearly has feature F. The third premiss, the proportional analogy, is the key premiss.

Arguments of this kind are useful because they can represent thought experiments in testing theses. This is especially common in ethics. Since ethical principles, like conceptual rules, are projective, that is, they can be applied to new cases, we can test them by concocting imaginary, but realizable, cases. Such cases can be formulated so that undesirable distracting features of real cases are not present. This procedure is akin to the design of a controlled experiment in science. But the ability to generate fictitious, conceptually "sanitary," examples brings with it the prospect that the relationship of y to Y (the real case) differs in some crucial respect from that of x to X (the made-up case). This is because there will often be more features involved in the y-Y relationship, by virtue of our failure to produce an analogue that is as rich in features as our real case.

Consider this example discussed by Govier (1989, 143): "In seeking protection from Eastern's creditors in bankruptcy court, Lorenzo (chairman of financially troubled Eastern Airlines) is like the young man who killed his parents and begged the judge for mercy because he was an orphan. During the last three years, Lorenzo has stripped Eastern of its most valuable assets and then pleaded poverty because the shrunken structure was losing money" (letter to *Time*, 10 April 1989). We can schematize this argument as follows:

P_1 The young man who killed his parents is related to his judge in the following way: he intentionally created his own bad situation that he is using as the basis for his mercy plea.

P_2 If he intentionally created his own bad situation that he is using as the basis for his mercy plea, then he does not deserve mercy.

P_3 Lorenzo's relation to his bankruptcy court is the same as the young man's relation to his judge.

C Lorenzo does not deserve mercy.

In this argument we can challenge P_3. It may be true that Lorenzo's misfortune, like the young murderer's, is his own doing, but in the latter case there is no one else who would be harmed by a failure to show mercy. This is not so in Lorenzo's case. He is an agent for a company, and a failure to show mercy would result in harm to others. If the airline went out of business, many employees would be laid off and suffer financial hardship. Indeed, it may well be that, as one who is acting for a company at the highest level, Lorenzo will suffer no financial harm at all. Again, this is not true of the young murderer.

Thus, the analogue seems to lack important relevant features of the actual case. That is to say, it is not a satisfactory analogy. Perhaps a better analogy would be this: the young man who has murdered his parents pleads with the judge for mercy on the ground that he has younger siblings who need him at home. Of course, this analogy lacks the power to outrage the hearer, so reliance on it would not persuade anyone to accept the original conclusion. This example illustrates the potential for abuse afforded by arguments that rely on analogy.

Legal argumentation sometimes relies on analogy. In common-law legal systems we try to argue a case by citing precedent. In the easiest cases this can take the form of citing earlier decisions that are similar to the case being tried. To argue for the same verdict is to produce a predictive analogical argument. In harder cases, there will not be any sufficiently similar cases, so that arguments using proportional analogies may be resorted to. Consider this case "in which a steamboat proprietor was held liable for money stolen from a passenger's room. The precedent cited consisted of previous cases in which innkeepers had been held liable for money stolen from the rooms of guests."[19]

In the form given above, the argument is written like this:

P_1 An innkeeper is related to his or her guests in the following way: s/he has contracted to provide secure accomodation for them.

P_2 If an innkeeper has contracted to provide secure accomodation for a guest, then the innkeeper is liable for the loss of guests' money from the accomodation.

P_3 The relationship between proprietors of steamboats and their passengers is the same as that between innkeepers and their guests.

C Proprietors of steamboats are liable for the loss of passengers' money from their accomodation.

The only significant respect in which the analogy here may fail is that proprietors of steamboats contract to provide transportation, rather than accomodation. But this difference seems to be irrelevant, especially when an extended journey is being taken which requires overnight accomodation.

If we schematize arguments relying on proportional analogies in the above fashion, the most likely point of weakness is the analogical claim itself. Evaluating this particular premiss involves thinking of relevant ways in which the analogy is not adequate.

7.6 SYNOPSIS

In this chapter I have, in a sense, tried to do the opposite of identifying inductively fallacious patterns: I have tried to identify the inductively satisfactory patterns that we use. In attempting to provide outlines of these patterns in a systematic way, I have relied heavily on the approach of Ehninger and Brockreide in their *Decision by Debate*. I identified nine patterns (effect to cause, cause to effect, sign, and so on) in terms of the distinctive inference-claim warrant that each depends on. Then I relied on their classification of assertions to identify eight distinctive types. Finally, I reviewed the possible premiss-conclusion combinations that could occur with each inference pattern. Some combinations were rejected because the premiss was irrelevant. Some were set aside because the premisses were judged to be more in doubt than the conclusion. The ones remaining were considered to be useful patterns (to varying degrees) for persuasion.

This chapter is intended to be seen as programmatic. As I have argued elsewhere (Grennan 1991), study of inductively satisfactory argument patterns, in contrast to inductive fallacies, is a seriously neglected area of logic. A review of almost any informal logic or Copi-style text will confirm that most of the patterns outlined here are not discussed. It is hoped that the dissemination of this material will encourage other logicians and rhetoric scholars to do more research on these patterns. After all, they are the ones we rely on in everyday life.

8 Premiss Evaluation

The third step of the recommended argument evaluation procedure is the evaluation of the individual uninferred premisses. The outcome of this step is a rating for each premiss, assigned either directly or by selecting a verbal equivalent from the premiss-rating table (Table 3) given in chapter 3.

8.1 EVALUATION STRATEGIES

At the most general level there are three strategies that might be considered suitable. First, and least satisfactory, is to ask, What supporting information does one have for *P*? or What reasons does one have for accepting *P* as true? This approach is apt to result in the assignment of a rating that is too high, especially when the premiss seems plausible at first sight. This phenomenon has been observed by psychologists, who note that people tend to be overconfident when confidence is high, apparently because we tend to look only for confirming evidence when a claim seems initially plausible. (Baron 1988, 203)

The other side of the logical coin is to follow the "evaluation-by-refutation" strategy, whereby one attempts to refute the premiss, then accepts it if one cannot refute. This has the virtue of encouraging a critical outlook, desirable when evaluators are uncritical. Since a good many novices are less critical than they should be, this advantage is a significant one. On the other hand, the refutational strategy is also somewhat one-sided, not requiring the evaluator to consider favorable evidence. This is apt to result in an inaccurate judgment, skewed downward, given what the evaluator knows. It is also intrinsically adversarial, a deficiency when arguments are introduced in the context of cooperative enterprises. However, research has suggested that if we attempt to refute a claim, our ultimate judgment of its probability is more accurate than if we seek only favourable evidence. (Koriat, Lichtenstein, and Fischoff 1980)

The third strategy is the "pro-con" one. We try to compile both favourable and unfavourable evidence with equal enthusiasm, then decide which set is epistemically "weightier," and to what extent. This is an intrinsically more accurate approach than the first one, in particular. However, as just formulated, it is limited in its practical application because of its generality. Most argument evaluation novices harbour erroneous beliefs about what is relevant to certain types of assertions. When they do, it is not helpful to direct them to rely on the favourable and unfavourable information they have in judging $p(P)$. I will cite two examples from my own experience.

If one asks novices to evaluate the assertion "Either this room is on the second floor or the third floor" when they know they are in a room on the second floor, a significant proportion will say, "This is false because we could be on the first floor." Apparently, they are construing the assertion as intended to exhaust the possibilities, so that citing a third one is seen as a providing a counterexample. Clearly, such a failure to understand the logic of alternations will prevent such people from applying the general strategy successfully when required to evaluate them. To ensure success they need to be given a strategy that is geared to alternations specifically.

A second example is this: if asked to evaluate "The president of the Flat-Earth Society believes Earth is flat," some will say, "This statement is false because Earth is round/spherical." There are several explanations for this error, but in any event, asking such people to weigh the favourable and unfavourable evidence for the claim will not be helpful, since they misunderstand the logic of belief attributions. Again, to ensure accuracy in judging $p(P)$, evaluators need to be given advice specific to this kind of assertion.

I contend, therefore, that to ensure reliability in premiss evaluation, a system must embody the general pro-con strategy tailored to the specific assertion types to be encountered. The task of setting out the main types of assertions and specific strategies for evaluating them is, however, complicated by the fact that there is no single typology that can be seen as correct. One's typology depends on the kind of criteria chosen for distinguishing types. In what follows I shall discuss claims classified along several different dimensions.

8.2 CATEGORICAL CLAIMS

In the last chapter I utilized the Ehninger and Brockreide claim classification to develop the following classification of categorical claims:

1 Obligation claims, expressible in the form "*S* must (must not) do *A*."
2 Supererogatory claims, expressible in the form "*S* ought (ought not) to do *A*."
3 Prudential claims, expressible in the form "*S* ought (ought not) to do *A*."
4 Evaluative claims. Grading claims are expressible in the form "x_1 is a $G(X)$." Ranking claims are expressible in the form "x_1 is an $R(X)$." Comparison claims are expressible in the form "x_1 is a $C(X)$ than x_2."
5 Physical-world claims, expressible in a variety of ways. They report either empirical or institutional states of affairs or events.
6 Mental-world claims, expressible in the form "*S* is *M*," where *M* is a mental predicate and *S* normally refers to a person or group of persons.
7 Constitutive-rule claims, which involve definitions and other necessary truths and falsehoods.
8 Regulative-rule claims, expressible as "*A* is obligatory" or "*A* is prohibited." These claims may represent either enacted or unenacted rules.

As argued above, I advocate the pro-con approach to uninferred premiss evaluation: we identify all of the facts we can that are relevant to a premiss, both favourable and unfavourable, then intuitively weigh them to arrive at a value for $p(P)$. In what follows I attempt to identify the types of facts that are favourably and unfavourably relevant to each of the above types of claim.

Part of the task of identifying forms of favourable evidence has already been done. Each of the different conclusions in the argument-patterns set out in the last chapter can be thought of as a claim and their premisses as favourably relevant items of evidence for them. However, to provide a more comprehensive treatment, I will also include indirect evidence, that is, the types of claims that serve as backing for the direct evidence. For example, direct evidence for "Sam must be home by 6:00 P.M. on the 23rd" could be "Sam promised to take his wife to the opera on the 23rd." Indirect evidence for it is "Sam said to his wife three weeks ago 'If you get the opera tickets for the 23rd, I'll take you.'"

The same claim types that can be favourable evidence for any particular type can also be exemplified as unfavourably relevant claims. This is because the negative counterpart of an affirmative claim is of the same type as the affirmative, and unfavorably relevant claims for a claim C are favourably relevant claims for the negation of C. For example, physical-world claims are favourably relevant to mental-world claims. For example, "Sam has turned red" is favourably relevant to "Sam is embarrassed." Thus, there are potential unfavourably relevant physical-world claims for any mental-world claim. For example, "Nothing has been said that would embarrass Sam" is unfavourably relevant to, or undermines, "Sam is embarrassed."

8.2.1 *Obligation Claims*

Obligation claims can be expressed in the form "S must (must not) do A." Claims of the following kinds are especially relevant:

1 Claims reporting obligations based on a sampling of those referred to in the original claim. "Seventy percent of the 100 15-year-olds polled must not be out later than 10:00 P.M. on week nights" is favourably relevant to "Most 15-year-olds must not be out later than 10:00 P.M. on week nights." But "Thirty percent of the 100 15-year-olds polled must not be out later than 10:00 P.M. on week nights" is unfavourably relevant.

2 Claims reporting obligations of observed individual(s) of the class referred to in the original claim. "Most professors in Canada must teach three courses each term" is favourably relevant to "Professors at Dalhousie University must teach three courses each term." "The more research-oriented universities in Canada tend to require a lesser teaching load" is unfavourably relevant.

3 Claims attributing obligations to the individual referred to in the original claim, which are obligations that can be met by meeting the obligation mentioned in the original claim. "Sam must allow the security guard to inspect his luggage" is favourably relevant to "Sam must unlock his suitcase." "Sam must ensure that the classified documents he is carrying are not read by anyone" is unfavourably relevant.

4 Evaluative claims. "In this situation, Q-KB7 is the best move" is favourably relevant to "The move you must make is Q-KB7." Unfavourably relevant is any move that may actually be better.

5 Physical-world claims, institutional or purely physical, that have a bearing on the conduct specified in the original claim. "The streets are very icy" is favourably relevant to "Sam must not drive his daughter to the movies." "Sam promised to drive his daughter to the movies" is unfavourably relevant.

6 Mental-world claims that either attribute a mental predicate to the referent of the original claim, or to someone else. "Sam dislikes people of Jones's race" is favourably relevant to "Sam must not accept a place on the jury." "Sam is not aware of any of the evidence to be presented in the case" is unfavourably relevant.

7 Regulative-rule claims that apply to the act mentioned in the original obligation claim. "Turning right on a red light is prohibited" is favourably relevant to "I must not turn right while this light is red." "Turning right on a red light is permissible" is unfavourably relevant.

8.2.2 *Supererogatory Claims*

Supererogatory claims are expressible in the form "*S* ought (ought not) to do *A*." Claims of the following kinds are relevant:

1 Other supererogatory claims of the form "*S* ought to do *B*," where *B* is an effective means for *S* to do *A*. For example, someone might say to me, "You ought to make a generous contribution to the United Way campaign." To persuade me in the event that I do not readily agree, that person could add, "Because you ought to support the local agencies that provide financial and psychological help for people in the area." "I have been out of work for a month" is unfavourably relevant.

2 Evaluative claims. For example, someone might say to me, "You ought to make a generous contribution to the United Way campaign." To persuade me in the event that I do not readily agree, that person could add, "Because it is the best way of helping the needy in this area." Unfavourably relevant is any claim that specifies a better way to help the needy.

3 Physical-world claims. In general, supererogatory claims entail a claim that someone needs help. The kind of evidence exemplified here serves as an explanation of the need for the help. "We ought to buy the children across the street some toys for Christmas, because their parents cannot afford to get them much" is an example. Unfavourably relevant is any claim reporting a negative outcome of the supererogatory act, such as "Doing this would be very embarrassing for the parents."

4 Mental-World claims. Example: "We ought to take your aunt for a Sunday drive. She is fed up with staying at home." Unfavourably relevant is any claim reporting a negative outcome of any act. In this case, "She will do nothing but complain" is unfavourably relevant.

8.2.3 *Prudential Claims*

Relevant claims that serve as backing for prudential claims, which can be expressed in the form "*S* ought (ought not) to do *A*," include

1 Obligation claims reflecting the existence of prior obligations that restrict or permit acting in self-interest. For example, I obtain confidential information that my company has landed a large contract and that this will be announced tomorrow. I think, "I ought to buy some company shares today." "I must provide for my family" is favourably relevant. On the other hand, "I must not take unfair advantage of other share traders," is unfavourably relevant.

2 Supererogatory claims that the act mentioned in the prudential claim help to make possible or impossible. For example, the claim "Physicians ought to treat highway accident victims when they encounter an accident while driving," is a good reason to support the claim "Physicians ought to carry their medical bag in their car." Unfavourably relevant supererogatory claims are ones that advise actions in the interests of others when one cannot act on the advice to further one's own interests without precluding acting in the interest of another. Altruism conflicts with selfish or self-benefiting acts. For example, "You ought to give the $5000 you won to your church" counts against "I ought to use the $5000 to get a newer car."

3 Other prudential claims that can be seen as advice implemented by the advice given in the original claim. For example, a reason in support of the claim "Canadians ought to eat fewer animal fats" is the claim "They ought to avoid heart disease." "Canadians ought to support the Canadian beef cattle industry" is unfavourably relevant.

4 Evaluative claims that provide a rationale for or against the original prudential claim. For example, if I know someone is in the market for a medium-priced sedan, I might say, "You ought to get a Honda Accord." If asked to justify this claim, I might say, "It is an excellent medium-priced sedan." Unfavourably relevant evaluative claims either (i) represent a negative grading judgment of something (an object, a state of affairs, an event) recommended in a prudential claim, or (ii) a negative ranking of such a "thing," or (iii) an unfavourable comparison of that "thing" with something else. For example, "A Jaguar is quite unreliable" counts against "I ought to get a Jaguar as my next car."

5 Physical-world claims that describe a situation for which the action advised in the prudential claim is a rational response. For example, I say to my walking companion, "We ought to walk around the pond rather than cross on the ice." In support of this recommendation I

might say, "The ice is too thin to carry us." Unfavourably relevant physical-world claims represent states of affairs that undermine the value of the action advocated in the prudential claim. For example, the claim "We ought to sail your boat from Halifax to Bermuda and back in July" is undermined by the claim "July is the start of the hurricane season."

6 Mental-world claims, especially those that report the existence of a desire that might be satisfied by doing A. For example, the claim "We ought to turn left here" is supported by the claim "We want to take the shortest route home." Unfavourably relevant mental-world claims undermine the value or appropriateness of the action advocated in the prudential claim. For example, the claim "We ought to have a drink before heading home" is undermined by the claim "My wife is expecting me home at the usual time."

7 Regulative-rule claims are relevant because we often have to pursue our goals within a framework of rules. For example: "You ought to report this extra income on your tax return." "Why?" "Because it is legally obligatory to do so." Unfavourably relevant claims exclude, or make questionable, a proposed course of action as immoral, illegal, and so forth. For example, a fellow employee says to me, "We ought to buy company shares today, a big contract award will be announced tomorrow." This claim is undermined by the fact that insider trading is legally prohibited.

8.2.4 *Evaluative Claims*

As noted in the last chapter, there are three kinds of evaluative claims: gradings, rankings, and comparisons. In what follows I will give examples of favourably and unfavourably relevant claims for each type of evaluative claim, in the context of listing the different kinds of claims that are relevant. Relevant to evaluative claims are claims of the following kinds:

1 Other evaluative claims that refer to a sample of the class of things referred to in the original claim. A statistically expressed evaluative claim about a total population is supported or undermined by another such claim that is based on a representative sample.

Grading-claim example: "30% of the apples in this box are Grade A" is favourably relevant to "30% of the entire crop is Grade A." On the other hand, it is undermined by "20% of the apples selected at random from 100 boxes are Grade A."

Ranking-claim example: "These peaches from tree 79 are the best in the orchard" is favourably relevant to "The peaches on tree 79 are the best in the orchard." On the other hand, it is undermined by "These randomly selected peaches from tree 79 are only average quality."

Comparison-claim example: "The students in introductory psychology at Ivy College are more intelligent (on average) than the ones taking that course at Enormous State University (ESU)" is favourably relevant to "Students at Ivy College are more intelligent (on average) than those at ESU." On the other hand, the claim is undermined by "The students in introductory psychology at ESU are more intelligent (on average) than the ones taking that course at Ivy College."

2 Other evaluative claims that refer to observed instances of the thing(s) referred to in the original claim.

Grading-claim example: "Most policemen in Canada are good marksmen" is favourably relevant to "Most policemen in my town are good marksmen." On the other hand, the claim is undermined by "Most policemen in Canada are only average marksmen."

Ranking-claim example (1): "Freshmen from that high school are, on average, the best we get" is favourably relevant to "The freshmen coming from that school next year will be the best."

Ranking-claim example (2): "George, entering our university from high school X, will do well here" is undermined by "Students from high school X have, in the past, been average performers here."

Comparison-claim example (1): "Observed bear cubs raised in the wild flourish better there than ones raised in captivity" is favourably relevant to "That cub living with its mother in the wild will flourish better there than this orphaned one here at the zoo."

Comparison-claim example (2): "Observed bear cubs raised in the wild flourish better there than ones raised in captivity" undermines "The orphaned cub in our zoo will be fine when released in the wild as an adult."

3 Evaluative claims that refer to a parallel case of the same kind as the referent in the original claim.

Grading-claim example: "The peach I just ate was delicious" is favourably relevant to "This peach from the same basket will be delicious." On the other hand, "The peach I just ate was sour" undermines it.

Ranking-claim example: "Lendl, who is eligible to enter any of the top tennis tournaments, is one of the ten best players in the world" is favourably relevant to "MacInroe, who is also eligible, is one of the ten best players in the world." On the other hand, "Connors, who is also eligible to enter any of the top tennis tournaments, is not one of the ten best players in the world," undermines it.

Comparison-claim example: "The peach from the red basket was tastier than the one from the blue basket" is favourably relevant to "This peach from the red basket will be tastier than this one from the blue basket." However, "The peach from the red basket was tastier than the one from the blue basket" undermines it.

4 Physical-world claims that attribute good-making qualities to the referent of the evaluative claim.

Grading-claim example: "The Jaguar sedan accelerates and decelerates quickly" is favourably relevant to "The Jaguar is a great luxury performance sedan." However, "The Jaguar has inadequate cornering power" undermines it.

Ranking-claim example: "In the luxury performance sedan category, the Jaguar is second-best in acceleration" is favourably relevant to "The Jaguar is one of the top three cars in this category." On the other hand, "The Jaguar has only the seventh-highest cornering power" undermines it.

Comparison-claim example: "Graf has beaten Navratilova in most of their matches in the past year" is favourably relevant to "Graf is currently a better tennis player than Navratilova." On the other hand, "Navratilova has beaten Graf as often as Graf has beaten her this year" undermines it.

5 Mental-world claims that predicate valuable mental qualities of the referent of the evaluative claim.

Grading-claim example: "Sam likes women as persons" is favourably relevant to "Sam is good marriage material." On the other hand, "Sam prefers the company of men" undermines it.

Ranking-claim example: "Gorbachev is one of the shrewdest and most politically knowledgeable Russians" is favourably relevant to "Gorbachev was one of the best Russian leaders." However, "Gorbachev wanted to preserve the USSR" perhaps undermines it.

Comparison-claim example: "Sam knows more about the company's product line than Marvin" is favourably relevant to "Sam is a better candidate for promotion than Marvin." But "Sam is not as enthusiastic about the company's product line as Marvin" undermines it.

6 Regulative-rule claims in which the act referred to in the evaluative claim is said to be obligatory or prohibited.

Grading-claim example: "Corporal punishment of older children is permitted" is favourably relevant to "Corporal punishment is a good approach to molding childrens' behaviour," whereas "Corporal punishment of two-year-old children is morally prohibited" undermines it.

Ranking-claim example: "Rewarding for good behaviour is morally permissible" is favourably relevant to "Positive reinforcement is the best way of molding children's behaviour," whereas "Bribery is morally prohibited" undermines it.

Comparison-claim example: "Child abuse is morally prohibited" is favourably relevant to "Corporal punishment of children is as bad as child abuse," whereas "Corporal punishment of children is morally permitted" undermines it.

8.2.5 *Physical-World Claims*

Physical-world claims have the general form "*X* is *F*." Since their truth or falsity is independent of human desires and rules, favourably and unfavourably relevant propositions are either other physical-world propositions or mental-world propositions. These include the following:

1 Claims about a sample of the population referred to in the original claim. For example, "10% of the students in my logic class are left-handed" is favourably relevant to "10% of the human population is left-handed," but "20% of the students in my logic class are left-handed" undermines it.

2 Claims about observed members of a class of things that are relevant to a claim about another individual (or group) of that class. For example, "10% of all those whose hand preference has been noted favour their left" is favourably relevant to "10% of those in my logic class are left-handed," whereas "20% of all those whose hand preference has been noted favor their left" undermines it.

3 Claims about another individual of the same kind as the individual referred to in the original claim where the individuals are similar in other relevant respects. For example, "Alvin, Edgar's twin, is excitable" is favourably relevant to "Edgar is excitable," whereas "Their brother Elmar is phlegmatic" undermines it.

4 Claims that might report the cause of the event/state reported in the original claim, or claims that might represent a cause of a different event/state outcome from that reported in the original claim. For example, "The fog is getting thicker at the airport" is favourably relevant to "Our flight will be delayed," whereas "The aircraft has arrived from its previous stop" undermines it.

5 Claims that might be a causal sign of a state/event reported by the original claim or of a different state/event. For example, "The sky is clearing" is favourably relevant to "We will have a fine day tomorrow," but "The wind has shifted toward the east" is unfavourably relevant.

6 Claims that might report the effect of an event/state reported in the original claim, or of a different event/state. For example, "Business bankruptcies increased again last month" is favourably relevant to

"The economic recession is continuing," whereas "The monthly value of machine tool orders has increased" undermines it.

7   Mental-world claims that can be regarded as an individual's (or a group's) reason for the act reported in the original claim or some act incompatible with it. For example, "Sam has a toothache" is favourably relevant to "Sam won't be good company at dinner tonight," but "Sam is in a good mood today" undermines it.

8   Mental-world claims that can be regarded as having a sign-event relationship to the original claim or a relationship incompatible with it. For example, "Canadians are fed up with their prime minister" is favourably relevant to "The party in power will lose the next election," but "The main opposition party is not well thought of" undermines it.

9   Mental-world claims that might serve as an explanation of an act/state reported in the original claim or ones that explain an act/state incompatible with it. For example, "Suzy is sad" is favourably relevant to "Suzy did not get the job she was interviewed for last week," but "Suzy has been in a good mood the last few days" undermines it.

8.2.6 *Mental-World Claims*

Mental-world claims can be expressed in the form "S is M." The following claim types are relevant:

1   Mental-world claims about a sample of the group of persons referred to in the original claim. For example, "Most of the players I talked to are unhappy about their coach being fired" is favourably relevant to "Most players on the team are unhappy about the coach being fired," but "Most players interviewed by the other reporter feel it was time for a change" is unfavourably relevant.

2   Mental-world claims about observed instances of the class of persons to which the individual (or group) referred to in the original claim belong. For example, "Most Canadian college freshmen interviewed feel insecure" is favourably relevant to "Suzy, a freshman here, feels insecure," whereas "Most Canadian college freshmen interviewed feel confident" undermines it.

3   Mental-world claims that represent a parallel case. For example, "Jill's friend Joan is upset with her" is favourably relevant to "Jill's friend, June, is probably upset with her." However, "Jill's friend Jane is happy for her" undermines it.

4   Obligation claims attributing an obligation to the person referred to in the original claim. For example, "Sam must apologize to Sue tonight" is favourably relevant to "Sam is apprehensive about the dinner party tonight," whereas "Sam must visit his sick mother tonight" undermines it.

5   Evaluative claims that can represent an explanation for the original claim. For example, "Sam had a good round of golf today" is favourably relevant to "Sam will be in a good mood tonight," whereas "Sam had a poor round of golf today" is unfavourably relevant.

6   Evaluative claims that might, or might not, be explained by the original claim. For example, "Sam is playing well today" is favourably relevant to "Sam is concentrating well today," whereas "Sam is playing poorly today" is unfavourably relevant.

7   Physical-world claims that might, or might not, produce the mental state reported in the original claim. For example, "Sam burned the steaks" is favourably relevant to "Sam's wife will be angry with him," whereas "Sam is going to give his wife an expensive present tonight" undermines it.

8   Physical-world claims that might be a sign of the state of affairs reported in the original claim, or a sign of something incompatible with that state of affairs. For example, "Sam's gaze is wandering" is favourably relevant to "Sam is bored by his wife's story," but "Sam is grinning" undermines it.

9   Physical-world claims that might be evidence for or against the mental state reported in the original claim. For example, "The Israelis continue to let Jews settle in the West Bank area" is favourably relevant to "The Israelis do not intend to allow the West Bank to be a Palestinian homeland." "A willingness to discuss the future of the West Bank" is unfavourably relevant.

10 Regulative-rule claims of two kinds: claims that S believes that s/he must do (refrain from doing) A, and claims that S (or a group) believes that A is desirable (undesirable) conduct. An example of the first kind: "Exceeding 50 kph past my house is legally prohibited" is favourably relevant to "My neighbors believe that exceeding 50 kph past my house is prohibited." "Exceeding 70 kph past my house is legally prohibited" is unfavourably relevant to it. An example of the second kind: "Exceeding 70 kph past my house is legally prohibited" is favourably relevant to "My neighbors believe that refraining from exceeding 70 kph past my house is desirable." "Exceeding 50 kph past my house is prohibited" undermines it.

8.2.7 *Constitutive-Rule Claims*

Constitutive-rule can be written in the form "D counts as W" or "D constitutes W" or "'D' means the same as 'W,'" where D represents a definition of W. Relevant claims include

1 Physical-world claims of the form "Things that are describable as D are called W's." For example, "Women who have never married are

called spinsters" is favourably relevant to " 'Spinster' means the same as 'a woman who has never married.' " "Unmarried women are called spinsters" is unfavourably relevant.

2 Physical-world claims of the form "In the rules of I, D counts as W," where I is an institution constituted by rules. For example, "The rules of golf state 'a swing intended to strike the ball counts as a stroke' " is favourably relevant to "A swing intended to strike a ball counts as a stroke." "The rules of golf state 'a swing intended to strike a ball in play counts as a stroke' " is unfavourably relevant.

3 Mental-world claims that can be written as "Speakers of the language L believe that 'W' means the same as 'D.' " For example, "Speakers of English believe that 'bachelor' means the same as 'a man who has never married' " is favourably relevant to " 'Bachelor' means the same as 'a man who has never married.' " "Speakers of English believe that 'bachelor' means the same as 'unmarried man' " is unfavourably relevant.

8.2.8 Regulative-Rule Claims

Regulative-rule claims can be written as "A is prohibited" or "A is obligatory." Relevant claims include

1 Other regulative-rule claims about a sample of the referent of the original claim. For example, "Half the people over seventy-five at the seniors complex are prohibited from driving" is favourably relevant to "Half the people over seventy-five are prohibited from driving." On the other hand, "None of the people over seventy-five living in my apartment building are prohibited from driving" is unfavourably relevant.

2 Other regulative-rule claims about observed instances of the kind referred to in the original claim. For example, "Two-thirds of the u.s. states require the use of car seatbelts" is favourably relevant to "Six of the nine most populous states require the use of car seatbelts." On the other hand, "One-third of the u.s. states require the use of car seatbelts" is unfavourably relevant.

3 Other regulative-rule claims about acts that are parallel cases to those mentioned in the original claim. For example, "Copying chapters of novels without permission is legally prohibited" is favourably relevant to "Copying chapters of textbooks without permission is legally prohibited." However, "Copying sections of newspapers is legally permissible" is unfavourably relevant.

4 Other regulative-rule claims referring to acts related to the act mentioned in the original claim. For example, "Theft of information is prohibited" is favourably relevant to "Copying chapters from text-

books is prohibited." On the other hand, "Acquiring information for educational purposes is permissible" undermines it.

5 Obligation claims of the form "As an X, S must (must not) do A." For example, "Sam must remove his spiked golf shoes before entering the golf club bar" is favourably relevant to "Entering the bar wearing spiked shoes is prohibited." On the other hand, "Sam is permitted to wear his golf shoes in the bar" is unfavourably relevant.

6 Physical-world claims, when the original claim cites a rule based on a statute/enactment. For example, "Section 309(1) of the Criminal Code of Canada specifies that the possession of burglary tools under suspicious circumstances is an offence" is favourably relevant to "Possession of burglary tools is legally prohibited in Canada." But "There is no article in the Criminal Code pertaining to possession of burglary tools" is unfavourably relevant.

7 Claims about people's behaviour, when the original claim cites an un-enacted rule. For example, "In Britain, people queue when waiting for buses" is favourably relevant to "In Britain, queueing for buses is morally obligatory." However, "People who improve their positions in a bus queue are not criticized for doing so" is unfavourably relevant.

8 Physical-world claims that members of a society regularly censure those who engage in a particular form of behaviour. For example, "Local people clamoured for the laying of charges when a man dropped a kitten from a fourth-floor window for amusement" is favourably relevant to "Harming animals for amusement is prohibited here." On the other hand, "There was no indignation when someone dropped a snake from a fourth-floor window for amusement" is unfavourably relevant.

9 Mental-world claims attributing beliefs about A being prohibited, obligatory, or permissible. For example, "Experienced golfers believe that a player may not change balls during a game" is favourably relevant to "Changing balls during a hole is prohibited." However, "Many golfers believe that a player can change balls at any time during a hole" is unfavourably relevant.

8.3 GENERALIZATIONS

Most of the nine types of claim discussed in chapter 7 can take general as well as singular forms. Generalizations can be classified in three groups: (1) universal, (2) qualified, and (3) non-qualified.

8.3.1 Universal Generalizations

Universal generalizations are inclusionary (All S's are F) or exclusionary (No S's are F). The exclusionary version is equivalent to "All S's are not F," so we can write all universal generalizations in the form "All S's are ..."

Assigning a $p(P)$ value can often be straightforward because if we can identify a clear counterexample, we know that $p(P)$ = o. Thus, if I were to say "All members of my logic class are right-handed," this statement could be shown to be false by a left-handed person identifying himself as such. However, even when all the S's known to us are F, we can regard the generalization as true only when it is highly likely that there is no prospect of counterexamples being discovered. When there is such a possibility, we must assign a lower value, depending on how large a sample we think the observed S's represent.

For example, suppose someone claims "All swans are white." The evidence relied on might be "All the swans I have seen are white," or even "All the swans seen by everyone I know are white." The second claim is better evidence because it is probable that it is based on a larger percentage of existing swans. But even so, the percentage is low, leaving a lot of room for possible counterexamples. For centuries Europeans were willing to claim that all swans were white – until black ones were found in Australia.

When no counterexamples can be identified, the evaluator can best proceed by asking "What is the probability of finding a counterexample?" For example, faced with the claim "All humans with AIDS die within three years of contracting it," we might not know of a counterexample, but figure that the probability of finding one with a thorough search is 10%, based on our knowledge that there are always people who confound the medical experts with their resistance to disease. Thus, we would make $p(P)$ = o.9.

8.3.2 Qualified Generalizations

Qualified generalizations are prefixed by a modifying term other than "all" or "no" or their synonyms. In English there are quite a few nonnumerical expressions that we may employ to tailor the strength of our claims to the known evidence. There seem to be two kinds, claims referring to a proportion of a class and claims referring (however vaguely) to quantities. Among the former we have "Nearly all S's are F," "Most S's are F," "Most S's are not F," "Almost no S's are F," and so on. Among the latter we have "Many S's are F" and "A few S's are F."

8.3.2.1 *Proportional Qualifiers.* Evaluating generalizations that have proportional qualifiers is tricky because the generalizations are quite vague. In what follows I shall try to give some guidance for each of the forms just mentioned, leaving it to the reader to extend the advice to other expressions.

The form "Nearly all S's are F" entails that not all S's are F. The upper limit of proportion, then, is "under 100%." There is obviously no precise lower limit, so in picking a figure one must rely on one's linguistic intuitions. Perhaps 90% is appropriate, since 80% seems a bit low. So we "define" the range for this form as "At least 90% of S's are F, but less than 100% are F." The most appropriate form for refuting a claim of this form is one phrased as "less than N% of S's are F," where N is a value distinctly below 90%. Because of the vagueness, I would not consider 80% to be a clearly refuting value. Intuitively, it seems that "Nearly all S's are F" is clearly refuted when it has been shown that at least 25% of S's are not F.

The form "Almost no S's are F" seems to be the logical contrary of "Nearly all S's are F" since the latter seems to be synonymous with "Almost all S's are F." Thus, it can be clearly refuted by showing that at least 25% of S's are F. For example, if someone claims that "In Canada almost no law school graduates are women," this claim could be considered disproved by the true claim that "More than 25% of law school graduates are women."

The expression "Most S's are F" is, if anything, vaguer than the ones just discussed. It is not clear that it is a contrary of "Almost all S's are F." It would be inaccurate to say that "Most airline crashes are caused by pilot error" when almost all are caused by pilot error, but, on the other hand, the latter (if true) does not seem to clearly refute the former. "Most S's are F" does seem to be a contrary of "All S's are F," since the former recognizes the existence of S's that are not F. Furthermore, "Most S's are F" contradicts "Less than half of S's are F," showing that the lower limit of "Most S's are F" is "More than half of S's are F." Thus, we are able to say only that "Most S's are F" means that more than 50% but less than 100% of S's are F. Its contradictory, "Most S's are not F," therefore, means "More than 0% and less than 50% of S's are F."

This discussion of conditions of refutation for the four selected qualifiers is, I think, theoretically sound. However, it does not represent a very practical means for evaluating these kinds of claims, because we are frequently not in a position to know what proportion of S's are F. To know such a thing, strictly speaking, requires observation of all S's, and the class in question may be a large one, even an indefinitely large one. The most obvious practical solution is to rely on a representative sample, normally one selected by some expert such as the government or a social scientist or a professional pollster. When our sample is representative, Table 29 applies.

Table 29
Proportional Qualifier Refutations

Assertion	Refuted by
Nearly all S's are F.	At least 1/4 of observed S's are not F.
Almost no S's are F.	At least 1/4 of observed S's are F.
Most S's are F.	Less than 1/2 of observed S's are F.
Most S's are not F.	More than 1/2 of observed S's are F.

In relying on prior experience in evaluating these kinds of assertions, we are relying on a sample of S's, and if we are to be accurate in our judgments, the sample must be representative of the class of S's. How do we know when it is? In gathering samples, experts can proceed in one of two ways. One way is to select S's randomly. For example, to conduct a poll by phone, we could pick phone numbers out of the phone book by calling the first number at the top of each column on each page. Since there is no principle that is used to determine whose number is at the top of a column, this is a random procedure. However, there is a danger of sample-selection bias here.

Suppose we wanted to poll women on the question of whether they favour abortion on demand. We use the phone number selection procedure just described, calling only residences. We set aside the male respondents and females under 19. We make our calls in the daytime. We get answers from 1000 women. Is our sample representative? There is a distinct possibility it is not. About half the women in this country have jobs outside the home. Many of those who do not are older women, or younger ones who have chosen to be homemakers, perhaps because they have a number of children. These people are more likely to oppose abortion on demand than younger women who work. But of course our survey does not reach the employed people. A more representative sample would be obtained by calling in the evening.

To be representative, a sample must involve no selection bias. In addition, it must be large enough to avoid an accidental bias. If we are considering buying a particular kind of car, we might ask people we see in the local shopping mall parking lot if they have had any problems driving this kind of car. Suppose we encounter five of them and they all report trouble-free experience. Unanimity is always impressive, so we might judge the car to be reliable. But it may be that all but one of these people drove their vehicles very few kilometers per year, whereas we would drive ours much farther. Since reliability is partly a function of mileage, we might be misled. A larger sample might have included more owners who drive as much as we do.

When we make judgments about generalizations by relying on our experience, we are usually relying on small samples. If we choose not to gather more evidence, we need to ask ourselves if there are any biases built into the sample we have. We can avoid errors arising from selection bias by relying only on paradigm, or typical, cases. If we have the concept of an S, we are thereby equipped with the ability to distinguish the typical S from things that are not.

It is obvious, of course, that a single ordinary counterexample cannot refute a qualified assertion such as "most physicians are rich." On the other hand, if we are acquainted with the standard of living of several physicians who seem typical of the group and we regard them as being "comfortable" rather than rich, we have a basis for assigning $p(P)$ a relatively low value. Accuracy in particular cases depends on having identified genuinely typical cases. The general assumptions being relied upon in making such inferences require classifying cases as being of three kinds: (1) typical cases, for example, the middle-aged nonspecializing physician who has an average client load; (2) clear instances that are not typical, by virtue of lacking an attribute necessary for being typical, for example, a physician just beginning practice; (3) borderline instances, those for which there are reasons for not counting them as members of a class, as well as reasons for counting them as members, for example, people with physician qualifications who teach in medical schools but do not practise.

When we claim to have refuted an assertion of the form "Almost all S's are F" by citing typical cases of S's that are not F, we are assuming that there are more individuals in the typical group than in either of the other two. If more than one-third of S's are not F, the generalization is false.

In the case of "Most S's are F" the assumption being relied on is that more than half the class members are typical cases. This is a less defensible assumption, but it is often acceptable. Many classes are relatively homogeneous, especially "natural kinds" classes such as cats, roses, gold, and so forth. Some are clearly not homogeneous, such as Wittgenstein's example, games.[1] While we may, with some diffidence, want to claim that there are typical board games (Monopoly?) and typical athletic games (soccer?), we seem to recognize that there is no typical game per se. Nonetheless, if all, or a high proportion of the typical cases of S's that we have encountered are counterexamples to a proportionally qualified generalization, we have good grounds for giving the premiss a low rating.

Table 30
Nonproportional Qualifier Relationships

Assertion Form	*Refuted by*
Many *S*'s are *F*	Few *S*'s are *F*
	No *S*'s are *F*
Few *S*'s are *F*	Many *S*'s are *F*
	No *S*'s are *F*
Some *S*'s are *F*	No *S*'s are *F*

8.3.2.2 *Nonproportional Qualifiers.* Other qualifying expressions that prefix qualified generalizations include "many," "a few," and "some." These expressions do not seem to refer, even vaguely, to proportions of classes. If they did, "many Americans" and "many Canadians" would refer to groups much different in size, since Americans outnumber Canadians ten to one. But they do not seem to refer to groups much different in size. One million Canadians can be said to be "many Canadians," but one million Americans can be said to be "many Americans" too.

It does seem clear that "Many *S*'s are *F*" and "A few *S*'s are *F*" are contraries, the truth of one entailing the falsity of the other. This seems to be because "many" is synonymous with "a large number of" and "a few" is synonymous with "a small number of." But the synonyms also reveal why they are only contraries and not contradictories. If "A large number of *S*'s are *F*" is false, this falsity is compatible with "A small number of *S*'s are *F*" but also with "No *S*'s are *F*," which contradicts "A few *S*'s are *F*." Conversely, if "A small number of *S*'s are *F*" is false, this falsity is compatible with "A large number of *S*'s are *F*," and also with "No *S*'s are *F*."

The term "some" is even vaguer than the other two. "Some *S*'s are *F*" is compatible with "many *S*'s are *F*," "Few *S*'s are *F*," and even "Some *S*'s are not *F*." "No *S*'s are *F*" is a contradictory, providing the only definite refutational move that might be available. Unfortunately, assertions of this latter form are universal generalizations, which are difficult to sustain in many cases. Consider "Some humans have telekinetic powers." It is not practically feasible to refute this by showing that no human has such power. Fortunately, we can proceed by identifying those whose behaviour serves to back the premiss, then regarding it as of low probability if they do not exhibit genuine telekinetic powers. Table 30 summarizes the clear relationships between "few," "many," and "some" and their refutations.

8.3.3 *Non-Qualified Generalizations*

Very few applied logic texts discuss strategies for dealing with premisses of the form "*S*'s are *F*," yet assertions of this form are at least as common as overtly qualified generalizations. It is also common for critics to treat these assertions as logically equivalent to universal generalizations. It may be correct to do so in the case of some utterances, but frequently speakers do not intend their utterances to have a suppressed "all" prefixing it, as is made clear on occasions when counterexamples are brought forward and the speaker clarifies the original utterance by adding a qualifier rather than recognizing a refutation. The clarification usually takes the form of a qualifier such as "*In general, S*'s are *F*" or "*The typical S is an F*," or "*Most S*'s are *F*."

The frequency with which people protest that they "did not mean" that all *S*'s are *F* makes it appropriate to be charitable in evaluating non-qualified generalizations. This charity should take the form of treating the utterance as a qualified generalization with a suppressed qualifier. But what qualifying expression should we "read in"?

There seem to be two different kinds of expression that could be read in. One kind can be seen in the following exchange:

Sam. Cats aren't very friendly pets.
Hiram. My cat Felix is pretty friendly.
Sam. But he's a Siamese.

In this case the response to the counterexample suggests that "*S*'s are *F*" should be regarded as a shortened version of "The typical *S* is an *F*," or "Typically, *S*'s are *F*." Sam's response suggests that he thinks there is something abnormal, untypical, about Felix by virtue of his being a Siamese.

The second kind of qualifier that can be imputed arises from exchanges like this:

Suzy. Cats aren't very friendly pets.
Heloise. Ed's cat Muffin is friendly.
Suzy. Well, there are some exceptions.

Here Suzy is not suggesting that Muffin is untypical. Rather, she is implying that she meant "Most cats aren't very friendly pets" or "Generally cats aren't very friendly pets."

The identity of the qualifier being suppressed ought to be a matter of arguer testimony. If the arguer is not available, the evaluator selects one on the arguer's behalf, depending on which of the two dialogues might be most likely to occur if the arguer were present and challenged.

8.4 ALTERNATIONS (DISJUNCTIONS)

In what follows I shall discuss the simplest form of the alternation, the one with only two disjuncts: "Either *A* or *B*." Here "*A*" and "*B*" stand for propositions that are not individually asserted. That is, if I say "Either my logic class is the largest philosophy class, or it is the second-largest philosophy class," I am not asserting that this class is the largest philosophy class. Nor am I saying that it is the second-largest. The characteristic use of alternations is to convey information when it is not clear which proposition ought to be accepted, based on the evidence.[2]

Alternation premises of the form "Either *A* or *B*" are true when at least one alternate is true. Sometimes both alternates are true, that is, they are inclusive. In such cases the assertion could have been expressed in the form "Either *A* and/or *B*." For example, the nonfinancial requirements for a student loan where I live can be stated as "Either you are not living in your parents' home or you are enrolled in a postgraduate degree program." Sam has his own apartment and is doing a BA, so only the first proposition is true of him. Only the second is true of Sally, because she lives with her parents but is enrolled in the BEd program (a postgraduate one). But both are true of Eloise because she is in the MBA program and has her own apartment.

More commonly, the alternates are exclusive. If one is true the other is not, and vice versa. For example, suppose it is late and two people are walking toward a bus stop to catch the bus. One observes an oncoming bus in the distance and says "Either we get this bus or we walk home." Obviously, they will not be able to ride the bus and walk home, so only one of the two propositions is true. On the other hand, the alternation itself is false if there happens to be another bus.

The procedure for obtaining ratings for premises of the form "Either *A* or *B*" depends on the following probability rule:

$$p(A \text{ or } B) = p(A) + p(B) - p(A\&B)$$

Now we can calculate $p(A\&B)$ in two ways:

$$p(A\&B) = p(A) \times p(B/A), \text{ or}$$
$$p(A\&B) = p(B) \times p(A/B).$$

Since $p(A\&B) = p(B\&A)$, it does not matter which way we do it. I will use the first version in what follows. We can now write

$$p(P) = p(A \text{ or } B) = p(A) + p(B) - p(A) \times p(B/A).$$

In using the equation, four distinct situations can arise, and our procedure must reflect this.

1 A and B are exhaustive: if there are no other possibilities that deserve a rating of at least 0.1, then regardless of what values $p(A)$ and $p(B)$ have, we can say that $p(A \text{ or } B) = 1.0$. Thus, we do not have to bother assigning values to A and B individually. However, a deliberate effort needs to be made to try to identify another plausible alternative. Otherwise, if there is one, we will have overrated the premiss.

2 A and B are exclusive: if A and B cannot be true at the same time, $p(A\&B) = 0$, so we can calculate $p(A \text{ or } B)$ as the sum $p(A) + p(B)$. However, we must keep in mind that $p(P)$ cannot exceed 1. If the sum exceeds 1, we have assigned values that are too high. Cognitive psychologists have found that when we must assign probability values individually to the disjuncts in an alternation, we frequently assign values that result in the alternation having a value greater than one (Robinson and Hastie 1985). One way to avoid this is to add another exclusive alternative (C), such that "A or B or C" is exhaustive. That is, such that $p(A \text{ or } B \text{ or } C) = 1$. Then we assign values to each proposition, taking the others into account to make sure the sum is 1. The values for $p(A)$ and $p(B)$ are then summed to get $p(A \text{ or } B)$. For example, some people have lately claimed that Elvis Presley is alive; more cautious ones have asserted, "Either Presley is dead or he is in hiding." Symbolized as "Either A or B," we can judge A and B to be exclusive, but not exhaustive. Presley might be living in the open in a disguise (C). These three possibilities are mutually exclusive and jointly exhaustive. (There is also the possibility that he has been preserved cryogenically until some appointed date when he will be "revived," but I do not regard this as being even 5% probable, so I set it aside.) Now we assign values to A, B, and C. My information leads me to make these assignments: $p(A) = 0.8$; $p(B) = 0.1$; $p(C) = 0.1$. I can now calculate $p(A \text{ or } B)$ as $0.8 + 0.1 = 0.9$.

3 A and B are independent but not exclusive: in such cases $p(B/A)$ equals $p(B)$, since A does not make B more likely. So here $p(A \text{ or } B)$ $= p(A) + p(B) - p(A) \times p(B)$. For example, I cannot find my copy of John Locke's *Essay Concerning Human Understanding*, so I ask a colleague who might have one. She says "Either s.c. has one or a.p.m. has one," which is symbolized as "Either A or B." We note that A and

B are compatible alternatives but not exhaustive, as I have other philosophy colleagues as well. Furthermore A and B are logically independent, so that $p(B/A) = p(B)$. My discovery that s.c. has a copy would neither increase nor decrease the likelihood that a.p.m. has one. I decide that $p(A) = 0.9$ since s.c. teaches material from Locke. I decide that $p(B) = 0.9$, also, since a.p.m. has a good collection of early modern philosophy books. Therefore,

$$p(A \text{ or } B) = 0.9 + 0.9 - 0.9 \times 0.9 = 0.99.$$

Since we get the rating by rounding off to one decimal, the rating for $p(P)$ is 1.0. For practical purposes P can be regarded as certain.

4 A and B are related but not exclusive: if A and B are compatible but not independent, we shall have to assign values to $p(A)$, $p(B)$, and $p(B/A)$. Then we use the formula

$$p(P) = p(A) + p(B) - p(A) \times p(B/A).$$

Here is an example. It is early August 1990 and the Persian Gulf crisis is in full swing. A commentator says, "Either Iraq will attack Saudi Arabia next, or it will attack Jordan, so America must have a strong military presence in the Persian Gulf." The premiss can be symbolized as "Either A or B," where A = Iraq will attack Saudi Arabia next, and B = Iraq will attack Jordan next. The first issue is whether or not A and B are exhaustive. It is clear that they are not. There is also the possibility that Iraq will not attack any country, and even the possibility that it will attack Israel. The next issue is whether A and B are inclusive (compatible). In my view they are, since Iraq's military resources relative to its neighbors are such as to make it at least conceivable that it could attack both Saudi Arabia and Jordan simultaneously. The American presence in Saudi Arabia dictates that a value of 0.2 is appropriate for $p(A)$. Comments made on Iraqi TV suggest to me that Saddam Hussein is more likely to attack Jordan so as to come to grips with Israel and gain access to the Gulf of Aquaba, which leads me to assign $p(B)$ a value of 0.4. The probability of Jordan being attacked given that Saudi Arabia is attacked is much less than the probability of only Jordan being attacked, because of military considerations, so I make $p(B/A) = 0.1$. Thus,

$$p(A \text{ or } B) = 0.2 + 0.4 - 0.2 \times 0.1 = 0.58.$$

This value corresponds to a rating of 0.6, since we round off to the nearest decimal place. This represents a judgment that the premiss is somewhat more likely to be true than false.

Table 31
Alternation Probability Formulas

Situation	$p(A \text{ or } B)$
A and B exhaustive (no other alternatives)	1.0
A and B exclusive but not exhaustive	$p(A) + p(B)$
A and B not related but not exclusive and not exhaustive	$p(A) + p(B) - (p(A) \times p(B))$
A and B related but not exclusive and not exhaustive	$p(A) + p(B) - (p(A) \times p(B/A))$

This completes the discussion of alternation ratings. Table 31 summarizes the possibilities.

8.5 CONDITIONALS

Most conditional assertions can be cast in the form "If X then Y." Although there are quite a few stylistic variants of this form, including "If X, Y," "X only if Y," "Y if X," "X provided that Y," and so on, I shall conduct my discussion of conditionals in terms of the "If X then Y" form and its elliptical equivalent "If X, Y."

In section 3.1.2 I argued that the four conditionals examined by Copi in making his case for a material implication interpretation of "If X then Y" can be written in the form "The truth of X (when true) guarantees the truth of Y." This includes his counterfactual conditional. Subjunctively expressed conditionals can also be written in this form, according to Brian Ellis, who also claims that Robert Stalnaker shares this view: "Robert Stalnaker and I hold that indicative and subjunctive conditionals are basically similar. Neither kind of conditional is truth functional, and the same general account can be given of both" (Ellis 1984, 50).

This thesis certainly seems correct when applied to Copi's examples (1982, 291). In subjunctive form they look like this:

A If all humans were mortal and Socrates were a human, then Socrates would be mortal.
B If Leslie were a bachelor, then Leslie would be unmarried.
C If blue litmus paper were placed in acid, then the litmus paper would turn red.
D If State were to lose the homecoming game, then I would eat my hat.

Each of these conditionals could be written in the form "If it were true that X, then it would be true that Y," with X and Y being cast in indicative form, in appropriate tenses: for example, "If it were true that State will lose the homecoming game, then it would be true that I will eat my hat." Here the truth of "State will lose the homecoming game" is being said to guarantee the truth of "I will eat my hat," which amounts to the same logical claim as the original indicative version.

As I observed in section 2.1.1.2, conditionals are infrequently uttered in everyday argument. Perhaps for this reason, and because logicians regard their logical analysis as controversial, writers of informal logic and critical thinking texts seldom include much advice for evaluating conditional claims. Formal logic texts, on the other hand, do devote space to analyzing conditionals. But, as we saw in chapter 2, with Copi, they discuss natural language conditionals only to justify symbolizing them as material implication. This is done to make propositional and predicate logic more powerful. Given this aim, their accounts leave much to be desired as advice for evaluating conditionals.

Having, I hope, persuaded the reader in chapter 2 that $p(Y/X)$ is the correct parameter for assigning probability values to conditionals of the form "if X then Y," it is now necessary for me to provide some advice on how to arrive at a value for $p(Y/X)$. One approach is to try to show that X is true and Y is false. If this can be done, the conditional is rated 0.0. However, though effective when it can be applied, this approach is not useful when X is false or when Y is true. Nor is it useful when we judge $p(Y/X)$ to be between 0 and 1.

Another approach is to identify the favourable and unfavourable evidence with a view to assigning a value to $p(Y/X)$, but this brings with it the risk of allowing other evidence for Y to affect our judgment of "If X then Y." Consider the example "If Quebec chooses to secede from Canada, then the rest of the country will not resist." In arriving at a value for $p(Y/X)$, we take into account such things as the attitudes of Canadians outside Quebec as known through reputable polls, our personal discussions with other Canadians, and what we know of the policies of the federal and provincial governments.

The alternative to the "pro-con" approach is the one presented in the chapter 6, the rebuttal factor technique for inference-claim evaluation. I repeat that procedure here:

Step 1 If X is not relevant to Y, rate the claim 0.0. If it is relevant, identify all the significant rebuttal factors that you can.

Step 2 Identify the rebuttal factor you regard as most probable, given X. This is R_1. Assign a value to R_1 from the premiss rating table in chapter 3 (Table 3) by identifying the verbal rating that is best supported by your information, given X and the context associated with the utterance.

Step 3 If the appropriate rating for R_1 is above 0.2, count the total number of significant rebuttal factors (including R_1). "Significant" = "meriting a rating above 0.2," so that ones that are "highly unlikely" are not counted. Use "$(1 - R_1$ rating$) - (0.1 \times N)$" to calculate the conditional rating.

Step 4 If the rating for R_1 is 0.2 (you consider it to be highly unlikely), identify any other rebuttal factors that deserve that rating. The total number, including R_1, is N. Use the formula to calculate the conditional rating.

Step 5 If the rating for R_1 is 0.1, the inference rating is 0.8 regardless of any other rebuttal factors.

I will present one example to illustrate the procedure. At the moment, the governments of Britain and the Republic of Ireland are holding talks with a view to removing British army troops from Northern Ireland. Suppose someone is presenting an argument about the situation in Ireland and uses this assertion as an uninferred premiss: "If the troops are withdrawn from Northern Ireland, there will be a big escalation of sectarian violence."

At step (1) I decide that the antecedent (X) is relevant to the consequent (Y). Two plausible rebuttal factors come to mind: "The government of Northern Ireland is able to prevent a big escalation of sectarian violence" and "The IRA chooses not to increase its terrorist activity."

At step (2) I identify the most probable rebuttal factor (R_1), given X, and determine a value for it. In my (less than well-informed) judgment, "it is as likely to be false as true" (from the premiss-rating table) that the government of Northern Ireland can prevent a big escalation, even with some cooperation from the Republic and the British government. I judge this factor to be R_1, because I regard the other factor as highly unlikely, or even less probable than that. So for the formula, R_1 is rated 0.5 and $N = 1$.

At step (3) I calculate $p(Y/X)$:

$$p(Y/X) = 1.0 - (0.1 \times 1) - 0.5 = 0.4.$$

Now the 0.4 rating would be entered on the diagram next to the uninferred conditional premiss.

Because of the value of $p(R_1/P)$, steps (4) and (5) are not applicable here.

To summarize, the best two ways to arrive at a rating for conditional premisses, irrespective of whether they are indicative, counterfactual, or subjunctive, is the "pro-con" method and the rebuttal-factor method.

8.6 "$p(P)$" AND ARGUER CREDIBILITY

Any uttered argument can be regarded as having the form "P, so C," where P and C stand for the propositional content of the two respective assertions, so that they are independent of any particular language. They must, of course, be expressed in some language, but they can have the same content value when expressed in a variety of languages.

Thus far in this chapter, and throughout most of this book, I have discussed the evaluation of arguments as propositional complexes. In this section I wish to discuss the impact on the rating of uninferred premises of taking into account something external to the argument as a propositional complex – arguer credibility. Arguer credibility may be the most important factor in premiss evaluation, since we frequently accept claims used as premisses on the implicit ground that the arguer knows what s/he is talking about, even when we disagree with the arguer's claim that the premisses are adequate to prove the conclusion. And, of course, the information we bring to bear in arriving at a value for $p(P)$ is usually second-hand (or nth-hand, where "n" is a surprisingly large number!) itself, gleaned from media sources and other persons we come in contact with. Ethos, then, must be accomodated in any theory of uninferred premiss evaluation.

8.6.1 *Assessing the Impact of Credibility*

In judging $p(P)$ while attributing credibility to S, we can think of P as having an a priori ("prior") probability, which is "the probability of [P] apart from our knowledge of the fact that the witness [S] has asserted it" (Keynes 1921, 183). The prior probability value is determined by all of the relevant information we have about P. The a posteriori ("final") value will be the prior value adjusted upward or downward for the reliabilty of the arguer.

As I argued in section 7.4.1, the discussion of argument from authority, the appropriate way of making this adjustment is to use Bayes' Theorem. It was pointed out there that, assuming the prior probability of a claim is 0.5, attempting to accomodate witness/speaker reliability intuitively can result in overrating the probability of a claim because of our tendency to commit base-rate fallacies. (When 0.5 is, in fact, the appropriate value to assign, the final probability will be the "hit rate" of S, but only when 0.5 is appropriate.)

As presented in section 7.4.1, a useful version of Bayes' Theorem can be expressed as follows:

$$p(C \, / \, S \text{ affirms that } C) = [p(C)_i \times (1 - E)] \, / \, [(p(C)_i \times (1 - E)) + (E \times (1 - p(C)_i)].$$

Here $p(C)_i$ = the probability of C prior to taking S's testimony into account; E = the error rate of S in judging the truth of matters such as C. "E" has the value "$1 - R$," where R = the reliability of S, that is, S's "track record" in being correct about such judgments.

On exploring the outcome of the Bayes equation for realistic values of $p(C)_i$ and E in 7.4.1, it was found that a relatively simple formula gave accurate results, so long as $p(C)_i$ was not below 0.1, or R greater than 0.9:

$$p(C \,/\, S \text{ affirms that } C) = p(C)_i - (R - 0.5).$$

To arrive at an accurate rating for P, then, we can follow this procedure:

1 Assign a probability value to P based on all relevant information that one has, but disregarding the fact that it has been asserted by S. This is $p(P)_i$.
2 Assign a value to E, S's error rate. Considerations relevant to S's reliability were presented in 7.4.2 and 7.4.3.
3 Use the formula "$p(P)_i - (R - 0.5)$" to calculate an approximate value of $p(P)$, rounding it off to one decimal place to get P's rating.

8.6.2 Examples

In this section I will illustrate the use of this procedure for evaluating the premisses of two arguments having the same conclusion. In one case the arguer is considered to have observer knowledge, in the other, expert knowledge. I will draw upon the discussion of factors influencing reliability arising from these two sources that was presented in sections 7.4.2 and 7.4.3.

Consider a trucker transporting a heavy load of goods through a remote area. He comes to a bridge on his route which is in such poor condition that it raises doubt in his mind whether he can cross safely, since his total vehicle weight is forty tonnes. He stops to investigate, but not knowing much about bridge design, he decides to rely on the knowledge of others. He accosts a passerby who says "A truck as big as yours crossed here yesterday, so it is safe for you to cross." Not yet satisfied, he phones the highway maintenance office and speaks to the engineer who inspects bridges and who says "That bridge can carry a load of sixty tonnes, so it is safe for you to cross." The trucker considers the other route available to him as a relatively unattractive alternative because it is much longer and he would fail to meet his schedule if he used it. On the other hand, he is not disposed to accept the arguments directed to him as acceptable without detailed evaluation.

The argument involving P_1 ("The passerby asserts that a truck as big as yours crossed here yesterday") is an example of one of two broad kinds of cases in which an arguer (S) has some epistemic authority. The individual is in a position to know the truth value of the premise by virtue of having observed the alleged event (or state of affairs). I call this "observer" knowledge. In contrast, the argument involving P_2 ("The engineer asserts that this bridge can carry a load of sixty tonnes") is an example of someone having a different kind of epistemic authority. The engineer supposedly qualifies as an expert on the matter of the bridges in his jurisdiction. I call this sort of knowledge "expert" knowledge.

The first argument the trucker has to deal with is "A passerby asserted that a truck as big as mine crossed here yesterday, so a truck as big as mine crossed here yesterday." The rating of the premise in this argument depends on observer credibility. Five factors were identified in section 7.4.2 as influencing such credibility: (1) the observer (O) was in the appropriate place at the right time; (2) O had nondefective sensory modalities; (3) O attended to the event/state; (4) the event/state was observed recently; (5) given these four factors, humans in such a situation are not prone to sensory deception.

To decide whether to accept the premise and thereby acquire a (nearly) conclusive ground for inferring that he can cross safely, the trucker could inquire of the passerby whether that person actually saw the other truck cross. If s/he did, the trucker might then ask about the time of day (was it daylight or dark?) and also make a judgment about the person's visual acuity. Being satisfied on these points, he could then check with others living nearby to see if they would corroborate the testimony. If they disagree, then he might wish to discreetly inquire about the first individual's reliability. If they do corroborate on the basis of observation, he can judge the witness's error rate to be relatively low. Suppose in light of the above inquiries he assigns it a value of 0.05; that is, he concludes there is a 5% chance that the testimony is incorrect.

To apply the premise-rating procedure, he must first choose a value for the prior probability of the premise "A truck as big as yours crossed here yesterday." Here he would have to rely on what he knows of truck traffic patterns in the area to judge the frequency of truck crossings and the proportion of trucks that carry a load as heavy as his. Suppose, setting aside the testimony, he decides that the prior probability of the claim is 0.1. (If he had judged it to be high, he would not likely have solicited information in the first place.) Now he can use the simplified formula given above to calculate $p(P)$:

$$p(P) = 0.1 + (0.95 - 0.50) = 0.55.$$

From this value we infer that the premiss rating is 0.6. (Using the Bayes equation for more accuracy we would have found $p(P)$ to be 0.68, which yields a rating of 0.7.)

If the trucker rates the premiss supplied by the observer as 0.7, it will be, at best, marginally sufficient for concluding that the bridge will support his truck. The inference is of high quality: if a truck as big as his crossed yesterday, then it is highly likely that the bridge will carry his truck, especially if such trucks cross regularly. But he may still want to consider the engineer's evidence.

The engineer's testimony is in the category of expert knowledge (if it is knowledge). In section 7.4.3 I identified three considerations relevant to judging the reliability of an expert: (1) E must have the appropriate credentials, that is, training or education; (2) E must be trustworthy; (3) E's claim must not be controversial among his or her fellow experts.

The engineer's argument was, "That bridge can carry sixty tonnes, so it can carry your forty-tonne truck." In this case a careful trucker might wish to establish the engineer's qualifications: How long has he been in charge of bridge maintenance? Is he a graduate civil engineer? Has he done bridge design? How regularly does he check his bridges? If the answers he receives sound satisfactory he can probably trust the engineer, since the latter would have no reason to give bad advice; indeed, if the bridge did fail the engineer would be in serious trouble. To be really sure the trucker might wish to ask people in the area if there had been any qualified persons who had recently expressed negative views about the safety of the bridge.

If the information gleaned does not raise any misgivings about the engineer's competence, the trucker might attribute an error rate of, say, 0.001 $(R = 0.999)$ to the engineer. That is, he might think that there is only one chance in a thousand that the engineer is mistaken.

On the other hand, he might assign a fairly low value to the prior probability of the claim. Prior to consulting the engineer, if he had been asked to set a probability value for the claim that the bridge would carry sixty tonnes, he might have said 0.1. After all, he was concerned about his truck, which weighs only forty tonnes. To determine $p(P)$ he cannot use the simplified formula used above, since R exceeds 0.9. But since E is only 1/100 of $p(C)$, he can rate P as 1. (Using the Bayes equation, $p(P) = 0.991$, which also yields a rating of 1.0.) Since the inference in the engineer's argument deserves a 1.0 rating, the trucker can accept the engineer's argument and proceed with relative equanimity. He is not, after all, faced with proceeding on the strength of the observer's argument.

8.6.3 *Conclusion*

To take into account the credibility of the arguer when evaluating the premisses of his or her argument, we must utilize Bayes' Theorem. In this section I have showed how a simplified version can be used to obtain accurate premiss rating results. The examples presented show that authoritative testimony can alter our initial premiss ratings. Using the simplified formula, the change in $p(P)$ is equal to "$R - 0.5$." In chapter 7 I called this parameter "authority support," in contrast to the "evidence support" represented by $p(P)_i$.

However, it must be remembered that even the most reliable person cannot make highly implausible premisses very plausible. If I regard a person as being 99% reliable and if I think that there is no more than one chance in a thousand that an alien spacecraft would land in my neighborhood, that person's statement to me that one did land recently would authorize me (using Bayes) to admit only that there is a 10% chance that it actually occurred.

9 Missing Premisses

Arguments depend not only on their premisses to persuade *H* that *C* is acceptable. Every argument, if it is to be satisfactory, requires also that *H* agree with *S* on a variety of other implicit assumptions. Some logicians regard some of these assumptions as missing premisses, and if they are correct, their position has repercussions for argument evaluation theory: "Anyone who has tried to evaluate natural arguments will know that these missing premisses ... must be formulated, for the strength or weakness of the argument very often depends on what they are" (Blair and Johnson 1980, 18).

9.1 MISSING-PREMISS CONCEPTS

The most fundamental distinction between implicit assumptions for the purposes at hand is the distinction between ones the arguer "had in mind" or relied on but did not state and the ones that the argument as a propositional complex relies on if it is to be a good argument. The two types of missing premiss are called "used" and "needed" assumptions by Ennis: "Sometimes implicit assumptions are propositions that are needed to support the conclusion, to make the argument a good one ... On the other hand, sometimes they are unstated reasons that a person actually used consciously (or subconsciously, if you believe in subconscious reasons) as a basis of argument or action" (1982, 63).

The distinction can also be labelled as one between "arguer's assumptions" and "argument's assumptions" (Hitchcock 1985, 89). Arguer's assumptions will normally concern the argument evaluator only in the context of a dialogue with the arguer or when the arguer is otherwise accessible to respond to inquiries about the content of the argument or when we are engaged in an exegesis of a scholarly text. The existence of arguer's assumptions is an empirical matter: "Claims that a used assumption has been identified are empirical mental event or state claims about the thinking of a person" (Ennis 1982, 64). In what follows I shall continue to be concerned with arguments as propositional complexes, so I will talk exclusively about "needed" or "argument's" assumptions.

9.1.1 *Missing Premisses as Gap-Fillers*

One kind of implicit assumption is the "premiss-type" assumption. According to Ennis, "Premise-type assumptions are at least of two types: those that provide backing for a proposition already thought to be part of an argument ('back-ups'), and those that join with one or more other premises in giving support to the conclusion ('gap-fillers')" (1982, 62–3). Although Ennis is a bit vague in saying what "support" amounts to, it seems that he has inference quality in mind. At one point he says, "A gap is filled when one can infer without any question a conclusion ... from its support" (1982, 70). In discussing an example, he says that the assumption "is needed in order to make a valid argument out of the one given" (1982, 65). Thus, the implicit assumptions required to make the inference satisfactory are the gap-fillers of an argument.

In a follow-up to Ennis' paper, Govier argues that gap-fillers ought to be called "missing premises," and in the interest of clarity she argues that "It is a serious mistake to identify unstated premises with unstated assumptions. Many assumptions which are required in order for arguments to work are not required to fill inference gaps – the standard role for missing premises. Thus, it is better to speak of missing or unstated premises rather than of missing or unstated assumptions" (1987, 82–3).

Govier defines a missing premise as a proposition whose truth is "a necessary condition for properly inferring the conclusion from the stated premises" (1987, 92). This definition is similar to the definitions of a number of textbook authors: "Natural arguments are usually incomplete. They make leaps from supporting reasons to claims based on them that would be plausible only if certain other assertions, which they do not mention, were also accepted ... these missing premises must be formulated" (Blair and Johnson 1980, 18).

Scriven raises the issue of whether we should "fill in what are called "missing premises," namely, the further assumptions that are required, in many cases, to make an inference satisfactory" (1976, 81). Hitchcock observes that sometimes "the author of the argument has left un-stated certain factual information or a general principle which, if added as an extra premiss, would make the argument valid" (1983, 73). He calls these "tacit premises". Schwartz advises that "you may find a number of ways to supply tacit premises – a number of sets of fairly plausible statements, any one of which would make the argument valid if added to the expressed premisses" (Schwartz 1980, 152).

I have chosen to quote Hitchcock and Schwartz because Johnson and Blair have commended their approaches to identifying missing premisses (1985, 189). Others could also be quoted to the same effect, that missing premisses qualify as such because they are needed to make the inference acceptable.

However, this account is too general. Consider an example. We go to my car, but when I try to start it the engine does not "turn over" fast enough to start. I say, "The starter won't turn the engine over fast enough, so the battery is discharged." You know enough about cars to realize that the inference is a bit shaky so you say, "It could be a wiring problem." I turn on the headlights and go around front to see if they are working properly. I find they are very dim, whereupon I say, "The starter won't turn the engine over fast enough to start it and the lights are dim, so the battery is discharged."

In this argument the additional premiss "The lights are dim" im-proves the inference to an acceptable level, so it could be conceived as a missing premiss, given the foregoing definition. But it is an addi-tional ground for the conclusion, not a gap-filler. I believe that the lo-gicians referred to above share this view about adding new evidence: "in response to the query 'how many missing premisses can we allow?' we would propose, as many as are needed to begin an adequate cri-tique as long as you do not begin expanding upon the text by inserting fresh material" (Gough and Tindale 1985, 103).

A proposition functioning as a missing premise must be either sup-port for a stated ground or support for a conclusion or support for the inference claim. The first kind is a back-up, not a gap-filler. The sec-ond is a new ground. So it would seem that missing premisses are war-rants or other backing for the inference claim. This is clearly Scriven's view: "missing premisses ... serve as the link between the original given premisses and the conclusion of the argument. For this reason they are often said to be 'inference licenses'" (1976, 83).

The other authors cited above can have this view imputed to them by virtue of the examples they discuss. Here are some examples:

1 "Capital punishment must be unjust, because it has not been shown to be an effective deterrent." Tacit premiss: "A punishment is unjust

if it has not been shown to be an effective deterrent" (Schwartz 1980, 8).

2 "The stone was an emerald, therefore the stone was green." Tacit premiss: "All emeralds are green" (Schwartz 1980, 147).

3 "The costs of going to war always outweigh the benefits of going to war. Therefore we should go to war no more." Tacit premiss: "We should do nothing whose costs outweigh its benefits" (Schwartz 1980, 154).

4 "The extra cost is about $0.75 per week. Therefore, the extra cost is not much money." Tacit premiss: The sum of "$0.75 per week is not much money" (Hitchcock 1983, 73).

5 "K percent of the members of sample S, drawn from population P, have property X. [So] K percent of the members of population P have property X." Suppressed premiss: "Sample S is representative of population P in incidence of property X" (Thomas 1973, 150).

In each of the examples, the alleged tacit premiss can be seen as a warrant, in the sense that it entails the inference claim of the stated argument. Furthermore, each is a generalization, and in each argument the premiss and conclusion have the same referent. These features permit us to construe each argument as a syllogism whose major premiss is unstated. These are what Copi identifies as "first-order enthymemes" (1982, 254). In what follows I will discuss only these kinds of arguments. The emerald example given above (example 2) can serve as an illustration when needed.

9.1.2 *Diagramming Syllogisms*

Given the diagramming conventions of this book, how is a syllogism to be diagrammed? Obviously, the minor premiss can be regarded as providing independent evidence/support for the conclusion. In the emerald example of the last section "The stone was an emerald" seems to be good, perhaps conclusive, evidence for "The stone was green." Thus, we can draw an arrow from "P" to "C" in our diagram.

Now, what about the major premiss? Can we simply regard it as a second premiss that results in a v-shaped two-premiss argument? There are both logical and epistemic considerations that suggest that this would be inappropriate. From an epistemic point of view it can be argued that the major premiss (taken by itself) is irrelevant to C and therefore cannot be evidence/support for it. (This is not the same as being irrelevant to the *argument.*) Consider the emerald example. Intuitively, "All emeralds are green" does not appear to be relevant to "The stone was an emerald," probably because the generalization is not explicitly about the stone in question. The evidence given for claiming a thing has a property is usually the fact that it has some other property or the fact that some causally related state of affairs or event exists/occurs. (For example, evidence for "The Boston Red Sox baseball game will be postponed" is "It is raining in Boston.")

It might be suggested that someone might say "All emeralds are green, so the stone was green" in a particular context and the recipient of the argument would become convinced that the stone was green as a result. Should we say that in such contexts the generalization functioned as evidence? No. In such cases the arguer is relying on the recipient knowing that the stone was an emerald. In face-to-face contexts, this knowledge could be depended upon. But it makes more sense in such cases to say that the recipient consciously (or unconsciously) added the unstated premiss in the course of reaching the conclusion. As genuine evidence for the conclusion in the context, there is no objection to regarding "The stone was an emerald" as unstated support for it.

I conclude that the minor premiss and the major premiss of a syllogism have different logical roles. Whereas the minor premiss serves as independent evidence or support for the conclusion, the major premiss does not. Textbook authors are somewhat aware of this difference. Copi, for example, recognizes that "Not every premiss in an argument provides ... independent support for the conclusion ... Some premisses must work together to support their conclusion. When this happens, the cooperation they display can be exhibited in the argument's diagram ... by connecting [the premisses] with a brace ... with a single arrow leading from the pair of them to the conclusion" (1982, 21).

The problem with this form of depiction is that it does not reflect the different roles of the two premisses. If the roles of the two premisses of a syllogism differ and the minor premiss can be seen as evidence/support for the conclusion, what, then, is the role of the major premiss? To identify this we must view the syllogism from the viewpoint of logic rather than from the epistemic viewpoint.

From a logical point of view the form of the "Barbara" syllogism can be written as "All S is M and all M is P, so all S is P." The major premiss is the second one. In the emerald example this is "All emeralds are green." Now "All M is P" is logically equivalent to (or at least entails) the conditional "If a thing is M, then it is P" (taking the standard modern interpretation). This conditional, in turn, entails "If this particular thing is M, then this particular thing is P." This step represents what is called the rule of "universal instantiation" in most versions of the predicate calculus. Thus, in our example about the stone, "All emeralds are green" is logically equivalent to "If a thing is an emerald, then that thing is green." This proposition, in turn, entails "If the stone is an

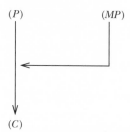

Fig. 25.   Missing-premiss model

emerald, then the stone is green." But this last proposition represents the inference claim of the enthymematic version of the argument (the version containing only the minor premiss as a premiss). Thus, the major premiss entails the inference claim of the enthymeme. That is to say, it provides (if true) conclusive evidence or support for that inference claim. And this being so, it cannot be conclusive evidence or support for the conclusion itself, since "If P then C" is not logically equivalent to C, nor does it entail C.

We now have the answer to how to accomodate "major premisses" in the adopted diagram format. They cannot be represented as a second independent premisses, and since they support the inference claim of the enthymeme, which is represented by the arrow from P to C, it is appropriate to draw an arrow from the major premiss (MP) to the arrow between P and C, as shown in Figure 25.

The most important point to be derived from the exercise of establishing how to diagram a syllogism is that when the major premiss is unstated (that is, when we have an enthymeme) and we choose to call it an unstated premiss of the argument, its role in the argument is not that of a gap-filler but that of a backup. According to Ennis, it will be recalled, a backup "provides backing for a proposition already thought to be part of the argument" (1982, 62). That proposition is, in this case, the implicit inference claim.

9.1.3 Are Enthymemes Complete Arguments?

Can an enthymeme be a complete argument by conceptual standards? That is, given our concept of an argument, is an enthymeme such as "The stone was an emerald, so the stone was green" a clear instance of an uttered argument, or is it a borderline case, or even, by virtue of missing a part, not a case at all?

Textbook authors generally define "argument" in such a way that enthymemes do count as clear instances. Copi's definition is typical of those found in logic textbooks: "An argument ... is any group of propositions of which one is claimed to follow from the others, which are regarded as providing support for or grounds for the truth of that one ... The simplest kind of argument consists of just one premiss and a conclusion" (1982, 6–7).

Textbook authors, then, seem prepared to accept arguments with one premiss as completely stated. And just as we can have a complete argument without any backing for the single premiss, by parity of reasoning it would seem that no backup is required for the inference claim either. Thus, an enthymematic syllogism is a complete argument. (Of course, it is not a complete *syllogism*.) In referring to completeness here I am talking about conceptual completeness. However, the case for major premisses as needed parts of enthymematic arguments involves the notion of logical completeness, not conceptual completeness. I will evaluate those arguments shortly, but first I want to mention some pragmatic considerations in favour of not regarding major premisses as unstated premisses of enthymemes.

If major premisses have the role described above, we can explain why people frequently utter enthymemes rather than complete syllogisms, and why, as Hitchcock observes, "we are unaware of having omitted a premiss when we advance an enthymeme" (Hitchcock 1985, 94). That is, they are a backup for argument that get stated only when the validity of the inference is challenged.

Arguments are frequently uttered with a view to persuading someone else to accept a claim that we judge they believe is dubious or false. In the interests of logical efficiency we utter only the propositions that we think are necessary to persuade. If we think the audience will accept a premiss as true because of information they have that supports it, we do not provide any backup for the premiss. Furthermore, if we think they might regard that premiss as providing adequate support for the conclusion (that is, if we think they would regard the inference claim as true), we do not state the major premiss as another premiss. It, and premiss backups, are considered to be logically redundant in the context.

Our practice of stating syllogisms enthymematically, then, is explained by an intuitive understanding that major premisses are backups for inference claims, and when we fail to state the gap-filler, we are manifesting our belief that the audience will accept our inference claim, that is, that they will regard C as following from P because of information they already have. Were I to try to prove to a relative that a missing heirloom ring contained a green stone and if I knew that this person was knowledgeable about gems, I might give as a reason for this claim, "The stone was an emerald." I would see it as unnecessary to also state the backup "All emeralds are green" if I believed my relative knew this.'

Before detailing some objections, conceptual and methodological, to the gap-filler approach to argument evaluation, it is appropriate to consider the logical grounds given in support of saying that major premisses are unstated premisses of syllogistic enthymemes. The main one is contained in the quotation from Johnson and Blair in section 9.1.1 (above): gap-fillers are relied on to infer C from P.

This thesis seems to be true, but it must be remembered that to prove their conclusions, arguments rely on many propositions being true, most of which are clearly not premisses.[1] In any case, if major premisses are really backups for inference claims, the question whether they are unstated premisses is the same question that arises for backups for stated premisses. Are backups for stated premisses to be regarded as unstated premisses?

In terms of their logical properties, we have no way to distinguish backups that are premisses from backups that are not. If we take every backup to have its own backup when added to the argument, we must take the view that any argument has an indefinite number of premisses. If, instead, we deny that there is an infinite regress, then we must take some such view as that a completely stated argument must begin with self-evident premisses. The former choice is absurd and the latter is not much better. It is better to adopt a third choice: we take the argument to be complete with the original stated premisses. And since the major premiss is really a backup for the inference claim, we are led to the view that an uttered argument can be complete without it.

Even if it is granted that they are backups, it will be objected here that major premisses are a special kind of backup; that is, their addition to an argument produces an argument with a valid inference. And since an argument must have a valid inference if it is to prove its conclusion, the gap-filler is an unstated premiss in any argument that is not formally valid as it stands. This thesis is questionable. Another way of stating it is to say that an inference claim is acceptable only when it is necessarily true by virtue of its logical form. But an argument must be judged as proving its conclusion whenever we accept its stated premisses and its inference claim as true, whether necessarily or contingently. Perhaps some examples of arguments with these kinds (or degrees) of validity will clarify this claim.

The following is an example of an argument that is formally valid: "The stone was an emerald, and all emeralds are green, so the stone was green." It is formally valid because it can be written in such a way as to correspond to a valid syllogism pattern, and to a valid pattern in first-order predicate calculus. However, arguments can be deductively valid without being formally valid. Consider an example of an argument that has a necessarily true inference claim, but whose truth arises from the meaning of the words used to state it: "Al is older than Bill. Bill is older than Charlie. Therefore, Al is older than Charlie." Copi says that the proposition " 'Being older than' is a transitive relation" is a missing premiss because it is needed to make the argument formally valid (1967, 155). Govier challenges this interpretation: "But this must be wrong. The argument ... is in fact deductively valid as stated. Copi's account goes beyond deductivism in that he seeks to make the argument not just deductively valid, but deductively valid in virtue of its form as identified within a specific system of logic. The stated premises do entail the conclusion. It is just not formally provable that this is the case" (1987, 93).

Besides cases in which we have deductive validity without formal validity (following Govier, we can call these arguments "semantically" valid), there are cases in which the inference claim is contingently true: for example, "The stone was an emerald, so the stone was green." The backing for the inference claim is "All emeralds are green," which is true, so the inference claim is true. However, in some logically possible worlds the generalization is false, so that the truth of the premiss does not guarantee the truth of the conclusion in those worlds. The argument is valid only in those worlds in which all emeralds are green. For these reasons, such examples can be called "contingently" valid (or, following Govier, "materially" valid).

Thus, the gap-filler method involves the use of a standard (formal validity) beyond that required for proof. The use of such a standard results in the search for unstated premises in cases in which none are required: specifically, when semantic rules or empirical facts ensure that the inference claim is true. This must be regarded as a serious defect in the missing-premiss approach.

Another problem with the gap-filler method is that adopting it commits us to several unwelcome implications: (1) all fully stated arguments are formally valid; (2) argument evaluation is solely a matter of premiss evaluation; and (3) there are no fallacies, only arguments with unstated premises. The first implication seems to be incompatible with much of what has been said about the nature of logic as a subject, that is, that the task of applied logic is to establish whether or not inferences are valid. The second position follows from the first, and given the role of applied logic as just described, it would follow that argument evaluation is not the main business of logic! The third position also follows from the first and is incompatible with the theory and practice of those engaged in the study of fallacies (Govier 1987, 85).

Lastly, there is a methodological difficulty in using the method: the formulation of the gap-filler. The proposition identified as the gap-filler will frequently be a stronger claim than we may want to impute to the arguer, given the information we think they have. For example, if an argument is a syllogistic enthymeme of the "Barbara" type, the gap-filling major premiss will be a universal generalization. Suppose we are in a world in which about 1% of the emeralds in circulation are blue and the rest are green, and this is general knowledge. Given the argument "The stone was an emerald, so the stone was green," the proponents of the gap-filler approach would identify "All emeralds are green" as the gap-filler that secures formal validity. The arguer who knows of the existence of the blue emeralds would not find this claim acceptable, and would deny that it is a premiss in the argument.

Someone who supports the gap-filler approach would respond that the arguer *must* accept the generalization as a premiss, otherwise the argument does not have a valid inference. This response is correct. The argument is neither formally valid nor semantically valid nor contingently/materially valid. But the arguer could respond that the stated premiss, although it does not entail the conclusion, is a very good reason to believe the conclusion.

At this point a deductivist might complain that there is an unstated qualifier in the conclusion. That is, the arguer ought to have said something like: "The stone was an emerald, so, almost certainly, the stone was green." The addition of the qualifier can be seen as justified by the truth of the strongest defensible inference backup: "Nearly all emeralds are green." While the deductivist seems to be right about imputing unstated qualifiers in cases like this, qualifiers are not premisses. We can regard the major premiss as entailing the inference claim of the argument with its unstated qualifying expression added, but the major premiss itself is still backing for the inference claim and, as such, is not a gap-filler.[2]

9.1.4 *Machina on Missing Premisses*

The conceptual oddness of the deductivist view of missing premisses, when dealing with inductive arguments, is illustrated by an example from a text by Kenton Machina. He introduces a distinction between "tight" inductive arguments, and ones that are not tight:

In determining whether a particular argument satisfies the definition of "tight argument" one must consider only what is included in the argument itself, without bringing to bear any additional background information or beliefs one might have concerning the subject matter under discussion. In this regard, the evaluation of arguments with respect to tightness parallels their evaluation with respect to [deductive] validity, for in the latter case the argument was considered valid only when it contained within itself sufficient support for its conclusion to render the conclusion certain given the premises. Accordingly, the following argument is not tight: That man is standing there with a smoking gun in his hand. [So] he recently fired the gun. (1982, 307)

Machina goes on to say that this argument is not tight because "There is no probable connection presented by the argument between a gun's being fired and smoke ... As far as this argument itself goes, smoke could come from guns all the time, as from chimneys, without any shooting."

The "probable connection" that Machina thinks must be included might be expressed as "Guns emit smoke immediately after, and only after, being fired." This claim would provide excellent support for the inference claim, since it is in fact true. It is some such claim that Machina is referring to when he says "The argument may seem tight, but only because you are assuming some extra things about smoking guns not stated in the argument." Now if we judge the argument to have a fairly good inference, we are no doubt relying on the warrant-like claim I formulated. But is this illegitimate, as Machina alleges? I will argue it is not.

A distinction must be made within what he calls "background information." Machina's view would be correct if all relevant background information was regarded as additional evidence (Toulmin's "grounds") for the conclusion. But clearly, if the warrant-like claim is evidence, it is evidence for the inference claim, not the conclusion. In providing support for the inference-claim, the warrant is logically analogous to backing that might be cited in support of the premiss. As such, I contend that the argument is no more deficient in not providing inference-claim support than it is in not providing backing for the premiss. That is to say, it is not seriously deficient. All arguments must have a starting point, and the most immediate starting points are the stated uninferred premises and the (necessarily) implicit inference claim. It is one thing to say that an argument relies on a fact not included in the utterance of it, and another to say that it is incomplete (and therefore flawed) because that fact is not included. Persuasive arguments inevitably rest on a base of information that supports the premises used and the inference made.

Machina ought to have realized that there is something odd about his view when he concluded that "In order to make the above argument tight, it would be necessary to add a great many premises" (1982, 307). Any policeman who accepted the argument in its original form and was then accused by Machina of not being logically rigorous would be bemused, if not indignant.

We can consider this question from another perspective, that of someone evaluating the argument. We reach a value for $p(P)$ by bringing to bear all the information we have that is relevant to it. Analogously, we reach a value for $p(C/P)$ by utilizing all the information relevant to the inference claim. In Machina's example, the evaluator will judge $p(P)$ to have a value of 1.0, based on observation (assuming she is in the company of the person who uttered the argument). In arriving at a value for $p(C/P)$, she could rely on, among other beliefs, the fact that guns emit smoke immediately after being fired, and only then. This process should seem quite natural and appropriate to the reader, but evidently Machina would hold that we are illegitimately reading things into the argument.

It is correct to say that we must not rely on additional evidence for the conclusion when we evaluate an argument. It would be improper, for example, to take into consideration that a bystander reported seeing the man firing the gun. But the fact that guns emit smoke immediately after firing is not in this category.

Where does this leave us on the issue of whether some arguments have missing premisses? If neither the premiss backing nor the inference-claim backing needs to be regarded as a missing premiss, am I committed to denying that there are arguments being uttered that have missing premisses? In the next section I will present three kinds of situations in which uttered arguments have missing premisses.

9.2 ARGUMENTS WITH MISSING PREMISSES

I have argued that warrants are not missing premisses when absent from a stated argument. There are, however, arguments that can be said to have missing premisses.

As I noted in chapter 1, the arguer is committed to affirming three propositions: (1) P, (2) if P then C, and (3) C. The inference claim must be implicit in the uttered argument, so it cannot be a missing premiss. The conclusion is not a premiss, of course. P, the ground for C, on the other hand, is an essential part of the argument, and when absent from the utterance, it qualifies as a missing premiss.

Since natural languages permit arguers to take liberties in stating their arguments, there are three situations in which a genuine ground P may be missing from a stated argument. They can be diagrammed as shown in Figure 26. To discuss each situation concretely, I will adapt an example from Johnson and Blair (1983, 14). The propositions are designated as follows:

P = This (their book) is a textbook.
W = Textbooks don't usually contain jokes.

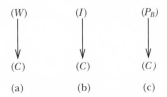

Fig. 26.   Missing-premiss argument-forms

P_B = This book was written for college students.
C = It is unlikely that there are jokes in this book.
I = If this is a textbook, then it is unlikely that there are jokes in this book.

Situation (a) would occur when this argument is uttered: "Textbooks don't usually contain jokes, so it is unlikely that there are jokes in this book." The required ground P (This book is a textbook.) is not included in the utterance. P is required because the first assertion (W) is not direct evidence for C. To be direct evidence in an inductive argument, an assertion must normally mention the same thing referred to in the conclusion. In adding P to the stated argument we are not supplementing the evidence for C that has already been presented. None has been given. We are adding the evidence that, given the original utterance, the argument relies on.

Situation (b) would arise when the uttered argument is "If this is a textbook, then it is unlikely that there are jokes in this book. So it is unlikely that there are jokes in this book." Here again no direct evidence is provided for C. C is a categorical claim and normally, hypothetical claims cannot prove categorical claims, in spite of the fact that by the standards of the propositional calculus this argument is formally valid. (See chapter 5 for discussion of this matter.) The proposition to be added as a missing premiss explicitly appears, of course, in the stated argument as the antecedent of the first assertion (I), which is the inference claim. But it was not originally asserted.

Burke presents an argument of this sort in his discussion of unstated premisses: "This wine can't be port. If it were, it would be sweet" (1985, 107). Here C = "This wine can't be port." The second assertion (I) qualifies as the inference claim because, relying on the rule of transposition, it can be written as "If this wine is not sweet, then this wine is not port." The missing premiss P is "This wine is not sweet."

Situation (c) is less common. An assertion in an argument-passage is a backing premiss when there is some other assertion entailed by it, which assertion in turn entails the conclusion. Here P, when added, provides a linking function. The situation would arise if someone were to say "This book was written for college students, so it is unlikely that there are jokes in this book."

It is characteristic of arguments of this third kind that evaluators sometimes have difficulty seeing the relevance of one assertion to the other. What, in this case, is the connection between being written for college students and not containing jokes? This connection becomes clearer when the missing premiss *P* is added, because it "links" the two stated assertions. The argument can now be stated as "This book was written for college students, so it is a textbook; therefore it is unlikely that there are jokes in this book."

All three of the above patterns can be found in everyday argumentation, though not with equal frequency. The process of identifying the missing premiss in each case supports the view of Gough and Tindale that missing premisses are extracted from the text: "It is not so much that we recognize an argument as incomplete but that insofar as we do recognize the argument, we understand part of it to be hidden within the meaning of the author's stated assertions" (1985, 100).

To summarize this section: I have presented three argument formats that have missing premisses. In each case the missing premiss is the ground for the conclusion. This being the case, it is correct to say that any argument that can be diagrammed in one of these formats is incomplete. The missing premiss to be added is to be inferred from the assertions in the argument utterance.

9.3 AN EVALUATION PROCEDURE USING SUPPLEMENTARY PREMISSES

In chapter 6 I presented the rebuttal-factor approach as a superior alternative for inference evaluation. In this section I will show how the rebuttal-factor concept can be used to develop an added-premiss procedure for argument evaluation that can replace the "add-the-warrant" procedure favoured by most textbook authors.

In chapter 6 I pointed out that rebuttal factors are related to $p(C/P)$ through the following relationship: "If P then C, unless R_1 or R_2 or ... R_n." (Here "n" is the total number of plausible rebuttal factors associated with a particular argument of the form "P, so C.") Some algebraic manipulation and several probability axioms enabled me to get a formula relating $p(C/P)$ to rebuttal-factor probabilities:

$$p(C/P) = p(\text{not-}R_1/P) \times p(\text{not-}R_2/P) \times \ldots p(\text{not-}R_n/P).$$

The relationship between the rebuttal factors and inference validity expressed in this formula can be the basis for identifying premisses that can be added to improve inference validity prior to argument evaluation. Since $p(C) = p(P) \times p(C/P)$, we can write $p(C)$ as

$$p(C) = p(P) \times [p(\text{not-}R_1/P) \times p(\text{not-}R_2/P) \times \ldots p(\text{not-}R_n/P)].$$

The rules of arithmetic allow us to drop the square brackets in a case like this, so we may write $p(C)$ as

$$p(C) = p(P) \times p(\text{not-}R_1/P) \times p(\text{not-}R_2/P) \times \ldots p(\text{not-}R_n/P).$$

Now this formula represents the way we would calculate $p(C)$ for an argument that has a valid inference and premises P, not-R_1, not-R_2 ... not-R_n. Thus, if we take the stated argument "P, so C" and add the other premises, we will have made the original argument valid, because there are no rebuttal factors remaining. We can think of the supplementary premises as "blocking" the influence of the rebuttal factors.

This result can be confirmed by example. Suppose a particular argument is deemed by the evaluator to have three rebuttal factors, judged to have the following probabilities: $p(R_1/P) = 0.4$; $p(R_2/P) = 0.3$; and $p(R_3/P) = 0.2$. In its original form the argument would have a $p(C/P)$ value of $(1 - 0.4) \times (1 - 0.3) \times (1 - 0.2) = 0.336$, a rating of 0.3. If we add "not-R_1" as a premiss, there will be only two rebuttal factors, so that $p(C/P) = (1 - 0.3) \times (1 - 0.2) = 0.56$, a rating of 0.6. If we also add "not-R_2" as a premiss, $p(C/P) = 1 - 0.2 = 0.8$, a rating of 0.8. If we also add "not-R_3," we will not have any plausible rebuttal factors left, so that the inference will be satisfactory. By adding the negations of identified rebuttal factors as premisses, we can bring the inference to a satisfactory level, then evaluate the argument by rating only the premisses (original and added).

It might be objected that this technique involves adding new evidence to improve the argument, but two considerations suggest otherwise. First, the negated rebuttal factors represent support for the original inference claim, not direct support for the conclusion. Secondly, although adding negated rebuttal factors as premisses improves inference validity, the value of $p(C)$ does not change, as the above equations show. While validity increases, the probability values of the added premisses exactly offset that increase. Another objection arises from the fact that, although supplementing the original premises of arguments with negated rebuttal factors improves their validity, the method cannot yield formally valid arguments. It cannot because "$(P \,\&\, (-R_1 \,\&\, -R_2 \,\&\, \ldots)) \supset C$" is not a logical truth.

Those who incline to formal deductivism ("The only good arguments are arguments with formally valid inferences") might at this point dismiss the rebuttal-factor method because it does not yield gap-filling premisses that make the original argument formally valid. We could respond that although the method does not yield arguments with formally valid inferences, the inferences will be materially deductively valid if we add all rebuttal factors with a probability greater than zero. But the critic could point out that many inferences (for example, causal ones) are open-textured in the sense that there can be an almost indefinite number of rebuttal factors ranging from the probable to the barely conceivable. Must we include premisses to block all of these? If so, how then can we have a practically useful yet logically effective procedure?

Consider again the argument about Harry: "Harry was born in Bermuda, so he is a British subject." A knowledgeable critic might think, "unless both his parents are not British subjects or unless he has changed his nationality." Depending on what the critic knows about Harry either or both of these possibilities might be negated to serve as a supplementary premiss. But it would also be intelligible to regard "Harry is dead" as an rebuttal factor, or even "Harry is not a human being." These propositions could be converted into the premiss candidates "Harry is alive" and "Harry is a human being," respectively. To make the inference as valid as possible we would need to add these and perhaps many more, as Machina would suggest, so that the method seems to be too unwieldly for practical application.

The response to this objection is simply to say that a satisfactory argument need not be even deductively valid, much less formally valid. To think it must is a symptom of deductivist bewitchment. It is to think, in effect, "We can't plug all the logical holes in the dike of argument, so what's the use of building it in the first place?" But of course those of us who have been to the Netherlands know that a dike with some small leaks can be just as useful as one with none.

Another theoretical issue that must be addressed is a challenge from Michael Burke, who argues that "needing to be true for validity" is not a correct criterion for identifying missing premisses. Burke discusses several concepts or theories of missing assumptions. One of them is identified with Michael Scriven's views as found in *Reasoning* (1976) where, it appears, Scriven uses the rebuttal-factor strategy as part of his evaluation procedure. For instance, part of one of Scriven's examples is "He is a homosexual; hence, he is prone to blackmail." Scriven then goes on to say that the argument "assumes that the individual is not already known to be a homosexual." This assumption represents the negation of a rebuttal factor: if he is a homosexual then he is prone to blackmail, unless he is already known to be a homosexual. Burke complains that "Scriven has given no reason for thinking that the homosexual argument ... needs to contain as a premise the ... implausible assumption which ... needs to be true if its inference [is] to be justified" (1985, 114).

One's first reaction to this comment is that Burke is rejecting the gap-filler concept of a missing assumption, but the remarks that follow it show that he is really saying that "needing to be true if the inference is to be valid" cannot by itself be the criterion for acceptable missing assumptions. His evidence takes the form of adducing counterexamples, one of which is "There is at least one thing that is either an inference or a polar bear."

Burke's counterexamples decisively establish his point, I think, but they do not undermine the rebuttal-factor approach. The products of the effective application of the approach do indeed need to be true if the inference is to be valid, but the procedure has another criterion that eliminates Burke's counterexamples as contenders for missing-assumption status. For example, the rebuttal factor associated with the counterexample just given is "It is not the case that at least one thing is either an inference or a polar bear." This proposition has a probability of zero, so its negation cannot be put forward as a missing premiss of that argument. Adding it will not improve the level of validity.

Now if an argument can be useful and respectable even if it is not deductively valid, a practically useful procedure can be developed from the rebuttal-factor concept. If we identify all possible rebuttal factors for any argument and rank them R_1, R_2, R_3, etc., in order of decreasing probability (given P), we need only generate premises to block the more probable ones so that the inference meets some acceptable standard short of deductive validity.

Consider again the supposed argument that is deemed by the evaluator to have three rebuttal factors judged to have the following probabilities: $p(R_1/P) = 0.4$; $p(R_2/P) = 0.3$; and $p(R_3/P) = 0.2$. Now suppose further that there are two other rebuttal factors with $p(R_4/P) = 0.1$ and $p(R_5/P) = 0.05$. In its original form the argument has an inference rating of 0.3 (0.287 rounded off). If we add not-R_1 as a premiss, the rating goes up to 0.5 (0.479 rounded off). If not-R_2 is added, the rating becomes 0.7 (0.684 rounded off). Adding not-R_3 raises it to 0.9 (0.855). Adding not-R_4 raises it to 0.95.

The pattern exhibited here indicates that as we take account of more of the low-probability rebuttal factors, the inference rating converges toward 1.0. That is, there is a smaller and smaller change in $p(C/P)$ as we add more rebuttal factors. In terms of a trade-off between complexity and validity, we need to choose a value for $p(C/P)$ that is considered satisfactory, so that rebuttal factors below some level can be safely ignored. I will return to a discussion of what that level might be, shortly.

Two practical problems must now be addressed: (1) How are we to choose among the rebuttal-factor candidates in generating blocking premises? (2) How many premises need to be added?

Which rebuttal factor should we begin with in generating premises? By starting with R_1 and proceeding in order, we will upgrade the inference by adding the fewest premises. This is desirable on four grounds: (1) the original argument ought to be changed as little as possible to avoid a complaint by the arguer that the suggested assumptions result in an argument s/he no longer considers to be his or hers; (2) for purposes of criticism it is generally less laborious to evaluate fewer assumptions rather than more; (3) more seriously, if we do not choose on the basis of relative probability, we will have no criterion for choice at all and the method would be unusable; (4) as a vehicle for argument criticism, there is no point in a critic suggesting the addition of a premiss based on what s/he takes to be a low-probability rebuttal factor, since s/he would not consider it to be criticizable.

Given this criterion for the order of selection among identified rebuttal factors, how many premises ought to be added? My view is that we should add them until the value for $p(C)$ is within about one rating level of the value calculated by taking all rebuttal factors that we can identify into account. What is needed is a rule that directs us to stop adding premises beyond not-R_p when the value of $p(R_p/P)$ is such that ignoring less probable rebuttal factors does not result in an inference rating much below 0.9, say. To be more specific, if $p(R_p/P)$ is at the cutoff point, so that we add "not-R_p" as a premiss, but no others, the value for $p(C/P)$ is

$$p(C/P) = (1 - p(R_{p+1}/P)) \times (1 - R_{p+2}/P) \times \ldots (1 - R_n/P).$$

In the last example we stipulated that there were five rebuttal factors identified, having the following probabilities: $p(R_1/P) = 0.4$; $p(R_2/P) = 0.3$; $p(R_3/P) = 0.2$; $p(R_4/P) = 0.1$; and $p(R_5/P) = 0.05$. Suppose we accept a rule of exclusion that directs us to ignore any rebuttal factor with a rating below, say, 0.3. In this case we would add premises "not-R_1" and "not-R_2." Having done so, we find that $R_3 = R_p$, so that inference quality is

$$p(C/P) = (1 - 0.2) \times (1 - 0.1) \times (1 - 0.05) = 0.684 \text{ (rating: 0.7)}.$$

A rating of 0.7 is not awfully close to validity, but if we treat the inference as valid for purposes of evaluation, then the conclusion-support rating (stipulating that the rating for P is 1.0) is

$$p(C) = 1.0 \times 0.6 \times 0.7 = 0.42 \text{ (rating: 0.4)}.$$

The correct value for $p(C)$ without adding any premises would be

$$1.0 \times [(1 - 0.4) \times (1 - 0.3) \times (1 - 0.2) \times (1 - 0.1) \times (1 - 0.05)],$$

which is 0.2873 (rating: 0.3). Therefore, in treating the inference as valid after the two premises have been added, the conclusion-support rating is within one rating level of the true value. This result may seem strange, given that the inference rating is a significant amount below 1.0, but it is explained by the mathematical "dominance" of the higher-probability rebuttal factors in the calculation of $p(C)$.

On the other hand, if we add a third premiss "not-R_3," the value for $p(C/P)$ would be 0.855 (rating: 0.9), so we are rather closer to validity. Assuming the inference is actually valid, $p(C)$ based on all premises is 0.336 (rating: 0.3). This is the correct rating, taking all rebuttal factors into account.

The results of choosing different cutoff values for excluding rebuttal factors in this example show that when we look for an exclusion principle, we are engaged in a trade-off. From the point of view of the labour involved, the fewer premises we add, the better. On the other hand, the fewer we add, the less accurate will be our conclusion-support rating. By adding three instead of two, we improve inference validity to a higher level and end up with the correct conclusion-support rating.

The rebuttal-factor inference-rating procedure I developed in chapter 6 led to a relatively simple formula for calculating inference ratings:

Inference rating = $1.0 - R_1$ rating $- (0.1 \times$ number of rebuttal factors rated above "0.2").

The formula was simple in part because it was found that when R_1 is rated above 0.2, the rebuttal factors rated 0.2 and lower had negligible impact on the inference rating.

Based on this formula, the policy I advocate here is that we add premises for R_1 and each of the other rebuttal factors rated 0.3 or higher, and add only "not-R_1" when R_1 is rated 0.2. We add none when R_1 is rated below 0.2.

9.3.1 A Procedure for Argument Evaluation

The procedure I advocate is based on the rebuttal-factor procedure presented in chapter 6, but whereas there we identified rebuttal factors in order to make an inference-rating judgment about a stated argument, here we transform them into supplementary premises, with a view to getting an argument that has an acceptable inference. Having done so, we then evaluate the premises (new and original) to obtain the conclusion-support rating. In effect, the only step of the original procedure given in chapter 3 (section 3.3.2) that needs to be structurally altered is step (2), although the form of response made at step (5) will be different.

Step 1 Construct a structural diagram for the argument.
Step 2 Inference evaluation:
    (a) Identify all "plausible" rebuttal factors (those that warrant a rating of 0.3).
    (b) Add the negation of each rebuttal factor as a premiss in the argument.
    (c) If the most plausible rebuttal factor, R_1, is rated 0.2, add only it to the argument.
    (d) If the most plausible rebuttal factor is rated 0.1, do not add any premisses.
Step 3 Evaluate P and enter the ratings for the supplementary premisses on the diagram. Their ratings will be calculated as "1.0 − rebuttal factor rating."
Step 4 Calculate the product of the premiss ratings. Rounded to one decimal place, this value is the conclusion-support rating.
Step 5 Generate a response that includes a critique of the original premiss, if appropriate, along with something of the following form: "The conclusion follows only if it is assumed that P_1, P_2, etc. But P_1 is [verbal rating from the premiss rating scheme, Table 3, sec. 3.2.4] because [evidence against P_1]. And P_2 ..."

    To illustrate the arithmetical validity of the procedure, I will consider an argument situation with a given set of rebuttal factor ratings. Suppose we have an argument in the form "P, so C," which we judge to have four rebuttal factors with these values: $R_1 = 0.5$; $R_2 = 0.3$; $R_3 = 0.2$; and $R_4 = 0.1$. The procedure dictates that we ignore the last two factors and add two premisses, "not-R_1" and "not-R_2," to the diagram. At step 3 we enter the ratings 0.5 and 0.7, respectively, and the rating for P, which I suppose to be 1.0. At step 4 we calculate $p(C)$: $1.0 \times 0.5 \times 0.7 = 0.35$. This value is rounded to a rating of 0.4.
    Now, suppose instead of adding the premisses, I had simply calculated $p(C/P)$ using the accurate formula

$$p(C/P) = (1 - 0.5) \times (1 - 0.3) \times (1 - 0.2) \times (1 - 0.1) = 0.252.$$

The rating 0.252 is rounded to 0.3, which is the "true" rating. Thus, in ignoring the lower-valued rebuttal factors, I have made a significant gain in simplicity, at the cost of a small amount of inaccuracy.

Now I want to discuss an actual argument in a context of dialogue to show the usefulness of this approach.

Suppose two British immigrant acquaintances of Harry are speculating about his present nationality. All three live in Canada. Both discussants know that Harry was born in Bermuda and that he has been living in Canada for some time. *S* says "Harry was born in Bermuda, so Harry is a British subject." *T* is familiar with the British Nationalities Act, which excludes a person from British subject status when (a) neither of the person's parents are British subjects, or (b) the person has become nationalized in another country. As a practioner of the rebuttal-factor approach, *T* thinks, "unless Harry has become a Canadian citizen, or Harry's parents were not British subjects." He remembers that Harry once told him that he was filling out the papers to obtain Canadian citizenship. He also remembers that Harry told him that he comes from a long-established Bermudian family. Thus, *T* selects "Harry has become a Canadian citizen" as the most probable of the two rebuttal factors by a considerable margin. In his mind he rates this 0.4 which corresponds to "more likely false than true" in the premiss rating scheme of chapter 3 (Table 3, sec. 3.2.4), because even though Harry had said he was filling out the papers, he thinks Harry would have told him if he had acquired Canadian citizenship. He rates the other factor as almost certainly false, or 0.1.

T then adds the negation of the rebuttal factor (Harry has not become a Canadian) as a premiss, which is rated 0.6. His conclusion-support rating is $0.6 \times 1.0 = 0.6$. This rating has a verbal equivalent in the conclusion-support table (Table 6, sec. 3.2.6) of "somewhat likely." Thus, *T* might respond to *S* by saying "your conclusion would follow if you make the assumption that Harry has not become a Canadian, but this is hardly more likely to be true than false. I recall that Harry once told me that he was filling out a Canadian citizenship application." If *S* had evidence, not possessed by *T*, that supported or proved the supplementary premiss, he could now bring it to *T*'s attention and perhaps thereby persuade *T* that Harry is indeed still a British subject.

The reader can note that the wording used in *T*'s response does not allege that *S* has assumed that Harry has not become a Canadian. This may not have been a used, but unmentioned, premiss at all. It is simply that *T* believes that it is needed to make the inference valid.

9.3.2 *Sufficiency, Preservation, and Plausibility*

In this section I want to see whether this missing premiss approach yields missing premiss candidates that meet three commonly accepted criteria for adding missing premisses: sufficiency, preservation, and plausibility.

The sufficiency requirement is that "the unstated premises must be sufficient to validate, or at least to strengthen, the inference" (Burke 1985, 107–19). Enough has been said already to indicate that the method can be used to meet the weaker version of this requirement.

The preservation requirement is that "we should try to preserve the role of the stated premises" (Burke 1985, 108). In using the rebuttal-factor approach, it was said, we try to complete a sentence of the form "If P then C unless ..." The items that are logically adequate for completion are the rebuttal factors associated with the argument. It should be obvious that the approach not only preserves the role of the stated premises, it relies on them in the sense that the original inference claim (If P then C) determines what is logically acceptable to follow "unless." For example, in the argument about Harry, "Harry was born in Canada" could not qualify as a rebuttal factor because it is incompatible with "Harry was born in Bermuda," the original premiss. A case can even be made for saying that reliance on stated premises should replace preservation as a criterion: a procedure that does not rely on stated premises effectively ignores them, even if it does not interfere with their role in the argument, and to this extent it amounts to ignoring the original argument.

As regards the plausibility criterion, it dictates that where a choice between two otherwise acceptable premises must be made, the principle of charity requires us to select the more plausible. This would not only result in the inference being improved a certain amount, it would also improve premiss quality. Now the rebuttal-factor approach involves blocking the most probable rebuttal factor first, then the next most probable, and so on. Since the added premises are negations of R_1, R_2, etc., this approach amounts to choosing the least likely premiss first and proceeding to the more likely. This seems to be, on the face of it, a most uncharitable method. However, as I have already demonstrated, adding any negated rebuttal factor alters the conclusion support to the same extent, that is, not at all. Choosing the most probable rebuttal factor as the basis for a premiss results in having the least probable premiss, but it is the one that improves inference validity most.

To summarize this part of the discussion: the rebuttal-factor method for missing premiss identification meets the sufficiency criterion and the preservation criterion. However, because of the conservation-of-proof feature that is peculiar to the method, it violates the plausibility criterion. But since it results in bringing to the arguer's attention the most serious inference problems in the argument, this should not be regarded as a deficiency.[3]

9.3.3 *Concluding Comments*

The example about Harry shows how the rebuttal-factor method shifts the target of criticism from inference to premisses. One adds needed premisses until the inference is satisfactory, then evaluates these premisses. As was shown earlier, the method features conservation of degree of proof. The degree of proof does not change when rebuttal-factor based premisses are added, but the inference becomes more acceptable. Whatever deficiencies are located in the original inference are shifted to the added premisses. In any event, the product of the process is one or more premisses that must be present for the inference to be satisfactory. If the evaluator finds the original inference unsatisfactory, s/he then considers the added premisses questionable.

The last statement might invite a question from some readers: Must the evaluator consider the added premisses questionable? The answer is "Yes."

Suppose the evaluator does not regard not-R_1 as questionable. It follows that s/he must consider R_1 to be false. Now proper use of the method precludes us from selecting such a claim as a legitimate rebuttal factor. If this claim is the most plausible candidate that can be identified, the arguee is committed to regarding the inference as acceptable.

An important advantage of the rebuttal-factor approach is that it requires critics to discriminate among candidates for extra premisses in terms of how much each would improve inference quality. In being taught the technique, students come to realize that not just any favourably relevant proposition should be put forward as a supplementary premiss. It is insisted that, given the content of the original argument and the knowledge they have that is pertinent to the topic, some candidates are better than others, and they must decide which.

A more fundamental question that could be asked is this: why use a supplementary-premiss approach in argument evaluation rather than an inference-evaluation approach? In terms of logical adequacy there is nothing to choose between the two approaches. In terms of ease of application, inference criticism has a slight edge, in that the added-premiss approach requires an extra step: we must generate the missing premisses from the identified rebuttal factors. This is not particularly difficult, however, as the above example shows.

The supplementary-premiss approach has one important and often-overlooked advantage: it enables the critic to formulate argument deficiencies in a way that is clearer for most people. Very few untrained people, I have found, can recognize or do good inference criticism, but many can recognize and do good premiss criticism. Apparently this difference is to be explained by a poor grasp of the logic of conditionals and certain factors that influence our judgments of them.[4] By shifting the target of criticism from inference to premisses it is possible to make criticism more intelligible to the arguer, and thus more persuasive if it is well founded.

10 Conclusion

Since the goal of this book has been to present a system, including strategies, for argument evaluation, it is not possible to state some particular thesis that I regard as having been proved. It is more appropriate to provide a brief outline of the system developed and to indicate how the various chapters are relevant to different aspects of it. And since I conceive of the essay as a work in informal logic, it seems appropriate to indicate the problems that it addresses within the subject.

10.1 THE ARGUMENT-EVALUATION SYSTEM

This book presents a formal procedure for argument evaluation, intended to enable argument "consumers" to accurately judge how well arguments support conclusions, in light of the information they have. It is a five-step procedure (outlined in chapter 3) employing probability estimates for uninferred premisses and inferences, so as to arrive at a "degree-of- support" judgment for the final conclusion.

Step 1 (sec. 3.3.2) is concerned with constructing a diagrammatic representation of an argument. Among other things, this involves becoming clear about the content and structure of the argument. I do not discuss this facet of the procedure, except the issue of adding missing premisses (see chapter 9). There are several texts that provide guidance in argument analysis.[1] I do discuss (chapter 4) the two main diagram formats that have gained favour in the textbooks, concluding that the "Scriven-type" diagram is better suited for purposes of argument evaluation.

Step 2, inference evaluation, has as its goal assigning a probability value to each inference claim. The sequence recommended is

(a) Explore the possibility that inferences are formally valid. The common techniques for assessing formal deductive validity were described and evaluated in chapter 5. It is worth keeping in mind that
   (i) an inference embodies a valid syllogism only if it refers to three classes and has two premisses with one class mentioned in both, but not in the conclusion;
   (ii) an inference embodies a formally valid pattern in propositional deduction only if it contains a conditional assertion or an alternation (disjunction), or an assertion logically equivalent to one of these.
(b) Are the premisses relevant to their conclusions? This question might be answered by utilizing knowledge of the "fallacies of relevance" obtainable from a number of sources.[2] If there is a single premiss for a conclusion and it is irrelevant, that inference can be rated o.o. If any member of a set of premisses is irrelevant, it can be ignored in evaluating the inference.
(c) If premisses are relevant, we should make a judgment of the inductive strength of the inference. Several procedures for doing this were described and evaluated in chapter 6. I advocated the use of the rebuttal-factor approach, which is based on Toulmin's model of argument. Just as acquaintance with the classical fallacies is useful in identifying irrelevant premisses, acquaintance with the presumptively valid patterns presented in the inductive argument typology of chapter 7 can help in arriving at a value for $p(C/P)$.

Step 3, evaluation of uninferred premisses, is discussed in chapter 8. I have presented considerations favourably and unfavourably relevant to each of the eight kinds of propositions identified in chapter 7.

Step 4, determining conclusion ratings, directs the evaluator to calculate conclusion ratings using the product rule "$p(C) = p(P) \times p(C/P)$." Although step 4 is the simplest step to execute, it is crucial for accuracy, given the almost universal incidence of the conjunction fallacy (see chapter 3). The effect of committing this fallacy is to assign conclusion-support ratings that are too high.

Step 5, formulating a response to the argument, involves formulating a verbal equivalent for the support rating of the final conclusion (see the conclusion-support table (Table 6) in chapter 3) and justifying that "verdict" by citing concisely the main weaknesses of the argument as identified at steps 2 and 3.

10.2 PROBLEMS OF INFORMAL LOGIC ADDRESSED BY THIS BOOK

The value of what is contained in this book might be assessed in terms of a list of problems formulated by Johnson and Blair in their discussion of the nature of informal logic as a discipline at the First International Symposium on Informal Logic. Although they modestly say that they present only a "partial list of problems and issues" (1980, 25), I regard it as quite comprehensive. Indeed, it seems to provide something like an enumerative definition of the field of informal logic.

In what follows I will try to say how this book addresses some of the problems and issues they mention.[3]

1 *The theory of logical criticism*
(a) What is the purpose of logical criticism? The use of the definite article presupposes that there is a single purpose, or at least a single main purpose. It is doubtful that logical criticism has only one purpose. I regard its main purpose as ascertaining the support that arguments provide for their final or main conclusions. But logical criticism can have other purposes too. For instance, in formal debating contests and in court trials, an individual's purpose may be to undermine the arguments of an opponent.
(b) Can an overall theory of logical criticism be developed? The answer implied in this essay is "No," if such a theory involves the use of a single general strategy to be relied on in evaluating all inferences. Given that the purpose of logical criticism is to arrive at inference-quality judgments for any argument (that is, values of $p(C/P)$), we must face the fact that, although content is the main determiner of inference quality in everyday argument, logical form can also determine quality, in the sense that formal deductive validity is sufficient to determine the inference rating in particular cases. Thus, as the procedure outlined in the last section reflects, our repertoire of logical criticism and inference evaluation strategies must be pluralistic.
(c) What are the criteria to be invoked in logical criticism? The most general criterion is that of premiss sufficiency, which for most natural argumentation is a matter of adequate evidence.[4] However, this criterion is far too general to bring us reliably to specific critiques of actual arguments. In the case of inductive argument, the criteria used are dependent on the kind of inference pattern we are dealing with. In chapter 7 I provide a typology of patterns and identify the rebuttal factors whose absence must be established if we are to judge an inference to be acceptable to us.

2 *The theory of argument*

(a) What is the nature of argument? In chapter 1 I follow van Eemeren and Grootendorst in holding that the utterance of an argument
constitutes the performance of an illocutionary act complex, with S's
intention being to bring about the perlocutionary effect of convincing H that C ought to be believed because P is alleged to be true.
This is the "argument-as-act" concept. The other concept of argument, the one of primary interest in this essay, has a process-product
relation to the first. It is the propositional complex concept.

(b) How is argument related to reasoning? I do not deal with this
question, but one plausible answer to it is that the utterance of an argument is an outcome of a reasoning process. On the recipient's
(H's) part, arriving at a conclusion-support judgment after following
the five-step procedure represents the outcome of a reasoning process, that is, an argument evaluation.

(c) Is there a value to developing a typology of argument? I think
anyone who sees value in fallacy classification from the purely academic or theoretical point of view must say "Yes." Chapter 7, where I
present a typology of inductive argument, shows that I also think so.
To be thorough in developing argument-evaluation strategies, we
need to identify argument patterns systematically. Identifying principles of classification and applying them is essential for comprehen-
siveness in the identification and individuation of patterns.

(d) What are the standards that arguments (especially mundane arguments) should meet? I have been at pains to argue that rationality
of belief and action does not require an argument to be deductively
valid to be acceptable. I think it is rational to regard a conclusion as
true for purposes of acting when we judge $p(C)$ to be 0.8 or greater.
The deductivist standard has, for much of the history of Western
philosophy, been the professed standard for inference quality, its
prominence waxing and waning with the influence of logicians in
the discipline. However, the actual argumentation that has led to
progress on philosophical issues over the centuries suggests that the
deductivist standard is commonly professed but not so commonly invoked. But the influence of deductivism runs deep, and, to the extent that one is under its influence, one will find much to object to
in this essay.

(e) What principles should be decisive here? I will respond to this
only by referring to, not stating, the principles that should be decisive: the principles of rationality governing action. My $p(C)$ value of
0.8 or greater, mentioned above, meets the standard of rationality at
least in the sense that, if one were asked to say whether a particular
conclusion ought to be accepted or rejected, it would be reasonable

to accept it if one thought the argument made $p(C)$ at least 0.8. It would be entirely unreasonable to choose to reject it. Of course, having accepted it, one might subsequently find unforeseen decisive evidence to the contrary. But rationality does not require withholding a judgment until all the evidence is in. It only requires us to be reasonably thorough in gathering it.

3 *The theory of fallacy*

What is the nature of fallacy? Can the conditions of individual fallacies be identified? Can fallacies be individuated? How should fallacies be classified? Is there a correct principle of fallacy classification? Should the notion of fallacy be junked?

I do not address the issues raised in this connection. However, to the extent that the patterns in chapter 7 that I call "presumptively valid" represent what Scriven might be referring to as "the face of the coin whose reverse is the fallacies approach" (1987, 17), I am committed, by parity of reasoning, to saying that conditions of fallacies can be identified and that they can be individuated. I did argue in chapter 2 that an exclusively fallacy-oriented approach to inference evaluation is not adequate.

4 *The fallacy approach vs the critical-thinking approach*

What are the merits, and drawbacks, of each approach? As I argued in chapter 2, when we are doing argument evaluation, the fallacy approach is probably not adequate by itself. Several reasons were given: (1) the principle that an argument that is not an instance of some recognized fallacy is valid (or inductively strong) is controversial, relying on the questionable assumption that our fallacy typology is exhaustive; (2) preparing students to judge argument quality by acquainting them only with fallacious inference patterns frequently induces a belief that all arguments are defective, which manifests itself when they claim there is fallacious reasoning when there is none. I do not directly discuss the critical thinking approach, except insofar as it is exemplified in the "new wave" texts I talked about in chapter 2.

5 *The viability of the inductive/deductive dichotomy*

(a) Are mundane arguments inductive or deductive? I have argued and presented data for the view that almost no mundane arguments are deductively valid, owing mainly to the fact that people seldom employ conditionals and alternations (disjunctions) in arguing. Most deductively valid arguments that do appear are probably materially deductively valid.

(b) Are the validity/soundness criteria of evaluation inappropriate or outmoded? If so, what should replace them: effective argument? successful argument? plausible argument? persuasive argument? what? As my comment on the last question implies, requiring arguments to meet a deductive standard for acceptance is inappropriate, considering that we are persuaded by some arguments we encounter, and do not consider ourselves to be duped or logically "slack" in most such cases. As regards replacing the validity/soundness criteria, I argued explicitly that the two-term grading pairs "valid" or "invalid," "true" or "false," and "sound" or "unsound" are far too crude, given the fact that we often have good but insufficient evidence for our claims. And a deductively invalid argument can still include good grounds for its conclusion. For these reasons I have advocated probability-based rating schemes that can accomodate both deductive and inductive arguments. Such a system of grading terms probably amounts to a form of plausibility grading, although not exactly in Rescher's sense.[5]

Accomodation to, and recognition of, the "dichotomy" is built into the evaluation procedure at step (2). Following Hitchcock (1980), I take the view that deductive arguments are really only arguments that are deductively valid.[6] There is no non-normative class designated "deductive arguments." On this view, an argument that embodies the affirming-the-consequent fallacy is not a deductive argument.

6 *The ethics of argumentation and logical criticism*
Under the heading of the ethics of argumentation and logical criticism Johnson and Blair are most concerned with the problem of formulating a defensible principle of charity. This issue is not addressed in this book, but in my evaluation system it is relevant at step 1, where we try to state the argument clearly and fairly in our diagram. It does not arise in connection with the formulation of missing premises, as I take the position that the formulation of missing premises can be avoided (see chapter 9). It does not even arise in a major way if my own supplementary premise-based procedure is used, once the meaning of the uttered assertions has been fairly and clearly expressed.

7 *The problem of assumptions and missing premisses*
(a) What exactly is a missing premiss? I address this question in chapter 9, where I argue that only missing grounds are missing premisses and that propositions that support inference claims need not be treated as missing premisses, even if their inclusion yields an argument with a formally deductively valid inference.
(b) What different kinds of assumptions can be distinguished in argumentation? I do not address this issue.

(c) Which assumptions are significant for argument evaluation? My failure to address (b) is explained by the fact that in discussion of argument-evaluation strategies, one's concern is mainly with only one type of assumption – missing premises. Other kinds of assumptions[7] must be shared for an utterance to result in the illocutionary effect (H grasps that S has uttered an argument containing certain assertions having certain logical relationships – see chapter 1), but in general the only assumptions that have a bearing on one's evaluation are the missing premises added at step 1.

(d) How are missing premises to be identified and formulated? One approach that seems to be feasible was presented in section 9.3, developed from Toulmin's concept of a "rebuttal" (rebuttal factors). Following the identification of plausible rebuttal factors, one adds their denials, starting with the most plausible, until the inference has an acceptable degree of validity.

(e) Are these just practical and pedagogical questions, or theoretical as well? This question was not addressed, but if there is an issue about what qualifies as a missing premiss, it is a conceptual issue, and therefore theoretical.

8   *The problem of context*
The problem of context is not addressed in detail. Features of context have a bearing at step 1 of the procedure, since they influence what propositions (and their logical relationships) we take to be part of an argument. In this book I am primarily concerned with steps 2 and 3. Psychological aspects of context were discussed in chapter 1 in setting out the conditions for successfully uttering an argument.

9   *Extracting arguments from context*
Methods for extracting arguments from context are not discussed here. Elsewhere I cover this in some detail, from a practical rather than a theoretical perspective.[8]

10   *Methods of displaying arguments*
Methods of displaying arguments are addressed in chapter 4, where I argue for the practical superiority (from an evaluation point of view) of the Scriven-type diagram over the Toulmin type.

11   *The problem of pedagogy*
Pedagogical considerations have influenced the development and discussion of the argument-evaluation techniques presented here. The practical effectiveness of a technique is partly a function of

how easily it can be imparted and retained. All of the techniques advocated have been tested in my course on argument evaluation.

The expression "the problem of pedagogy" can be regarded as ambiguous, given the informal logic literature. In the above paragraph it has been used in the sense of "technique". But there is another, more fundamental, sense in which the problem is that of motivating students to acquire not just the use of logical skills but also the desire to use them. I have not addressed this important problem here.[9]

12 *The nature, division, and scope of informal logic*
The scope of informal logic has not been explicitly discussed. This book focuses specifically on argument evaluation. The subject of argument evaluation overlaps with, but is not identical with, applied informal logic. If we take the term "informal" literally and seriously, formal logic techniques would not count as part of informal logic. Yet they are sometimes useful and legitimate techniques of inference evaluation, which is one aspect of argument evaluation.

13 *The relationship of informal logic to other inquiries*
(a) The relationship of informal logic to formal logic was not discussed, but see the previous paragraph.
(b) Epistemology is not discussed, but clearly epistemological concepts such as evidence have a key role in the discussions of theoretical issues in informal logic.
(c) As for the philosophy of language, pragmatics, especially speech act theory, has an essential role to play in theories of argument, as chapter 1 shows.
(d) The literature on rhetoric and speech communication contains valuable information that most informal logicians are not aware of. Most people who regard themselves as doing informal logic are philosophers trained in the Anglo-American tradition (myself included). Rhetoric, as a field of study, has not been given adequate recognition or respect in our tradition. Apparently we are never exposed to the rhetoric studies literature because our tradition, which takes a highly analytic approach to problems in philosophy and consequently values clarity and stylistic simplicity, embodies the view that rhetoric is about techniques of persuasive speech and writing that are characteristically nonlogical.[10] My explorations in that literature in the course of writing this essay does leave an impression that rhetoric scholars are not preoccupied with the normative aspects of persuasion, but this is probably explained by their awareness that this is logicians' "turf." In any case, the reader will

have noted that I have taken advantage of the literature on rhetoric theory at various points, especially in chapters 7 and 8, where I rely heavily on the taxonomical work of Ehninger and Brockreide.

(e) Writings on the theory of debate appear to be part of the field of rhetoric studies. The literature is of value to informal logicians writing about practical argument evaluation issues and techniques, and those interested in argumentation as a dialectical activity.

(f) The psychology of reasoning, a specialty within cognitive psychology, has a direct bearing on argument-evaluation studies. Psychologists take a much more empirical approach to how ordinary people reason than do informal logicians.[11] In particular, the work of logicians on fallacies is much more like "armchair theorizing" than that of cognitive psychologists. The fallacies studied by logicians tend to be chosen for study because they have been written about by our predecessors, irrespective of the frequency of their commission.[12] This conservatism has prevented us from identifying some of the fallacies humans are susceptible to and apportioning our efforts according to frequency of occurrence. But the progress of cognitive psychology in this century has established it as the discipline that identifies fallacious reasoning patterns and attempts to explain scientifically why we use such patterns. Its findings are valuable to informal logic in at least two ways. First, the informal logic text designed to promote good reasoning will be more efficient if it trains the student to avoid the common reasoning errors humans actually make. Second, the findings of cognitive psychology in this area can provide grist for the fallacy-theory mill. At least one finding of cognitive psychology has had a big impact on the system of argument evaluation presented in this essay. I refer to the "conjunction fallacy" described in chapter 2: it leads people to assign a value to $p(C)$ by averaging the $p(P)$ and $p(C/P)$ values they have obtained. But the correct value of $p(C)$ is the product of the latter two, which is always of lesser magnitude, except when they are both exactly 1. A second fallacy not given much attention by logicians is the "base-rate" fallacy, which interferes with correct statistical reasoning. It is described in section 7.4, where I discuss its impact on evaluating arguments from authority.

The foregoing comments are intended to indicate to the reader how this essay fits into the informal logic corpus. This is, as far as I know, the first attempt to intensively exploit probability theory in the cause of argument evaluation. I hope to have shown that the potential of such an approach ensures that if this is the first word, it will not be the last.

Notes

1 Throughout, I will follow the convention of referring to the utterer of an argument as "S," and the individual or group to whom it is addressed as "H." When oral arguments are presented, S = speaker and H = hearer, on some occasions. However, it is not always the case that a person hearing an argument uttered is the person to whom it is addressed. (Think of spectators in court, for example.)

There seems to be no satisfactory pair of terms in use at this time to name the two parties in a persuasion context. Rhetoricians commonly use "speaker" and "audience" (e.g., Perelman and Olbrechts-Tyteca 1969), but the latter term in its standard use can include third parties, in the way "hearer" does. And of course "speaker" does not normally refer to authors. Perhaps the most appropriate pair of terms is "persuader" and "persuadee," although the latter is a neologism whose use would no doubt grate the sensibilities of traditionalists. Even so, I think this pair of terms (and their equivalents in other languages) ought to become standard usage in argumentation studies.

2 The derivation of this formula will be given in section 3.1.

3 The reader unfamiliar with speech act theory can obtain an efficient introduction by reading Searle's "What Is a Speech Act?" (1965).

4 The suppressed illocutionary force indicator for assertions is "it is asserted that." In the case of some illocutionary acts the force indicator is regularly used, for example, "I promise that," "I request."

5 Van Eemeren and Grootendorst (1983, 41) mark this distinction as one between "recognizable" (= clear) and "correct" (= paradigmatic).

6 Fogelin thinks that it is inappropriate to say that arguments contain assertions. He prefers to say that "in the argument 'p, so q,' one affirms 'q' on
the basis of the proposition 'p' that one also affirms" (1967, 17). His reason for preferring "affirm" to "assert" is the claim that "nothing is asserted
by the construction 'p so q.'" This claim seems unpersuasive because question-begging. There are differences between the two concepts. One can affirm without asserting; for example, if I say to someone "Do you think it will
rain today?" and s/he says, "Yes," s/he has affirmed that it will rain, but s/
he has not asserted, "It will rain." On the other hand, it seems that whenever one asserts that P, one is affirming that P. These differences make "assert" more suitable here.

7 Van Eemeren and Grootendorst (1983, 195–14) use "conclusion" as a synonym for "an expressed opinion following an argumentation and linked to
it." My usage will be the logician's one: a proposition claimed to be entailed by others, which serve as its premises.

CHAPTER TWO

1 According to Johnson and Blair, "Copi's *Introduction to Logic* … is the best
known and so stands as the preeminent example of this approach to logic
and informal logic … [His text] structure is repeated almost identically
time and again in introductory logic textbooks" (1980, 11).

2 The deduction system used by modern textbooks was pioneered by Ger-
hardt Gentzen (1934). He called it "natural" deduction, because the inference rules are thought to represent ones that untrained people use in
reasoning.

3 I am concerned here with evaluating logic texts, primarily. By virtue of
their contents, this involves, to some extent, an evaluation of formal logic
techniques as techniques for evaluating everyday argumentation. It must
be noted here that rhetoricians (rhetoric scholars) have, in favourable contrast with logicians, debated the usefulness of formal logic for this purpose.
Among the more notable debates, Anderson and Mortensen (1967) and
Shepard (1966) argued the negative; Mills and Petrie (1968) responded in
defence of symbolic logic, and Petrie (1969) elaborated and extended
their case.

4 Taken in a broad sense, syllogistic includes the square of opposition and a
set of immediate inferences arising from it. Thus, syllogistic can confirm
the validity of patterns other than standard syllogisms. But this additional
capability is not of much practical utility. For example, not many everyday
arguments have simple forms such as "All S are P, so it is not the case that
no S is P."

5 Examining the contents of the print media will confirm this, judging by a brief survey I made. I took one issue of the Toronto *Globe and Mail,* one of the London *Sunday Times,* and one Sunday edition of the *New York Times* and identified occurrences of conditionals and alternations in their editorials, opinion pieces, and letters. One would expect the greater amount of argumentation to appear in these sections. Of a total of 807 sentences examined, there were only 20 conditionals, only two of which appeared in arguments! Only two alternations were found, both within one argument.

6 To a great extent it is these considerations that have led cognitive psychologists to conclude that everyday inference making cannot be modelled on extant logical calculi: "it is clear that no conventional notion of logical form is viable for the analysis of ordinary deduction" (Wason and Johnson-Laird 1972, 93).

7 "I shall concentrate on deductive logic. I shall accept the contention that deductive logic – formal logic – is a body of necessary truths" (Goldman 1985, 4).

8 "[B]y the beginning of the 1970s a second generation of introductory texts had begun to appear ... this second wave of texts [is] devoted to informal logic as their main focus" (Blair and Johnson 1980, 11).

9 I believe I am especially qualified to do this by virtue of having used each one as an informal logic text prior to publishing my own.

10 Since *Reasoning* was published, Scriven has apparently come to see the need for attention to good patterns of inductive inference: "what we need is the face of the coin whose reverse is the fallacies approach. The fallacies approach is specific and can be very useful ... but it is essentially negative. It needs a better half, a more positive half" (1987, 17). He refers to this other part of informal logic as "probative logic." My chapter 7 qualifies as probative logic, I think.

11 Of the newer texts, Govier (1992) provides good detailed guidance on premiss acceptability and relevance and some very general guidance for dealing with ordinary inductive arguments. As I argue in chapter 7, specific advice for inference evaluation of inductive arguments can be done effectively only when we distinguish the more useful inductive patterns. Like the others, Govier seems to recognize only the inductive patterns found in the traditional texts. As chapter 7 shows, there are many more.

CHAPTER THREE

1 A restriction must be placed on the formula: P and C cannot be the same proposition. This restriction is necessary to deal with arguments involving petitio principi.

2 A number of writers have developed formulas for quantifying the support a new item of evidence adds to a given claim (hypothesis). See Kyburg (1964).

One of the most appealing formulas has been developed by Brian Ellis (1970). Where $p(C)_i$ is the prior probability of C, the support for C given by P is expressed as

$$S(C/P) = [p(C/P) - p(C)_i]/[1 - p(C)_i].$$

In the most impressive case, when H regards C as false, prior to the utterance of the argument, and accepts P as entailing C, $p(C)_i = 0$; $p(C/P) = 1$. Thus, $S(C/P) = 1$. The argument provides maximum support. At the other extreme, when $p(C/P)$ equals $p(C)_i$, $S(C/P) = 0$.

3 See Johnson (1987) for evidence to support this claim.

4 Roderick Chisholm has probably put more effort into developing scales of epistemic appraisal than anyone. See Chisholm (1973, 226–9), for example, and an alternative presented in response by Lucey (1976). Unfortunately, neither writer tries to correlate his terminology with probability values. The same is true of Rescher, who presents a seven-point scale ranging from "impossible" to "certain" (1964, 58).

5 Other writers are also aware of the problem, but not of course, as a difficulty for my evaluation system: Freeman notes that "convergent arguments may have false premises and yet still establish their conclusions." He depicts a convergent argument with three premises and imagines this situation: "Suppose statements (1) and (2) are both true and provide weighty evidence for (4), evidence sufficient to carry the day. Suppose, on the other hand, that statement (3) is false. Now although we may urge that the presence of (3) in this argument is a flaw, that the argument would be better off without it ... this does not mean that the argument is fallacious, that it does not establish its conclusion" (1991, 240).

CHAPTER FOUR

1 Toulmin's model has been extensively discussed in the literature. Ehninger and Brockreide (1960) introduced it to rhetoric and speech-communication scholars, who have found it to have considerable merit, judging by the number of texts that rely on it: "By mid-1968 Toulmin's model had been discussed in at least eight speech textbooks, five doctoral dissertations, and several articles" (Trent 1968, 252). Trent makes the astute observation that "The great appeal of Toulmin's model appears to be the emphasis on material validity which is achieved by de-emphasising formal validity" (255).

Philosophers and logicians have not been as enthusiastic, but some negative reactions are due to a failure to understand. Cowan (1964), for example, does not seem to realize that grounds and warrants are different in that the latter are support for the inference claim, rather than the conclusion.

An extended critique of the model is given by van Eemeren, Grootendorst, and Kruiger (1984). They take issue with Toulmin's sloppy use of important terms such as "valid" and "sound." They also argue that it is difficult in actual cases to distinguish data (ground) and warrant. I do not think it is as difficult as they do, as I will argue below.

2 There is no standardized term in the literature for what I am referring to. Govier follows Hitchcock in calling it "the associated conditional," but this term seems to imply that it has a somewhat peripheral role in argumentation. "Implicit conditional" might be better, but "inference claim" is more specific.

3 Ryle provides a compatible, but somewhat different, account of the role of the inference claim. He asks, "How does a valid argument require the truth of the corresponding hypothetical statement?" and responds " 'p, so q' does not embody 'If p then q' as a component of its premiss but rather applies it" (1950, 329). On this view, we might think of having two propositions, "P," and "If P then C," that we think H would believe and "applying" them to prove C to H.

4 It is this feature of inference claims that Lewis Carroll illustrates in his cautionary tale "What the Tortoise Said to Achilles" (1895), directed to those who believe that logic can compel belief. Govier also cites Carroll in arguing that "every argument 'assumes' the associated conditional" (1987, 96).

5 See Scriven (1976), Johnson and Blair (1983), Copi (1986), and Freeman (1988), among others.

6 See Scriven (1976, 50); Copi (1988, 21).

7 The Elvis example is an instance because we can word it as "*All things that are Elvis* are men. All men are mortal. So *all things that are Elvis* are mortal."

8 The appropriateness of applying the warrant/ground distinction to deductive logic derivations, and the example used here, were brought to my attention by a reviewer for the Aid to Scholarly Publications Program.

9 It appears that Freeman accepts this principle: "One conclusion, one case, one argument" (1991, 237).

CHAPTER FIVE

1 For some arguments containing relational predicates, the truth-tree method cannot provide a decision. For example, "Everyone loves someone, therefore Alma loves herself" is invalid, but the truth tree method does not yield this result (Jeffrey 1981, 127).

2 This alternative was brought to my attention by a reviewer for the Aid to Scholarly Publications Program.

3 A reviewer for the Aid to Scholarly Publications Program believes that accepting these into the fold as valid patterns creates a problem for my theory of how warrants are individuated in valid syllogisms.

In chapter 4 I argue that one of the premisses in a syllogism is actually a warrant for the inference claim generated by taking the other premiss as the evidence for the conclusion. I argue that the warrant is the "premiss" that does not contain the subject-term of the conclusion.

The problem the reviewer identifies is illustrated using the AAI-3 pattern:

All true Christians are happy with their state.
All true Christians are persecuted.
Therefore, some who are persecuted are happy with their state.

According to my criterion, the major (first) premiss is the warrant because it does not contain the referring expression of the conclusion. But the reviewer claims that this syllogism is "logically equivalent to"

All true Christians are persecuted.
All true Christians are happy with their state.
Therefore, some who are happy with their state are persecuted.

By my criterion, the first premiss is still the warrant, but now it is a different premiss in content. The reviewer argues that "It seems very harsh to say that this simple rewording switches ground and warrant."

Presumably, the two syllogisms are logically equivalent as syllogisms because their premisses are the same, and their conclusions are logically equivalent. The conclusions are indeed logically equivalent by conversion. However, they are not equivalent in one way that is important here: in uttering the two conclusions, the acts of reference and predication are different. The first one is about people who are persecuted, and the second is about people who are happy with their state.

4 Gerritsen makes this point in a general way: "What's more, Hitchcock himself indicates that the universal generalization thesis is to some extent indeterminate ... it is not always clear which terms in the associated conditional [that is, inference claim] should be generalized ... In formulating his thesis, Hitchcock therefore must make certain reservations ... These exceptions limit the use of Hitchcock's thesis, for how are we to decide in practice what is plausible or whether the context indicates a restriction or not?" (1991, 483).

5 This problem is expressed by Govier: "Since the generalization necessarily goes beyond what is said in the original, there is always the question of whether the author is really committed to it. This seems to me to constitute a real objection to Hitchcock's approach" (1987, 104n).

CHAPTER SIX

1 One who does is Freeman (1987, secs. 6.3, 8.1), although he takes them only as devices for deciding whether to evaluate an argument deductively or inductively.

   Surprisingly little has been written about the criteria for inference evaluation of such arguments. Benjamin (1982) argues that these qualifiers can be regarded as illocutionary-force indicators, but unfortunately I have been unable to examine his paper. Charles Caton discusses qualifiers in terms of what their use commits us to. For example, when one uses a moderately strong qualifier such as in "It is likely that p," one cannot go on to say "It is likely that not-p." Caton also expounds the axiom that "The epistemic qualifier on the conclusion ... cannot be stronger than that on the most weakly qualified premise, if the latter is essential to the argument" (1987, 309). This follows from the product rule for $p(C)$, since the product "$p(P_1) \times p(P_2) \times ... p(P_n)$" cannot exceed the value of the premiss having the lowest probability.

2 One might think that since inductive arguments can make their conclusions only more or less likely, everyday argument would be rife with modal qualifiers. But there is documented evidence that it is not. Trent, for example, writes, "Hastings [1962] found few qualified arguments when he examined a variety of sources. Smith [1962] found few in a Congressional debate, and Trent [1966] found none in an examination of 347 pages of courtroom argument" (Trent 1968, 259).

3 I believe he would use "inference claim" as I do, although he never writes an inference-claim down, apparently being content to identify them by referring to the inference claims of particular arguments.

4 This suggests that in using this method, we ought to consider the question of premiss relevance before seeking rebuttal factors. Here there is a need for acquaintance with the more common fallacies of relevance in inductive inference evaluation.

5 I wish to thank Dr Walter Finden of the Mathematics Department, Saint Mary's University, for confirming that the series is convergent on some value greater than zero.

CHAPTER SEVEN

1 For a very brief history, see Kienpointner (1987, 280–3).

2 The scholar currently most active in developing argument typologies is Dr Manfred Kienpointner (University of Innsbruck). He has developed (1992) a more adequate typology by modifying the Perelman and Olbrechts-Tyteca typology using Toulmin's model for argument (presented at the Second International Conference on Argumentation, Amsterdam 1990).

3 The philosopher Gilbert Harman discusses these as "inference from the best explanation" and "inference to the best explanation," respectively (1986, 67–8). It is interesting that he evinces no acquaintance with the extensive work done on these patterns by rhetoricians. I do not think he is untypical of philosophers in this respect.

4 A variant of this has been described by John Wisdom, whose version is discussed by Govier (1987, chap. 4). It can be written in the form "Case x has features a, b, c. Case y has features a, b, c also. Case x is of type e. Therefore, case y is of type e also."

5 Statistically based inferences have been studied intensively. Most informal logic and critical thinking texts provide some guidance for their evaluation. Among the more thorough are Govier (1992, 326–34) and Barry and Soccio (1988, 257–84). The latter is especially thorough.

6 Though there are no doubt cases that prevent us from drawing a sharp conceptual line between physical- and mental-world claims, I accept Strawson's way of making the distinction. In discussing predicates that can be ascribed to persons, he distinguishes "M-predicates" from "P-predicates": "The first kind of predicate consists of those which are also properly applied to material bodies to which we would not dream of applying predicates ascribing states of consciousness … The second kind consists of all the other predicates we apply to persons" (1959, 100). Thus, mental-world claims involve the ascription of P-predicates, and physical world claims involve the ascription of M-predicates, that is, predicates that are ascribable to material objects (including humans qua material beings).

7 Govier has drawn attention to some work of Carl Wellman, who identifies what he calls "conductive" argument. According to Govier: "In conductive reasoning where there are several supporting premises, we draw together these independently relevant factors to support a conclusion" (1987, 66).

8 A good discussion of excuses and justifications is provided in Heintz (1981).

9 A recent book-length study of issues related to supererogation is Heyd (1982). Montague (1989) presents an analysis of the concept of supererogation itself.

10 This is a topic on which there is a considerable philosophical literature. See Raz (1978). His introduction is especially helpful in that he makes some distinctions that are important for the evaluation of practical inferences. He faces squarely the fact that we are often faced with conflicting action-guiding reasons. He defines a reason for acting in a particular situation as "a fact which by itself is sufficient to necessitate a certain course of action, provided no other factors defeat it." Defeating factors (which qualify as rebuttal factors) are of two kinds: (1) conflicting reasons, that is, ones for refraining from the act, and (2) other facts that are not reasons for an incompatible act. He calls the latter "cancelling conditions." Given the argument "John promised to do A, so John ought to do A," "Doing A will

insult John's father" is a conflicting reason, and "John was released from his promise" is a cancelling condition (12).

Writers in the social policy field have done valuable work on prudential arguments as policy arguments. Gasper (1991), for example, provides a very useful detailed account of the criteria that such arguments must meet. May (1991) offers a useful discussion of some of the classical quasi-syllogistic patterns of ends-means reasoning.

11 Ethical claims involving "right," "wrong," "good," "evil," and the like, are evaluative, but I will not discuss them specifically. The role of ethical evaluative terms in ethical reasoning has been discussed extensively by philosophers, especially in the English-speaking world since World War Two. Perhaps the most important figure here is R. M. Hare.

Writers in other disciplines have also made contributions, shaped by their interests. For example, Tuman (1987) provides an account of considerations relevant to constructing arguments for value propositions in a formal debating situation.

12 Some philosophers would regard this inference as illegitimate because they hold some version of the principle that one cannot derive a value claim from a "factual" one. I believe that John Searle has shown this principle to be incorrect, at least where stipulative definitions are involved. Contrary to Urmson (1950), Searle argues that when an apple meets criteria *A*, *B*, and *C*, this entails that it is Extra Fancy Grade (in Britain) by virtue of a formal definition of this evaluative expression by the British Ministry of Agriculture and Fisheries. Searle recognizes that the utterance of "This apple meets criteria *A*, *B*, and *C*" amounts to an illocutionary act of description, and that the utterance of "This apple is Extra Fancy Grade" amounts to an illocutionary act of evaluating, but argues, "But the fact that the two utterances have characteristically different illocutionary forces is not sufficient to show that the proposition expressed in the first utterance does not entail the proposition expressed in the second" (1969, 136).

It might be objected that the example differs importantly from everyday arguments for evaluative claims, in that it relies on a stipulated definition representing a constitutive rule. That is why the entailment relation exists. But we do not need to claim that the relationship is entailment in informal evaluative cases. We need only to say, following Searle, that the proposition containing the criteria represents evidence for the proposition expressed in the conclusion.

13 For an up-to-date treatment, see Walton (1989).

14 This point was made by David Hume in his "Of Miracles," section x of *An Enquiry Concerning Human Understanding*: "[When] the fact which the testimony endeavours to establish partakes of the extraordinary and the marvellous – in that case the evidence resulting from the testimony admits of a diminution, greater or less in proportion as the fact is more or less unusual ... 'I should

not believe such a story were it told to me by Cato' was a proverbial saying in Rome ... The incredibility of the fact ... might invalidate so great an authority." For discussion of Hume's views on miracles from the perspective of Bayes' Theorem, see Sobel (1987) and Owen (1987).

15 Ennis (1962, 90) provides a concise but detailed account of criteria for reliability of observation statements.

16 See Aristotle *Prior Analytics* 69a; Whately (1851, 27–8); Mill (1978, 555–61).

17 See Aristotle *Poetics* 1475b, and *Topics* 108a; Whately (1851, 27–8); Mill (1978, 554–5); Govier refers to proportional analogies as a priori analogies (1989, 141–9).

18 See Barker (1989, 187–8).

19 See Brown (1989, 169–70).

CHAPTER EIGHT

1 See Wittgenstein (1951). The example was intended to show that useful concepts need not have any necessary conditions governing their application.

2 This condition apparently rules out the pattern "*A*, so *A* or *B*" as acceptable, even though it is valid in the propositional calculus.

CHAPTER NINE

1 For a comprehensive list of kinds, see Govier (1987, 92)

2 Much of the material in the foregoing sections of this chapter appeared in Grennan (1995).

3 I wish to thank two referees from *Informal Logic*, Robert Ennis and an anonymous referee, for constructive comments on an earlier version of section 9.3.

4 Cognitive psychologists have identified several illegitimate influences we are prone to in judging inferences. Miller reviews the literature and concludes that "there is considerable evidence that an individual's attitude toward the content of an argument influences his judgment of its logical soundness" (1969, 283). Janis and Frick (1943) studied syllogistic inference evaluation and found (1) if the evaluator accepts the conclusion, s/he is more prone to accept as valid arguments that are invalid, and (2) if s/he rejects the conclusion, s/he is more prone to reject valid arguments as invalid.

CHAPTER TEN

1 See especially Thomas (1973) and Grennan (1984, chap. 8).

2 Among textbooks, Michalos (1970) and Damer (1980) are comprehensive sources.

3 In the remainder of this section, the questions with which I begin each item in the list are from Blair and Johnson (1980, 25–6).

4 Philosophers and logical theorists have not given a great deal of attention to analyzing our ordinary concept of evidence, considering its importance. A modern *locus classicus* is Achinstein (1983), an anthology in which the editor includes an important essay, "Concepts of Evidence" (22–45). A recent paper that critiques and builds on it is Phillips (1991).

5 Rescher considers that the plausibility of a thesis, as he conceives of it, is distinct from its probability: "The plausibility of a thesis will not be a measure of its probability – of how likely we deem it ... Rather, it reflects the prospects of its being fitted into our cognitive scheme of things in view of the standing of the sources or principles that vouch for its inclusion herein" (1977, 38). He goes on to say that "the probative strength of confirming evidence could serve as yet another basis of plausibility" (39). Rescher's theory is nicely summarized in McKerrow (1987).

The *Concise Oxford Dictionary* (1990) defines "plausible" as "(of an argument, statement, etc.) seeming reasonable or probable," and "probable" is defined as "likely." Thus, usage sanctions the term "plausible" for my applications. However, I chose not to use it because of a suspicion that in logic Rescher has preempted it.

6 Skyrms shares this view: "Deductive and inductive logic are not distinguished by the different types of arguments with which they deal, but by the different standards against which they evaluate arguments" (1986, 13).

7 See Govier (1987, 92) for a list of such assumptions.

8 See Grennan (1984, chap. 8).

9 The need to recognize this pedagogical problem for informal logic and critical thinking has recently been vigorously argued by Shelagh Crooks (1995). She draws our attention to challenging, if not distressing, research indicating that students cannot be assumed to share our epistemic values, and she suggests ways of "converting" them, so as to ensure that they will use what they learn.

10 Note that the second entry for "rhetoric" in *The Concise Oxford Dictionary* (1990) is "language designed to persuade or impress (often with an implication of insincerity or exaggeration, etc.)."

11 The best "entry-level" source for logicians is Baron (1988), who provides syntheses of the primary literature. Important book-length primary sources include Evans (1982), Johnson-Laird and Wason (1968), Johnson-Laird (1983), and Nisbett and Ross (1980), Kahneman, Slovic, and Tversky (1982), and Hogarth (1987). The latter provides an excellent classified bibliography (appendix E) on decision making, reasoning errors, and related topics.

12 There is active debate on how frequently fallacies are committed. Finocchiaro (1981) argues that they occur only in logic textbooks! Govier (1987, chap. 9) provides a thorough account of the issue, including a response to Finocchiaro.

Bibliography

Adams, E.W. 1975. *The Logic of Conditionals.* Dordrecht: Reidel.

Achinstein, P., ed. 1983. *The Concept of Evidence.* Oxford: Oxford University Press.

Allen, D. 1988. "Inferential Soundness." *Informal Logic* 10(2): 57–67.

Anderson, R.L., and C.D. Mortensen. 1967. "Logic and Marketplace Argumentation." *Quarterly Journal of Speech* 53: 143–51.

Barker, E. 1989. "Beardsley's Theory of Analogy." *Informal Logic* 11(3): 173–85.

Baron, J. 1988. *Thinking and Deciding.* Cambridge: Cambridge University Press.

Barry, V.E., and D.J. Soccio. 1988. *Practical Logic.* New York: Holt, Rinehart & Winston.

Beardsley, M. 1950. *Practical Logic.* New York: Prentice-Hall.

Bedell, G. 1976. "Teaching the Material Conditional." *Teaching Philosophy* 2(3–4): 225–36.

Behn, R.D., and J.W. Vaupel. 1982. *Quick Analysis for Busy Decision Makers.* New York: Basic Books.

Benjamin, R.L. 1982. "The Sentence Adverb as an Illocutionary Act." Western Speech Communication Association Annual Convention, Denver, Colorado.

Benoit, W.L., and J.J. Lindsey. 1987. "Argument Fields and Forms of Argument in Natural Language." Chapter 24 in *Argumentation across the Lines,* edited by van Eemeren, Grootendorst, Blair, and Willard. Vol. 3A.

Blair, J.A., and R.H. Johnson, eds. 1980. *Informal Logic: The First International Symposium.* Inverness, CA: Edgepress.

Brown, W.R. 1989. "Two Traditions of Analogy." *Informal Logic* 11(3): 161–73.

Burke, M. 1985. "Unstated Premises." *Informal Logic* 7(2–3): 107–19.

Burleson, B.R. 1979. "On the Analysis and Criticism of Arguments: Some The-
    oretical and Methodological Considerations." *Journal of the American Forensic
    Association* 15(3): 137–47.

Carroll, L. 1895. "What the Tortoise Said to Achilles". *Mind* 4: 278–80.

Caton, C. 1987. "Is There an Epistemic Theophrastean Rule for Actual Argu-
    ments?" Chapter 34 in *Argumentation across the Lines*, edited by van Eemeren,
    Grootendorst, Blair, and Willard. Vol. 3.

Chisholm, R.M. 1973. "On the Nature of Empirical Evidence." In *Empirical
    Knowledge*, edited by R.M. Chisholm and R.J. Swartz. Englewood Cliffs, NJ:
    Prentice-Hall.

Cohen, L.J. 1981. "Can Human Irrationality Be Experimentally Demon-
    strated?" *Behavioral and Brain Sciences* 4: 317–30.

Copi, I.M. 1967. *Symbolic Logic*. 3d ed. Toronto: Collier-Macmillan.

– 1982. *Introduction to Logic*. 6th ed. New York: MacMillan.

– 1986. *Informal Logic*. New York: MacMillan.

Cowan, J.L. 1964. "The Uses of Argument – An Apology for Logic." *Mind* 73:
    27–45.

Cox, J.R., and C.A. Willard, eds. 1982. *Advances in Argumentation Theory and Re-
    search*. Carbondale, IL: Southern Illinois University Press.

Crooks, S. 1995. "Developing the Critical Attitude." *Teaching Philosophy* 18(4):
    313–25.

Dale, A.J. 1974. "A Defence of Material Implication." *Analysis* 34(3): 91–5.

Damer, T.E. 1980. *Attacking Faulty Reasoning*. Belmont, CA: Wadsworth.

Eemeren, F.H. van, and R. Grootendorst. 1983. *Speech Acts in Argumentative Dis-
    cussions*. Dordrecht: Foris.

Eemeren, F.H. van, R. Grootendorst, J.A. Blair, and C.A. Willard, eds. 1987. *Ar-
    gumentation across the Lines of Discipline: Proceedings of the Conference on Argu-
    mentation, 1986*. 3 vols. Dordrecht: Foris Publications.

– 1991. *Proceedings of the Second International Conference on Argumentation*. 3 vols.
    Amsterdam: SICSAT.

Eemeren, F.H. van, R. Grootendorst, and T. Kruiger. 1984. *The Study of Argu-
    mentation*. New York: Irvington.

Eemeren, F.H. van, and T. Kruiger. 1987. "Identifying Argumentation Schemes."
    Chapter 8 in *Argumentation across the Lines*, edited by van Eemeren, Grooten-
    dorst, Blair, and Willard. Vol. 3A.

Ehninger, D., and W. Brockreide. 1960. "Toulmin on Argument: An Interpre-
    tation and Application." *Quarterly Journal of Speech* 46: 44–53.

– 1963. *Decision by Debate*. New York: Dodd, Mead & Company.

Ellis, B.D. 1970. "Explanation and the Logic of Support." *Australasian Journal
    of Philosophy* 48(2): 177–89.

– "Two Theories of Indicative Conditionals." *Australasian Journal of Philosophy*
    62(1): 50–66.

Ennis, R. 1962. "A Concept of Critical Thinking." *Harvard Educational Review*
    32(1): 81–111.

– 1982. "Identifying Implicit Assumptions." *Synthese* 51: 61–86.

Evans, J.S.B.T. 1982. *The Psychology of Deductive Reasoning*. London: Routledge & Kegan Paul.

Finocchiaro, M. 1981. "Fallacies and the Evaluation of Reasoning." *American Philosophical Quarterly* 18(1): 13–22.

Fisher, W.R. 1978. "Toward a Logic of Good Reasons." *Quarterly Journal of Speech* 64: 376–84.

Fogelin, R.J. 1967. "Inferential Constructions." *American Philosophical Quarterly* 4(1): 15–27.

Freeley, A.J. 1966. *Argumentation and Debate*. 2d ed. Belmont, CA: Wadsworth.

Freeman, J. 1988. *Thinking Logically: Basic Concepts for Reasoning*. Englewood Cliffs, NJ: Prentice-Hall.

– 1991. *Dialectics and the Macrostructure of Arguments*. New York: Foris.

Gasper, D.R. 1991. "Policy Argumentation – On Practical Theory and Teachable Tools". Chapter 107 in *Conference on Argumentation*, edited by van Eemeren, Grootendoorst, Blair, and Willard. Vol. 1B.

Gentzen, G. 1934. "Untersuchungen über der logische Schliesen." *Mathematische Zeitschrift* 39: 121–76. Published in translation as "Investigations Into Logical Deduction." *American Philosophical Quarterly* 2: 288–306.

Gerritsen, S. 1991. "Problems of Unexpressed Premises in Writing Argumentative Texts." Chapter 63 in *Conference on Argumentation*, edited by van Eemeren, Grootendorst, Blair, and Willard. Vol. 1A.

Goldman, A. 1985. "The Relation between Epistemology and Psychology." *Synthese* 64(1): 29–68.

Gough, J., and C. Tindale. 1985. "'Hidden' or 'Missing' Premisses." *Informal Logic* 7(2–3): 99–107.

Govier, T. 1981. "Rigor and Reality." *Queen's Quarterly* 88(3): 525–35.

– 1987. *Problems in Argument Analysis and Evaluation*. Dordrecht: Foris Publications.

– 1989. "Analogies and Missing Premisses." *Informal Logic* 11(3): 141–53.

– 1992. *A Practical Study of Argument*. 3d ed. Belmont, CA: Wadsworth.

Grennan, W. 1984. *Argument Evaluation*. Lanham, MD: University Press of America.

– 1985. "Testing Syllogisms with Venn-Equivalent Truth-Table Methods." *Teaching Philosophy* 8(3): 237–9.

– 1986. "A Logical Audit Scheme for Two-Premiss Arguments." *Informal Logic* 8(3): 125–32.

– 1991. "An Unrecognized Part of the Informal Logic Program." Chapter 45 in *Conference on Argumentation*, edited by van Eemeren, Grootendorst, Blair, and Willard. Vol. 1A.

– 1995. "Are 'Gap-Fillers' Missing Premisses?" *Informal Logic* 16(3): 185–96.

Grice, P. 1957. "Meaning." *Philosophical Review* 66: 377–88. Reprinted in P.F. Strawson, ed. 1967. *Philosophical Logic*. Oxford: Oxford University Press.

- 1975. "Logic and Conversation." In *Syntax and Semantics 3*, edited by P. Cole and J.L. Morgan. New York: Academic Press.

Hample, D. 1977. "The Toulmin Model and the Syllogism." *Journal of the American Forensic Association* 14(1): 1–8.

Harman, G. 1986. *Change in View.* Cambridge, MA: MIT Press.

Hart, H.L.A. 1961. *The Concept of Law.* New York: Oxford University Press.

Hastings, A.C. 1962. A Reformulation of the Modes of Reasoning in Argumentation. PhD diss., Northwestern University.

Heintz, L. 1981. "The Logic of Defenses." *American Philosophical Quarterly* 18(3): 243–9.

Heyd, D. 1982. *Supererogation.* Cambridge: Cambridge University Press.

Hitchcock, D. 1980. "Deductive and Inductive: Types of Validity Not Types of Argument." *Informal Logic Newsletter* 2(3): 9–11.

- 1983. *Critical Thinking: A Guide to the Evaluation of Information.* Agincourt, ON: Methuen.

- 1985. "Enthymematic Arguments." *Informal Logic* 7(2–3): 84–97.

- 1989. "A General Theory of Good Inference?" *Third International Symposium on Informal Logic.* University of Windsor.

Hogarth, R.M. 1987. *Judgment and Choice.* New York: Wiley.

Jacobs, S., and S. Jackson. 1982. "Conversational Argument: A Discourse Analytic." In *Advances in Argumentation Theory and Research*, edited by Cox and Willard.

Janis, I., and F. Frick. 1943. "The Relationship between Attitudes towards Conclusions and Errors in Judging Logical Validity of Syllogisms." *Journal of Experimental Psychology* 33: 73–7.

Jeffrey, R. 1981. *Formal Logic: Its Scope and Limits.* 2d ed. New York: McGraw-Hill.

Johnson, R.H. 1981. "The New Logic Course: The State of the Art in Non-Formal Methods of Argument Analysis." *Teaching Philosophy* 4(2): 123–43.

- 1987. "Logic Naturalized: Recovering a Tradition." Chapter 3 in *Argumentation across the Lines*, edited by van Eemeren, Grootendorst, Blair, and Willard. Vol. 3.

Johnson, R.H., and J.A. Blair. 1980. "The Recent Development of Informal Logic." In *Informal Logic*, edited by Blair and Johnson.

- 1983. *Logical Self-Defence.* 2d ed. (1st ed. 1977). Toronto: McGraw-Hill.

- 1985. "Informal Logic: The Past Five Years, 1978–1983." *American Philosophical Quarterly* 22(3): 181–96.

Johnson-Laird, P.N. 1983. *Mental Models: Towards a Cognitive Science of Language, Inference, and Consciousness.* Cambridge, MA: Harvard University Press.

Johnson-Laird, P.N., and P.C. Wason, eds. 1968. *Thinking and Reasoning.* Harmondsworth, England: Penguin.

Kahane, H. 1971. *Logic and Contemporary Rhetoric.* Belmont, CA: Wadsworth.

Kahneman, D., P. Slovic, and A. Tversky, eds. 1982. *Judgment under Uncertainty: Heuristics and Biases.* Cambridge: Cambridge University Press.

Kapitan, T. 1982. "On the Concept of Material Consequence." *History and Philosophy of Logic* 3: 193–211.

Keynes, J.M. 1921. *A Treatise on Probability.* London: MacMillan.

Kienpointner, M. 1987. "Towards a Typology of Argumentative Schemes." Chapter 24 in *Argumentation across the Lines*, edited by van Eemeren, Grootendorst, Blair, and Willard. Vol. 3.

– 1992. "How to Classify Arguments." Chapter 17 in *Argumentation Illuminated*. Amsterdam: International Centre for the Study of Argumentation.

Kneale, W., and M. Kneale. 1962. *The Development of Logic*. Oxford: Clarendon Press.

Kneupper, C.W. 1978. "On Arguments and Diagrams." *Journal of the American Forensic Association* 14(4): 181–7.

Koriat, A., S. Lichtenstein, and B. Fischoff. 1980. "Reasons for Confidence." *Journal of Experimental Psychology (Human Learning and Memory)* 6: 107–18.

Kyburg, H. 1964. "Recent Work in Inductive Logic." *American Philosophical Quarterly* 1(4): 249–87.

Lichtenstein, S., and Newman, J.R. 1967. "Empirical Scaling of Common Verbal Phrases Associated with Numerical Probabilities." *Psychonomic Science* 9(10): 563–4.

Little, J.F., L.A. Groarke, and C.W. Tindale. 1989. *Good Reasoning Matters.* Toronto: McClelland & Stewart.

Lucey, K.G. 1976. "Scales of Epistemic Appraisal." *Philosophical Studies* 29: 169–79.

Machina, K. 1982. *Basic Applied Logic.* New York: Scott, Foresman.

May, J.D. 1991. "Practical Arguments." Chapter 34 in *Conference on Argumentation*, vol. 1A, edited by van Eemeren, Grootendorst, Blair, and Willard.

McKerrow, R.E. 1987. "Rescher's Plausibility Thesis and the Justification of Arguments." Chapter 28 in *Argumentation across the Lines*, edited by van Eemeren, Grootendorst, Blair, and Willard. Vol. 3.

Michalos, A.C. 1970. *Improving Your Reasoning.* Englewood Cliffs, NJ: Prentice-Hall.

Mill, J.S. 1978. *A System of Logic, Ratiocinative and Inductive.* In *The Collected Works of John Stuart Mill*, edited by J.M. Robson. Vol. 7. Toronto: University of Toronto Press.

Miller, G.R. 1969. "Some Factors Influencing Judgments of the Logical Validity of Arguments: A Research Review". *Quarterly Journal of Speech* 55: 276–86.

Mills, G.E., and H. Petrie. 1968. "The Role of Logic in Rhetoric." *Quarterly Journal of Speech* 54: 260–7.

Montague, P. 1989. "Acts, Agents, and Supererogation." *American Philosophical Quarterly* 26(2): 101–11.

Mortensen, C.D., and R.L. Anderson. 1970. "The Limits of Logic." *Journal of the American Forensic Association* 7: 71–8.

Nisbett, R.E., and L. Ross. 1980. *Human Inference: Strategies and Shortcomings of Social Judgment.* Englewood Cliffs, NJ: Prentice-Hall.

O'Keefe, D.J. 1982. "The Concepts of Argument and Arguing." In *Advances in Argumentation Theory,* edited by Cox and Willard.

Owen, David. 1987. "Hume versus Price on Miracles and Prior Probabilities: Testimony and the Bayesian Calculation." *Philosophical Quarterly* 37: 187–202.

Perelman, C., and L. Olbrechts-Tyteca. 1969. *The New Rhetoric: A Treatise on Argumentation.* Translated by J. Wilkinson and P. Weaver. Notre Dame, IN: University Of Notre Dame Press.

Petrie, H. 1969. "Does Logic Have Any Relevance to Argumentation?" *Journal of the American Forensic Association* 6: 55–60.

Phillips, H.E. 1991. "On Appealing to the Evidence." *Philosophical Forum* 22(3): 228–41.

Pollock, J.L. 1975. "Four Kinds of Conditionals." *American Philosophical Quarterly* 12(1): 51–9.

– 1990. *Nomic Probability and the Foundations of Induction.* New York: Oxford University Press.

Pospesel, H. 1974. *Introduction to Logic: Propositional Logic.* Englewood Cliffs, NJ: Prentice-Hall.

Raz, J. 1978. "Introduction." In *Practical Reasoning,* edited by J. Raz. Oxford: Oxford University Press.

Rescher, N. 1964. *Hypothetical Reasoning.* Amsterdam: North-Holland.

– 1977. *Dialectics.* Albany, NY: SUNY Press.

Rieke, R.D., and M.O. Sillars. 1975. *Argumentation and the Decision Making Process.* New York: Wiley.

Robinson, L.B., and R. Hastie. 1985. "Revision of Beliefs When a Hypothesis Is Eliminated from Consideration." *Journal of Experimental Psychology; Human Perception and Performance* 11: 443–56.

Ryle, G. 1950. "If, So, and Because." In *Philosophical Analysis,* edited by M. Black. Ithaca, NY: Cornell.

– 1954. *Dilemmas.* Cambridge: Cambridge University Press.

Schellens, P.J. 1987. "Types of Argument and the Critical Reader." Chapter 4 in *Argumentation across the Lines,* edited by van Eemeren, Grootendorst, Blair, and Willard. Vol. 3B.

Schwartz, T. 1980. *The Art of Logical Reasoning.* New York: Random House.

Scriven, M. 1976. *Reasoning.* New York: McGraw-Hill.

– 1987. "Probative Logic: Review and Preview." Chapter 1 in *Argumentation across the Lines,* edited by van Eemeren, Grootendorst, Blair, and Willard. Vol. 3.

Searle, J.R. 1965. "What Is a Speech Act?" In *Philosophy in America,* edited by M. Black. Ithaca, NY: Cornell University Press. Reprinted in J.R. Searle, ed. 1971. *The Philosophy of Language.* Oxford: Oxford University Press.

– 1969. *Speech Acts.* Cambridge: Cambridge University Press.

Shepard, D.W. 1966. "Rhetoric and Formal Argument." *Western Speech* 30(4): 241–7.

Skyrms, B. 1986. *Choice and Chance: An Introduction to Inductive Logic.* 3d ed. Belmont, CA: Wadsworth.

Sloman, A. 1964. "Rules of Inference, or Suppressed Premises?" *Mind* 73, 84–96.

Smith, R.G. 1962. The Arguments over Abolition Petitions in the House of Representatives in December 1835: A Toulmin Analysis. Ph D diss., University of Minnesota.

Sobel, J.H. "On the Evidence of Testimony for Miracles: A Bayesian Interpretation of David Hume's Analysis. *Philosophical Quarterly* 37: 166–186.

Strawson, P.F. 1959. *Individuals.* New York: Methuen.

Tapscott, B.L. 1976. *Elementary Applied Symbolic Logic.* Englewood Cliffs, NJ: Prentice-Hall.

Thomas, S.N. 1973. *Practical Reasoning in Natural Language.* Englewood Cliffs, NJ: Prentice-Hall.

– 1990. "New Advances in Natural Logic." Paper presented at the Second International Conference on Argumentation, Amsterdam.

Tomko, T. 1979. "Informal Logic: A Review." *Educational Theory* 29(4): 351–8.

Toulmin, S.E. 1958. *The Uses of Argument.* Cambridge: Cambridge University Press.

Toulmin, S.E., R. Rieke, and A. Janik. 1984. *An Introduction to Reasoning.* 2d ed. New York: MacMillan.

Trent, J.D. 1966. Stephen E. Toulmin's Argument Model as an Instrument for Criticism of Forensic Speeches. Ph D Diss., Purdue University.

– 1968. "Toulmin's Model of an Argument: An Examination and Extension." *Quarterly Journal of Speech* 54(3): 252–9.

Tuman, J.S. 1987. "Getting to First Base: Prima Facie Arguments for Propositions of Value." *Journal of the American Forensic Association* 24: 89–94.

Tversky, A., and D. Kahneman. 1982. "Evidential Input of Base Rates." In *Judgment under Uncertainty,* edited by Kahneman, Slovic, and Tversky.

– 1983. "Extensional versus Intuitive Reasoning: The Conjunction Fallacy in Probability Judgment." *Psychological Review* 90: 293–315.

Urmson, J.O. 1950. "On Grading." *Mind* 59: 145–69.

Walton, D. 1989. *Informal Logic: A Handbook for Critical Argumentation.* Cambridge: Cambridge University Press.

Wason, P.C., and P.N. Johnson-Laird. 1972. *Psychology of Reasoning: Structure and Content.* London: Batsford.

Weddle, P. 1991. "Resurrecting the Practical Argument." Chapter 35 in *Conference on Argumentation,* edited by van Eemeren, Grootendorst, Blair, and Willard. Vol. 1A.

Wenzel, J.W. 1977. "Toward a Rationale for Value-Centered Argument." *Journal of the American Forensic Association* 13(3): 150–8.

Weston, A. 1982. "A Pattern for Argument Analysis in Informal Logic." *Teaching Philosophy* 5(2): 135–9.

Whately, R. 1851. "Rhetoric." In *Encyclopedia Metropolitana.* London.

White, A.R. 1975. *Modal Thinking.* Ithaca, NY: Cornell University Press.

Willard, C.A. 1976. "On the Utility of Descriptive Diagrams for the Analysis and Criticism of Arguments." *Communication Monographs* 43: 308–19.

– 1979. "Propositional Argument Is to Argument What Talking about Passion Is to Passion." *Journal of the American Forensic Association* 16: 21–8.

Williams, B.A.O. 1985. *Ethics and the Limits of Philosophy.* Cambridge, MA: Harvard University Press.

Wittgenstein, L. 1951. *Philosophical Investigations.* Oxford: Blackwell.

Wyer, R.S., and L. Goldberg. 1970. "A Probabilistic Analysis of the Relationships among Beliefs and Attitudes." *Psychological Review* 77(2): 100–20.

Zarefsky, D. 1977. "The Role of Causal Argument in Policy Controversies." *Journal of the American Forensic Association* 13(4): 179–191.

– 1982. "Persistent Questions in the Theory of Argument Fields." *Journal of the American Forensic Association* 18: 191–203.

Index

Adams, E.W., probability of conditionals, 50

Allen, D., validity as true inference claim, 132

alternations: concepts of, 240; evaluating, 240–3

analogical arguments: Copi on, 22; predictive version as parallel case pattern, 215–16; proportional 216–18

argument: defined, 3; as utterance act, 4; as product of utterance act, 4; dialogical, 5; as illocutionary act complex, 5–7,13; responsibility condition, 9; paradigmatic cases 7–8; analogous to chemical compounds, 7; conditions for satisfactory utterance of, 7–9; utterance effects of, 10; illocutionary effect of, 10–12; as speech act product, 13–15; Toulmin's model of 66–8; the T2 model, 68–9, 76; theory of, 278–9

argument diagrams: Willard on, 64–5; for syllogisms, 65–6, 74–6; for linked-premiss arguments, 71–4; Toulmin format versus Scriven format, 89–92

argument evaluation: elements of, 2, 34–68; in informal logic texts, 31–2; Scriven's procedure, 32, 54–7; proposed procedure, 57–60; argument quality, 35, 36, 38; procedure, 131–2, 146, 275–6; by adding rebuttal-blocking premisses, 264–71;

argument forms, classified by diagram structure: convergent, 72–3; linked premiss, 76; divergent, 86; serial, 86

argument patterns: Perelman and Olbrechts-Tyteca on, 152–3; classified by field, 153–4; Ehninger and Brockreide on, 154–8; classified by warrant, 154–8; revised classification, 163–5

arguments, everyday, 19; quality of, 35, 36, 38; as analogical (Copi), 22

assertion, as illocutionary act, 5–6

authority, argument from, 201–15; and news media, 201; errors in evaluating, 203, 206–8; evaluating inference of, 211–12

base rate, 202–6

Bayes' Theorem, 148–50, 204, 206, 208, 215, 294; simplified version, 247–8; evaluating uninferred premisses using, 246–7

Behn, R.D., and J.W. Vaupel, modal term numerical definitions, 45–6

Benjamin, R.L., on modal terms, 291n1

Benoit, William, and J.J. Lindsey, on Toulmin's argument fields, 154

Blair, Anthony, and Ralph Johnson: on informal logic texts, 27; on missing premisses, 251–3; on